Towards **social** adjustment

Labour market issues in structural adjustment

Towards **social**

adjustment

Labour market issues in structural adjustment

Edited by Guy Standing and Victor Tokman

International Labour Office   Geneva

Standing, G. and Tokman, V.
Towards social adjustment: Labour market issues in structural adjustment
Geneva, International Labour Office, 1991

Impact of /Structural adjustment/ on /Labour market/, /Developed country/s, /Developing country/s. 13.01.2
ISBN 92-2-107745-4

ILO Cataloguing in Publication Data

Printed in Switzerland   ICO

Foreword

*by Hans Singer**

"Structural adjustment" is an inevitable part of economic growth and development and as such has always been recognised and analysed in the development debate. However, it has now acquired a narrower and more definite meaning, i.e. the kind of policies now recommended to indebted developing countries - or developing countries struggling for other reasons with balance of payments deficits - to enable them to pay their debts, become credit-worthy again and lay the foundations for subsequent sustainable growth. There is a consensus that these policies have a major impact on employment and labour markets, and that the latter in turn have an effect on structural adjustment which should be taken into account when shaping these policies. These are matters of legitimate - indeed mandatory - concern to the ILO; many of us feel that the voice of the ILO has not been heard loudly and clearly enough in the adjustment debate so far. The present volume should help to rectify this situation.

One can adopt two positions on adjustment. One is the "TINA" position "there is no alternative". Debts, high interest rates, poor terms of trade, capital flight, protectionism, slowed growth of the world economy and all the other international causes of balance of payments difficulties are "facts of life" which must be faced by developing countries - the objective then is to protect employment, labour conditions and job security to the greatest possible extent. This is the starting position of this volume - part of a broader movement to give adjustment a "social dimension" or a "human face".

The other position is to question more fundamentally the justification for the structural adjustment programmes and the unilateral pressures on deficit countries. On this view, the role of the international organisations should not just be to help deficit countries adjust to the facts of life, but to *change* the facts of life and return the world economy to a path of growth and full employment. This wider task is not directly considered in this volume, but it should not be forgotten; the ILO also has a mandate to participate in this wider task.

* Institute of Development Studies, University of Sussex, United Kingdom.

The scenario for the present volume is a widespread, and often drastic, decline in real wages in the modern industrial sector, a rise in unemployment both open and hidden in the swelling informal sectors, a decline in both legislative and effective protection of labour conditions and minimum wages, a trend to privatisation, cutbacks of public sector employment and to deregulation and informalisation of labour markets. All these developments have desirable and undesirable features setting a task to preserve and maximise the former and avoid or minimise the latter. The contributions to this volume represent a major effort to rise to this task and provide a foundation for further systematic work in the future, in the ILO and elsewhere. One would hope that this material will be carefully studied by those more directly involved in the formulation and negotiation of structural adjustment programmes. There is a risk that in a headlong rush for deregulation and flexibility of labour markets the baby of productive employment will be thrown out with the bathwater of rigidity.

There is also plenty of evidence that rising unemployment - particularly among the young and educated - creates threats to the political and social stability which is a precondition for the success of structural adjustment programmes. Reduction of poverty is now increasingly recognised - some of us would say remembered - as a prime objective of adjustment policies. A productive job securely held in a good working environment is the most important single barrier against poverty. Unemployment is also an inexcusable waste of resources which is often overlooked when denouncing the waste of resources arising from bad macroeconomic policies. Employment and labour market problems are thus at the crucial intersection between growth and poverty alleviation. This volume will have performed a great service in reminding us of this central role.

Contents

Introduction

For what seems a very long time, "structural adjustment" has been at the forefront of international economic debates. Yet remarkably few attempts have been made to integrate the labour market concerns into the competing approaches, even though in recent years there has been growing concern over the apparent neglect of social dimensions of adjustment strategies.

The orthodox approach, to the extent that one can be clearly identified, essentially treats the "labour market" like any other market. That is, forces of supply and demand should be enabled to operate to ensure the efficient allocation of resources, so that policies should be implemented to ensure high levels of labour mobility at low cost and flexible labour markets. This raises some awkward questions, especially for those who believe that the principle enshrined in the ILO's Philadephia Declaration that "labour is not a commodity" is a recognition that the quest for labour security is a legitimate objective that should be not be sacrificed, and that as such, market mechanisms may need to be circumvented in the interest of social values.

A "social adjustment" approach would favour flexible labour practices subject to the preservation and enhancement of labour security and labour standards. Those involved in the debates on how labour processes should evolve recognise that abuses and lack of decent safeguards should not be tolerated, but most policy-makers also recognise that in low-income developing economies "ideal" standards envisaged by their counterparts in highly-affluent, industrialised economies cannot be attained for some considerable time. Yet, unless socially-defensible practices and structures are pursued consistently as explicit objectives, they are likely to be neglected, with lasting adverse consequences for the more vulnerable in their societies. In short, social progress and labour standards should not be sacrificed in the name of efficiency.

It was in that spirit that a group of labour specialists, mostly economists, were invited to prepare papers on specific themes to present to a three-day workshop on labour market issues in structural adjustment, convened at the ILO in Geneva and attended by over 50 people. Not all the papers presented at that workshop are included in the following volume, for reasons of length and balance, rather than quality. Although many ILO officials participated in the ensuing debates, there was no intention to make the outcome an explicitly ILO perspective. However, the values and objectives of the ILO figured prominently and the underlying intentions were, first, to highlight the principal elements of what might be a social adjustment approach to labour policies, and second, to identify an agenda for future work in the ILO and elsewhere. It was a basic premise of the workshop that the structural adjustment debate was as relevant in Western industrialised countries and in Eastern European economies undergoing transition as in developing countries, whether or not they were formally operating a negotiated World Bank-IMF type structural adjustment programme. This view was supported by the extent of common concerns expressed by participants from very different parts of the world. It was nevertheless decided beforehand to leave to a separate occasion the complex questions of transition in Eastern Europe that were thrown into sharp relief by political events around the time of the workshop. Indeed, a major international conference on closely-related themes was organised in Moscow towards the end of 1990, the proceedings of which will be published during 1991.

The papers in the structural adjustment workshop were intended to highlight issues perceived to be priorities in various countries around the world. Mostly, they focused on a particular region or country. But it is hoped the reader will find that the policy concerns raised with respect to one country or group of countries are relevant more widely, albeit in different forms or degree. This seemed particularly true of such themes as "informalisation", "deregulation" and "privatisation", three topics that figured prominently in the debates.

A long workshop can be a formal set-piece occasion or an animated set of discussions of longer-lasting benefit. We certainly hope that this was the latter, and believe that the discussions and papers helped clarify priorities for ILO labour market research. For that, considerable thanks are due to the participants. In addition, we would like to thank Heribert Maier, Deputy Director-General of the ILO, who opened the meeting, and who participated in its final stages, and Douglas Poulter, Chairman of the ILO's Governing Body, who participated in the concluding session. We would like to give special thanks to Loretta de Luca, who commented on all the papers and acted as rapporteur for the Conference. Finally, all participants would join us in thanking Jo-Ann Bakker, whose organisational skills and other assistance were greatly appreciated.

Most of the papers that follow reflect the outcome of long-term research projects and/or the output from programmes in the ILO's Regional Employment Teams in Africa, Asia and Latin America. We hope they will be read in that context and that readers will be able to refer to the supportive empirical studies and reports. Above all, it is to be hoped that in the 1990s policy-makers and their advisers will be able to refine what we have called a social adjustment strategy that puts social values and equity more clearly and consistently at the forefront of macro-economic and development policies.

Guy Standing   and   *Victor Tokman*
Employment Planning and   Director,
Population Branch,   Employment and Development Department
ILO, Geneva   ILO, Geneva

Conceptual perspectives

1

Structural adjustment and labour market policies: Towards social adjustment?

by Guy Standing [*]

Introduction

"When I use a word, it means just what I choose it to mean." Lewis Carroll: *Alice through the looking glass* (London, Dent, 1979).

For over a decade "structural adjustment" has been a euphemism embracing an impressive set of euphemisms that include "decentralisation", "deregulation", "labour flexibility", "income decompression", "price distortions", "fiscal neutrality", "financial repression" and the like, all of which have a meaning somewhat different from that conveyed to the uninitiated. The trouble arises because too many of us use the terms to mean what we want them to mean, or receive messages from their use that may be contrary to what was intended, or would reject the implications if we knew what the user meant by his or her use of them. After all, at an abstract level, who could be against structural adjustment or labour flexibility? But these terms do not mean what a literal interpretation would imply.

In this paper, we will use the term "structural adjustment approach" interchangeably with "supply-sideism", since the orthodoxy of the 1980s focused on altering the constraints, incentives and barriers to micro-level behaviour. The *essence* of this approach is that resource allocation and economic outcomes should be left to "the market", that macro-economic policy should be geared primarily to monetary stability and that government should concentrate on the preservation of a legal framework in which "business" can be done. We will consider the defining characteristics of this approach in the next section. But it is worth stressing that, according to many who use the term, "labour flexibility" implies its application to the labour market; that is, by removing certain types of government (protective) regulation the employers'

* Employment Planning and Population Branch, Employment and Development Department, International Labour Office. Thanks for comments are due to Loretta de Luca, Samir Radwan, Derek Robinson, Victor Tokman, Jan Vandemoortele, Wouter van Ginneken and Frances Williams.

costs of change will be reduced, labour mobility between sectors, regions, enterprises and jobs will be accelerated and relative prices adjusted accordingly. Both structural adjustment and labour flexibility in the orthodox view represent an enthronement of the market, or if we wished to indulge in the playful invention of euphemisms, "market populism". Indeed, this term may be more appropriate than supply-sideism, in that some Keynesians - notably in Sweden - argue that they have practised a supply-side approach to the labour market all along.

The main objective of this introductory paper is to identify and contrast the labour market policies and labour developments that could be expected to correspond to the supply-side approach and those that one might expect from an alternative "social adjustment" perspective. Because we are dealing in ideal types we will make some simplifications, and hope that this will not do injustice to the essence of the respective arguments.

Before turning to labour market policies, however, it seemed potentially useful to sketch alternative macro-economic policy frameworks that might be seen as alternative routes to structural adjustment, in the sense of enabling the economy and its industrial and labour market structures to respond to external shocks and pressures.

Alternative macro-economic policy frameworks[1]

For many years the dominant macro-economic framework was what might be called "social Keynesianism". Since the economic upheavals of the 1970s, not only has that framework been rejected in many countries and international institutions but it has become clearer that there are various macro-economic regimes competing for intellectual pre-eminence.[2]

For our purposes there is no need to discuss the intricacies of alternative macro-economic frameworks. The objective in this section is merely to identify the principal strategies and the logic underlying them so as to determine whether certain types of labour and employment policies could be anticipated in different macro-economic policy contexts, and whether those contexts have implications for the success or failure of the labour market policies adopted.

At the outset, it is worth reminding ourselves that *all* macro-economic strategies - models or frameworks - have both growth and distributional properties. One cannot divorce consideration of economic stabilisation from consideration of distributional objectives, whether those consist of progressive redistribution, an unchanging pattern or a regressive shift in the functional distribution of income. For instance, most variants of social Keynesianism include a long-term objective of progressive income redistribution via fiscal policy and social expenditure.

Social Keynesianism

The essence of social Keynesianism is that macro-economic monetary and fiscal policy should be geared to secure full employment, while micro-economic policy is expected to regulate inflation. Most macro-economic regimes have followed the Tinbergen dictate of setting one type of policy for one objective and having an equal number of policy instruments and macro-objectives. But the outstanding feature of Keynesian macro-economic policy is that fiscal policy is treated as a counter-cyclical stabilisation device, involving tax cuts in recessionary phases to boost aggregate demand and tax increases in booms to curtail economic overheating.[3] The tax structure is expected to be progressive, partly for redistributive reasons and partly to correspond to the nature of the aggregate consumption function. Long-term social adjustment is pursued in part by the growth of public social expenditure, geared to the extension of the welfare state, with the *long-term* objective of providing social security "from cradle to grave". For many years, adherents of social Keynesianism saw little need for *active* (i.e. counter-cyclical) labour market policy, although there was a place for long-term productivity-enhancing employment policies were promoted. It was presumed that with macro-economic "fine tuning", full employment could be ensured while industrial enterprises would be sufficiently motivated to train workers and to pay for the required labour mobility. In effect, it was assumed that industrial growth would be "structurally stable", in the sense that the industrial structure would change only gradually and not require massive labour mobility. As such, social Keynesianism could be said to be more appropriate to an economy based on large-scale industrial enterprises in a situation of industrial stability and a labour market in which the great majority of workers are in regular, full-time employment. Some observers have claimed that the adoption of Keynesianism has depended on the existence of a strong working class, and that elsewhere Keynesian principles have not been institutionalised or perceived as particularly relevant.

Another feature of social Keynesianism has been the acceptance and promotion of a "mixed economy", in which public investment and public ownership of some industries coupled with public social expenditure have been seen as complementary to private investment and private ownership of other economic spheres. Above all, public expenditure has been seen as facilitating long-term growth and industrial development.

As for the role of the welfare state, with social Keynesianism there is a commitment to what Richard Titmuss called an "institutional redistributive model" of social welfare, based on the principle of universal entitlement to social benefits. Related to that, one of the underlying issues for Keynesianism has been the type of market mechanisms being promoted, and the preference for collective rather than individualistic mechanisms has always been a feature of the underlying model.

The major predicament for social Keynesianism has been its apparent tendency to generate accelerating inflation. Keynes himself said that economists could be divided into "little deflationists" and "little inflationists". Keynesianism undoubtedly has a bias towards inflation. The Phillips-curve relationship suggesting a trade-off between the level of unemployment and price inflation was taken to show that counter-cyclical fiscal and monetary policy had to stabilise aggregate demand somewhere below an economy's full capacity. But it became clear that the inverse relationship between unemployment and inflation was neither stable nor very predictable and that there was a tendency for the curve to become more vertical or shift to the right, as the effect of a given level of unemployment on behaviour in the labour and consumer goods markets wore off. This led to theories of "rational expectations" and "hysteresis", which need not concern us here, although we might consider the latter when discussing the appropriateness of alternative labour market policies. The point is that the apparent trade-off led Keynesian policy-makers to give an increasingly prominent role to statutory incomes policy as the means of overriding that trade-off and enabling governments to maintain a level of aggregate demand that would generate something close to full employment. It also meant that corporatist institutional mechanisms figure prominently.[4]

Finally, there is a characteristic regulation policy associated with social Keynesianism. This is sometimes described as "Fordism"; and has spawned what is usually seen as the French *regulation* school of analysis. One does not have to agree with all of this literature, but it has attempted to come to terms with crucial elements of what we are calling social Keynesianism. In effect, part of the social compromise is that in return for macro-level employment and labour market security - near-full employment and a system of employment protection regulations - workers, and unions in particular, accept management's right to modernise, with the presumption that workers and employers share the benefits of productivity growth. The primary mode of regulation under Fordism is wage-oriented - or negotiated - rather than market-oriented via competition involving bankruptcies, redundancies and price wars. For this to work efficiently and smoothly there must be a high degree of social consensus on objectives, notably income distribution. But the framework is also in a sense conservative, being more suitable to eras of stable economic growth and slowly changing industrial structures than to one of industrial dislocation and structural change. If employment security and job security are integral parts of the macro-economic system, then there may be resistance to rapid and wholesale structural change.

An inadequately stressed aside of social Keynesianism links the regulatory stance with international trade policy. Because dissimilar levels of labour rights and regulations undermine the principle of free trade, a "social tariff" is needed, as advocated by the founding father of American labour economics, John Commons, and subsequently supported by Keynes in 1933. It is important in the context of this paper, because it implies a commitment to take social policy out of international competition. Those countries in which labour rights are systematically abused or undeveloped should not be enabled thereby to gain growing shares of international trade. As such, social protectionism could be a consistent aspect of social Keynesianism. However, this is a controversial issue even for those adhering to a Keynesian model, since while some see the tying of fair labour standards as a form of protection by the advanced industrialised countries against imports from developing countries, others see it as a legitimate means of improving human rights internationally.[5]

Market Keynesianism

All variants of Keynesianism stress counter-cyclical fiscal policy, but one can draw a distinction between social (or welfare) and "market Keynesianism". The difference is epitomised by institutional developments in the United States in the 1945-79 era, compared to most of Western Europe and several other parts of the world where the development of the welfare state was given priority.

Whereas social Keynesianism puts the institutional redistribution of income high on the politico-economic agenda, that objective has been incidental or rejected in the market Keynesian model. It has given precedence to a pronounced division of social functions, with management preserving the right to manage and with labour only allowed to bargain about the effects of management decisions. Thus, the cornerstone of labour market policies in such contexts is a law - the prime example being the US National Labour Relations Act (the Wagner Act) - that not only limits government intervention in private enterprises but also puts strong curbs on the bargaining rights of trades unions.

As for fiscal policy, under market Keynesianism, governments have eschewed nationalisation and the acquisition of private capital either for redistributive purposes or for counter-cyclical reasons. This passive stance could be expected to result in greater fluctuations in economic activity, meaning more bankruptcies and unemployment in recessionary periods and more dynamic spurts in times of economic growth. Relatively inefficient or unprofitable sectors would not be preserved, or at least not to the same extent as under social Keynesianism.

With market Keynesianism, short-term fiscal policy could be expected to act primarily by stimulating consumption, which despite implying a low savings ratio (a feature of the United States) is far less problematical in a relatively closed economy in which the balance of payments constraint is non-existent or only a minimal irritant.

In sum, market Keynesianism results in a less stable economic environment and a much reduced propensity to progressive income redistribution. There is thus a greater onus on labour market policy to reduce inequalities and labour market disadvantages of marginalised groups, such as ethnic minorities, women and migrants.

Scandinavian Keynesianism

Two variants of social Keynesianism have been named after the countries in which they have been most assiduously applied. The first is what is called "the Swedish model" - sometimes miscalled the "Scandinavian model" - which was much admired in the 1960s and again by many in the 1980s. While it gives a pivotal role to counter-cyclical fiscal policy, macro-economic policy is intended to stabilise aggregate demand at a level *below* full employment, precisely to prevent the emergence or intensification of inflationary pressures. Even so, the overriding socio-economic objectives are full employment and a progressive redistribution of income and welfare. To ensure full employment, a critical role is given to *active labour market policy,* where the active refers to its counter-cyclical character. The number of workers covered by such measures as labour market training and subsidised employment schemes is expected to rise in recessions and periods of structural change, and to fall in periods of rapid economic growth. Active labour market policy is also expected to be an instrument in controlling cost-push inflation, primarily by facilitating various forms of labour mobility and reducing their cost.

In the Swedish model, statutory incomes policy is ruled out as a macro-economic means of controlling inflation, on the grounds that it introduces rigidities into the labour market. Instead, reliance is put on what are usually called "neo-corporatist" mechanisms of centralised bargaining and consensus. Accordingly, the success of macro-economic policy depends on the institutionalised and socially responsible participation of representative organisations of employers and workers. Either the government can be a regular partner in the bargaining process or, as preferred in the Scandinavian countries, it can be a passive participant, providing macro-economic guide-lines and indicators at the appropriate time but otherwise intervening only at times of seemingly irreconcilable differences between employers and unions. So, whatever the merits of the Swedish model, it could not work without a sense of social consensus, a fairly organised solidarity of the respective organisations of employers and workers, and the existence of a strong trade union movement legitimately representing the majority of workers. Thus this may be a dubious model for societies undergoing industrialisation or in a state of social or economic flux.

Another aspect of the Swedish macro-model is a concern to promote simultaneously progressive income redistribution and labour market efficiency. Besides a progressive fiscal policy and a welfare state based on principles of universal entitlement to an extensive range of social transfers, income redistribution is sought through a "solidaristic wage policy" whereby the lower-paid groups are gradually expected to close the gap with their better-paid counterparts. At the same time, centralised wage bargaining is supposed to adhere to what is variously known as the "Scandinavian inflation model", the "EFO model" or, most correctly, the "Aukraut model", whereby overall wage rises are set by the growth of productivity in the export sectors. The emphasis given to a distinction between the export sector and the import-substitution and other sectors geared to domestic consumption is another difference from the traditional Keynesian model, and highlights the common belief that the Swedish model is most relevant to small open economies dependent for growth on their trade performance.

The Swedish model also differs from conventional social Keynesianism in its regulation policy. Under the latter the emphasis of regulation is on the preservation of macro-economic stability. The emphasis in the former is on facilitating economic change without deserting the basic Fordist principle underlying all variants of Keynesianism - an institutional preference for wage-oriented, or negotiated, rather than market-oriented methods of regulation. In the Swedish model the labour market organisations are obliged to negotiate structural change, whether in the field of technology, organisational structure, industrial relocation, job structures or employment changes. Most critically, these issues become matters for negotiation at a centralised as well as a decentralised, or firm, level, and are institutionalised via legislation and, in effect, labour market planning.

Austro-Keynesianism

Another variant of social Keynesianism is what is known as "Austro-Keynesianism". Whereas the Swedish model has in practice depended on an undervalued exchange rate as a means of boosting exports, a differentiating feature of Austro-Keynesianism is an explicitly hard-currency policy, designed to prevent the growth of imported inflation by lowering the cost of imported consumer and capital goods as well as to impose discipline on bo unions and industrial enterprises in setting wages and prices.[6]

A second differentiating feature of Austro-Keynesianism concerns the role of the State in the productive system. Social Keynesianism favours a mixed economy, but in the Swedish model private ownership of industry is preserved, whereas in the Austrian variant a far greater role has been given to the nationalisation of production. In other words, while private enterprise is the main engine of economic growth in the Swedish model, with light taxation of capital and profits, public ownership has been a central aspect of Austro-Keynesianism, a basic intention being that the State would capture the economic surplus, to be used for reinvestment and for redistribution. This difference has implications for the character of any negotiated incomes policy and for the regulation system.

Austro-Keynesianism gives incomes policy the primary role of helping to avoid balance of payments deficits, through maintaining price competitiveness. Otherwise there is a rather specific assignment of policy instruments to economic objectives, primarily because in small open economies inflation is mainly imported. According to conventional economic theory, an expansionary fiscal policy along Keynesian lines coupled with a strong currency policy inevitably leads to external disequilibrium and growing balance of payments deficits. This theoretical conundrum puts tremendous strain on the wage bargaining process and on labour market policies to moderate wages and/or facilitate labour mobility and rising labour productivity.

Besides inflation, which is the bugbear of all variants of Keynesianism, there is a distinctive problem for each variant. The critical tension in social Keynesianism is structural change, hindered through its focus on the preservation of stability, which in the longer term leads to an erosion of technological competitiveness; the critical tension in the Swedish model is the distribution of economic surplus, because of the acceptance of high profits as a motivation for rapid economic growth; and the critical tension in Austro-Keynesianism has been the persistent search for price competitiveness.

Social market models

Moving away from social Keynesianism, one finds macro-economic strategies in which the social welfare and regulatory elements of Keynesianism coexist with economic policies that are quite different. One particular macro-economic policy framework involves a pro-cyclical fiscal and monetary policy combined with a negotiated, centralised incomes policy involving employer and union confederations, coupled with a mixed economy and a commitment to long-term redistribution via progressive direct taxation and a universalistic welfare state. In such cases the pursuit of monetary stability may well lead to greater cyclical fluctuations in aggregate demand than in Keynesian regimes and thus involve more unemployment. This policy combination would arise where the monetary institutions are independent of government, so that the central bank pursues an orthodox finance strategy while the government may be committed to full employment and state regulation of the economy.

Such a macro-economic policy combination implies more emphasis on supply-side adjustments in the interest of boosting employment and economic growth. Being neither Keynesian nor consistently market-oriented, this is not a strategy that has commended itself to any large number of economists or policy-makers, but is one that has been in effect in several countries (e.g. Finland until the 1980s), whether by design or institutional accident.

Supply-sideism

As we know, in the 1970s there was an onslaught on Keynesian methods, assumptions and values. Out of monetarism developed the supply-side perspective that crystallised in the orthodox stabilisation structural adjustment strategy that has been promoted zealously in both developing and industrialised countries in the 1980s. This orthodoxy should be called supply-sideism because of the overwhelming concern for adjustments on the supply-side of capital and labour markets to what is supposed to be a stable macro-economic policy environment. According to the new orthodoxy, the Keynesian pursuit of full employment and rapid growth by macro-economic policies induces not only accelerating inflationary pressures but rigidities that arrest structural and labour market adjustments, undermining industrial competitiveness and intensifying price distortions. According to the supply-side view, fiscal and monetary policy should not be counter-cyclical but rather be geared to the reduction of government deficits, with the objective of securing a balanced budget. This is partly because otherwise public expenditure would "crowd out" private expenditure, particularly investment, and push up interest rates beyond the market-clearing level.

A key difference between the supply-side and the Keynesian policy frameworks is a reversal of instruments and objectives, the supply-side belief being that macro-economic monetary and fiscal policy should be targeted on the control of inflation while micro-economic policy is expected to influence employment and the underlying (or "natural") rate of economic growth.[7] Indeed, a premise of the supply-side approach is that macro-economic policy *cannot* determine the level of employment and unemployment, or the level of economic activity, and that there is a "natural" rate of unemployment ground out by the institutional and regulatory structure of the labour market and the behavioural adjustments that occur in it.

Consistent with their faith in market forces, adherents believe in decentralisation of economic decision-making and in a particular type of (labour) market *regulation*, not deregulation as is commonly claimed.[8] Mechanisms such as minimum wages are "rigidities" that introduce price distortions and raise the "natural" rate of unemployment. Adherents also regard trades unions as interfering with market forces and thus to be curbed as "monopolistic" entities, through the statutory restriction of their role and "power". That is one sense in which the supply-side school believes in regulation. It also believes that, in the interest of flexibility, hiring-and-firing decisions should be the prerogative of management, with minimal restrictions, and that union interference in such matters should be prevented, by regulations if necessary.

The supply-side approach accepts the existence of wide income differentials to maximise incentives to factor mobility, and for similar reasons advocates low direct tax rates. It advocates privatisation of economic and welfare activities and a dismantling of the institutional-redistributive welfare state, turning it initially into a "residual" welfare state geared to selective ("targeted") protection for the most disadvantaged. Given the balanced-budget objective, only selective employment measures are feasible, either as counter-cyclical or as longer-term development measures.

The supply-side approach was the dominant one in the 1980s, shaping structural adjustment strategies and stabilisation policy in many parts of the world. As will be seen, it entails a particular view of labour market policy, in terms of both the desired objectives and its components.

Dualistic industrialisation: The Lewis model revisited

The success of a small group of economies that have moved from being agrarian to "newly industrialised" has been attributed to all sorts of factors, ranging from cultural background to wholesale reliance on market forces or the extensive provision of foreign aid. No doubt cultural and geo-political factors have been relevant, but the macro-economic policy parameters have been distinctive.

Foremost has been an expansionary long-run fiscal policy, in that public investment has been crucial to accumulation and industrialisation, whether through public enterprises or through hefty subsidies to private, often foreign, direct investment. Countries that have successfully pursued export-led industrialisation have relied on fiscal policy to mobilise and invest savings for key industries.

They have also implemented policies that intensify economic and labour market dualism. This applies not only to monetary, credit and fiscal policies but to the design and implementation of the regulatory system. In sectors selected for export-led industrialisation, regulations restricting the freedoms of workers have been extensive, most of all in export processing zones.

The denial of social benefits and labour rights has had the objective of lowering non-wage and wage labour costs, supposedly to secure or maintain competitiveness in international trade and accelerate industrialisation. But there is an explicit dualism in regulation policy, since outside the export-oriented and public sectors there have been minimal labour regulations, or minimal implementation of supposedly-national regulations. This informal, unregulated sphere has been expected to bear the brunt of cyclical fluctuations, expanding in recessions to absorb those displaced in export industries, as well as providing an "unlimited" supply of wage labour in times of industrial expansion. The export industries are also enabled to reduce production costs and associated risks by the proliferation of an informal economy in which small-scale firms are linked via sub-contracting chains to export enterprises, providing low-cost components or services, sometimes on a regular basis but probably most in times of export-led booms or when the export sectors run up against bottlenecks in their internal supply.

The Lewis-type model of macro-economic policy has been held to be relevant both to developing and to affluent countries such as Italy, particularly since the international upheavals of the 1970s when many economies became more open to international trade and competition.

Typically, short-run variations in government fiscal policy are hard to make in low-income economies with a macro-economic stance geared to export-led industrialisation, aided by extensive development expenditures and direct state investment designed to capture economies of scale or to nurture infant industries. Governments intent on reducing budget and current account deficits in periods of structural change or recession have relied on a restrictive monetary policy, pushing up interest rates, often to ensure that the money markets absorb government bonds being sold to finance the budget deficit. That regularly puts a brake on investment, which in turn leads to pressure on the informal economy to absorb displaced labour and to accept the loss of income in units attached to large enterprises. But in the longer-term, fiscal policy has been crucial. Cuts in public expenditure, whether by slashing social services or more directly productive activity, or by privatisation, have been intended to release resources for export industries, including certain types of (educated) labour, and to enable governments to concentrate aid on export-oriented industries.

A difficulty with this dualistic model arises as the nature of the demand for labour changes within export industries. As the industrial structure moves "upstream" technologically, while automating at the bottom, enterprises cannot easily obtain or retain an increasingly qualified or functionally flexible labour force in an environment in which the workforce is both technically uneducated and oriented to informal or subsistence survival. Increasingly, educated workers attuned to urban lifestyles and the incentive appeal of mass consumption are unlikely to put up with the denials of labour rights and the tight labour regulations implicit in the dualist macro-economic approach. Thus after some point in the industrialisation process, the pressures on the system of maintaining low non-wage labour costs will almost certainly become overwhelming, inducing a crisis which leads governments to shift regulatory policy in one of two directions. They either resort to tighter controls over the workforce (including the banning of unions, the removal of any right to strike and the tightening of workers' contractual obligations), or they face up to the need for a reorientation of labour regulations away from restrictions towards worker protection. The sooner governments take the latter course the lower the social costs of doing so.

Macro-economic policy must then begin to play a different role, probably involving a more active fiscal policy. Unless government can underwrite the costs of transition - the costs of training, labour relocation, protection of workers and their working environment, etc. - the dislocation costs could block continued industrialisation. One can foresee that labour market and social welfare policies will be most needed in medium-sized firms, because they could least afford the social costs of transition in labour relations, necessitating subsidies if mass lay-offs are to be avoided. The country that has reached this phase of industrialisation most dramatically is the Republic of Korea. Extremely rapid industrialisation and urbanisation left many of the disadvantaged more deprived and vulnerable because those modernising forces had undermined the social bonds of kinship and community support. In response, fiscal policy has been altered with a remarkable alacrity. For instance, the Ministry of Health and Social Affairs' expenditure has increased by nearly 30 per cent in each of the past three years (1986-89), and the ratio of tax to GNP is scheduled to rise. The example of the Republic of Korea highlights both phases of the reaction to the "turning point" of dualistic industrialisation.

Macro-economic policy in impoverished economies

The scope for coherent macro-economic policy may seem to be dauntingly narrow in those very low-income economies in which "subsistence" production and forms of employment predominate. The classic countries of this type are most of those in sub-Saharan Africa. Of course, there are many features of such economies that undermine the relevance or potential efficacy of many pet prescriptions of macro-economic policy-makers elsewhere, and perhaps the major constraint to *any* approach to adjustment is simply that the economic and social costs to those living on the bare margin of human existence are impossible to bear.

An institutional feature of such economies is that there is no bond market, which means that there can be little difference between monetary and fiscal policy. There is little alternative to financing government debt other than by "printing money". A second feature is that fiscal policy is limited largely to taxes on exports and imports, since the monetised economy is rather a small component of the total. Given these constraints, some countries of this type have nevertheless practised a sort of counter-cyclical fiscal policy in the Keynesian tradition, pump-priming development projects or emergency works schemes, essentially to compensate for declines in the terms of trade. But it has been extremely difficult for governments to adhere to any short-run fiscal policy, because the nature of most government expenditure is essentially long-run and rather inflexible, being mainly development expenditure. The interest rate is also a rather unimportant variable - making it a limited policy instrument - because of the economy's predominantly quasi-subsistence and localised nature, and because such economies are *supply-constrained*. This makes arguments about government expenditure "crowding out" private investment not so much right or wrong but largely irrelevant, simply because most investment is not financed through raising funds on local money markets and is constrained by the absence of appropriate means of production. In particular, most smallholder farmers cannot obtain access to inputs to respond to whatever changes are made to relative prices. Structural non-price constraints are far more important than price distortions, whether those refer to domestic prices or the exchange rate.

Considering the socio-economic and land structure of such economies, it is ironic that those advocating a price-reform approach to macro-economic policy and adjustment may have to acknowledge that this would require and involve large numbers of smallholders being pushed off the land. Land consolidation would tend to accompany more use of price mechanisms and any major shift from non-tradeables to tradeables. This would have implications for the labour market and the required policy.

One must also consider labour market policies in such economies in the context of an extensive regrowth of virtually undifferentiated economic activities. Prolonged stagnation and economic involution have forced many more workers and families, kinship groups and communities to pursue survival strategies that involve a combination of types of work and types of work status, often mixing individual work with exchange labour and communal labour outside any concept of a labour market. Often that has meant combining work schedules across geographical areas, perhaps in a town at one moment and in a distant rural area at another, making distinctions between rural and urban labour markets dubious guides to policy.

Macro-economic monetary and fiscal policy in such economies can neither be expected to achieve very much very quickly nor be blamed for most of the economic ills, which are essentially structural in their origin and persistence. Even so, sharp devaluations could be expected to have severe inflationary effects while having only a small and slow effect on the supply of tradeable goods. This is because of the supply constraints and because of the institutional and economic structures that put a high premium on personal risk, when bare survival is precarious for the vast majority of the population.

The conventional wisdom is that such economies should become more "outward-oriented". The most common prescription involves devaluations designed to make exports more price competitive and raise returns to export-goods production, coupled with a shift of government support to tradeables, away from basic consumer goods. If many countries pursued that course simultaneously, the price elasticity of demand for primary exports is such that there would be little gain in foreign earnings for those countries as a whole. The terms of trade would merely be tipped further against them. Surely a broadly-based stimulus to the emergence of an internal set of markets for domestically produced goods and services is essential for renewed growth and productive labour absorption.

Whether or not a *more* export-led policy is desirable, the relevant concern is identification of the type of labour policy and employment structure that could be expected or be required with a shift of macro-economic policy. For instance, a more outward-oriented development path is likely to create a more fragmented labour structure. A small wage labour market, requiring certain types of training and worker habituation policies, would coexist with an enlarged spectrum of groups relying on diverse means of survival, whereby households, kinship groups and communities combine forms of economic activity outside the realm of regulatory policy instruments. This was the reality of many impoverished economies at the end of the 1980s. Labour policy has to be made more relevant and helpful for those thereby exposed to exclusion and informalisation.

Development and structural adjustment strategies

Accompanying loss of faith in Keynesianism and the enthronement of market mechanisms, there has emerged a corresponding orthodoxy on appropriate development strategy.[9] However, the typical stabilisation and "structural adjustment" package has been superimposed on countries pursuing different development strategies that correspond to national social, political and economic structures. The labour market implications will depend not only on the relative emphasis given to the components of the stabilisation-adjustment package - as well as the order and pace of their introduction - but also on the preceding development strategy.[10]

In all cases, three questions need to be addressed. In the short- and medium-term, will the adjustment strategy boost economic growth and income per capita? What are the welfare consequences of such strategies, for poverty, income distribution and the level and type of employment and unemployment, again in the short- and medium-term? And are there better alternatives, in terms of growth and distributional outcomes, for the type of economy under consideration?

Beyond these is the nagging, insufficiently asked question: If the stabilisation and structural adjustment policy urged on individual countries were to be adopted simultaneously by a large number of low-income countries, what would be the likely outcome for the average country involved? What might "work" in some sense if only one country adopted the strategy might have very different consequences if 20 or 30 others did the same.

To set the scene for consideration of labour market implications and policies, it may be useful to recall the principal "development strategies" and then compare the most relevant elements of the orthodox "structural adjustment" (or "supply-side") strategy with those of what might be described as a "social adjustment" strategy. The differences between those two ideal types are quite substantial.

As far as development strategies are concerned, one can distinguish four distinctive patterns, each of which reflect the social and political structures and economic endowments of various countries. The first is *agro-export production*, based on large estates and powerful landlords or agro-enterprises. Many countries, notably in Central America, still adhere to something like this structure. In such cases, one finds an impoverished "peasantry" supplying seasonal or migratory wage labour, a concentration on export crops to the relative neglect of domestically-consumed food crops, and a very limited growth of industrial capacity. Since urban-industrial labour absorption is restricted, as is the public sector, policies that altered relative prices and returns to investment *could* lead to a reallocation of resources to urban areas. But devaluations would scarcely rectify balance of payments deficits, given the low price elasticity of demand for agro-exports. Cutting public expenditure as a means of freeing resources for private, industrial investment would also have a limited role, since the public sector in societies dominated by agro-export production is typically rather small. Sustained economic development in such countries cannot be envisaged without fairly fundamental reform of the economic structure, and more widespread access to land, credit, technology and markets.

A second development strategy, also rural-oriented, is what might be described as *neo-populist autonomy*, whereby an attempt is made to delink the economy from the international division of labour and pursue "balanced" economic growth through communal production and distribution. Countries pursuing something of this kind have had some success in redistribution but have had far less satisfactory results in terms of growth. A feature of such systems has been bureaucratisation of production, the mechanism by which state-organised redistribution of economic surplus has limited income differentiation. There has been little surplus for productive investment, while a "motivational crisis" has arisen, reflecting the lack of incentives for investment or for dynamic labour supply. Among the labour consequences has been structural underemployment in rural areas and then a growing pool of urban unemployed, the latter partly reflecting the absence of basic consumer goods in rural communities. In short, the strategy has run into major problems. Yet to impose an orthodox supply-side structural adjustment package on such countries would have chaotically disruptive effects on the economy and political system.

A third development strategy is *import-substitution industrialisation,* designed to free foreign exchange for the acquisition of capital and technology for autonomous economic growth. This has, in practice, depended on the prior creation of a mobile labour force supplying labour at low cost in urban, industrialising areas. Among the conventional criticisms of this strategy is that it is not based on a country's comparative advantages and involves adoption of inappropriately capital-intensive techniques of production. It has tended to result in high urban unemployment, segmented labour markets and a chronic proliferation of small-scale "survival" (or informal) activities in the slums and other areas that surround the small number of relatively high-paying enterprises subsidised to produce goods that are supposed to displace imports. It is countries that have been pursuing this development path that those advocating the supply-side adjustment package most often have in mind.

It is the fourth principal development strategy that has been most widely advocated, namely *export-led industrialisation.* This has sometimes been based on a phase of accumulation through import substitution, as exemplified by the Republic of Korea. But export-led growth depends on international competitiveness. That has led to overwhelming emphasis on measures to alter relative prices, and in particular wage rates. To be successful, export-led industrialisation *seems* to necessitate some rather painful changes. Countries pursuing this strategy have depended on the initial creation of a large surplus population available to provide a flexible, low-cost labour force and to act as a disciplining threat to those in employment. Moreover, to ensure a low-cost, efficient labour supply, not only have wages been held down, but measures have been used to limit workers' rights and their bargaining power over working conditions.

To the extent that export-led industrialisation leads to labour absorption, the dynamics of an open labour market could be expected to drive up wages, inducing labour-saving technological change, a restructuring of production or a slowdown in the growth of exports. Whatever the exact mix of those effects, the rising costs of production would help other, less-developed industrialising economies to acquire a share of the international market for those goods on which that country's initial industrial spurt had been based.

However, in countries where export-led industrialisation has flourished to the point where they could be classified as "newly-industrialised", the labour market has been circumvented, notably by policies and institutions devised to check the incipient growth of labour's bargaining power. Are such measures necessary or even the most "efficient" for sustained export-led industrialisation? Normally, means of restraint have included restrictions on trades unions activities or the suppression of unions altogether, a ban on industrial action, promotion of increased labour intensity through, for example, the sanction of long work-weeks in export industries, the bypassing of health and safety regulations and the non-provision of fringe benefits. Many workers end up "over-employed", working 60 hours a week as a condition of employment.[11] Other workers have been pushed into insecure, low-income jobs, with little chance of avoiding a lifetime of insecurity and deprivation.

Even more than with import-substitution, this development strategy has relied on low-cost female labour. Typically, young women have been drawn or pushed into the urban-industrial labour market, commonly to do semi-skilled jobs, to assemble imported components or to work on semi-automated production lines. In industrial export zones, set up in many countries pursuing export-led industrialisation, women often account for three-quarters of total employment. The social and labour market implications are profound. In the absence of extensive systems of industrial craftsmanship, one rarely finds the emergence of a skilled male "labour aristocracy" of manual workers, with the type of income and status associated with wives and children, and even older relatives, outside the labour force. Indeed, the nature of such industrialisation has meant a general mobilisation of labour supply, from women, from migrants, even from children, but only a limited development of a skilled labour force. Other measures have been needed to ensure such development and the emergence of a more diversified productive structure.

Of the four development strategies, export-led industrialisation, if successful, appears to offer the best prospect for sustained labour absorption. There is more doubt about the necessity for the labour market policies countries have put in place. Some also doubt whether more than a few countries could successfully follow suit in the near future, *partly* because if many developing countries did manage to increase their share of world manufacturing trade by substantial amounts, the (short-term) disruption to more industrialised countries would lead to protective responses to limit their imports. Although it is customary to discuss this latter doubt as a "fallacy of composition", it is one of the dilemmas arising from a global strategy of economic growth through trade liberalisation. Another is the problem of transition, particularly for middle-income developing countries such as the Philippines.[12] Among the countries that have attempted to move from an import-substitution strategy to export-oriented industrialisation based on trade liberalisation and a structural adjustment package, some have floundered in part because they have been hit by the imports from technologically advanced countries *and* by those from lower-cost developing countries.

Supply-side and social adjustment labour policies

Thus there are two complementary orthodoxies in place - an outward-oriented development policy and a supply-side stabilisation and adjustment policy. Stabilisation policy essentially means a tight monetary policy to combat inflation and hold down domestic demand, so limiting imports. That means lowering many people's living standards and employment in the short-term. Coupled with that is an outward-looking development policy, which means trade liberalisation, by nominal and real exchange rate devaluation, by cutting selective and general protection and by a shift in relative prices between tradeable and non-tradeable goods and services.

In recent years the pressure for adjustment to external economic shocks and the belief in outward-oriented development have led to a sustained critique of many labour market policies long perceived as desirable attributes of development. As a consequence of the supply-side critique, we have witnessed the juxtaposition of two perspectives on labour market policy, which we will characterise as a "social adjustment" model and the "supply-side" model.[13] It may be useful to contrast the main elements of each view.

For a long period, the dominant mode of economic thinking could be summarised as the social adjustment perspective. The underlying assumptions were Keynesian, backed by a social democratic ethos and a belief that markets could and should be circumvented or moderated by institutional and other regulatory devices in the interest of both equity and long-run economic growth.

For well-known reasons this perspective was thrown onto the defensive by the economic upheavals of the 1970s and 1980s and the pressure for rapid and extensive adjustments to internationally-transmitted economic shocks and instability.[14] The result was the global triumph of the supply-side perspective, based on an overwhelming faith in markets untramelled by protective regulations, collective organisations or other institutional interventions. The pursuit of outward-oriented development became a global panacea, with earnest economists everywhere diligently searching for "rigidities" - particularly but not only associated with trade unions and labour regulations - that were alleged to be raising production costs and undermining the competitiveness of country x or y. This perspective has been pervasively influential during the past decade, but one can anticipate a continuing debate between its exponents and those of a reemerging social adjustment model more concerned with distributional issues, institutional structures and the labour process itself.[15]

The following discussion attempts to contrast the views of the two perspectives on labour market policies. The intention is to identify competing hypotheses, provide a tentative research agenda, and clarify the underlying assumptions and values of the alternative views.

Price versus social distortions

The essence of a conventional social adjustment strategy is "growth with social protection." Among its elements are the following labour-related aspects. First, to alleviate poverty of the most basic kind, there are usually food subsidies and price support systems to encourage the production of domestically-consumed food. Supply-side critics say that these are "market distortions." Second, there is usually some minimum-wage protection machinery, designed to reduce exploitation and alleviate poverty. Critics say that this is a market distortion, raising wages above the market clearing, equilibrium level, deterring employment by favouring capital-labour substitution and increasing "inequalities between the formal and informal sectors." Third, there are institutional forms of labour security protection - safety-and-health standards, employment security regulations, limits on working time, etc. These are also intended to protect workers from exploitation and, by ameliorating working conditions, enhance productivity. Critics say they amount to market distortions, since they represent non-wage labour costs and rigidities that impede labour mobility and thus efficient resource allocation.

Fourth, a social adjustment approach would foster freedom of association and the legitimacy of collective organisations. Trade unions should be given an active role, to strengthen democratic tendencies, ensure more equitable income distribution, restrict discrimination, and promote social integration. Neoclassical critics see such organisations as market distortions in that they limit the ability of firms to react to market forces, limit the realisation of high profits that could boost investment, and limit "individual freedom". Fifth, in the social adjustment model public expenditure is regarded as complementing private expenditure, as potentially productive and as a means of mobilising and retaining resources for national development. Critics say this too is a market distortion, arguing that it results in "financial crowding out" of private investment and growth, while being unproductive, unresponsive to market forces and an inappropriate standard setter for wages and conditions of employment.

By contrast with the social adjustment model, the labour-related policies associated with the supply-side strategy focus on price mechanisms and overcoming what are depicted as price distorting statutory interventions. Thus governments should cut subsidies to basic consumption goods because they distort market signals. Critics from the social adjustment perspective might say that the removal of subsidies results in "social distortion", and a loss of welfare.[16] They might also argue that subsidies on "non-tradeables" promote productivity of the current and future workforce and lower the optimal efficiency wage in export and import-substitution industrial sectors. The evidence is far from conclusive that cutting such subsidies, thereby altering the relative prices of tradeables and non-tradeables, is unequivocally beneficial for industrial development.

Minimum wages and wage differentials

Traditional social concerns over wages have included (a) the need to protect those in low-paid, low productivity jobs from poverty, (b) the need to protect vulnerable groups from wage discrimination, (c) the desirability of reducing wage differentials, and (d) the need to ensure productivity-enhancing stability and predictability of earnings. These concerns lead to advocacy of minimum wages, anti-discriminatory measures, collective bargaining and so on.

By contrast, the supply-side view is that you need to be harsh to be kind. It focuses almost exclusively on "cost competitiveness" and stresses that nominal and real wage flexibility is essential for structural adjustment and low unemployment.[17] It is also believed that wage differentials must be wide and that measures to combat group-specific wage inequality harms the employment prospects of the "low productivity" groups. In short, if market clearing wages were allowed, unemployment above the "natural" level (defined by structural and frictional factors) would be short-lived. A crucial part of their labour market analysis is the presumption of a labour market dualism in which formal sector wages are held up by minimum wage and other "price distorting" mechanisms, notably trade unions and statutory obligations on employers.[18] Much the same analysis has been applied to both industrialising and industrialised economies.[19] Stripped to essentials, their policy prescription is to "deregulate" the formal sector, reduce or remove "non-wage labour costs", decentralise wage bargaining to the individual worker-employer level if possible, and remove or erode minimum wage machinery, so that labour costs will fall and the "quasi-voluntarily" unemployed queueing for formal sector jobs will filter back into available informal sector jobs.[20]

This view of wage determination in industrialising countries is a little like a punchbag, absorbing empirical punishment from a host of institutional realities. We will consider the role of labour regulations and standards later. Here we will concentrate on the wage-labour supply nexus.

First, it must be reiterated that industrialising countries hailed as examples of supply-side success have relied in part on wage repression, not unregulated market clearing, on negative regulations, not deregulation. Thus in Singapore collective bargaining over fringe benefits was restricted, union leaders jailed for years and strikes outlawed, while the government-dominated National Wages Council and the National Trades Union Congress held down wages.[21] In the early 1980s wage repression was briefly reversed "to restore wages to market levels", so as to induce technological restructuring away from labour-intensive production, which demonstrated that early industrialisation had not been based on market clearing, open labour markets. The Government took actions to "distort" the price of labour by lowering the social wage, through housing subsidies for workers and the provision of other social welfare, such as education and health care.[22] In the Republic of Korea, the government long controlled union activity and pressured employers to prevent wage rises, both directly and through the banks.[23] In Taiwan, China, the Union Act made unionisation of factories mandatory, and it is not too fanciful to believe that was solely to restrict workers' rights; strikes for wage increases were outlawed. In Malaysia and in other industrialising countries, differential labour regulations have been applied in export processing zones so as to lower labour costs in export-oriented manufacturing plants. In short, it is disengenuous to claim that "price distortions" have been avoided in successful cases of industrial growth.

All this recalls an old debate about the transition to industrialism in Western Europe, when State actions created a surplus population free in the double sense - free from the means of production and free to hire out their labour. In effect, wages were driven down by measures to lower the supply price of labour. In today's developing countries, perhaps the most elegant study of such a process was Arrighi's historical analysis of Rhodesia. Of course, most cases of successful industrialisation have been preceded by land reform that has loosened ties to the land of a large part of the population. To focus on market-clearing wages or to cite wage distortion as the crucial variable is moot when interventions have lowered the supply price of labour to the low-income informal economy by the creation of surplus labour conditions. The social adjustment view is that measures should be introduced to raise opportunity incomes in the low-income, "informal" economy, not reduce the wages of those for whom some wage protection had been achieved. The supply side retort would be that a developing country cannot afford that route. But in a sense that would merely shift attention further away from the structural-institutional variables.

In both industrialising and industrialised economies one can cite numerous ways by which wages have been depressed in the interest of "pricing people into work", by wage subsidies, fiscally supported "two tier" wage structures and so on. The pragmatic justification of such measures is at odds with the declared aim of letting markets work.

Wage protection by contrast is attacked for disrupting market mechanisms. Statutory minimum-wage machinery has been eroded in many parts of the world, and minimum wages have generally fallen relative to average wages.[24] The supply-side view is that minimum wages cause unemployment and sluggish labour mobility, partly by pricing goods out of the market produced by low-productivity workers.

However, familiar objections are unanswered. Minimum wages have multiple functions, including that of raising productivity. Low wages encourage low productivity, as demonstrated in the American economy in the past decade, and also favour enterprises unconcerned with long-term employment relations. Minimum wages pressurise firms to find ways of raising productivity, whether by technological change or by the provision of training. Such effects are often neglected. Thus, one influential labour economist recently stated:

> "So long as we have unskilled workers, the only way they will remain in work is if their relative wages adjust."[25]

This is nonsense. Lowering the wages of the unskilled is one way of ensuring they remain unskilled, whereas one way of ensuring that they remain in work is by providing them with the skills; another is by altering the job structure to utilise the skills that they undoubtedly have as human beings. It is one example of an overbearing focus on prices.

The supply-side view ignores the role of wages in securing labour commitment, on which there has been a neglected literature going back many years. Commonly, a dualism is postulated in which the minimum wage in an ill-defined "formal sector" is above the average income in the residual "informal sector", and then the analyst proceeds on the presumption that the price of labour is distorted in the former. That the dualism is arbitrary is one well-rehearsed problem. Perhaps equally importantly, this view neglects the role of wages in securing an optimum effort bargain from workers in enterprises and jobs requiring high commitment, efficiency and skill application. Thus, although minimum wages may be above the average income received outside modern, export-oriented industrial enterprises, or above the "aspiration wage" of unemployed job-seekers, it cannot be presumed that they exceed the optimum "efficiency wage", the wage at which the average worker works with optimal effort.[26] Minimum wages also deter the use of low-productivity workers such as children, and thus reduce labour force segmentation and encourage firms to concentrate on efficiency.

Critics of the supply-side emphasis on reducing real wages also observe that lowering unit labour costs can either be achieved by lowering wages with constant productivity (or with a lower decline in the latter) or by raising productivity with constant wages (or even allowing a rise in the latter, if they rise less than productivity). Research suggests that minimum wages lead to narrower wage differentials at the top end, compressing the wage structure, rather than leading to a loss of employment at the minimum wage level.[27] Have those who believe that minimum wages should be eroded or abandoned considered both the potential employment effects and the impact on wage differentials? *If* the impact is mainly on wage differentials and *if* that creates some labour immobility, then a social adjustment approach would entail some other mobility enhancing policies, not cuts in the minimum wage.

A related supply-side line of reasoning is that country x has failed to achieve export-led industrial growth because high labour costs do not justify the fixed infrastructural costs of moving into export markets (e.g. extending harbours, railways, roads).[28] Jamaica has been mentioned in this regard, leading to calls to lower manufacturing wages.[29] Given the paucity of reliable national data in such countries, closer examination might reveal a rather different picture. Thus a survey of export-oriented manufacturing factories in Kingston, Jamaica, indicated a pattern of low productivity, high absenteeism and low money wages.[30] Labour costs were high because there was a high ratio of fringe benefits to money wages, which encouraged absenteeism (in some cases to over 20 per cent a day), while skill formation was limited not by narrow wage differentials but by a lack of regulations on skill classifications and

pervasive market-led poaching of partially-trained workers. Poaching (a feature of flexible, unregulated labour practices) discouraged firms from investing
in training, which could have raised productivity and lowered the product wage.
Employers had responded to market signals, in that they had raised the ratio
of fringe benefits to wages to combat labour turnover, which could be attributed
in part to a lack of regulations and public expenditure on education and
training. The general point of such examples is that it is simplistic to focus on
wage rates without looking at underlying institutional mechanisms.

The supply-side approach also emphasises a need for relative wage
changes, or adjustment in the "equilibrium" structure of real wages. The
reasoning goes something like this. Real wages of skilled workers in protected
import-competing industries have to decline, to encourage such workers to shift
to export industries, while the wages of skilled workers in the latter should
stabilise, or rise *if* inter-sectoral labour mobility is slow. With nominal exchange
rate devaluations, the price of tradeables rises relative to non-tradeables,
leading labour to flow into the tradeable sectors, theoretically leaving relative
wages unchanged. If wages of some sectors are protected, this distributional
neutrality will not follow. If wage differentials are reduced by minimum wage
or other mechanisms, then the returns to education or training will be reduced
to the point where the incentive to invest in them is insufficient. This is further
reason, in their view, to whittle away at minimum wage machinery.

However, this reasoning runs into some familiar objections. At the
micro-level, real wages may be below the efficiency level, so resulting in
stagnant productivity. The link between wages and induced technological
change is peculiarly omitted in the neoclassical paradigm. At the macro-level,
it is too easy to *assert* that high unemployment (in whatever form) is "classical".
It may actually be largely "Keynesian", even in low-income countries or in
economies with high inflation. In that case, if real wages rose, not only would
there be efficiency gains in export or tradeable industries, but aggregate
demand for goods produced outside the export-oriented sectors would rise.
Structural adjustment could be aided, because the demand for such goods
would rise, probably boosting small-scale, productive enterprises; higher real
wages would not have any "crowding out" effects on investment in tradeable
sectors, but could create a virtuous growth path of accumulation in low-income
parts of the economy.

What then of inter-sectoral labour mobility? In the supply-side view,
wages are supposed to adjust, creating the appropriate mobility for adjustment
without prolonged high unemployment. Attention has concentrated on labour
market segmentation as an obstacle to successful structural adjustment programmes. Riveros invites us to focus on the "two basic questions":

> "Is the presence of distortions associated with labour market segmentation a
> factor that may hinder the effectiveness of exchange rate policies? Is labour
> market segmentation a factor that may foster a detrimental equity impact of
> typical adjustment policies?" [31]

From a dualistic model applied to the Philippines, he concluded that "nominal devaluations broaden the formal/informal wage gap" while "labour market distortions exert a negative effect on the real exchange rate" and "labour market segmentation, which derives mostly from government intervention", leads to the policy implication that there is a "need for deregulating the labour market".[32]

A basic difficulty lies in the procedure of conceptualising labour markets in dualistic terms. Why focus on a two-sector rather than on an n-sector approach? In most economies, the main forms of labour mobility are something like the following (each being in both directions): (i) Rural - urban; (ii) International (e.g. "brain drain"); (iii) Public - private; (iv) Small establishments ("sweatshop/survival units" and "flexible specialists") - large; (v) Less "skilled" - more skilled.

Collapsing all "segments" into a contrived dualism may perhaps be justified, but surely we cannot know that a priori. For instance, if wages were reduced in some "formal sector", mobility under (ii) could be adversely affected (a major problem in small open economies), as could mobility under (v). Another basic point about moving from non-segmented theorising to segmentation approaches (which is what much of the structural adjustment literature on labour markets seems to entail) is that one cannot analyse segmented labour markets without linking that process to labour stratification and segregation, or the social division of labour.[33] Labour mobility between sectors or job clusters may be limited not because of wage protection but because social groups are occupationally or sectorally segregated. For instance, in *all* cases of successful export-led industrialisation the "formal sector" has relied on the mobilisation of female labour, coming from rural areas, low-income marginal activities or from outside the recognised labour market. Male workers have not shifted into tradeable sectors because of labour force segmentation, not labour market (sector) segmentation. The main labour market "distortion" comes from the payment of sub-subsistence wages to young female workers, not from excessive wages in "male" jobs.

Another common proposal is that to increase mobility into sectors producing tradeables, relative wages should change and that, because relative wages are "sticky", governments should concentrate on lowering public sector wages because they have little control over private-sector wages. This has been one justification for the tremendous cuts in public sector wages in many parts of the world.

However, do real wages of workers in non-tradeable sectors have to fall in the pursuit of labour mobility? The social adjustment view would be that labour market policies, notably (re-)training and mobility assistance, could avoid any need for wider wage differentials, even if there was labour immobility *and* that it was of the type in the theoretical model. Indeed, by *reducing* wage differentials, labour mobility from low to high productivity sectors might be accelerated, not slowed, if only because that would raise the relative and absolute return to high productivity sector investment, while higher costs in low productivity industries would squeeze such firms out of business. One could also question the claim that by narrowing wage differentials, minimum wages deter skill acquisition by reducing the return to education. There are many non-wage benefits of higher education, and in any case since schooling is a job screening device, it is the enhanced access to job opportunities that maintains high individual economic returns to education and training.

In sum, the combination of low wages plus wider wage differentials is not a panacea for labour market adjustment. But this leads us back to a concern for a renewed social adjustment model, for there has been an erosion of wage protection, pushed by some governments and international institutions and as a result of more flexible labour systems.

Wage and payment system flexibility

Another key supply-side theme is that wages should be allowed to fluctuate and that, if they were tied more to economic performance and profits, not only would employment be stabilised cyclically, but it would do so at higher levels than with fixed wages. The policy preference is decentralisation of wage determination, erosion of collective bargaining, and the introduction of flexible payment systems such as "profit-related pay". These trends have been widespread in both industrialised and low-income countries. Thus, for example, under the structural adjustment regime in Chile both centralised and sectoral collective bargaining were banned; recently, bargaining has been allowed at plant level only.

However, decentralised, market-oriented wage determination does not produce more wage flexibility than centralised consensual systems. Wage flexibility has been shown to be greatest in the most centralised, "corporatist" economies, followed by those with the most decentralised systems, with intermediate cases being the least flexible.[34] There is also substantial research showing that "social corporatism" achieves better macro-economic performance in terms of employment, inflation and wage dispersion than decentralised systems. There is also evidence that not only is the "atomistic and competitive labour market" the worst case for employment but that the wider the range of issues subject to centralised bargaining the better the macro-economic outcome, since the economic actors can make Pareto-improving deals.[35]

Second, decentralisation coupled with payment systems tying wages to profits runs into familiar objections.[36] A social adjustment view would be that as long as workers do not at least have a share in the decisions over investment or productive strategy, it would be unjust for them to have to bear the risk. Moreover, if payment systems are made more flexible - as is happening in some countries pursuing structural adjustment strategies - then a likely consequence would be a widening of earnings differentials between those in high-tech sectors and those outside them. There is evidence of this.[37] For some, that may be acceptable, but not from a social equity point of view. Flexible payment systems may also result in extremely low and uncertain earnings for those in low-productivity jobs and may slow structural change rather than accelerate it, to the extent that capital is tied up in inefficient, low-productivity production.

These strictures on decentralisation and individualistic flexible payment systems should perhaps lead us to consider renewed consideration of alternative forms of "incomes policy", a much abused term in the past decade or so, and alternative forms of productive organisation, notably co-operative forms that pool risk, reward and work organisation.[38] The challenge surely is to move towards systems that promote adjustment, productivity and flexibility while maintaining rather than disrupting progress towards social equity and co-operative solidarity.

In that context, the position and role of trade unions have been controversial. For those taking a supply-side, neo-liberal view, unions are the source of wage rigidity, lowering productivity through restrictive practices and the pursuit of employment security in place of flexibility. Some taking the supply-side view take a slightly more nuanced position, but feel that on balance unions impede adjustment, so that their monopolistic position should be curtailed.

By contrast, the social adjustment perspective depicts unions as not only necessary social agents, but as a source of dynamic efficiency, forcing enterprises to pursue an efficiency wage policy, obliging them to avoid the low-wage, low-productivity route and pressurising them to be technologically and organisationally innovative. Ultimately, even *if* the economic arguments were the only ones that mattered, the outcome is empirical and anything but predetermined. The issues deserve more balanced research than has shaped some policy prescriptions in recent years.[39] The paper by Lucio Geller in this volume addresses some of the critical issues and highlights how unions can play an indispensable role in securing employment changes in the context of rapid structural change.

The public sector, privatisation and labour market implications

The supply-side approach to structural adjustment involves a substantial reduction and a redirection of public expenditure, as well as a shrinking role for the public sector. Privatisation has become a global crusade, with over 100 countries having privatisation programmes, many of which are part of structural adjustment programmes. In the process, it sometimes appears to have been forgotten that there were a set of compelling reasons for nationalisation, including a desire to stabilise employment and reduce economic dependency on foreign capital. Now it is more often believed that privatisation will promote efficiency.

Cutbacks in public expenditure have often proved the most resented and hard-to-implement component of a structural adjustment package. For example, after the 1989 General Election in Jamaica, the outgoing Prime Minister, Edward Seaga, attributed his defeat to the obligation under the IMF structural adjustment programme to make sharp cutbacks in social services, particularly education, the longstanding source of hope for the poor in the country. The Government of Sri Lanka in 1989 resisted an IMF stabilisation and adjustment package because it wished to introduce a poverty alleviation scheme to cushion the poor, which would mean maintaining public expenditure as a high proportion of GDP. Such agonising, in fact, flows from an orthodoxy that denigrates the public sector and public expenditure.

The supply-side view is that the public sector as a vehicle of public expenditure is a market distortion, "financially crowding out" private investment and growth, while being unproductive, unresponsive to market forces and an inappropriate standard setter for wages and conditions of employment.[40] In the social adjustment model, public expenditure is regarded as largely complementing private expenditure, as potentially productive, as a means of mobilising and retaining resources for national development and as a counter-cyclical policy.

Public expenditure cuts have almost invariably adversely affected public sector employment. Often it has been a condition of IMF-World Bank structural adjustment loans that the Government should cut or freeze public service sector recruitment, as was done for instance in Zambia in the mid-1980s, where it seems one consequence was that public service efficiency declined.[41] Such declines often arise because the cuts result in structural mismatches, with critical vacancies being left unfilled. However, in most industrialised and low-income countries the brunt of the deterioration has been in average wages rather than in employment; in general, public sector wages have fallen sharply relative to equivalent private sector wages. Such trends can easily induce the stagnation in productivity that is used to justify further cuts and privatisation. The almost incredible declines in public sector wages and terms of employment in many parts of Africa have led to widespread "daylighting" and other responses by civil servants that seriously erode public sector productivity.[42] In some industrialised countries similar patterns have been unfolding. If public sector cutbacks are pursued on narrow efficiency grounds, then surely cutting public sector wages while maintaining employment is inappropriate. That is what has been done under many supply-side structural adjustment programmes. It could be described as stabilisation policy "making prices wrong".

As for reducing public sector wages, this may *or* may not be justified economically. In recent years, just as it is too easily *presumed* that the size of the public sector is "bloated" and that it is socially unproductive, it has been too easily taken as an article of faith that public sector wages and fringe benefits are excessive. It *may* be that wages should be reduced; it *may* be that wage rates should be maintained but the level of public employment cut to raise efficiency; it *may* be that wages and employment should be cut relative to expenditure on other inputs involved in social service provision, for example. All these responses are possible. But the choice should not be made without prior analysis of which, if any, such action makes economic and social sense. As far as we know, such analysis has rarely preceded the action taken.

One should also be wary about justifying public sector wage cuts by reference to higher productivity in the private sector. *If* high profits in some private firms were produced by such low wages and poor working conditions that workers could only be productive for short periods before having to leave or before reaching the point where employers sought their replacement, then cutting public sector wages could compound a longer-term trend towards stagnant labour productivity in the economy. Again, one cannot presume that if relative prices are in imbalance, the higher one should be lowered. Another reason for having reservations about efficiency claims is that those closely involved with privatisation advocate efficiency run-downs prior to sell-offs. As the internationally-influential Adam Smith Institute put it:

> "Micropolitics is the art of generating circumstances in which individuals will be motivated to prefer and embrace the alternative of private supply".[43]

One insufficiently considered aspect of public sector employment policy is that, while salaries, benefits and employment security of a core of public sector employees may be favourable, beyond that privileged group are numerous workers whose wages are low by comparison with private sector workers and whose employment security is minimal. With cuts in public expenditure those workers will probably be the first to suffer and to suffer the most. Yet they may be the least skilled technically and thus the least able to transfer from the non-tradeable to the tradeable sectors. Moreover, one of the main forms of privatisation has been the contracting out of employment, and there are widespread fears that this results in more insecure working conditions.[44]

The public sector has been a source of labour security, both directly and through welfare services; it has reinforced social mechanisms of income support, rather than leaving them to "households". So, indirectly and inadvertently, privatisation may have a disruptive effect on social survival networks, both in developing and industrialised countries.

Privatisation also has implications for inequality, labour force stratification and for labour and consumer rights.[45] The public sector has been a major source of social equity, both in terms of its provision of social services to the poor and through its role in the labour market. For instance, the female share of public sector employment has tended to be higher than in the private sector, while gender wage differentials have been smaller.[46] Paradoxically, privatisation may have increased the feminisation of public sector employment, probably because of the deterioration of wages, benefits and labour security.[47] But this may well be associated with worsening gender-related inequality.

It is not to argue for or against privatisation to suggest that, in the absence of appropriate safeguards, it may lead to erosion of wages and employment security, an increase in labour force segmentation and a growth of external labour flexibility. When welfare implications of structural adjustment are considered, those possibilities should surely not be neglected. In some countries privatisation has been accompanied by obligations on the new private corporations to preserve employment or wage levels for a certain period. That seems to reflect an expectation that otherwise they would decline or that the workforce would be subject to increased labour insecurity.

Adjustment, labour regulations and labour market fragmentation

"The successful use of competition as the principle of social organisation precludes certain types of coercive interference with economic life, but it admits of others which sometimes may very considerably assist its work and even requires certain kinds of government action." [48]

One of the myths of the past decade lies in the notion of deregulation. Both the neoclassical supply-side theorists and any respectable variant of social adjustment believe in regulation and regulations.[49] In reality, the neoclassical synthesis believes in individualistic regulations (i.e. *anti*-collective) while the social adjustment perspective believes in solidaristic, protective regulations (i.e. *pro*-collective).

Both the supply-side and social adjustment perspectives give a pivotal role to labour market "dualism" or "segmentation". According to the former, excessive regulations and minimum wages are shown by the growth of the "informal sector" and the stagnation of the "formal", tradeable sector. They advocate dismantling of such regulations so that more of the informal can become formal, or vice versa, and so that employment can rise. By contrast, the social adjustment view is that the long-term objective should be the extension of social protection to those currently uncovered and surviving in petty units of production or in other peripheral activities, whether productive or merely survival-oriented. Priority should be given to anti-discrimination and protective regulations designed to reduce the marginalisation of socially vulnerable groups, notably women, children, migrants and ethnic minorities.

A few conceptual distinctions are worth making about labour regulations. First, it seems useful to distinguish between *protective, repressive* and *paternalistic* regulations. In practice, supply-siders do not believe in labour deregulation, but in regulations designed to restrict collective action on the part of labour. Many advocates of "deregulation" have been remarkably silent on repressive regulations.

The Republic of Korea is a good example of the mix of types of labour regulations. It is after all the ideal type of export-led industrialisation. For many years it relied on a mix of repressive and paternalistic labour regulations. The former included police enforcement of factory discipline in the 1940s and 1950s, the disbanding of independent unions in 1961, the "temporary" law of 1970 - which lasted until May 1986 - restricting labour rights in foreign-owned firms, and the 1971 Law Concerning Special Measures for Safeguarding National Security, which inter alia banned all collective action and extended compulsory arbitration to all industries.[50] When the IMF pushed for a stabilisation policy in the early 1970s and urged wage restraint, the Government backed up its interventions by introducing paternalistic regulatory measures, including company-specific welfare schemes to strengthen worker commitment, measures to bolster company-appointed unions over independent unions, the Factory Saemaul (New Community) Movement by which work team (Quality Control, Zero Defect) organisations were created to reduce costs and improve productivity, and an ideological campaign promoting the "enterprise as family" which meant more labour through unpaid overtime, longer working hours, abolition of summer holidays, etc.

Another case is Chile. Under Allende, the Labour Law established a centralised system of collective bargaining and labour rights, and provided protective regulations on employment security and income security. Subsequently, under Pinochet repressive regulation, not deregulation, was pervasive; collective bargaining was eliminated, as were union activities, and no employment security was allowed; later, decentralised wage bargaining was made obligatory under the 1979 *Plan Laboral*, while public sector workers were banned from striking. To call such measures deregulation would be a misuse of language.

A second distinction should be made between *explicit* and *implicit* deregulation, the latter referring to the non-enforcement of (protective) regulations, the former to their formal abolition. Implicit deregulation is pervasive. For instance, there is no doubt that the Republic of Korea also had protective regulations that elsewhere would be held up as distorting non-wage labour costs impeding industrial growth. Under the Labour Standards Law of 1953, there was an 8 hour working day, a limit of 48 hours a week, paid holidays, severance pay, safety and health regulations, protection of women and young workers, etc. Later some loopholes were introduced, so that for example workers could work up to 60 hours a week by "mutual agreement" with their employers. But the reality was non-enforcement. In 1986, the mean average working week in manufacturing was nearly 55 hours, giving Korea the distinction of having the longest work week among countries for which data are available.

A third distinction should be made between types of worker security to which protective regulations are supposed to apply. There are various forms of labour security, and critics tend to lump them together and then take a one-sided view of the alleged effects on employment and structural adjustment. One should distinguish between:
  (i)   labour market security;
  (ii) employment security;
  (iii) job security;
  (iv) work security;
  (v)   labour representation security;
  (vi) income security.

Labour market security is high when job changing involves only modest personal costs and reasonable prospects of subsequent benefits, and is typically inversely related to the level of unemployment. Employment security is high when workers cannot be dismissed without either costs to employers or the satisfaction of pre-specified conditions. Job security is high when workers have rights to particular niches within enterprises, and where unions or other institutions safe-guard craft barriers or skill levels. Work security is high when working conditions are safe and healthy. Labour representation security is high when employment-related changes are subject to negotiation between equally strong, representative groups, or when workers are able to influence the pace and direction of change. Finally, income security is high when workers have their wages or income protected from fluctuations either by indexation, collective bargaining or other institutional protection.[51]

The crucial difference between the current orthodoxy and a social adjustment view is that the former sees protective regulations as costs and barriers to growth, whereas a social adjustment view is that they express social objectives in themselves and are also instrumental in pushing firms to be more dynamic and co-operative in nature.

All six forms of security have *potential* costs and *potential* benefits for enterprises and for the pursuit of structural adjustment and economic growth. Because it is their alleged costs that have been stressed in recent international debates, it may be appropriate to highlight the potential benefits.

Take, for example, job security. Many firms have introduced job security arrangements precisely because they were perceived as conducive to productivity growth; this was the essence of Taylorist management, since narrowly-defined job classifications enabled employers to have closer control over output, work input and labour costs. Accordingly, one should not presume that the erosion of job security regulations is always desired even on efficiency grounds. Moreover, job security to a certain extent surely encourages the development of technical skill within jobs, because workers can expect a return to training and informal learning on the job. Against that, if job demarcation results in workers resisting technological change and redeployment, then regulations or union agreements protecting job security could hinder structural adjustment and impair economic growth. As it is, there seems to have been a global trend towards reduced job security, often involving a tremendous collapsing of job classifications.[52]

However, it is employment security that most critics have in mind when castigating "job security regulations", on the grounds that workers in secure employment have less incentive to be productive,[53] are immobile in the face of a need for structural adjustment,[54] or have to be compensated to such an extent that the potential benefits of resource reallocation are lost. It is also claimed that employment security regulations discourage enterprises from hiring workers and encourage them to opt for more capital-intensive techniques of production, and that they prevent wage flexibility because of the "insider-outsider" divide.[55] This is a set of strong claims. Yet employment security regulations also have potential economic benefits:

(a)　They can improve workers' commitment to the enterprise and thus raise work motivation and productivity;

(b)　They may reduce the "transaction costs" of employment, by reducing labour turnover, especially important where productivity rises with on-the-job learning;

(c)　They may encourage worker acceptance of productivity raising rationalisation and other modernisation measures

(d)　They may improve job and work flexibility, that is, improve the willingness of workers to accept (and even initiate) occupational and work environmentchanges;

(e)　They may induce greater acceptance of work disciplinary measures;

(f)　They almost certainly improve "dynamic efficiency", that is, the obligation on management to become more efficient and competitive by other means than by laying off workers;

(g)　They may induce workers to accept lower wage rises;[56]

(h)　They may reduce the probability of frictional unemployment by enabling workers made redundant to have adequate notice of impending job loss to seek alternative employment, thus reducing both the individual and social costs of mobility.

So, benefits of employment security regulations may well offset their alleged costs. In that context, one continuing element of the ILO's labour market research programme consists of establishment-level labour flexibility surveys in which the impact of labour regulations can be explored in detail. It is perhaps of interest that the results of a survey of over 2,600 manufacturing firms in Malaysia indicated that, according to the employers, the employment protection regulations there had scarcely any effect on employment; they had a small effect in encouraging a shift in the type of employment, mainly towards the use of more contract labour and temporary workers.[57]

Some economists have suggested that we should not be concerned with labour standards and protective regulations per se but only with "outcomes", once some minimal list of standards have been met.[58] This was an ingenious way of arguing for the abandonment of employment security regulations, on the grounds that they raise labour costs and decrease employment. This is somewhat unconvincing. It is not clear that such regulations do raise labour costs, rather than induce more effective allocation and development of human resources; they should induce more careful (cost-saving) recruitment practices, encourage labour stability and commitment, training, etc. Rather than the level they may affect the type of employment, degree of sub-contracting, and so on. In establishment surveys in Bombay and Malaysia, while the vast majority of employers reported that employment security regulations had no effect on the level of employment, a minority reported that their main effect had been to encourage greater use of contract labour and sub-contracting.

The view that one should only be concerned with outcomes not processes amounts to this: Why care about how you travel if in the long term all income strata are better off? The answer, of course, is that labour process security does matter, and that Keynes' quip about the long run still holds. Those living and working in the present do matter.[59]

Two common claims are that regulations lead to a dichotomy of a regulated and an unregulated sector and that they perversely harm those they are designed to protect, leading to substitution effects. It seems plausible that regulations reduce segmentation by setting standards in sectors where workers have least bargaining strength. In one recent review of the impact of structural adjustment programmes on women it was claimed, not for the first time, that protective legislation such as maternity leave have "the effect of limiting women's access to employment and reducing their earnings in the formal sector".[60] Is the logic that to promote women's employment, maternity leave should be prevented? A social adjustment retort would be that protective regulations should be coupled with other measures to reduce discrimination and to shift the costs, if they exist in net terms, from the employing unit to society.

Clearly, the debate on the role and impact of labour regulations is unresolved, although an impressive number of papers emanating from the World Bank and from the "Eurosclerosis" school have contended that they have adverse consequences.[61] What we do know is that there has been considerable erosion of protective labour regulations in industrialised, industrialising and low-income countries, in response to the growing openness of international trade and the changing international division of labour, under pressure from governments pursuing explicit and implicit protective deregulation, or as a consequence of enterprise-level restructuring of employment relations towards "external" labour flexibility.[62] The result of supply-side policies and corresponding enterprise strategies has been an erosion of all six forms of labour security. Thus, for example, technological-managerial options have grown, which easily leads to labour process insecurity and a decline of collective, co-operative bargaining.

The question of labour regulation cannot be divorced from the enormous growth in so-called informal economic activities in most parts of the world.[63] Part of that has been a reflection of the international recession, deflation and structural adjustment, whereby the unemployed have taken up small-scale employment, family enterprise production and the like, or whereby those whose formal employment earnings have fallen have supplemented them with secondary activities. A further part of the growth has been a reflection of the shift towards sub-contracting by larger enterprises, including State entities, done to reduce costs, or as an aspect of privatisation, or as a consequence of the increased uncertainty and risk in times of recession and structural adjustment.[64] At least part of the growth of small-scale firms is because the liberalisation measures have tended to strengthen large export-oriented firms and squeeze small-scale firms supplying domestic markets.[65] A further part may reflect resort to more informal and unprotected types of worker within, or working for, large enterprises, perhaps done to bypass regulations. Thus, there has been a growth of precarious forms of employment, by one means or another. In many economies, there has been a growing reliance on forms of contract and temporary labour, obliging workers to eke out an insecure existence and try to combine jobs, work statuses and income sources.

These diverse activity patterns of labour use highlight the likelihood that, unless designed to combat the tendency, protective regulations will be bypassed *if* firms perceive a need to do so. They also raise doubts about assumptions such as "that the informal sector is a producer of only non-tradeable goods and uses only unskilled labour". One recognises the need for simplifying assumptions for model specification, but if one derives important policy conclusions from an unrealistic premise one should surely stress that very explicitly.

A popular view, associated with De Soto, is that if only the State would remove all restrictions, notably tax and labour legislation, then the informal economy would become the leading source of economic growth. The evidence does not support such confidence,[66] and there is growing doubt that a massive self-sustaining network of "flexible specialists" could emerge in either developing or industrialised economies. Indeed, small business networks seem to require a very active State regulatory role, including subsidies via training assistance, credit and support for co-operative links between micro-units.[67] Even then, there are grounds for scepticism about their growth and labour absorptive potential.

If one disaggregates these various labour use and activity patterns, one can appreciate that assertions about the adverse effects of labour market regulations on employment levels should be treated with considerable reservation. This is important, for a key theme of the supply-side perspective on adjustment is that "fewer labour market regulations ... would promote labour market flexibility and higher employment" in developing countries, and that "rules on job security ... distort the labour market in ways that reduce employment and overall living standards".[68] Precisely the same argument is made for OECD countries.[69] In fact, regulations may have more impact on *types* of employment than on the level, and raise living standards by setting guidelines, which are by no means met everywhere, but which help to reduce the prevalence of poor working conditions, exploitation and oppression. They also have the potential of promoting social solidarity.

Some believe that because of changing technological and managerial strategies and options, traditional means for preserving and enhancing labour standards are "largely irrelevant".[70] That may be too strong, but it is likely that new forms of labour security are needed to promote flexibility and productivity growth. The challenge that comes to the fore in the context of concerns for structural adjustment is to devise mechanisms to move in the direction of greater and more widely shared access to labour market, employment, job, work, labour process and income security. Advocates of social adjustment must argue that only if workers can share in the decisions and in the benefits as well as the risks of investment can this issue be resolved. That is one reason for believing that there will be renewed interest in the creation of more co-operative organisational structures, where participation, risk taking and rewards are shared, in an environment geared to higher productivity and flexibility of response.

One cannot leave the area of labour regulations without returning to the question of labour rights and international trade. One reason given for removing protective regulations and labour process security, or for forestalling their introduction, is that they would undermine a country's competitiveness and adversely affect foreign capital's confidence in the country. This could easily lead to beggar-my-neighbour deregulation of protective standards and tighter repressive regulations. The problem is that the absence of labour regulations has been said to give some countries unfair trading advantages. Keynes proposed a "social tariff" to deal with such differences. Recently there has been debate about the feasibility of inserting a "social clause" in the next GATT round. A comparable debate in Europe is linked to the proposed Social Charter, which is supported by some EC countries because they support regulations for social adjustment reasons and by others because they fear "social dumping", whereby in a free capital market firms would move to where workers' rights were less developed. A similar fear is one reason cited for the United States linking trade preferences to respect for internationally-recognised worker rights under the 1984 amendment to its Generalised System of Preferences and the 1983 Caribbean Basin Initiative. Some developing countries have opposed such moves on the grounds of intrusion into their internal affairs. Some supporters of labour rights become ambivalent, others mix up the imposition of labour *costs* with the enhancement of labour *rights*. This is one reason for considering the option of positive inducements to encourage export-oriented countries at least to adhere to minimal standards of labour representation security.

Unemployment policies and structural adjustment

The supply-side school expects a period of resource reallocation - through trade liberalisation, market deregulation, etc. - to lead to a transitional period of high unemployment, particularly in economies previously following an import-substitution development strategy. Advocates and critics alike agree that such unemployment should be minimised.[71] But supply-side economists would expect the unemployment level to fall to its "natural" level as a result of market mechanisms, explaining any prolonged high unemployment as due to "market failure" or "voluntary unemployment". Social adjustment proponents would call for inadequate institutional mechanisms to secure labour reallocation, and thus would attribute high unemployment to inadequate labour market policies and inadequate institutional mechanisms for securing labour reallocation.

The appropriate policy response, of course, depends partly on the type of unemployment involved. Without wishing to go into classification issues, one must recall that the supply-side perspective draws heavily on such concepts as the "natural rate of unemployment" and "voluntary unemployment". Thus one widely used model is based on the claim that there is a dualistic labour market such that a wage gap between a formal, regulated sector and an informal, unregulated sector creates "quasi-voluntary" unemployment. From this it is suggested that open unemployment consists of "relatively skilled workers... unwilling to become employed in the low-paid informal sector", whereas the poor cannot afford to be unemployed. There are numerous World Bank and related papers and reports that take something like that view, and there are numerous analyses in the "Eurosclerosis" tradition asserting that much of European unemployment of recent years is voluntary. The logic is less than impeccable, for reasons elaborated elsewhere.[72] Despite assertions to the contrary, in both industrialised and developing countries the vast majority of the unemployed are not well-protected from destitution and in developing countries most of the unemployed are poor, landless people, while many of the "educated" unemployed are youths ill-equipped physically or technically to obtain a niche in informal productive activity.

However, by assuming that most of the unemployed are voluntarily idle, the supply-sider's policy response is likely to be one of neglect (it is not serious) or a regime of obligatory labour (they owe it to society). Indeed, in industrialised countries undergoing adjustment and / or chronically high unemployment, the persistence of unemployment has led many supply-side economists to support some form of "workfare", that is, the obligation to take low-paid employment in lieu of unemployment benefits.[73] This is not leaving the market to clear; it is clearing the market. If one assumes that the unemployment is voluntary, it is easy to claim that it does not exert downward pressure on wages and that the most appropriate response would be measures to reduce distortions that create the unemployment, rather than focus on the unemployed themselves. The unemployment disappears from policy concern through a focus on the employed, or at least those in relatively protected jobs. Alternatively, if one accepts the "hysteresis" view that the long-term unemployed are cut off from the labour market and thus raise the natural rate of unemployment by having no depressive effect on wages, then you go in the direction of selective fiscal or special employment measures oriented to the very long-term unemployed, which seems likely to raise the average duration of unemployment of the remainder and induce behavioural responses that could lead many more to be classified as voluntarily unemployed! Finally, if you assert that unemployment is voluntary and therefore not "real", then the next step is to dismiss the unemployed from the statistics: the market clears by the disappearance of the labour surplus.

These issues are important in assessing structural adjustment programmes and supply-side measures, in part because such arguments have been deployed to minimise concern over the unemployment consequences of expenditure switching and expenditure cutting. For that reason, among others, they should not go unchallenged.

However, in pursuing employment and output restructuring, one can conceive of four *modes of labour (market) adjustment:*
  (i)   External (mid-career) labour market;
 (ii)   Inter-generational;
(iii)   Internal labour market;
(iv)   Redeployment.

External labour market adjustment is generally painful, since it means existing workers being retrenched in some sectors and competing for jobs in others, during which overall and relative wages are expected to adjust in response to labour market disequilibria. This mode has been the norm in orthodox adjustment programmes. Given the existence of labour stratification and non-competing groups, those laid off in middle age are unlikely to find alternative wage employment or compete effectively with younger employed workers.

With the *second* mode, the existing workforce does not engage in mid-career job changes to any unduly large extent, but labour force entrants, mainly youths, are channelled into tradeable rather than non-tradeable sectors; in a period of adjustment, this means high youth unemployment and possibly accelerated "early retirement".

With the *third* mode, workers change jobs within enterprises, corresponding to product or technological changes or job restructuring. It is easy to presume that labour reallocation in the course of structural adjustment cannot be achieved by greater reliance on internal labour markets. But there is almost certainly scope for much more emphasis on this form of adjustment. Finally, the *fourth* mode, redeployment, places emphasis on the State or some other institutional mechanism to *direct* labour mobility, perhaps on a subsidised basis or with retraining.

The more that inter-sectoral and other labour mobility can be achieved by the third and fourth modes of labour market adjustment, the less likely it is that structural change will result in high unemployment. As that would also mean less reliance on relative wage rate changes, the more policy-makers can rely on modes (iii) and (iv), the less the need to widen wage differentials.

In discussing adjustment and employment recently, Streeten concluded,

> "There is one good aspect in conducting adjustment policies in the current environment of unemployment. It is easier to move unemployed workers into the right industries than to shift workers from one job to another. Redeployment and restructuring out of unemployment should be the programme for both developing and advanced countries."[74]

No doubt that conclusion was drawing small comfort from current adverse realities. But workers are rarely made more productive by experience of unemployment, especially if it is prolonged, and unemployed, impoverished workers are scarcely able to afford to indulge in optimal labour market mobility. A number of countries have shown that substantial structural adjustment can be achieved without any period of high unemployment, strongly suggesting that high unemployment is neither necessary for structural adjustment nor preferable to other forms of labour market adjustment. Those countries that have achieved structural adjustment without mass unemployment or severe cuts in wages could surely be emulated. Or could they?

Active labour market policies in "post-Fordism"

One of the most exciting prospects of a renewed social adjustment model is the positive reorientation of active labour market policy. Whether or not one accepts "post-Fordism" as a general trend, the growth of labour market flexibility implies abandonment of the old social Keynesianism version of full employment. But if we can foresee a need for worksharing, more labour mobility and a trend towards lifetime flexibility, we will have to focus on measures to make labour market services more flexible.

One longer term development may be the contracting out of the employment function. This is already happening in many places. But it has inherent dangers. A proliferation of temporary employment agencies can disempower workers by giving agencies and their hirer-clients a double bargaining power while workers are unable to develop any collective solidarity.[75] This points to the need for new forms of unionism representing communities of workers rather than specific crafts or industries. Another related danger is that the privatisation of employment services will lead to a stigmatised, residual public service and more intense marginalisation of vulnerable groups.

Another unresolved issue is the role of "special employment measures" and the provision of "job places" for the unemployed. There is little question that in some countries, notably Sweden, they have been used in an enlightened manner, both as counter-cyclical devices and as part of a bridging process of structural adjustment. But there is an inherent threat to labour process security implied by some closely-related trends. Special measures easily become unspecial: cheap labour schemes, dead-end jobs, ultimately coercive and potentially a means of undermining wages and working conditions at the lower end of the labour market.

As for social security, we have witnessed a transformation of its role in the supply-side era. It was long seen as not just a source of income security in times of recession and structural adjustment but as socially integrative and a means of reducing inequality. The fear now is that its regulative function in the labour process has become paramount. In very many countries conditionality for transfers has been tightened and "targeting" has been a euphemism for something more worrying, that is behavioural manipulation of individuals in the lower end of the labour market. To the extent that "workfare" replaces "welfare", labour obligation replaces labour rights, and the regulatory aspect of social security grows apace. As long as uncoerced reintegration is the guiding principle of "special measures", then they are to be welcomed. Once other labour market/regulatory objectives become prominent, the time to rethink has arrived.

The most topical labour market adjustment policy is training, universally favoured by supply-siders and social adjustment adherents. But there is a difference of emphasis. The supply-side view is that schooling and training should be geared to the needs of export, tradeable industries, and that policy-makers should take a fairly straightforward economic rate of return approach to educational investment. The social adjustment perspective would see education much more as a social end in itself, as well as a means of promoting development.

While tremendous stress has been laid on training and education policy as the means of accelerating labour force adjustment, a few words of caution are in order. It is conventional to argue that the economic rate of return to investment in schooling is higher than in "physical capital". This is comforting justification for boosting education. However, the effective use of educated or trained workers may be very sub-optimal, since access to many jobs may require an excessive level of schooling, simply because schooling attainment is a convenient, low-cost "screening" device in recruitment. More attention should be given to the effective deployment of educated workers. The sub-employment of relatively educated and technically-proficient workers in large corporations is probably a global phenomenon.

In the context of structural adjustment, we should also be wary about abuse of the educational system for short-term efficiency purposes. It is no coincidence that the word schooling means both taming and liberating. If schooling is used to produce docile, disciplined workers (as many stress as a primary objective),[76] then it may hinder the workforce's mobility and relearning potential in future eras of structural adjustment. This is another reason for having reservations about policies based on short-term economic rates of return. Similar problems arise in assessing the extent to which governments should invest in training, making it hard to conclude fairly that "some developing country governments have tended to expand higher-level vocational training too fast."[77] The difficulty is to identify the appropriate criteria for reaching such conclusions.

How can training policy facilitate structural adjustment? It has a triple function, that of raising productivity of workers in existing jobs, that of raising overall productivity of the labour force, and that of facilitating labour mobility as job structures change with technological change and productive restructuring. Several industrialising countries have reached a stage in export-led industrialisation when the Government has come to believe that concentrating on low-cost, labour-intensive industries is no longer appropriate. Singapore went through that phase at the end of the 1970s, when the Government launched a programme to achieve a new "industrial revolution" to go for high-tech, capital-intensive niches. A decade later Mauritius, for instance, reached a similar stage, launching a grandiose strategy for the 1990s named Operation Leapfrog, in which a new Industrial Training Strategy was seen as a crucial mechanism, designed to narrow a perceived skills gap with the established NICs.

Bearing such objectives in mind, training policy can be oriented towards either vocational (or craft) training or job training. In the former, the emphasis is on developing all-round capabilities of workers, whether through prolonged apprenticeship or institutional courses. In the latter, workers are trained solely for jobs they are required to perform in the immediate future. That is cheaper and has involved schemes that impart "modules of employable skill"; as such, it may make fewer demands on trainee and trainer alike, requiring less formal schooling and work commitment. However, it also leaves the worker less adaptable and less equipped to shift jobs or work status in times of industrial restructuring. In effect, the low-cost alternative may yield a lower longer-term social return. Moreover, it is widely believed that this option is becoming less viable, for technological, product cycle and organisational reasons, all of which appear to make skill flexibility more crucial than narrowly defined work capacity.[78]

Similarly, training policy should not be divorced from job structures within enterprises. If jobs are highly stratified, such that there is little use of internal labour mobility, the required amount of formal training will rise. In such circumstances, there has been a neglect of ways of promoting *internal* labour adjustment, through on-the-job learning, incentive structures, anti-discrimination regulations, etc. That could reduce substantially the need for government investment in training schemes. Too often too, it is assumed that if there is a perceived shortage of skilled labour the appropriate policy is more schooling or training. It should not be ruled out that a more appropriate and cost-effective approach would be a policy to alter job structures rather than alter the attributes of people required to fill them. It is technologically deterministic to focus exclusively on the need to train or retrain the workforce.

Finally, there is the form of training. Many economists would argue that labour market training schemes should be implemented by governments as a way of easing labour force adjustments. Undoubtedly, such schemes have a role to play. But they do have drawbacks. If governments subsidise the training of the unemployed, enterprises may simply substitute those trainees for others already trained or partially trained, implying a "substitution effect". Second, the subsidy may merely result in a number of workers being trained who would have been trained anyway, resulting in a "deadweight effect". Third, the trainees may be hired to do jobs for which their training is not really required, because the cost of the training is underpriced. Fourth, as a result of altering the effective "price" of technically-skilled workers, enterprises may alter their job structures to increase the relative demand for workers with those skills, thereby contributing to a persistent "shortage" of such workers. Because labour market training schemes are very rarely *evaluated*, they tend to be overvalued as a means of promoting labour market adjustment.

The principal alternative policy to facilitate labour mobility and adjustment is "in-plant" training. If, as is common, this involves the use of subsidies, the same problems arise, perhaps in more acute form since employers receive the subsidy directly, even though the public cost of this form of training may be lower because part of the cost may be borne by employers.[79] Here too, the challenge is to minimise substitution and deadweight effects.

These points suggest that, in encouraging enterprises to train more extensively, other policies are worth more active consideration, such as anti-poaching regulations - preventing other enterprises from offering financial inducements to attract newly-trained workers without bearing the costs of training - and statutory obligations on enterprises to train a stipulated percent-age of their workforce, perhaps distributed across the range of skills normally required. Such proposals would have to be carefully considered, so as to minimise costs and to maximise efficiency and dynamic flexibility. But moves in those directions must not be ruled out *if* a massive expansion of training is perceived as vital for labour force adjustment.

Concluding remarks: Industrial/organisational structure and labour policy

"The rule is jam tomorrow, and jam yesterday - but never jam today".
The White Queen, in Lewis Carroll: *Alice in Wonderland* and *Through the looking glass* (London, Dent, 1965).

If one conceives of labour market policy as a set of interventions to achieve labour mobility, productivity growth and the steady expansion of labour security in the sixfold sense described earlier, one must form a fairly clear image of the type of labour process involved. In recent years there has been an intense debate on Fordism versus post-Fordism, flexible mass production versus flex-ible specialisation, and so on.[80] The literature on these issues is tremendously fertile, if much of it abstract and speculative. What is clear is that the general trend in recent years, associated with the high flexibility of micro-electronic equipment and the ease with which it can be reprogrammed, is that (a) capital is far more mobile, (b) management-organisational options are more diversi-fied, (c) the balance of negotiating power has shifted from labour to capital, and (d) many forms of conventional labour regulations are not so much right or wrong as potentially irrelevant or enfeebled. For example, to the extent that there is an erosion of labour market and employment security because of increased external flexibility, national insurance-based social security income support becomes potentially anachronistic. To the extent that conventional means of labour-process security are undermined by the fragmentation of employment into various forms of informalisation and the probable coexistence of flexible specialist micro-enterprises, sweatshop sub-contractors and more flexible mass production, one has to think of alternative forms of union and alternative forms of co-operative and redistributive organisations that could reconstitute conditions for increased labour security.

A basic point about all this is the profound sterility of the neoclassical theory, with its narrow focus on prices and cost competitiveness, coupled with the innate authoritarianism of its leading advocates.[81] The supply-side macro-economic theory of natural rates of growth and unemployment is flawed, since on one definition (variants of hysteresis) it has no explanatory power and on another it is not operational.[82] In addition, however you define the natural rate in Walrasian terms, you cannot define it by reference to behavioural data on personal "reasons" for becoming unemployed. These theoretical points are crucial in undermining the macro-economic legitimacy of the supply-side approach, for if you eject the "natural" rate concept, it means demand-side policy *can* alter long-run output and employment.

So we are faced with a questionable macro-economic model, and a micro-level analysis that is institutionally impoverished and misleading. It is time to rethink. That there has been some "recovery" in the international economy does not alter the fact that, at the end of a decade of supply-side "experiments" in many labour markets in industrialised and low-income economies, poverty is more widespread, inequality and labour fragmentation greater, labour-related insecurity worse and unemployment chronically high.[83] It is time to rethink. Everyone seems to be in favour of "markets". But what sort of markets are desirable? Are collective institutions to have a role, and if so, what?

The harsh realities have led to a softening of tone by many of those wedded to or carried away by supply-side enthusiasm in the early 1980s. But, as Hans Singer puts it, they have not so much put on a human face as had a facelift. The trouble is that none of this softer tone represents a rejection of the underlying logic of the approach. To make much progress will require a clear alternative vision, based on a coherent macro-economic framework coupled with an institutional structure that focuses on the promotion of labour process security (consensus, co-operation, participation) and income security. In terms made famous by Albert Hirschman, there needs to be more emphasis on "voice" options and less on "exit", which seems to be the only language recognised by the neo-liberals. In the 1990s, reforms should be judged by whether or not they promote flexibility based on labour security, recognising that labour rights are part of development, rather than rigidities to be overcome or goals to be attained at some unspecified future date.

Notes

[1] For reasons of brevity and because it would have raised another set of issues beyond those associated with market-oriented strategies, no discussion is included of centralised planning systems.

[2] As an example of the scorn with which the previous views are now treated, see the special supplement on development in *The Economist*, 23 Sep. 1989.

[3] Recall that Keynes' preference for fiscal over monetary policy was due to liquidity preference and the fact that fiscal measures influenced expenditure directly and could be targeted to certain groups, regions or sectors.

[4] There has been an extensive literature on corporatism and its role in preserving stability, growth and social consensus in the post-1945 era, in particular. See, e.g. C. Crouch and R. Dore (eds.): *Corporatism and accountability* (Oxford, Clarendon Press, 1990).

[5] For a supportive statement, see S. Charnovitz: "Fair labour standards and international trade", in *Journal of World Trade Law*, Vol. 20, No. 1, Jan. - Feb. 1986, pp. 61-78.

[6] E. Walterskirchen: *Unemployment and labour market flexibility: Austria* (Geneva, ILO, 1991). This is one of a series of country studies examining how countries have adopted different labour market policy models in the pursuit of structural change.

[7] According to rational expectations theory, only unanticipated demand or monetary expansion can have real effects; the systematic use of demand policy to influence employment cannot work, and stabilisation policy can only reduce the variance of output and employment around "natural" levels.

[8] For example, supply-siders condemn import protection but often advocate (or do not criticise) export incentives. Why is one called a distortion and the other not?

[9] For a succinct summary, see "The Third World survey", Supplement to *The Economist*, 23 Sep. 1989, pp. 1-58.

[10] Within the supply-side school, there has been a long debate on the appropriate sequencing and pace of stabilisation and liberalisation policies. See, e.g. S. Edwards: "On the sequencing of structural reforms", in *OECD Economic and Statistics Working Paper*, No. 70, Sep. 1989.

[11] For instance, in the Republic of Korea, the *average* work week in manufacturing in 1982 was 55.4 hours for men and 56.3 hours for women. Hours had actually risen over the previous decade.

[12] R. E. Ofreneo and E. P. Habana: *The employment crisis and the World Bank's adjustment program* (Quezon City, University of the Philippines Press, 1987).

[13] Several participants in the conference, notably Samir Radwan and Christopher Colclough, made the valid point that there are divisions within the two schools. Others, such as John Weeks and Ben Harrison, argued that the bipolar approach did capture the essence of the debate. I would merely add that it seemed to be a way of making the analysis manageable. The intention in the following is to capture the essential *labour-related* differences as a way of moving towards a renewed social adjustment approach compatible with labour market developments in the 1980s and 1990s.

[14] For comparable perspectives on the causes of the end of the "social consensus" or "Golden Age", see A. Glynn, A. Hughes, A. Lipietz and A. Singh: "The rise and fall of the Golden Age", in S.A. Marglin and J. Schor (eds.): *The end of the Golden Age* (Oxford, Clarendon Press, 1990); and G. Standing: *Labour flexibility: Cause or cure for unemployment?* (Geneva, International Institute for Labour Studies, 1986).

[15] Recent manifestations of this debate include the furore over the IBRD-IMF SAPs in Africa and over the "Social Charter" in the EC.

[16] Thus the removal of price subsidies in structural adjustment programmes has had harmful effects on nutrition and health among the poor. J.R. Behrman: "The impact of adjustment programs", in D. Bell and M. Reich (eds.): *Health, nutrition and economic crises: Approaches to policy in the Third World* (Dover, Massachusetts, Auburn House, 1988). It is simply not true that subsidies mainly benefit the middle-classes, as is commonly claimed.

[17] M. Corden: *Inflation, exchange rates and the world economy* (Chicago, University of Chicago Press, 1977); E. Cardoso: *Inflation, growth and the real exchange rate* (New York, Garland Publishing Co., 1986); S. Edwards: "Terms of trade, tariffs and labour market adjustment in developing countries", in *The World Bank Economic Review*, Vol. 2, No. 2, 1988.

[18] S. Fisher: *Real balances, the exchange rate and indexation: Real variables in disinflation* (Washington, DC, NBER Working Paper No. 1497, 1984); D. Lal: *The real aspects of stabilisation and structural adjustment policies: Analytics and political economy* (Washington, DC, The World Bank, 1985, mimeo.); Edwards, 1988, op. cit.

[19] See, e.g. M. Burda and J. Sachs: *Labour markets and employment in West Germany* (Washington, NBER, 1987).

[20] R.A. Lopez and L.A. Riveros: *Expenditure and wage policies in a segmented labour market: A theoretical analysis* (Washington, DC, The World Bank, March 1989, mimeo.).

[21] F.C. Deyo: "State and labour: Modes of political exclusion in East Asian development", in F.C. Deyo (ed.): *The political economy of the new Asian industrialism* (Ithaca, New York, Cornell University Press, 1987), pp. 187-202; W. Galenson (ed.): *Foreign trade and investment: Economic growth in the newly industrialising Asian countries* (Madison, Wisconsin, University of Wisconsin Press, 1985).

[22] L.Y.C. Lim: "Social welfare in Singapore", in K.S. Sandhu and P. Wheatley (eds.): *Singapore: The management of success* (Singapore, Oxford University Press, 1989).

[23] M.-K. Bai: "Industrial development and structural changes in labor market: The case of Korea", in M.-K. Bai and C.-N. Kim (eds.): *Industrial development and structural changes in labour market: Korea and South-East Asia (Tokyo,* Institute of Developing Economies, 1985); J. You: *Labor standards and economic development: South Korean experience,* paper presented to Symposium on Labour Standards and Development, Washington, DC, Dec. 1988.

[24] On minimum wage systems in developing countries, see G. Starr: *Minimum wage fixing (*Geneva, ILO, 1981). Paldam and Riveros show that, except in Colombia, minimum wages fell dramatically, absolutely and relative to average wages in the major Latin American countries between 1970 and 1987. M. Paldam and L.A. Riveros: *The effect of minimum wages on average wages and inflation in Latin American economies* (Washington, DC, The World Bank, 1989, mimeo.), p. 8.

[25] R. Layard: "A cautionary tale of north and south", in *The Financial Times,* 22 Nov. 1989, p. 19. This was an article attacking a statutory minimum wage.

[26] Efficiency wage theories overlap with hypotheses relating high wages to increased productivity as a result of capital-labour substitution and better utilisation of fixed capital. Among the many analyses identifying the latter, see R. Sabot: *Labour standards in a small low-income country: Tanzania,* paper presented at the Symposium on Labour Standards and Economic Development, Washington, DC, Dec. 1988, p.16.

[27] This is relevant because it means women benefit disproportionately. P. Collier: *Women and development: Defining the issues,* (Oxford, University of Oxford, 1987, mimeo).

[28] G. Fields: *Labour standards, economic development and international trade: Links between the newly industrialising countries and the US,* paper prepared for the Symposium on Labour Standards and Development, Washington, DC, 12-13 Dec. 1988, p. 14.

[29] See, e.g. S. Chernick: *The Commonwealth Caribbean* (Baltimore, Johns Hopkins Press for the World Bank, 1978).

[30] G. Standing: *Unemployment and female labour* (London, Macmillan, 1981).

[31] L.A. Riveros: *Equity impact and effectiveness of adjustment policies with segmented labour markets: The case of the Philippines* (Washington, DC, The World Bank, 1989, mimeo.), p. 1.

[32] Ibid.

[33] Labour stratification is defined as the concentration of specific groups in particular clusters of jobs in an hierarchical fashion; segregation may occur without stratification.

[34] L. Calmfors and J. Driffill: "Centralisation of wage bargaining", in *Economic Policy*, No. 6, Apr. 1988, pp. 13-61.

[35] S. Bowles and R. Boyer: "A wage-led employment regime: Income distribution, labour discipline and aggregate demand in welfare capitalism", in S.A. Marglin (ed.): *The Golden Age of capitalism* (Oxford, Oxford University Press, 1989); S. Bowles and R. Boyer: "Labour market flexibility and decentralisation as barriers to high employment?", in R. Brunetta and C. Dell'Aringa (eds.): *Markets, institutions and cooperation: Labour relations and economic performance* (London, Macmillan, forthcoming).

[36] D.M. Nuti: "Profit-sharing and employment: Claims and overclaims", in *Industrial Relations,* Vol. 26, No. 1, Winter, 1987, pp. 18-29; G. Standing: "Would revenue-sharing pay cure unemployment?", in *International Labour Review*, Vol. 127, No. 1, 1988, pp. 1-18.

[37] See, e.g. D. Vaughan-Whitehead, *Partage des profits et marché du travail en France,* Labour Market Analysis Working Paper No. 28 (Geneva, ILO, April 1989).

[38] Among the more exciting developments in this area is James Meade's recent book on Agathotopia.

[39] For one well-known review, see R.B. Freeman and J.L. Medoff: *What do unions do?* (New York, Basic Books, 1984). For a tentative empirical study in an industrialising economy, see G. Standing: *Do trade unions impede or accelerate structural adjustment? Company vs. independent unions in an industrialising economy* (Geneva, ILO, 1990, mimeo).

[40] One economic model, devised by three World Bank economists, actually assumes that *all* public sector expenditure is unproductive. This is known as the Gelb-Knight-Sabot model. They used such terms as "an unproductive sink" to describe the public sector.

[41] C. Colclough, *The labour market and economic stabilisation in Zambia,* World Bank Working Paper Series No. 222 (Washington, DC, The World Bank, 1989), p. 21.

[42] J. van den Gaag, M. Stelcner and W. Vijverberg: "Wage differentials and moonlighting by civil servants: Evidence from Côte d'Ivoire and Peru", in *The World Bank Economic Review,* Vol. 3, No. 1, Jan. 1989, pp. 67-95. In Zambia, for example, the index of entry level salaries for university-trained public sector employees fell 78 per cent between 1975 and 1986. Colclough, 1989, op. cit., p. 29.

[43] M. Pirie: *Dismantling the State* (Dallas, National Centre for Policy Analysis, 1985), p. 29.

[44] See, for instance, European Trade Union Institute: *Privatisation in Western Europe* (Brussels, Apr. 1988).

[45] For a very worrying assessment, see H.J. Sullivan: "Privatisation of public services: A growing threat to constitutional rights", in *Public Administration Review*, Vol. 47, No. 6, Nov.-Dec. 1987.

[46] G. Standing: "Global feminisation through flexible labour", in *World Development*, Vol. 17, No. 7, July 1989, pp. 1077-95; R. Anker and C. Hein (eds.): *Sex inequalities in urban employment in the Third World* (London, Macmillan, 1986).

[47] See, e.g. M. Gogna, A.G. de Fanelli and E. Jelin: *Women workers in the public sector in Argentina: Feminisation and occupational segregation*, paper presented to the Fourth Conference of the Association for Women in Development, Washington, DC, 17-19 Nov. 1989.

[48] F. Hayek: *The road to serfdom* (London, Routledge, 1944), p. 27.

[49] It is most unfortunate that the double use of the term regulations has been encouraged. The Aglietta et al. notion of "regulation" relates to structure or system management, whereas regulations to many labour economists and labour lawyers relate to legislative rules and laws.

[50] J.M. West: "South Korea's entry into the International Labour Organisation: Perspectives on corporatist labour law during a late industrial revolution", in *Stanford Journal of International Law*, Vol. 23, Issue 2, 1987, pp. 477-546; You, 1988, op. cit., pp. 14-17.

[51] For an alternative conceptualisation that focuses on standards, divided into wage standards, workplace standards and process standards, see S.K. Tucker: *Beyond subsistence: Labour standards and Third World development* (Washington, DC, US Department of Labor, Jan. 1989), p. 15. That seems to leave out aspects of job and income security.

[52] For a more extended discussion, see G. Standing: *Labour flexibility: Towards a research agenda*, Labour Market Analysis Working Paper No. 3 (Geneva, ILO, Apr. 1986).

[53] P. Fallon and L.A. Riveros: *Macroeconomic adjustment and labor market response: A review of the recent experience in LDCs* (Washington, DC, The World Bank, Oct. 1988, mimeo.), p. 37. They claimed that, despite the widespread fall in wages, rules on compensation for redundancy, advance notice of plant closure, etc., were still obstacles to structural adjustment.

[54] R. Suarez: *Labor markets in Peru: An overview* (Washington, DC, The World Bank, March 1987, mimeo.); R. Lucas and P. Fallon: *Job security regulations and the demand for industrial labour in Zimbabwe* (Washington, DC, The World Bank, 1988, mimeo.).

[55] Fallon and Riveros, op. cit., p. 37. They also argue, "Firms will become less flexible in their adjustment to changing market conditions. This may apply to both employment and output levels."

[56] It has been suggested that this is why public sector wages were below private levels in Latin American countries. P. Fallon and L. Riveros: *Macroeconomic adjustment and labour market response: A review of the recent experience in LDCs*, Policy, Planning and Research Working Paper (Washington, DC, the World Bank, 1989). See also the chapter by Luis Riveros in this volume (pp. 23-24).

[57] G. Standing: *The growth of external labour flexibility in a nascent NIC: The Malaysian Labour Flexibility Survey*, Labour Market Research Working Paper No. 35 (Geneva, ILO, Nov. 1989).

[58] G. Fields, 1988, op. cit.

[59] Excuse the anecdote: In 1982, while conducting a survey of factories in a free trade zone, I visited a factory where about 5,000 young women were working on average 60 hours a week for pitifully low wages. The personnel manager claimed that the reason for

only employing young women was that they were the only workers who would put up with the tedious, low-paid but high productivity work, and because they were expected to stay for no more than about two years, which was deemed appropriate as they tended to suffer eyesight and back damage by then, lowering their productivity. At that point, they were encouraged to leave, to be replaced by new cohorts from rural areas. The problem for the women, of course, was that the social structure gave them little alternative, which drove down their "supply price". Many of these women suffered permanent damage. Was such an undistorted labour market necessary? And what measures to strengthen their bargaining power and rights could have been effective? To be unconcerned about labour processes and care only about long-term economic outcomes is characteristic of much of the structural adjustment literature.

[60] Joekes, 1989, op. cit., p. 5.

[61] For interesting and provocative reviews of employment security measures, see the various papers by Luis Riveros. For instance, L. A. Riveros: *International differences in wage and non wage labor costs,* Policy, Planning and Research Working Paper No. 188 (Washington, DC, The World Bank, April 1989).

[62] Various countries have relaxed employment protection laws for new hirings (e.g. The Federal Republic of Germany, Spain), implying an increased degree of labour force fragmentation. For a useful review of employment security regulations, which rejects deregulation, see M. Emerson: "Regulation or deregulation of the labour market", in *European Economic Review,* Vol. 32, 1988, pp. 775-817.

[63] See, e.g. A. Portes, M. Castells and L. Benton (eds.): *The informal economy* (Baltimore, Johns Hopkins Press, 1989).

[64] For a review of recent thinking and evidence on sub-contracting, see Chapter 13 of this volume. See also, B. Harrison: *The big firms are coming out of the corner: The resurgence of economic scale and industrial power in the age of "flexibility",* paper presented to the UNCRD Conference on Industrial Transformation and Regional Development in an Age of Global Interdependence, Nagoya, Japan, 18-21 Sep. 1989.

[65] This seems to have been a consequence of liberalisation in Sri Lanka. ILO-ARTEP: *Structural adjustment: By whom, for whom* (New Delhi, ILO, 1987), pp. 40-44. It has also occurred in Malaysia.

[66] A. Portes and L. Benton: "Industrial development and labour absorption", in *Population and Development Review,* Vol. 10, 1984, pp. 589-611; A. Portes: "Latin American urbanisation during the years of crisis", in *Latin American Research Review,* 1989, pp. 7-44.

[67] See the papers by Capecchi and Benton in Portes and Castells, 1989, op. cit. There is now a huge literature on the Third Italy consisting of "industrial districts" of interdependent networks of small, innovative firms. For a positive view, see C. Sabel: "Flexible specialisation and the reemergence of regional economies", in P. Hirst and J. Zeitlin (eds.): *Reversing industrial decline* (Oxford, Berg, 1989).

[68] IBRD: *World Development Report 1987* (Washington, DC, Oxford University Press, 1987), pp. 32.

[69] For example, H. Fest: "Economic policy and the move towards markets", in *The OECD Observer,* No. 158, June-July 1989, pp. 28-32; OECD: *Economies in transition: Structural adjustment experience in OECD countries* (Paris, 1989).

[70] M. Piore: *Labour standards and business strategies,* paper presented to Symposium on Labour Standards, Bureau of International Labour Affairs, Department of Labour, Washington, DC, 12-13 Dec. 1988.

[71] Some influential neo-liberals seem to suggest that no institutions should be responsible for the welfare of those affected by restructuring, because of the imperatives of

economic efficiency. This seems to be the view underlying the Chicago school of law and economics. For a representative statement, see R. Posner: *Economic analysis of law* (Boston, Little, Brown and Co., 1986, 3rd edition).

[72] G. Standing: "The notion of voluntary unemployment", in *International Labour Review,* Vol. 120, No. 5, Sep. 1981, pp. 563-79; see also M. Godfrey: *Global Unemployment* (1986).

[73] See, e.g. P. Minford: *Tackling European unemployment,* paper presented at the Conference on The Art of Full Employment, University of Limburg, Maastricht, 5-7 Sep. 1989.

[74] P. Streeten: *Employment and macro-economic policies,* paper prepared for the UNDP, July 1988, mimeo., p. 27.

[75] This is part of the rationale behind ILO Convention No. 96, which calls for the opposite of the current trend.

[76] IBRD, 1987, op. cit., p. 63

[77] Ibid.

[78] e.g. C. Heckscher: *The new unionism: Employment involvement in the changing corporation* (New York, Basic Books, 1988).

[79] It is probably not uncommon for the "subsidy" to exceed the cost of training.

[80] It has never been clear whether "flexible specialisation" is a prediction, as an ideal type model of future patterns of production, or a proposed development (and redevelopment) strategy.

[81] Recall that Hayek advocated a *strong* State to ensure his vision of "spontaneous order" based on individualism and the removal of collective institutions. Hayek, 1944, op. cit.

[82] Recall that Friedman defined it in Walrasian (perfect competition) terms and then said that it depended on "market imperfections". As for hysteresis effects, there are so many factors that can cause current unemployment to depend on past or current unemployment that a natural rate becomes a mirage. As Solow concluded, "A natural rate that hops around from one triennium to another under the influence of unspecified forces, including past unemployment rates, is not "natural" at all. "Epiphenomenal" would be a better adjective". R. Solow: "Unemployment: Getting the questions right", in *Economica*, Vol. 53, Supplement, 1986, p. S33. See also O.J. Blanchard and L.H. Summers: "Beyond the natural rate hypothesis", in *American Economic Review, Papers and Proceedings*, Vol. 78, No. 2, May 1988.

[83] See, e.g. Worldwatch: *Poverty and the environment: Reversing the downward spiral* (Washington, DC, 1989). Dependence on social assistance has risen enormously in the majority of EC countries since the early 1970s. G. Room, R. Lawson and F. Laczko: "New poverty in the European community", in *Policy and Politics*, Vol. 17, No. 2, 1989, pp. 167-168.

2

The myth of labour market clearing

by John Weeks [*]

Introduction

This paper addresses itself to one of the themes specified for the workshop, namely the advantages and disadvantages of alternative conceptualisations of labour processes.[1] The ultimate purpose of the analysis begun in this paper is to understand the working of labour markets in underdeveloped countries. However, in pursuing this goal, one immediately encounters a major obstacle to theoretical analysis: the neoclassical concept of "labour market clearing". A brief discussion of characteristics of labour markets in underdeveloped countries is presented in the next section. The purpose is to show that theoretical concepts should not be shifted between developed and underdeveloped countries without appropriate qualifications and changes. In other words, labour market analysis for developed countries is a special case. Central to this special case is "market clearing", which occupies the rest of the paper; for notwithstanding the limitations of this special case, it is applied to the underdeveloped countries as if it were the general and universal case.

While the argument that follows refers only in passing to the structural adjustment debate,[2] the relevance should be clear. Structural adjustment programmes derive from an analysis that sees economies as constrained by relative prices; i.e., when an economy flounders this is because relative prices are wrong. This approach presumes that unregulated markets clear efficiently, and in an open economy this market clearing involves the convergence of internal and external relative prices. This policy prescription is based on four theoretical components:

(1)   the theory of comparative advantage, which determines the pattern and direction trade;

(2)   the quantity theory of money,[3] which determines the absolute price level and aggregate nominal demand;

(3)   Walrasian general equilibrium theory, which ensures market clearing; and

(4)   marginal productivity theory, which provides the factor market analysis.

[*] Middlebury College, Middlebury, Vermont.

Each of these, the Four Horsemen of neoclassical *a priori* theory, is in its own way analytically flawed. Yet they ride on through the fray apparently unscathed by the attacks of the critics. In what follows the last two will be considered in close detail, to demonstrate that it is ideology not science that keeps them firmly in the saddle.

Labour market in underdeveloped countries

For the purposes of this discussion, "underdeveloped countries" refers to economies in which a large proportion of the labour force is not engaged in formal wage employment. To simplify the discussion, the analysis will restrict itself to urban labour markets, thereby avoiding complications arising from different forms of land tenure and coercive rural labour systems.[4]

There has been little success in formal modeling of urban labour markets in underdeveloped countries in a manner that captures their salient characteristics. The most common approaches are either to presume a single market, or to dichotomise between a monopolistic capitalist sector (the "formal" sector) and a petty trade, artisanal sector to which are attributed the attributes of perfect competition (the "informal" sector). The latter is then treated as a residual employer, absorbing the excess supply of aspirants for jobs in the former. Neither homogeneity nor dichotomisation are very satisfactory in theoretical terms, for both tend to ignore the historical basis of the diversity of labour relations within urban areas of underdeveloped countries. A labour market is essentially an institutional phenomenon influenced by the social relations governing employment, which are themselves the result of a historical process. The danger of viewing markets and economic categories in general ahistorically is shown in the wage form of payment itself. While wages are a price of a particular type, this is not necessarily an allocative price, either from the point of view of the employer or the employee. For example, while there are wage payments in socialist economies, these do not serve to allocate labour or determine technique, so there is no labour market in any meaningful sense.

The labour market concept as used in the development country literature is based upon an institutional arrangement in which most people vend their labour services directly to employers for specified periods of time, with the exchange narrowly economic in character. The labour markets of neoclassical and classical theory presume that obligation of the employer to the employee (and vice versa) is a largely impersonal one, with the tie between them limited to the wage payment and the productive services rendered. This treatment of exchange as impersonal allows for the assumption that employers set the level of employment according to a profit maximisation (cost minimisation) criterion, and the workers select among jobs on the basis of payment, working conditions and desirability of the activity. Non-capitalist (and frequently small-scale) activities do not in general conform to this partitioning of economic considerations from the rest of social existence. Much non-capitalist activity is self-employment, with labour services vended indirectly, via a produced commodity. To include these people as part of a generalised urban labour market is conceptually invalid, for it results in a confusing mixture of product market and factor market adjustment processes.

Non-capitalist activities that involve subordination of labour to supervision frequently do not conform in their human relations to a model in which job choice and employer decisions are exclusively economic. This narrowly economic focus is but one form of the general category of subordinate labour relations. Many supervisor/subordinate relations involve kinship ties, perhaps the most personalised form of labour relations. Equally inconsistent with the pure economic model are various forms of apprenticeship. Even in cases in which apprenticeship is not based upon kinship, this form of subordination should not be cavalierly aggregated into formal sector market relations. While for some purposes it may be valid to treat formal sector labour allocation as primarily the result of relative wages, apprenticeship employment involves much more diverse forms of adjustment - period of service, transmission of customer relations, payment in kind, etc. While apprenticeship systems may adjust flexibility to changes in economic conditions, the mechanisms and speed of adjustment can be quite different from those characterising formal employment.

In consequence, the concept of labour markets breaks down for most underdeveloped countries. It is not so much that labour markets are fragmented or segmented, but rather that the pursuit of livelihoods involves a chaotic collection of different employment relations, frequently operating according to conflicting principles of rationality. This interpretation is in no way inconsistent with the principle that people pursue their self-interest and seek to optimise their position within the income-earning system. However, in doing so they encounter a wide range of decision-making variables, whose adjustment processes are not closely integrated. For example, one could argue that the rational agent would weigh the advantages of a more security-orientated apprenticeship position against higher-paid but less secure employment in the formal sector. While certainly people do this, the manner in which the adjustment mechanisms would act to equalise returns is not at all clear.

The foregoing analysis indicates that the central characteristic of urban labour markets in underdeveloped countries is that they are comprised of a heterogeneous collection of subordinate relations which, while they coexist and overlap, cannot be effectively integrated. Their non-integration is the result of different adjustment mechanisms, not all of which are economic in nature. In consequence, even were the neoclassical parable theoretically valid, one would not expect urban labour markets to clear. Further, it is difficult to specify rigorously what "clearing" might entail. In very underdeveloped countries such as those in Africa, south of the Sahara, open unemployment is relatively rare. For unemployment to exist, society must provide a manner for the non-employed to maintain themselves, which is absent in these countries. If "market clearing" does not imply the elimination of unemployment, then it becomes a very murky concept indeed. "Short-time" working is not an adequate substitute for at least three reasons: its arbitrariness (what are "normal" hours in a predominantly informal employment market?); its subjectivity (e.g., when does work end and non-work begin for kinship-based employment relations?); and the possibility that variations in working time may not be wage-related (e.g., hours may be limited by the state of a person's health).

In other words, in underdeveloped countries there is usually no direct and objective measure of excess supply in urban labour markets. Certainly there are indirect indicators, but the interpretation of these proves ambiguous. Consider, for example, the case in which a formal sector private employer advertises for workers and receives a flood of aspirants at the factory gate. Such a circumstance shows excess supply of a particular type (for those job openings at that time). It need not imply that the excess supply arises from government-inspired labour market distortions, but only that the different forms of subordinate employment relations are characterised by significant livelihood differentials.[5]

Further, it is invalid to presume that these livelihood differentials are evidence of market distortions. A host of literature indicates that private employers in the formal sector of underdeveloped countries consciously set wages to create an excess supply of applicants. The tactic allows employers a wider range of choice, and subsequently enables them to maintain low labour turnover. The differentials may reflect that labour is not homogeneous, and the excess supply illusory. An excess supply of hopeful applicants is consistent with a shortage of suitable employees: it may be that many of the applicants are unsuited by the criteria of formal sector employers. But even if most of the applicants are qualified, it does not follow that the differentials reflect "distortions". As argued above, livelihood differentials may reflect the absence of mechanisms to efficiently equalise returns across the different types of subordinate labour relations.

The neoclassicals view all labour markets in a particular way. Whatever the institutional and cultural arrangements for earning livelihoods, they presume that these can be synthesised within a Walrasian model in which the relative movement of a particular price, "the wage", is sufficient to clear the market and leave all agents content once equilibrium is reached. The analytical problems with this synthesis are many, any one of which is sufficient to annul the overall conclusions.

These are discussed in the next section. First, at any moment in time most workers do not sell their labour services, thus are not subject to the adjustment mechanism. Second, the demand for labour is unambiguously downward sloping only in a one-commodity world. Third, even were the demand for labour downward sloping, this applies to the nominal demand, not the effective demand. Fourth, in underdeveloped countries the institutional assumptions underlying the neoclassical labour market do not hold; and the wage category degenerates into a vague metaphor to include a wide variety of forms of compensation, usually poorly understood and rarely specified.

In consequence, the neoclassical labour market parable is at best a poor guide to understanding developed countries and is actually misleading for developing countries. Before it can be shown that depressing wages and removing protective labour legislation would facilitate market clearing, it must be shown in the abstract that, theoretically, unregulated labour markets clear. This cannot be demonstrated except under assumptions so restrictive as to be absurd. Put simply, market clearing is a myth. Like most myths it seeks to instill a lesson. The moral of the myth of market clearing is this: government policies that cancel the gains of organised labour and weaken the bargaining power of labour in general vis-à-vis capital in general are in the general interest.

Neoclassical labour market clearing

A. Introduction

The complexity of forms of employment and remuneration in urban areas in underdeveloped countries are subsumed in neoclassical theory under an analytical umbrella called "the labour market". Central to the neoclassical treatment of this market is the concept of "labour market clearing". I do not consider this concept, treating it at the aggregate level, where it produces its most policy-potent conclusions.[6] It will be argued that this neoclassical hypothesis involves a special case raised to the third power. It is a special case at the empirical level for the reason given above: developing country labour markets have features which require their own theoretical treatment. At the most abstract level a special case is involved because alternative theoretical approaches to labour markets do not in general involve the concept of market clearing. And market clearing is a special case within neoclassical analysis because it is not implied by the model in its most general form. Only through a series of extremely restrictive assumptions does it arise as a logical possibility in the neoclassical model.

Below I present the neoclassical hypothesis and develop the conditions under which it would hold as a logical outcome. I reach the conclusion that labour market clearing is unconvincing as a hypothesis even in the abstract. Special attention is given to the implications of the critique for policies seeking to foster labour market flexibility. Following that argument, we will later briefly consider an alternative to the neoclasical approach that shares its methodological framework, what might be called the "Walrasian disequilibrium" approach of Clower and Leijonhufvud. I argue that this approach provides profound insights, but is limited in its empirical and policy usefulness. A more promising alternative to the neoclassical labour market stories is treated in section V, where "classical" (Ricardian and Marxian) analysis is developed.

Before proceeding further, let the concept under scrutiny be defined: "labour market clearing" in the neoclassical sense refers to the process whose outcome is a situation in which there is no involuntary unemployment.[7] This outcome is achieved in the model *through the adjustment of relative prices*; and in the most common rendition of the process, the relative price adjustment in what is called "the real wage" relative to the return on capital (variously referred to as "the rental rate of capital", the interest rate, or the rate of profit). In one sentence, the labour market is cleared of involuntary unemployment by a fall in the real wage.[8] This hypothesis implies that unemployment is always a relative price phenomenon. Its existence (or persistence) results from institutional constraints upon relative price adjustment. These institutional constraints, in turn, are the result of *government* intervention in markets, since rational agents would never choose to impose them.[9] In brief, governments cause unemployment.

Here is a case of an abstract theoretical hypothesis that carries powerful policy implications: unemployment (and misallocation of labour in general) is the result of high wages (wage "distortion") and labour market interventions by the State. The hypothesis enjoys an extraordinary impact upon the makers of policy, and can be found repeated as if it were fact, not hypothesis, at the level of local, national and international policy. Since it is beyond the scope of this paper to treat empirical evidence, it will be asserted that the hypothesis cannot by its nature be verified or refuted by reference to reality. It is essentially a theoretical conclusion, and it is to the theory of market clearing that we turn in the following section. The discussion will at times become abstract to the point of apparent irrelevance. Throughout, the central question should be kept in focus: do "well-functioning" labour markets "clear" and, therefore, is unemployment the result of state intervention? Once it is demonstrated that neoclassical theory has no useful answer to this question (which it itself poses as the central problematic), it will be possible to pass on to more fruitful lines of inquiry. These will eventually allow tentative conclusions about the operation of labour markets in underdeveloped countries.

Before proceeding further a disclaimer is necessary. The discussion that follows does not refer to the application of neoclassical theory of labour markets to issues of efficiency under conditions of continuous general equilibrium in many markets. The issue under critique is *market clearing* as such at the aggregate level. Finally, I again stress that the issue is whether the labour market is cleared through relative price adjustments. Let us begin the neoclassical analysis with the labour market diagram well known to economic textbooks, shown in figure 1. On the horizontal axis are measured units of labour and on the vertical axis "the real wage", with the latter defined as the nominal wage divided by the price level. In the standard diagram, as here, the demand for labour is of negative slope and single-valued with respect to the vertical axis. Typically, the supply of labour is drawn upwardly sloping and monotonic, so that there is only one point of intersection. Above this intersection, the supply of labour exceeds the demand ("excess supply"). Below the intersection demand exceeds supply ("excess demand"). The story goes that an excess demand for labour provokes a rise in "the real wage", and an excess supply induces a

Figure 1

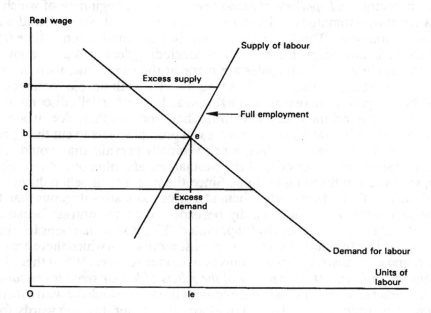

fall. Only at the intersection is excess demand (supply) zero, at which point a stable level of employment is achieved.

As simple and compelling as this story may seem, it is demonstrably false, the neoclassical equivalent of a fairy tale. First, even conceding the manner in which the curves are drawn, it cannot be demonstrated except under very restrictive assumptions that a movement of "the real wage" will eliminate excess demand or excess supply: the model has no convincing adjustment story that leads to equilibrium. Second, it can be shown that in general the demand for labour curve is not single-valued and monotonically downward sloping.

B. Trying to clear the market

In order to appreciate the problem of developing a reasonable story about how excess demand (positive or negative) might be eliminated, it is useful to consider a commodity other than labour services. Let us take the example of tomatoes. A positively sloped supply curve for tomatoes could be justified on the grounds that their production is subject to diminishing returns. The demand curve could be justified as downwardly sloping because of the subtitution effect in consumption (always negative) and an income effect less in absolute value than the former (so, if opposite to the former, it does not overwhelm it). The question then arises, what occurs if the offers of sellers and buyers do not coincide? The first step in formulating the answer is to determine

---

an initial offer price. Neoclassical theory deals with this problem through a fiction: it assumes a *hypothetical market period,* at the beginning of which all sellers arrive with tomatoes and all buyers with money, and where all trades are made simultaneously. This fiction, which involves the elimination of time from the analysis, avoids the problem of sellers concluding deals at a price above or below the equilibrium. If all trades are made at the same time, then one can conclude, for example, that all sellers would be left with unsold tomatoes for prices above equilibrium (excess supply), and all buyers partially discontent for prices below equilibrium (excess demand). Then, and only then, does it become reasonable to argue that unsold tomatoes will prompt sellers to cut their price.

Consider the case in which a price initially prevails that would allow sellers to dispose of 90 per cent of their tomatoes, and nine out of ten sellers do so, with the tenth selling nothing. Since the majority of sellers have concluded their deals, and concluded them at a price more advantageous than the equilibrium price, they could hardly be expected to re-contract because a minority of their fellow sellers is disappointed. This is what happens in labour markets. Assume the case of a totally capitalist economy in which there are only workers and capitalists, sellers and buyers of labour services. When there is 10 per cent unemployment, *90 per cent of the sellers of labour services are content with the market outcome,* indeed, more content than they would be with a market clearing wage, which by neoclassical rules would be lower. In other words, from a position of unemployment, market clearing would seem always to make the vast majority of workers (those employed) worse off.

This argument demonstrates that labour markets and non-labour markets do not function analogously. In the case of non-labour commodities, it is a reasonable fiction to presume that when some sellers (or buyers) are discontent, most are - for example, a 10 per cent excess supply of tomatoes results in all sellers being unable to vend one in ten of their tomatoes, rather than one in ten sellers being able to sell nothing. With all or most sellers discontent, a disposition to reduce price becomes a reasonable proposition. But it is not a reasonable proposition for the labour market, which even in moments of extreme oversupply has most sellers content (and, to repeat, more content than if the market cleared).

Then, how is the labour market cleared? Neoclassical theory achieves this by a *reductio ad absurdum* construction of the labour market so that it stimulates the tomato market, which itself required a fictional transformation before it would properly clear. The analysis assumes that the sellers of labour services enter each market period jobless, and the buyers arrive without a single employee on the rolls. The two groups then haggle until the market clearing wage is achieved. This is the famous Walrasian process of *tâtonnement* ("groping") in which an all-knowing "auctioneer" calls out offer prices which the participants mull over until the market clearing equilibrium is reached.

The postulated process is not credible. Most markets do not have auctioneers, and when they do the auctioneers do not behave in a Walrasian manner. Further, labour markets do not operate like non-labour markets: there is no market period, buyers and sellers do not contract continuously, and at any moment the overwhelming majority of workers are not in the market at all (they are employed). We can conclude that the neoclassical mechanism of labour market clearing is arbitrary, operating rather like a fairy tale in which magic powers permit anything to happen. The objection here is not that the theory is "unrealistic" (though certainly it is), but rather that its lack of realism is arbitrary. All theoretical abstraction is "unrealistic". The sin of neoclassical labour market theory in this case is that its lack of realism is unscientific. The purpose of the analysis is not to explore the workings of labour markets, but rather to conclude that they clear, and any aspect of labour markets that prevent clearing, either empirical (e.g., nature of labour contracts) or theoretical (e.g., the nature of aggregate production, see below) is ignored.

C. Market clearing and labour flexibility

Despite the arbitrary manner in which market clearing is achieved by the neoclassicals, one must entertain the argument that the fictional process might have policy implications. Consider the following argument: through appropriate labour market policies, governments could create a functioning approximation of the Walrasian market period; this would be achieved by breaking down institutional constraints that make labour markets relatively inflexible. Such policy measures would include legislation to facilitate part-time work ("flexible hours"), weakening of trade unions, and reduction of unemployment benefits ("raising the opportunity cost of leisure").

Close inspection of the shortcomings of the neoclassical analysis of labour markets shows that these measures would have no bearing on the logic of market clearing. Consider "flexible" working arrangements, and assume that they could have the effect of permitting (forcing) workers to vend their labour services in variable quantities, rather than for fixed periods. This would seem to bring reality closer to fiction, for the situation of workers would more closely approximate that of the hypothesised tomato sellers: instead of 90 per cent of the labour force fully employed and 10 per cent without work, one could in principle get the result of all workers employed at only 90 per cent of their desired level.

Even were this unlikely situation to present itself, it provides no help toward market clearing in logic, much less in practice. It must be remembered that the markets for non-labour commodities are constructed by the neoclassicals in a fictional manner even before the analogy is carried over to labour markets. The presumption that the seller sells and the buyer purchases in infinitely divisible quantities in no way affects the necessary condition for labour market clearing exchanges, namely that there be no "false trading",[10] at non-equilibrium prices. False trading is prevented by the intervention of the omniscient auctioneer, and whether labour services are sold in lumps or second-by-second is irrelevant to whether markets clear.

The problems attendant to false trading arise from the general equilibrium nature of market clearing. Not even in theory can the labour market clear on its own. In a pure capitalist economy the demand for labour is derivative from the demand for commodities. Beginning from a situation of excess labour supply, for a declining wage to clear the labour market the demand for commodities must simultaneously expand to stimulate the level of output consistent with a cleared labour market. This process, which requires a fall in the general price level and a drop in the rate of interest, must occur instantaneously with the decline in the real wage. This process of simultaneous adjustment of three markets (the labour market, the commodity market and the money market) is in no way facilitated in theory by more "flexible" conditions of employment. For example, a false trade in the commodity market prevents the labour market from clearing whether workers sell their services in discrete amounts or moment-by-moment, as will be discussed. To argue that labour markets clear on the basis of a Walrasian mechanism, then as a complement to argue that policies promoting flexibility facilitate this, is ideology.

What then is the result of greater "flexibility" in labour markets? The consequence is the perfectly straightforward one of reducing employers' labour costs and limiting the control of workers over their conditions of employment. Historically, the struggle by labour to limit the working day simultaneously served to guarantee the right to a full day's pay. "Flexible" hours in essence represent a return to the regime in which the employer unilaterally determines the length and regularity of service. At a more concrete level, it allows employers to undermine and avoid the rights of labour associated with full-time work: social security, unemployment benefits, medical care, seniority and severance pay (each of these depending on the specific institutional and legal arrangements in particular countries). Yet it would seem that our argument has contradicted itself. It began by concluding that "flexibility" did not facilitate market clearing, then argued that the effect would be to reduce labour costs. Is it not the case that lower wage costs would call forth more employment, which could not but aid in the clearing of labour markets? It is this argument that, *ceterius paribus,* lower real wages call forth greater employment that we consider in the next sub-section.

D.   Aggregate employment and aggregate production

Karl Marx coined the term "vulgar economy" to refer to economic analysis that investigated phenomena at the level of appearances. Keynes, while not using this term, provided a famous example in the "paradox of thrift" - at the individual level it appears that increased thrift means increased saving, but the opposite might be the case in the aggregate when the saving/income and investment/income relations are correctly specified. Similarly, the neoclassical analysis of demand for labour is vulgar: it generalises to the aggregate the observation that, other things being equal, employers prefer to pay less for labour than more.

At the risk of triviality, it should be stressed that the neoclassical treatment of employment requires that it be proved that the demand for labour is downward sloping, as in figure 1. If it cannot be established that the relationship between wages and employment is monotonically negative, then even the arcane world of Walrasian markets cannot save the analysis. In other words, if anything is central to neoclassical labour market analysis, it is that *ceterius paribus* more employment is obtained at a lower real wage. If this is not true, then unemployment is not a relative price phenomenon, and the entire discussion of market clearing is to little purpose.

Almost a generation ago the neo-Keynesian critics of neoclassical capital theory provided the elements to demonstrate conclusively that in general the demand for labour is *not* downward sloping with respect to the real wage. Unfortunately, they tended to focus their critique on neoclassical distribution theory, where it provides a relatively weak and ambiguous attack, rather than on aggregate employment theory, where it is irrefutable.[11] The refutation of the downward slope of the labour demand curve is easily demonstrated.

The justification of the downward slope lies in an argument involving the substitution between labour and capital in response to changes in relative factor prices. No serious neoclassical theorist views this substitution as occurring within a given technique; i.e., for a given set of machines and other means of production. It may or may not be that there are techniques which allow for the labour input to vary appreciably with nothing else changed. This is an empirical question that cannot be answered by theory and cannot be the basis to capital-labour substitution. Rather, the argument is that for any product (or set of joint products) there are at any moment a great variety of techniques, all of which are efficient and differ from each other by their respective capital-labour ratios. In theory, capital-labour substitution involves the switching among fixed-coefficient techniques in response to changes in factor prices.

This process of technique switching and its relationship to employment can be demonstrated in figure 2. The right-hand quadrant of the diagram shows the familiar "factor price frontiers" for three techniques, A, B, and C.[12] Each of these is derived from the distributional relation, value added equals wages plus profits.

$$y = wl + rk$$
$$l = y/k - w[l/k], \text{ and}$$
$$w = y/l - r[k/l]$$

Where

y = value added or net production
w = real wage rate
l = level of employment
r = profit rate
k = "capital stock"

Figure 2

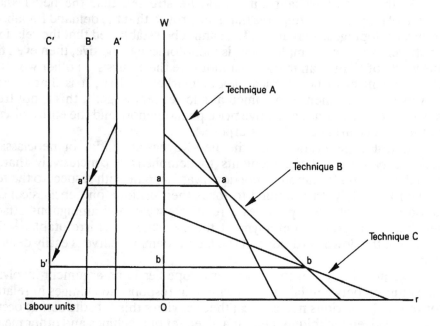

Since a technique is defined for fixed coefficients of production, k/l, y/k, y/l are all constants. The capital intensity of each technique can be inferred from the diagram. The vertical intercept of each technique is y/l, the average product of labour. The higher it is up the axis, the more capital-intensive the technique (a higher average product of labour implies a higher capital-labour ratio).[13] The diagram is read as follows: when the wage is above point "a" technique A yields the highest rate of return, r, for each wage; between points "a" and "b", technique B is the most profitable; and below "b", technique C is the most profitable. The left-hand quadrant shows the maximum level of employment associated with each technique on the assumption that each is employed with the same quantity of malleable capital. Vertical lines are used because each technique is defined for fixed coefficients. Thus the left-hand quadrant corresponds to the neoclassical "short run", when the capital stock is given, the relevant conceptual time period for neoclassical labour market analysis.

Figure 2 would seem to verify the downward slope of the labour demand curve: as the real wage drops, employers switch to a more labour-intensive technique, a technique which for any capital stock implies more people employed. If the aggregate supply of labour were C', then a real wage below level "c" would be consistent with full employment. Note that even as drawn, the story in figure 2 is not very convincing. It requires the assumption that capital is perfectly malleable, such that it can be transubstantiated (in the literal sense) into whatever means of production the employer wishes. But even were means of production silly-putty, figure 2 would not be an aid to the market clearing argument, for it represents a special case, the special case in which factor price frontiers are straight lines. Because they are straight lines, a technique, once abandoned (switched away from), never reappears as the most profitable.

The necessary and sufficient condition for linear factor price frontiers is that the economy in question has one and only one product. This assertion is easily proved. Consider an economy with two products, an output (final commodity) and an input. Presumably, few would argue that such a theoretical specification is not appropriate to investigate the generality of the story represented in figure 2. If the demand for labour cannot be shown to be downward sloping for a two-commodity economy, then one should hardly treat it as so in policies designed for actual, multi-commodity economies. For simplicity of presentation, it will be assumed that the input is completely exhausted in one production period. If the downward slope cannot be verified for this case, its invalidity applies even more to the three-commodity case in which there are also fixed means of production.

Each technique has two parts: the production conditions for the output and those for the input. These two relationships define a technique, and when switching occurs, a new capital-labour ratio for each is chosen. Using the standard notation, we can summarise some technique A as follows, where the level of output is defined as one unit and the two equations define the price of each commodity:[14]

$$pKa1 + wLa1 + rpKa1 = 1$$
$$pKa2 + wLa2 + rpKa2 = p$$

Where:

Ka1, Ka2 are the quantities of the input required to produce the output (commodity 1) and the input (commodity 2);

La1, La2 are the quantities of labour required to produce each commodity; p is the relative price of the input with respect to the output, or p2/p1;

r is the profit rate, the mark-up on non-wage cost,[15] assumed to equalise across sectors; and

w is the real wage rate which, because only commodity 1 is directly consumed, is a certain amount of that commodity; this, too, is assumed to equalise across sectors.

The factor price frontier is obtained by solving each price equation for p, then setting them equal. The result, so familiar to those versed in the so-called Cambridge controversy, is:

$$r = \frac{1 - wLa1}{Ka2 + w[Ka2La1 - Ka1La2]}$$

While the equation may appear complex, it can be interpreted by assuming [Ka2La1 – KaLa2] = 0. This will be zero if and only if Ka1/La1 = Ka2/La2; that is, if the input and the output have the same capital/labour ratio. In this case they are the same product and the expression reduces to (1/Ka2 – w[La1/Ka2]). Since we have defined the level of output as unity, this expression is the equivalent of the previous general expression for the factor price frontier, r = y/k – w[l/k]. We have shown that the factor price frontier will be a straight line only if the input and the output are the same - *if the economy has but one product.* Therefore, in general, factor price frontiers will be curved in towards the origin (if Ka1/La1 Ka2/La2, the input is more labour-intensive) or bowed out from the origin (if Ka1/La1 Ka2/La2, the output is more labour-intensive).

It is quite important not to become caught in the algebra. The algebra demonstrates a general point that will have disastrous consequences for the neoclassical specification of the demand for labour: one-commodity economies have factor price frontiers that are straight lines; for multi-commodity economies no theoretical generalisation can be made. The right-hand quadrant of figure 3 demonstrates the result of non-linear factor price frontiers. For a real wage above "a", technique A is the more profitable; between wage levels "a" and "b", technique B is the more profitable; *and below "b", technique A is again the more profitable.* This phenomenon is inherent in multi-commodity economies and is referred to as "reswitching". In the left-hand quadrant, define the level of employment for a given capital stock applied to technique A as A', and that associated with technique B for the same capital stock as B'. Let the aggregate supply of labour also be A'. Finally, assume that the real wage is "c", so employers chose technique B, with level of employment B' and an unemployment level of A'B'. In this two-commodity economy, *clearing of the labour market could be achieved either by a fall or a rise in the real wage; any* real wage above "a" or below "b" is consistent with full employment (shown by the arrows in the right-hand quadrant).

At the theoretical level this result is completely general: for multi-commodity economies the demand for labour cannot be specified as downward sloping. The shape of the labour demand curve, *including the sign of its slope over various ranges,* is an empirical question. The consequence for the relative price parable is disaster: since reswitching cannot be excluded *a priori,* there is no theoretical basis for arguing that an excess supply of labour implies that the real wage is too high; excess supply is equally consistent with the real wage standing *too low.*

This has been no arcane or esoteric exercise in algebra. The neoclassical labour market story requires that the demand for labour be downward sloping. If this cannot be verified theoretically, then the rest of the argument is irrelevant. It can be demonstrated, but only for a one-commodity economy; i.e., the neoclassical aggregate market clearing stories implicitly presume a one-commodity world. The stories break down in multi-commodity systems. Over 20 years ago, neoclassical economists conceded as much, and offered a line of defence: the existence and importance of reswitching is an empirical question.[16]

Figure 3

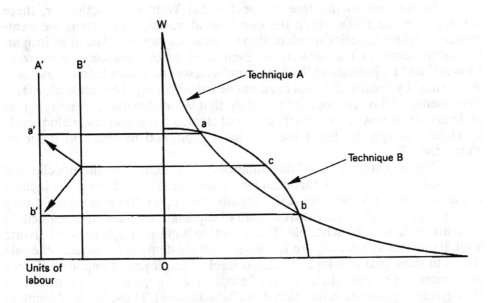

This is no defence at all; it concedes defeat. It grants precisely what we who have criticised neoclassical theory have always sought to establish: the relation between wages and employment is an empirical relationship about which no theoretical generalisation is possible.

E.   An epitaph for neoclassical market clearing

Where, then, are we left with regard to the ultra-neoclassical view that "labour markets work", or would do were it not for "distortions" and "rigidities" caused by state intervention? If these are empirical hypotheses, then they carry respectability. However, they are rarely derived from concrete investigation, but rather asserted as general truths based on *a priori* theorising. As theoretical generalisations they are false. Yet they are not only asserted by academic economists, but taken in hand as guides to policy. They are presented as the justification for policy conditionality by multilateral agencies, and governments are pressured to alter laws, issue decrees and dismantle protective labour legislation on the basis of theoretically suspect propositions.

It is not difficult to account for such an anomalous application of bad economic theory to economic policy. The virulent resurgence in the 1980s of labour market theory based on one-commodity systems with Walrasian auctioneers reflects the triumph of ideology over economic science.

Walrasian disequilibrium and labour markets

In reaction to the role of the fanciful Walrasian auctioneer, there developed in the 1960s within the neoclassical tradition an alternative treatment of markets generically referred to as "post-Keynesian". The most insightful contributors to this analytical revision of labour market theory were Clower[17] and Leijonhufvud,[18] whose approach was derisively labelled as "neo-Walrasian" by Brothwell,[19] but here will be called "disequilibrium Walrasian". The essence of this approach is the insight that Walrasian market theory serves to demonstrate why labour markets do not clear, a point also made eloquently by Hahn (though the latter has not been prompted to abandon it for an alternative).[20]

The objection by the "disequilibrium Walrasians" to the neoclassical analysis also involves the demand for labour schedule. Here the critique focuses not on whether it is monotonically negative in slope (strangely enough, they accept this), but rather on the treatment of expectations, implicit or explicit, in the construction of the schedule. The objection is quite straightforward on one level. If one looks back to figure 1, one sees that the demand for labour schedule claims to show that employers' desired level of employment implies different wage rates. Of course, these levels of employment impy levels of output (via the aggregate production function demolished above). These levels of employment will be desired if and only if employers believe that they can sell the associated levels of output.[21] Therefore, at least two markets have to clear simultaneously to move from one level of employment to another along the labour demand schedule: the labour market and the commodity market. A moment's reflection reveals that a third market must also clear: with a given money supply[22] a larger output can only be sold at a lower price level, which requires a rise in the interest rate.

Not only must all three markets clear simultaneously, *employers must believe in advance that this will occur.* It is not enough that employers be educated in neoclassical theory and trained to accept that there exists an interest rate, price level, and money wage uniquely associated with each point on the labour demand schedule; they must also have precognitive knowledge that all markets will clear to bring them about. In other words, employers (and workers, for that matter) must know the future.[23] This unlikely possibility prompts the "Walrasian disequilibrium" argument that markets tend to be *quantity constrained.* In this analysis, the reason for the failure of markets to clear instantaneously through price adjustment is that sellers view their exchanges as constrained by the quantity they can vend. In other words, exchanges involve "false trading". This false trading results in market clearing except for the labour market, in which the vendible article is unique in that it can go unsold indefinitely. This process, in which the failure to reach full employment general equilibrium manifests itself in an uncleared labour market, is the Clower/Leijonhufvud interpretation of Keynes' famous concept of "effective demand"

(and "the multiplier"). Specifically with respect to the labour market, the demand curve based upon perfect foresight (as described above) is *notional;* i.e., it is the demand curve which would prevail if all exchanges occurred at general equilibrium prices. The *effective* demand curve for labour is that which results from the actual prices governing non-labour exchanges (which determine the actual derived demand for labour).

The key analytical point in this argument is that under conditions of false trading (effective demand), labour markets are not wage-constrained; more explicitly, they cannot clear by a fall in the real wage (recall that the analysis accepts the downward slope of the labour demand curve). To put the matter more dramatically, in the Clower/Leijonhufvud analysis, *unemployment is not the result of conditions prevailing in the labour market.*

The existence of unemployment might be the result, for example, of a long-run rate of interest above the general equilibrium level due to excessively pessimistic expectations on the part of investors. This "inappropriate" rate of interest would have the effect of depressing current investment and, therefore, aggregate demand, below the level consistent with full employment. In such a circumstance, the real wage might be at its full-employment value,[24] but the demand for labour schedule might be depressed as a result of false trading in the securities market. In an open economy, the same result might occur if exporters anticipated a fall in the exchange rate and in consequence restricted current output.

The implication of this analysis is that, in general, unemployment is not the result of an "inappropriate" wage, but can stem from "disturbances" in any market.[25] This is a quite profound point, well-known in science outside the economics profession; things are not always what they appear to be. As put in a famous quotation, were things explainable on the basis of superficial appearances, science would be unnecessary. The problem of underutilised resources appears in the labour market. This does not imply, however, that the problem originates there.

The contribution of the Walrasian disequilibrium school is that it demonstrates that the cause of unemployment can arise in any market. Underutilisation of resources necessarily manifests itself in the labour market because of the relations of ownership in market societies (what Leijonhufvud euphemistically calls the "transactions structure" of the economy). The nature of capital is that it need not be exchanged to be employed in production. On the contrary, it is owned prior to production as a result of the very nature of private property in the means of production. Therefore, while capital can lie partly idle, it is not unemployed in the common sense of that term. Capital, even idle capital, is always part of the production process. One can talk of "capital services", and neoclassical theory is eager to do so to create the fiction that labour and capital are both socially equivalent factors of production. In practice, capital provides its services without any exchange (and unlike labour does so even when its return is zero or negative). In contrast, labourers must sell their services and do so repeatedly. Further, people are capable of maintaining and reproducing their capacity to work indefinitely in the absence of selling that capacity, due to the social nature of human existence. Therefore, any failure of the exchange system to generate full utilisation of resources *must,* by the nature of property relations, manifest itself in the unemployment of labour. To take this fact of the property relations of market society as the cause of unemployment is superficial *(vulgar)* in the extreme.

These insights, arrived at with clarity by Leijonhufvud, represent a major contribution, particularly in the light of the neoclassical aversion to anything vaguely associated with social relations of production. Important as these Walrasian disequilibrium insights are, it is unclear what they tell one about the operation of labour markets. The basic message is that unemployment need not be the result of labour market imperfections. This message does not tell one how labour markets operate though. Indeed, when the practitioners of this school turned to analyse labour markets as such, their approach tended to reinforce rather than weaken neoclassical arguments.

It is worth pausing to note what the Walrasian disequilibrium school demonstrated: namely, that in the absence of simultaneous[26] (and instantaneous[27]) clearing of all markets, there is no tendency for labour markets themselves to clear. This would seem to deliver the *coup de grâce* to neoclassical market clearing at least for policy purposes, since market exchanges take place over time and can never be simultaneous and instantaneous. The neoclassical response to this critique was to challenge their critics to demonstrate why markets do not clear simultaneously and instantaneously; in other words, to justify rejecting the impossible.

The burden of proof shifted to the critics, which effectively won the day for the neoclassicals. The proof offered by the Walrasian disequilibrium school involved a stress on "information costs", the argument being that no rational agent could or would spend the time necessary to reach trades at general equilibrium market clearing prices. This justification undermines the entire argument. It concedes that if sufficient information were available, markets would clear consistent with full employment. From this concession it is a small step to argue that the barriers to full information are "distortions" created by trade unions and governments. Further, whatever the barriers to full knowledge of market conditions, the "information costs" argument implies that unemployment is essentially voluntary.[28] Some critics of the critics have argued that the outcome of the Walrasian disequilibrium approach has been to fortify and generalise the neoclassical theory of market clearing.[29] Certainly the information costs critique of market clearing would lend support to policies designed to increase labour market flexibility.

The labour market of classical theory

The essence of the difficulty with neoclassical labour market analysis is the theory's concept of *markets*. Here, the word "market" is intended in the quite literal sense: "a gathering for the sale of goods or livestock ... a space or building used for this".[30] But at best the term "market" is a metaphor, and in the case of selling of labour services it is one that must be employed with great caution or not at all. As stressed in the critique of neoclassical market theory, in a pure capitalist economy most workers are at any moment employed, and not, strictly speaking, in the labour market. Thus, one fundamental characteristic of the labour exchange is that except under rare circumstances it is an excess supply market, in which only a small fraction of the commodity is actually on offer at any given time.

This was essentially the approach of the classical economists, particularly Marx with his concept of the "reserve army". This concept, implicit in the work of Ricardo, proves to be a powerful analytical tool. For the classical economists there was no tendency for labour markets in excess supply to clear through a wage adjustment. In Ricardo's analysis the real wage could not adjust downward because it always remained near subsistence level, an approach not very useful to pursue. Marx's treatment was considerably more developed, beginning with an analysis of wages themselves.

The sale of labour services involves an exchange between capital and labour, in which the worker obtains access to the means of production, and through that access to his or her means of livelihood. For the employer the exchange is the means by which production occurs, and upon sale of the product a profit is realised. Therefore, neither party to the exchange seeks its immediate consequence, the production of commodities. Rather, each enters into production as the necessary and unavoidable intermediate step to obtain a subsequent goal - consumption for the worker and profit for the employer. At the same time, the relationship is asymmetric. In response to increased wages the employer can attempt to raise productivity or pass the wage increase on in higher prices (depending on market conditions), while the worker's response to lower wages is to withhold his or her labour.

Wages are the particular form in a capitalist society by which workers obtain their necessities and non-necessities of life, which I shall call "the standard of living".[31] In all societies the labouring population must be supplied with the means to reproduce itself, both in the short run (maintain vigour and health) and the long run (biological reproduction and child-raising). In pre-market societies these functions were achieved in great part through direct provision by the working population itself. Such was (and is) particularly the case for agriculturalists, but also for the urban population. The development of market production and the decline of production for direct use requires that the wage cover an increasing number of commodities and services previously supplied by the household itself. This is particularly important in developing countries, where the spread of wage labour renders into commodities the necessities of life. This same process cannot be ignored in the developed countries, however. It is well documented in the United States that the increased participation rate of women over the last two decades increased the monetised component of the standard of living (child care being the most obvious example).

The commercialisation of life implies that over-time-rising average wages, even price-deflated wages, do not necessarily indicate a rising standard of living. One can go further and conclude that in the process of development and urbanisation, a rising "real wage" is the necessary condition for the standard of living of workers not to fall. In effect households find that they must progressively purchase more and more products and services that previously they themselves produced.

Having analysed the standard of living, we can turn to the wage as such. The capital-labour exchange is that for workers it represents the historical process by which the individualised reproduction of labour becomes socialised; socialisation here refers to integration of the non-biological aspects of reproduction into the market process. This, in turn, brings the discipline of competition and the force of technical change into the reproduction of labour. Unlike capitalists, workers do not directly compete to produce their vendible articles cheaper. Workers may offer their services at lower prices to undersell other workers, but unlike capitalists they cannot, through innovation and increasing the scale of production, reduce the cost of producing those services. They can accept wage cuts, but do not respond to competition by seeking to produce labour services cheaper, except in extreme circumstances. Even in these circumstances, the lowering of the standard of living (cost of producing labour services) is a response pressed upon the labouring population as a whole. The historic tendency in market economies has been for the standard of living to rise, not fall; in contrast, the tendency with other commodities has been for their unit cost to fall.

The technical change that cheapens non-labour commodities has an impact upon the cost of producing labour services, as opposed to the standard of living. For the moment, let us assume the standard of living of a labouring population to be given, and that all exchanges are in a currency directly convertible to gold (whose unit cost is constant). As non-labour commodities fall in cost due to productivity change, their gold prices will fall (an ounce of gold will buy more corn, for example). In consequence, the amount of gold that employers must pay workers in order to purchase the unchanged standard of living will fall. This, of course, was Ricardo's argument against the Corn Laws: if England could import cheap corn, then capitalists could pay workers lower wages. Marx, with his concept of "relative surplus value", generalised and endogenised Ricardo's process of the cheapening of wage costs. Marx pointed out that productivity change that cheapened wage commodities, or commodities that went to produce wage commodities,[32] would lower the real cost of labour services to capital.

We are now armed with the tools to construct a classical labour market. Classical labour markets are constructed in the context of expanding output, rather than static equilibrium. This reflects the classical insight that capitalist economies are inherently dynamic and never at rest. Let us begin from an initial situation of unemployment in an expanding system, with the standard of living constant. As the system expands, several things happen simultaneously. Expansion itself generates an increased demand for labour under prevailing techniques and a constant real wage (the latter implied by a constant standard of living). This process (which Marx called expanded reproduction) tends to reduce the pool of the unemployed. At the same time, productivity change is occurring,[33] reducing the demand for labour for a given quantity of output (Marx called this accumulation).[34] Therefore, the expansionary process simultaneously increases and decreases the demand for labour.

We have yet to consider the behaviour of wages in this expansionary labour market. Before doing so, it is necessary to clarify what has been established. It might be thought that nothing more has been said than increased output expands the demand for labour and productivity change decreases it. This would be wrong, rather like denigrating use of a budget line in consumer theory because all it shows is that one cannot buy more of everything with a given income. The contribution of classical labour market analysis is that it seeks to make a systematic specification of the interaction between output expansion and productivity change in the short run. Anyone who thinks that this is an unimportant contribution might refer to the experience of the European Community countries during the 1980s, when the short run productivity impact on employment was substantial.

Now, it is possible to analyse the role of wages in the classical labour market. Two forces are influencing their possible movement. On the one hand, the rate of output expansion compared to the rate of productivity change determines whether the pool of the unemployed contracts. If it does contract, then, *ceterius paribus,* an upward pressure on wages results. On the other hand, productivity change is also reducing the production costs of wage commodities, so that the real resource cost of producing the standard of living declines. To treat this process, again assume that all exchanges occur in gold, and gold has a constant unit cost throughout the analysis. If the standard of living remains constant, then the money (gold) wage will fall, absolutely reducing labour costs. Alternatively, the money wage could remain constant, thus increasing the standard of living. Which of these occurs depends upon the "tightness" of the labour market, itself determined by the rate of accumulation compared to the rate of productivity growth.

At some point in the accumulation process the pool of the unemployed contracts sufficiently to generate upward pressure on the money wage. The wage then serves to allocate labour: through rising wages labour shifts among different sectors of the economy. The wage in classical labour markets serves primarily as an allocative mechanism, not to determine technique as in the neoclassical analysis. In the latter, allocation is completely ignored in the aggregate labour market due to assuming a single commodity production function (or production in fixed proportions). Wage adjustments function to determine the desired capital-output ratio (technique), a singularly inappropriate role in a short-run model. In classical analysis, technique is established by product market competition - given the wage and other input prices, producers are forced to select the least costly technique.

One of the many weaknesses of neoclassical labour market analysis is that it makes no distinction between expanding and contracting markets with regard to market clearing.[35] Its labour market analysis is at the level of comparative statics. Stories about the performance of labour markets as unemployment varies - e.g., the Phillips Curve - are generally viewed by the neoclassicals as appallingly ad hoc. As a consequence, all emphasis is placed upon the wage-adjustment mechanism, though this is incorrect even in its own terms, as we saw in the previous section. Classical labour markets are dynamic, exhibiting asymmetry of behaviour when unemployment is contracting and increasing. When there is excess demand for labour, the market mechanism serves as an allocator of labour among industries. This function is performed relatively smoothly in part because the interests of employers and workers - an increase of wages - momentarily coincide.

However, when excess supply reigns, the allocative function of the labour market lies dormant, and the interests of employers and workers are in conflict. As we saw, it cannot be demonstrated even in theory (much less in practice) that the *ceteris paribus* demand for labour is continuously downward sloping; nor can it be demonstrated that rational employers would operate on their notional demand curves when output falls. Therefore, under excess supply conditions, the immediate effect of a downward wage adjustment may be neither allocative nor technique-determining (employment expanding). It is for these reasons and others that the asymmetric character of dynamic labour markets seems theoretically valid even without the pedestrian assumption of "downwardly rigid money wages".

The concept of "rigid wages" requires a disclaimer: it is not correct to say that classical analysis, be it Ricardian, Sraffian or Marxian, presumes wages to be rigid or ignores the wage adjustment mechanism. As explained, the wage adjustment mechanism plays a more important role here than in neoclassical analysis under conditions of excess demand. With regard to excess supply, wage adjustment is but one of a host of changes occurring that influence the demand for labour, and perhaps a relatively unimportant one. Further, theory tells us that the main impact of declining wages is to reduce the standard of living of workers, secondarily to reduce aggregate demand, and only far down the adjustment process, under certain circumstances (no reswitching), to stimulate employment. Only through an obsession with general equilibrium comparative statics, can one focus upon the wage as the mechanism that clears the labour market of the unemployed.

Notes

[1] The workshop guide goes on to suggest: "This should focus on whether one could or should draw on a wide variety of approaches or on one particular perspective ... Given the relative predominance of the neoclassical model in recent debates ... are alternative models richer or closer to reality in some respects ...?" Labour market workshop guide, p. 2.

[2] Structural adjustment is treated in detail in the chapter by Guy Standing.

[3] Reference is to the "quantity theory" broadly defined; i.e., the analysis of the money market based upon the view that there is a stable aggregate demand for money on the one hand (determined by various factors including "real output" and interest rates), and, on the other, an aggregate money supply autonomous with respect to the level of output and under the control of the "monetary authorities". I have critiqued this treatment of money markets in J. Weeks: *A critique of neoclassical macroeconomics* (London, Macmillan; and New York, St. Martin's Press, 1989), Ch. 3, passim.

[4] Elsewhere I have dealt with the coercive systems in rural Central America. J. Weeks: "An interpretation of the Central American crisis", in *Latin American Research Review* (Austin, Texas), Vol. 21, No. 3, 1986, pp. 31-53.

[5] The more commonly-used phrases, "wage differentials" and "income differentials" are not appropriate here, since they implicitly assume that the gains from different forms of subordinate employment can be rendered into a monetary equivalent. This is an arbitrary approach. Equally valid would be to render wage incomes into a non-monetary equivalent. Therefore, the more general term, "livelihood differentials" is used, that refers to standards of living associated with different employment activities.

[6] The analysis of this paper focuses on market clearing with respect to the labour market, not market clearing in general. This point should be clear subsequently.

[7] Strictly speaking, it implies that there are no frustrated sellers of labour services and no discontented buyers. The more technical definition of a cleared market is treated in the next section.

[8] It is beyond the scope of this paper to deal with the literature of the last decade on the "efficiency wage" approach to labour markets, epitomised in the work of Stiglitz. In any event, this contribution is derivative from the more "general" neoclassical analysis treated in the section on labour markets in underdeveloped countries, thus can be seen as a special case of a special case of a special case.

[9] One might think that long-term wage contracts negotiated by unions and capitalists represent an institutional constraint on labour market clearing freely entered into by private sector agents. Such is not the case, according to Barro, who argued that these are inconsistent with optimising behaviour on the part of workers and employers, and thus being irrational should be ignored in theoretical analysis. R.J. Barro: "Long-term contracting, sticky prices, and monetary policy", in *Journal of Monetary Economics* (Amsterdam), Vol. 3, No. 3, July 1977, pp. 305-316.

[10] Of all the ideologically-laden terms of neoclassical theory, this one must be among the most flagrant, yet not without its perverse charm for brazenness. Unless one thinks that the myriad markets of the world are in continuous equilibrium (indeed, *general* equilibrium), most exchanges are at disequilibrium prices. Therefore, what actually occurs is "false", and what occurs only in the mind is, by implication, "true". Even Descartes might have blushed at such a formulation of the mind and the material world.

[11] Frank Hahn pointed this out, expressing justified puzzlement over the failure of the critics to move in for the kill on the aggregate employment theory that they had so severely wounded:

What is at risk is a simplified neoclassical comparative static equilibrium analysis and a simplified neoclassical dynamics. Sraffa's point was a fine technical insight into neoclassical economics but ... [the critics] have not exploited it. ... [O]n the manner in which an equilibrium [at full employment] is supposed to come about, neoclassical theory is highly unsatisfactory ... The remarkable fact is that neither [Sraffa] nor the Sraffians have made anything of this.
F. Hahn: "The neo-Ricardians", in F. Hahn (ed.): *Equilibrium and macroeconomics* (Oxford, Basil Blackwell, 1984), pp. 383-384.

[12] For a simple but detailed derivation of the factor price frontier, see Weeks, 1989, op. cit., pp. 144-149.

[13] The capital-labour ratio itself can be deduced directly with a little trigonometry, for it is the tangent of the angle formed by each factor price line at the horizontal axis.

[14] One unit of the input is defined as the amount required to produce one unit of the output. This eliminates the need for two terms defining the level of production for each commodity.

[15] Profit could be calculated as $r(wl + rk)$, on all costs. The more common formulation is that in the text.

[16] This is argued in C.E. Ferguson: *The neoclassical theory of production and distribution* (Cambridge, Cambridge University Press, 1969), pp. XVII-XVIII.

[17] The essence of Clower's approach can be found in R.W. Clower: "The Keynesian counter-revolution: A theoretical appraisal", in F. Hahn and F.P.R. Brechling (eds.): *The theory of interest rates* (London, Macmillan, 1965).

[18] In my view the most important book on macroeconomics since *The general theory* is A. Leijonhufvud: *Keynesian economics and the economics of Keynes* (Oxford, Oxford University Press, 1968).

[19] In an important contribution to the debate over macroeconomic equilibrium, he argues that Clower and Leijonhufvud concede much too much to neoclassical theory. J.F. Brothwell: "A simple Keynesian's response to Leijonhufvud: Rejoinder to three comments", in *Bulletin of Economic Research*, Vol. 28, No. 2, Nov. 1976, pp. 123-126.

[20] "... [T]he recent meaning given to equilibrium (and disequilibrium) has had quite disastrous effects. Equilibrium is defined as Walrasian competitive equilibrium ... All other states are said to be disequilibrium." F. Hahn: *Equilibrium and macroeconomics* (Oxford, Basil Blackwell, 1984), pp. 8-9.

[21] And there is more to the story: it is presumed that they can sell all of these levels at the prevailing price level. If this were not the case, then one would not be justified in specifying the demand for labour in terms of the real wage. So specifying the schedule would be wrong because if it were anticipated that a lower price level was required to sell higher levels of output, price would be greater than marginal revenue. If price and marginal revenue are not equal, then it is not valid to divide the money wage by the price level; instead, it should be divided by marginal revenue. But a "real wage" obtained by dividing the money wage by marginal revenue is not the relevant real wage for the labour supply curve. However, this is rather a minor theoretical inconsistency that need not detain us.

[22] The assumption of a given money supply is absolutely necessary. If the money supply varies, then the clearing of the labour market is not the result of an adjustment of the real wage as such. Increases in the money supply stimulate greater aggregate expenditure, and though the real wage falls, this is the *result* rather than the *cause* of the expansion of employment.

[23] A variation on the perfect foresight approach is "rational expectations", as practised by the new classical macroeconomics. Treating this school of analysis is beyond the scope of this paper. See Weeks, 1989, op. cit., 130-142.

[24] "At its full-employment value" in the sense that if there were no false trading, this would be the unique real wage necessary to achieve full employment. Referring to the unemployment during the Great Depression, Leijonhufvud wrote:

> The essence of Keynes' diagnosis is this: the actual disequilibrium price vector initiating the contraction differs from the appropriate, hypothetical equilibrium vector in one major respect - the general level of long-term asset prices is lower than warranted ... Leijonhufvud, 1968, op. cit., p. 335.

[25] Again quoting Leijonjufvud:

> Keynes' point is that when the appropriate price relation does not obtain, it is in general not wages but asset demand prices that are out of line.
> Leijonhufvud, 1968, op. cit., p. 335.

[26] "Simultaneous" because a sequential clearing has to involve trading at non-general equilibrium prices: the price in each market is dependent on all other prices.

[27] "Instantaneous" because any actual process of "groping" for the general equilibrium price involves trades at non-equilibrium prices.

[28] Voluntary in the sense that workers are choosing not to be employed, albeit on bad information. It was exactly this interpretation of unemployment that Keynes explicitly rejected. J.M. Keynes: *The general theory of employment, interest and money* (London, Macmillan, 1936), p. 15.

[29] See B. Fine and A. Murfin: *Macroeconomics and monopoly capital* (Brighton, Wheatsheaf Books, 1984).

[30] M. Hawkins: *The Oxford Paperback Dictionary* (Oxford, Oxford University Press, 1984), p. 400.

[31] Wages are also paid in socialist economies; however, their function is different. They do not serve to allocate labour to any important extent, and much of the basic consumption of workers is only loosely related to wage payments (e.g., housing).

[32] These two categories of commodities (which leave out "luxuries", commodities not bought by workers directly or indirectly) comprise what is called the "basic system" in the Sraffian analysis. P. Sraffa: *The production of commodities by means of commodities* (Cambridge, Cambridge University Press, 1973).

[33] Neoclassical analysis treats productivity change as a "long-run" phenomenon that can be ignored in short-run comparative statics. If this is meant as a distinction in theoretical time, then it is not relevant to the classical approach, in which the theoretical short run includes productivity change. If it is meant as an empirical simplification (labour markets operate in a time frame for which technical change is not important), it is demonstratively false.

[34] To avoid diversionary arguments over whether technical change is "labour-saving" or "capital-saving", let it be arbitrarily assumed that it is neutral (Hicks or Harrod), in which case the statement in the text holds. For a discussion of the nature of technical change in classical models, see J. Weeks: *Capital and exploitation* (Princeton, Princeton University Press, 1981), pp. 182-186.

[35] This is partly because in neoclassical models growth almost invariably occurs at continuous full employment.

Labour market informalisation

As noted in Chapter 1, the orthodox structural adjustment and "deregulation" perspective has attached great importance to what it sees as labour market "rigidities" that supposedly impede employment expansion and output growth in the "formal" sector, inter alia. It also sees the "informal sector" as the actual and potential source of economic dynamism and labour absorption, if only regulations were relaxed or removed altogether. Critics, of course, are sceptical of both sets of claims.

In the three papers that follow, various aspects of labour market informalisation are highlighted. Jan Vandemoortele brings his long experience of working on "informal sector" issues in sub-Saharan Africa to argue that generalised informalisation has been extensive; labour market rigidities in those economies could scarcely be blamed, in his view, for unsuccessful adjustment programmes. Brian Roberts, who has carried out many empirical studies of labour market and social developments in urban areas of Mexico, argues that it is a continuing mistake to treat the informal sector as a homogeneous entity or as an unchanging one. Most crucially, export-led economic growth has coincided with rapid and widespread informalisation that has been associated with declining labour rights. This raises the problem of how to "bring the State back in", an issue taken up in Victor Tokman's paper, which deals with the issue of identifying the type of regulations appropriate for the informalisation that arises with structural adjustment.

3

Labour market informalisation in sub-Saharan Africa

by Jan Vandemoortele *

Introduction

Abba Lerner described the following nightmare. While walking along a straight avenue, Lerner saw a car approaching. The car stopped, the door opened and a passenger asked him whether he needed a lift. He looked into the car and noticed there was no steering wheel. "Of course we have no steering wheel" said one of the passengers, "we believe in democracy and cannot give anyone the extreme authority of life and death over all the occupants of the car. This would be dictatorship".[1]

Lerner believed that traditionalism, misunderstanding and vested interests by themselves do not prevent the use of the economic steering wheel. Instead, he argued that the main obstacles in the way of an economic steering wheel are dogma and timidity. Dogma of the right that says that it is improper for government to go into business or to interfere with business; dogma of the left that says that it is improper for private business to compete with government; and timidity on the part of those who say that we need a regulator of employment. He related timidity to the story of the emperor who was tricked by charlatans into parading without clothes before his people, but observed that in the real world it is not the emperor but the people who are made to go naked, hungry and unemployed.

Today, a new tide of the old laissez-faire approach is influencing the course of social and economic policy-making world-wide.[2] In the developing world, the new course is often associated with structural adjustment programmes supported by the IMF and the World Bank. As a consequence, labour market interventions and basic needs activities are increasingly considered as a Sargasso Sea of economic shipwrecks. For example, an authoritative World Bank report of 1984 on economic development in sub-Saharan Africa asserted that the policies of African governments have been redistributive only in the

* ILO/JASPA (Jobs and Skills Programme for Africa)/Addis Ababa. I would like to thank Guy Standing and Martin Godfrey for their helpful comments on an earlier draft.

sense that they have redistributed poverty, not wealth.[3] Emerging evidence indicates that new tidal wave is accompanied by unprecedented economic hardship and social regression. Even to the casual observer of today's situation in the developing world in general, and sub-Saharan Africa in particular, it would seem that Lerner's 40-year old nightmare is coming true.

The objective of this paper is to show how labour markets in sub-Saharan Africa have been gradually informalised in recent years. It first briefly touches on the debate on structural adjustment and employment in sub-Saharan Africa. Then it reviews some of the most important labour market adjustments that have taken place in recent years. The concluding section projects the employment trends for the 1990s. Based on the premise that the success of adjustment and recovery programmes will ultimately depend on the correct assessment of labour market behaviour and institutions, it suggests some of the major labour markets issues that will need renewed attention in the future if the formidable challenge of employment is to be met.

Structural adjustment and employment

Structural adjustment has become the watchword of the era in Africa. Over 30 countries are at different stages of implementing programmes of economic stabilisation and structural adjustment. There is a growing consensus that there is no escape from adjustment,[4] although most analysts agree that existing programmes are incomplete and sometimes faulty. Evidence is building up that they are not making satisfactory progress towards renewed growth and development in the region.[5] Among the reasons for the disappointing performance are (i) the too-much-too-soon syndrome regarding their design; (ii) the too-little-too-late syndrome about their implementation; and (iii) the continuing hostile international environment that increases a sense of adjustment fatigue. Countries that pursue strong reform programmes have not achieved a better economic performance.[6]

Standard adjustment programmes overlook the structural characteristics of African economies that arise from initial conditions of generalised poverty.[7] Typical adjustment programmes accord higher priority to short-term objectives than to longer-term development and structural change.[8] Often, the pressure to achieve immediate fiscal and monetary targets creates an atmosphere in which long-term development is overtaken by short-term fire-fighting, leading to a slowdown in economic growth because of declining human and physical investment and imports. Hence, existing adjustment programmes focus their objectives on symptoms rather than on the real causes of the crisis. Short-term efforts that narrowly focus on the improvement of domestic and external financial balances inevitably hinder longer-term development. Financial imbalances are mere symptoms of underdevelopment, not deep-rooted causes of the crisis.

There is clearly a need for reform in economic policies in most African countries, but to argue that such reforms will be sufficient to rectify the situation seems rather simplistic. Intuitively, the fact that the crisis affects virtually all African economies to a similar degree despite the heterogeneity in policy-making suggests that fundamental structural factors do play a crucial role. The real cause of the crisis is that Africa entered into the 1980s with several very serious structural, economic and social weaknesses which made the region ill-prepared and extremely vulnerable to the world economic crisis and the deteriorating external climate. The causes of the crisis go far beyond short-term financial imbalances. Structural transformation of African economies cannot and must not follow a smooth equilibrium path. Imbalances will necessarily be one of the fundamental characteristics of development in the future.[9] Human resources development, rehabilitation of economic infrastructure, diversification of exports, etc. will imperatively require more time and increased financial inflows - two of the most scarce resources in Africa today - than what is normally envisaged in standard adjustment programmes. Hence, there is an urgent need to move from the inadequate corrective approach of structural adjustment to the more appropriate directive approach because structural change and development are erratic, discordant and unbalanced processes.[10] A new generation of directive adjustment programmes is needed that will take greater care to incorporate the structural characteristics of the economy and mitigate the adverse social impact.[11] Existing programmes will have to evolve towards social adjustment programmes that will promote structural change, flexibility and productivity without jeopardising basic human rights, social progress and equity, as Guy Standing argues in Chapter 1. This will require fundamental reforms in economic policy-making in most African countries, including in the area of employment and labour market policies.

There is growing consensus that the employment problem looms as one of the most pressing development challenges of the 1990s in Africa. The region ended its so-called "lost decade in development" without any signal that the recession is abating, despite strong economic growth in the industrialised world. Between 1980 and 1989, per-capita GDP in sub-Saharan Africa dropped by approximately one fifth.[12] During the 1980s, the number of African countries belonging to the group of the Least Developed Countries increased from 16 to 28. Two decades of social and economic progress have been much eroded in a matter of years. Basic needs have been the first casualty of the crisis. For example, the gross enrolment ratio at the primary level decreased from 80 to 75 during the period 1980-87.[13] Available indicators suggest that there has been a social overkill in Africa regarding the social impact of the economic crisis. Latin America, which experienced an equally severe economic downturn as sub-Saharan Africa, managed to increase the gross primary school enrolment ratio from 105 to 108. Education trends indicate that Africa is seriously under-investing in human capital formation. Enrolment is lagging and the quality of education is falling, suggesting that the already low education profile of the labour force will decline in the future.

The nature of Africa's employment problem is primarily structural. The severe downturn in economic activity of the 1980s has merely aggravated an already precarious situation. Indeed, the employment crisis in the region is not new. The ILO mission to Kenya in 1972, for instance, which came when the economy was growing twice as fast as in the 1980s, had already discovered grave employment problems. The novelty is that the employment problem has become acute. Until the late 1970s, the employment crisis remained largely invisible because of the relatively rapid expansion of employment opportunities in both the modern and informal sectors. But the 1980s witnessed a sharp deterioration in the region's employment situation. When the labour force expands faster than the economy - as has been the case in sub-Saharan Africa since 1980 - the employment situation must worsen. It is estimated that the extent of open and disguised unemployment in the region increased by about a sixth between 1980 and 1988, four times faster than during the 1970s.

Labour markets do play a crucial role in the process of structural adjustment. The incorrect assessment of the functioning of labour markets has often been at the heart of the failure of adjustment programmes. Zambia represents a clear case of how faulty assumptions about labour market behaviour were at the heart of the failure of the programme. Indeed, one of the major objectives of Government's New Economic Recovery Programme, launched in 1987 after the abandonment of the IMF programme, was "to generate massive employment opportunities, combat youth unemployment and introduce practical skills training programme for school leavers".[14] The success of adjustment programmes depends, both on how efficiently labour markets operate and on how accurately the programmes reflect the behaviour of the labour markets and their institutional characteristics. The new conventional wisdom embodied in orthodox adjustment programmes is that output and employment are best determined by market forces. The aim of corrective structural adjustment programmes is to improve the competitive operation of the labour markets by removing existing distortions that result from government interventions. They usually assume labour mobility and wage flexibility. But flexibility and mobility are determined by the level of development and the development strategies pursued in the past.[15] These two variables cannot be altered in the short to medium term.

Therefore, another approach to adjustment is needed, namely the directive one. This approach argues that social adjustment will require selective interventions to steer and balance the process of structural change. So far, most of the existing structural adjustment programmes in Africa belong to the corrective type, although the circumstances call for a dose of directive adjustment. Indeed, labour markets and indigenous private entrepreneurs in sub-Saharan Africa are either non-existent or too weak to play the important role assigned by the corrective adjustment approach. Moreover, implicit or explicit labour market deregulation is fundamentally incompatible with the objective of growth with equity. Moreover, economic history shows that, in the long run, flexible wages have never been efficient or productive. Whereas orthodox adjustment programmes consider labour market regulations as costs and barriers to growth, a social adjustment perspective would regard them as instrumental in achieving the ultimate development goal.

Recent labour market adjustments

Since labour markets play a facilitating role in the process of adjustment and recovery, it is important to assess the recent changes that have taken place. The major labour market adjustments that have occurred in recent years can be summarised in the following four points: (i) erosion and compression of wages, particularly in the public sector; (ii) stagnation in modern sector wage employment; (iii) mounting unemployment; and (iv) saturation of the informal and agricultural labour sponges.

Erosion and compression of wages

Among the most important adjustments on the sub-Saharan labour markets is the rapid fall of real wages. Table 1 documents real wage trends in the modern sector. Out of the 27 countries for which recent data are available, only one has reported modest increases in real wages. The other 26 countries have all registered considerable losses in real wages. The decline has been steepest in Sierra Leone, Somalia, the United Republic of Tanzania, the Sudan, the Central African Republic (CAR), Zambia and Madagascar, where the average wage rate has dropped by 10 per cent or more every year since 1980. On average, real wages seem to have declined by approximately 30 per cent between 1980 and 1986.[16]

Moreover, the decline in real wages predates the downturn of the macro-economic indicators which started in 1980. For instance, non-agricultural real wages dropped by 57.8 per cent in Tanzania and 47.4 per cent in Swaziland between 1975 and 1980. This means that between 1975 and 1986, real wages dropped to almost unimaginably low levels, falling from index 100 to 44 and 11 in Swaziland and Tanzania respectively. In Zaire, the Central Bank's index of real wages in the public sector shows a drop from 100 in the base year 1975 to 15 in 1983.

Admittedly, wages and salaries give only a rough approximation of total earnings in most African countries as non-wage allowances and benefits (both in cash and in kind) constitute an important part of the pay system, especially in the public sector. Although attempts to trim allowances have met with considerable resistance,[17] evidence indicates that non-wage benefits have decreased since the mid-1970s and have not compensated for the fall in real wages.[18] Hence, wage trends can be considered as good proxy for trends in total earnings.

Table 1. Real wage trends in selected African countries (1980 = 100)

Country	Coverage	Year	Index	Annual change %
1. Botswana	Public sector	1984	85.3	− 3.9
2. Burkina Faso	Minimum industrial wage	1987	91.5	− 1.3
3. Burundi	Public sector	1987	70.4	− 4.9
4. Cape Verde	Public sector	1984	71.7	− 8.0
5. Central African Republic	Public sector	1985	52.8	− 2.0
6. Cote d'Ivoire	Minimum industrial wage	1988	69.7	− 4.4
7. Ethiopia	Civil service	1984	84.1	− 4.2
8. Gabon	Minimum industrial wage	1987	87.6	− 1.9
9. Gambia	Modern sector	1984	80.5	− 5.3
10. Ghana	Modern sector	1985	79.8	− 4.4
11. Kenya	Non-agricultural sector	1987	77.4	− 3.6
12. Lesotho	Civil service	1988	66.8	− 4.9
13. Madagascar	Public sector	1987	48.3	− 9.9
14. Malawi	Non-agricultural sector	1986	67.1	− 6.4
15. Mali	Public sector	1985	70.0	− 6.9
16. Mauritania	Civil service	1984	76.4	− 6.5
17. Mauritius	Non-agricultural sector	1986	93.7	− 1.1
18. Niger	Modern sector	1988	78.2	− 3.0
19. Senegal	Civil service	1985	70.0	− 6.9
20. Seychelles	Non-agricultural sector	1985	110.6	+ 2.0
21. Sierra Leone	Non-agricultural sector	1986	25.5	− 20.4
22. Somalia	Civil service	1986	28.4	− 18.9
23. Sudan	Civil service	1985	52.2	− 12.2
24. Swaziland	Non-agricultural sector	1986	83.2	− 3.0
25. United Rep. of Tanzania	Non-agricultural sector	1987	26.1	− 17.5
26. Zambia	Non-agricultural sector	1984	63.7	− 10.7
27. Zimbabwe	Non-agricultural sector	1984	88.9	− 2.9
Average		1986	70.4	− 6.0

Source: Compiled from ILO: *Yearbook of Labour Statistics* (various years), ILO Bureau of Statistics, government statistical abstracts, JASPA and World Bank country studies and various country profiles of the Economist Intelligence Unit.

There is also evidence that the decline in real wages has been accompanied by a strong compression in the wage structure. Lower income earners appear to have suffered less from falling purchasing power than higher income earners, leading to a narrowing in occupational wage differentials. In the civil service of Sierra Leone, for instance, the real income of a permanent secretary dropped by 88 per cent between 1980 and 1990. The ratio of this income to that of an unskilled worker in the civil service was nearly halved, from 15:1 to 9:1, during the same period. In Ghana, the real income of a principal secretary dropped by 88 per cent between 1977 and 1985, while that of a messenger fell

Table 2. Ratio of average to minimum wage in selected sub-Saharan African countries (1980 = 100)

Country	Year	Ratio
1. Burundi	1985	63.8
2. Ethiopia	1984	102.6
3. Kenya	1986	105.1
4. Madagascar	1986	82.9
5. Malawi	1986	61.6
6. Mauritania	1984	88.8
7. Senegal	1985	89.7
8. United Republic of Tanzania	1986	85.2
9. Zambia	1984	78.6
10. Zimbabwe	1984	76.0
Average		83.4

Source: ILO: *Yearbook of Labour Statistics* (various years), D. Ghai: *Economic growth, structural change and labour absorption in Africa: 1960-85,* UNRISD Discussion Paper No. 1 (Geneva, 1987).

by 52 per cent. In Senegal, the range between the minimum and maximum salary (including allowances) in the civil service decreased from 7.8:1 to 6.6:1 between 1980 and 1985. In Kenya, the income disparity among modern sector wage earners gradually declined between 1970 and 1985, with the Gini-ratio decreasing from 0.60 to 0.45.

A second indicator of the compression in the wage structure is given in table 2. This table indicates that the ratio of average to minimum wages declined in all but two of the ten countries for which data are available. On average, the differential between the average and minimum wage narrowed by over 15 per cent in the first half of the 1980s

Another indicator that illustrates the compression in the wage structure in sub-Saharan Africa consists of the ratio of non-agricultural over agricultural wages. Since agricultural wage labourers are typically among the lowest paid wage earners in the modern sector, the decline in the ratio would indicate that the income concentration among wage employees is becoming less skewed over time. Available data for six countries indicate that the average ratio has fallen continuously between 1975 and the early 1980s. According to table 3, the ratio decreased by 6 per cent in the period 1975-80 and by as much as 28 per cent in the first half of the 1980s.

These trends are confirmed by the results of a recent ILO survey of civil service pay in Africa which are summarised in table 4.[19] The data show that real basic salaries declined precipitously between 1975 and 1985.

The real basic salary for the lowest grade dropped by about one-half while that for the highest grade plunged by nearly two-thirds. As a consequence, the wage differential between the lowest and the highest grade narrowed by a

Table 3. Ratio of non-agricultural to agricultural wage rates in selected African countries

Country	Year		
	1975	1980	1985
1. Ghana	1.52	1.40	1.15
2. Malawi	4.00	4.44	3.57
3. Mauritius	1.06	1.05	0.76
4. Swaziland	9.76	8.22	5.21
5. Zambia	2.66	2.30	2.32
6. Zimbabwe	5.44	5.46	3.51
Average	4.07	3.81	2.75

Source: ILO: *Yearbook of Labour Statistics* (various years).

third over this ten-year period. The results also suggest that wage increments had a limited impact on both wage trends and wage disparities.

It is also important to note that since 1980 real wages have fallen more rapidly than per capita income. This means that the wage earners have borne a heavy burden of the recent economic crisis. Working people, especially in the cities, have been pauperised by inflation and devaluation. Table 5 confirms that their income position has worsened relative to that of other socio-economic groups. In the mid-1980s, an average wage employee in the non-agricultural modern sector earned about three times the country's per capita income, compared to a ratio of more than four in 1975. The ratio dropped by 20 per cent in the first half of the 1980s, against a decline of 10 per cent in the quinquennium 1975-80.

Table 4. Indices of real wages in the sub-Saharan civil service[1]

Grade	Year		Annual change %
	1975	1985	
Lowest grade			
Basic salary	100.0	52.4	− 6.3
Basic salary plus normal increments	100.0	64.0	− 4.4
Highest grade			
Basic salary	100.0	35.7	− 9.8
Basic salary plus normal increments	100.0	42.1	− 8.3

[1] Average indices are based on a sample of 12 countries.

Source: ILO: *World Labour Report* (Geneva, 1989), Vol. 4, table 4.1.

Table 5. Ratio of non-agricultural wages to per capita income in selected sub-Saharan African countries

Country	1975	1980	Most recent year
1. Burundi	6.81	5.67	4.96 (1987)
2. Ghana	2.30	1.50	1.53 (1984)
3. Kenya	5.71	5.10	5.01 (1987)
4. Madagascar	2.29	1.66	1.73 (1985)
5. Malawi	4.96	5.55	3.99 (1986)
6. Mauritius	0.68	0.80	0.58 (1987)
7. Sierra Leone	2.86	2.36	2.05 (1986)
8. Swaziland	4.62	3.85	4.04 (1986)
9. United Republic of Tanzania	6.86	5.26	2.55 (1986)
10. Zambia	4.76	4.67	1.68 (1984)
11. Zimbabwe	4.37	5.28	5.07 (1984)
Average	4.20	3.79	3.02

Source: ILO: *Yearbook of Labour Statistics* (various years), IMF International Financial Statistics, and JASPA country studies.

Informal sector earnings and rural incomes, on the other hand, have been relatively better protected than modern sector wages, largely because the former have benefited from a changing demand structure. Indeed, consumption patterns are changing in favour of less import-intensive and cheaper food items and everyday consumer goods. Consequently, the inter-sectoral income differentials have narrowed which has brought about a reallocation of labour to the informal and rural sectors. Hence, the dualistic division of the labour market into a high-wage modern sector and a low-wage traditional/informal sector is no longer valid.

However, wage erosion and wage compression have been more pronounced in the public sector than in private enterprises. Very often, reductions in the public wage bill have been one of the major targets of adjustment programmes. The easiest way of achieving this target is through a wage freeze rather than through a recruitment freeze or retrenchment. Data for sub-Saharan Africa indicate that the central government wage bill in real terms increased by only 5 per cent between 1980 and 1987, while total government expenditure rose by 23 per cent. Hence, the share of wages and salaries in total government expenditure declined by a seventh in a period of seven years.[20]

Wage trends in Africa are often very different for the public and private sectors. For instance, data on Kenya reveal that the drop in average real wages stemmed essentially from the public sector, while real wages in the private sector remained more or less constant. Between 1977 and 1987, private sector wages decreased by 4 per cent while public sector wages dropped by 25 per cent. In Côte d'Ivoire, private sector wages increased by 13.4 per cent between 1979 and 1984, whereas public sector wages decreased by 4.4 per cent. Therefore,

Figure 1. The fusion of urban labour markets*

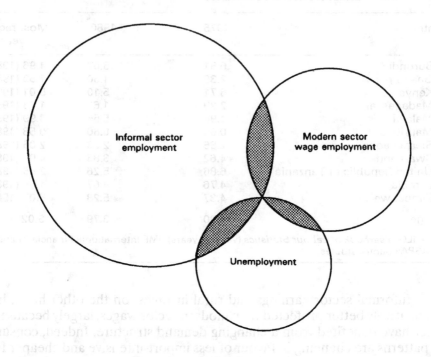

* This diagram does not consider the impact of the urban-rural exchange and international migration on urban labour markets.

the decline in real wages and the compression in the wage structure primarily stemmed from the public sector.[21] Consequently, as Christopher Colclough argues, there is compelling evidence that reductions in real wages have essentially been policy-induced, rather than resulting from market forces.

In short, real wage levels in Africa have not been rigid in the recent past, neither in absolute nor in relative terms. In some cases, real earnings have fallen below their "efficiency level". They often need to be supplemented by other income sources. A growing proportion of the wage earners are engaged in secondary jobs,[22] confirming the regularly observed phenomenon of moonlighting and occupational multiplicity. In addition, households increase their activity rate during periods of recession and adjustment - women and children in particular - and spread their income sources over a multitude of economic sectors that extend sometimes across international borders. The steady fusion of the urban labour markets explains a great deal about the absence of any serious social upheavals in the wake of the sharp falls in real wages in African countries during the 1980s.[23]

Table 6. Wage employment in selected African countries 1975-85 (thousands)

Country	Total wage employment			Industrial wage employment		
	1975	1980	1985	1975	1980	1985
1. Benin	33.1	66.2	80.8	6.3	14.6	15.3
2. Botswana	57.3	83.4	117.2	17.9	27.6	31.0
3. Burundi (Buja)	28.5	38.2	44.7	6.0	10.7	14.2
4. Côte d'Ivoire	340.9	470.2	415.5	55.0	73.5	65.9
5. Gambia	18.8	29.6	24.1	8.3	9.8	5.6
6. Kenya	819.1	1 005.8	1 174.4	152.4	217.0	231.2
7. Malawi	276.83	370.4	394.6	62.8	77.4	71.1
8. Mauritius	168.6	197.1	209.5	30.9	48.4	71.9
9. Niger	20.5	26.0	22.5	12.3	17.5	12.6
10. Seychelles	13.8	17.9	18.2	3.2	4.5	3.4
11. Sierra Leone	61.8	69.9	69.4	20.1	23.9	25.8
12. Swaziland	64.6	75.1	72.8	15.8	19.1	18.0
13 Zambia	393.5	379.3	361.5	186.0	162.6	143.4
14. Zimbabwe	1 050.2	1 009.9	1 039.4	286.3	274.5	276.4
Total	3 347.3	3 839.0	4 044.6	863.3	981.1	985.8

Source: ILO: *Yearbook of Labour Statistics* (various years), various government statistical abstracts, JASPA and World Bank country studies.

The fusion of urban labour markets is illustrated in figure 1. It is useful to distinguish three major employment statuses in urban areas, namely (i) modern sector wage employment, (ii) informal sector employment, and (iii) unemployment. About 60 per cent of the urban labour force are in the informal sector, either as proprietors, paid employees, unpaid family workers or apprentices; between 20 and 25 per cent are in modern-sector wage employment while the other 15-20 per cent are unemployed. These employment categories are not mutually exclusive in an African setting. The non-shaded areas in figure 1 represent workers who do not have major secondary income sources or the unemployed without an income-generating activity. The shaded areas of overlap illustrate the fusion of urban labour markets.

Observation in the region confirms that many modern sector wage employees are engaged in urban informal activities, including urban agriculture. Those operating in both the modern and informal sectors are represented by the shaded area I. The shaded areas II and III represent the unemployed who occasionally work in the informal or modern sector.[24] The overlap between unemployment and informal sector employment (area II) could be labelled "involuntary employment", since most of the unemployed take odd jobs in the informal sector for reasons of mere survival and consider their jobs as unsatisfactory and temporary. The overlap between modern sector wage employment and unemployment (area III) consists primarily of casual labourers in the modern sector who experience spells of unemployment.

Stagnating wage employment

The main objective of the restrictive wage policy has been to sustain modern sector wage employment, especially in the public sector. But despite the large decline in labour costs, wage employment growth in the modern sector has declined significantly since the early 1980s. Table 6 shows that wage employment growth in 14 sub-Saharan African countries decelerated from about 3 per cent per annum in 1975-80 to only 1 per cent between 1980 and 1985. The decline was steepest in the industrial sector, where employment growth decelerated from 2.6 to merely 0.1 per cent per year between the respective quinquennia. The number of new jobs created in the industrial sector as a proportion of all new jobs in the modern sector fell from 24 to 2 per cent. National accounts data on industrial output confirm that a process of de-industrialisation has started in the region.[25]

Although labour absorption in the modern sector during the 1970s was considerably faster than the labour force growth, modern sector wage employment in sub-Saharan Africa never accounted for more than 10 per cent of the labour force. Table 7 indicates that formal sector wage employment in 36 countries, representing 95 per cent of the sub-Saharan labour force, accounted for only 9.9 per cent of the labour force in 1980. As modern sector wage employment growth has actually lagged behind labour force growth in recent years, its relative importance has declined since 1980. It is estimated that wage employment accounts for no more than 8 per cent of the region's total labour force.

In many countries, the public sector is the most important wage employer. During the 1970s - and until the early 1980s - governments in the region have, to a large extent, played the role of employer of last resort. As a result, the public sector is often responsible for 50 per cent or more of modern sector wage employment. According to an international comparison, the share of public sector employees in non-agricultural wage employment was the highest in Africa (54 per cent), followed by Asia (36 per cent), Latin America (27 per cent) and the OECD countries (24 per cent).[26] The growth rates of public sector employment were often unsustainable and did not always correspond with the expansion in the demand for government services.[27]

However, the situation has changed radically since the early 1980s. The tight fiscal position has forced many governments to exercise a stricter control on recruitment. Indeed, public sector employment growth is reported to have decelerated in several countries. Hence, the slowdown in modern sector wage employment in recent years is essentially because the public sector - the engine of employment growth - has become increasingly unable to sustain the high rates of labour absorption of the 1970s and early 1980s. In some extreme cases, governments have been forced to retrench thousands of public sector workers. The retrenchment figures that are being quoted include 45,000 in Ghana; 40,000 in Guinea; 27,000 in the United Republic of Tanzania and 16,000 in Cameroon. The private modern sector, on the other hand, has not been able

Table 7. Importance of wage employment in sub-Saharan Africa in 1980 (thousands)

Country	Labour force	Wage employment	Share %
1. Benin	1 581	66.2	4.2
2. Botswana	288	83.4	29.0
3. Burkina Faso	2 963	50.0	1.7
4. Burundi	1 974	116.0	5.9
5. Cameroon	3 143	308.2	9.8
6. Congo	575	115.0	20.0
7. Côte d'Ivoire	3 119	470.2	15.1
8. Ethiopia	15 287	362.1	2.4
9. Gambia	2522	9.6	11.7
10. Gabon	448	110.1	24.6
11. Ghana	4 073	461.0	11.3
12. Guinea	2 285	157.5	6.9
13. Kenya	5 996	1 005.8	16.8
14. Lesotho	594	31.1	5.2
15. Liberia	635	121.0	19.1
16. Madagascar	3 552	337.7	9.5
17. Malawi	2 316	370.4	16.0
18. Mali	1 884	141.4	7.5
19. Mauritania	463	29.6	6.4
20. Mauritius	324	280.0	86.4
21. Mozambique	5 853	500.0	8.5
22. Niger	2 437	61.5	2.5
23. Nigeria	27 981	2 722.1	9.7
24. Rwanda	2 328	190.1	8.2
25. Senegal	2 240	110.4	4.9
26. Seychelles	23	17.9	77.8
27. Sierra Leone	1 184	69.9	5.9
28. Somalia	1 581	138.8	8.8
29. Sudan	5 365	600.0	11.2
30. Swaziland	214	75.1	35.1
31. United Republic of Tanzania	8 174	636.4	7.8
32. Togo	948	73.4	7.7
33. Uganda	5 239	362.8	6.9
34. Zaire	9 147	1 194.0	13.1
35. Zambia	1 690	379.3	22.4
36. Zimbabwe	2 555	1 009.9	39.5
Total	128 71	12 787.9	9.9

Source: Compiled from ILO: *Yearbook of Labour Statistics* (various years), government statistical abstracts, various JASPA and World Bank country studies.

to compensate for the job losses in the public sector. As a result, total wage employment is reported to have fallen in absolute terms in several countries, including the Central African Republic (– 33.6 per cent between 1980 and 1986), the Gambia (– 27.5 per cent between 1979 and 1986), Zaire (– 8.5 per cent between 1980 and 1984) and Zambia (– 5.4 per cent between 1980 and 1988).

Mounting unemployment

Stagnating or declining wage employment in the context of a rapidly expanding labour force leads inevitably to rising unemployment, especially in urban areas. Admittedly, unemployment in countries where there are no social security benefits for the unemployed may constitute a poor indicator for the overall employment situation. Nevertheless, the trend in many sub-Saharan African countries towards a growing prevalence of unemployment is undeniable. The urban unemployment rate in Kenya increased from 11.2 to 16.2 per cent between 1977/78 and 1986. In Zimbabwe, the urban unemployment rate stood at 18.8 per cent in 1987. Unemployment in Liberia rose from 12.8 to 17.9 per cent in the period 1980-84. In Côte d'Ivoire, where the number of modern sector jobs dropped by 12 per cent between 1980 and 1985, the rate of unemployment is estimated to have increased from 3 to 14 per cent. On average, the urban unemployment rate has doubled over the past 15 years, rising from 10 per cent in the mid-1970s to about 20 per cent today.

Hence, the common belief that unemployment in the region is not a widespread phenomenon is contradicted by the results of recent labour force surveys or population censuses.[28] Rising unemployment rates in the context of a rapidly growing workforce inevitably implies that the absolute number of unemployed persons is expanding extremely fast. The number of urban unemployed is currently growing by 10 per cent or more every year in many countries.[29] Unemployment can therefore no longer be dismissed as a relatively unimportant phenomenon in Africa.

The unemployed in the region have two important characteristics, namely their youthfulness and their high level of education. A large proportion of the unemployed population consists of young people. Under the international nomenclature, youths are defined as the age group between 15 and 24 years. Typically, youths represent between 60 and 75 per cent of the unemployed population in the region, although they account for only a third of the labour force. Their unemployment rate is universally higher than that for any other labour force category. Table 8 indicates that for the 15 countries for which information is available, youth unemployment rates are, on average, three times higher than adult unemployment rates.

It is important to know whether youth unemployment is essentially a transient problem or whether it is a sign of an emerging structural imbalance on the sub-Saharan labour markets. Evidence from labour force surveys

Table 8. Ratio of youth to adult unemployment rates in selected sub-Saharan African countries

Country	Coverage	Year	Ratio
1. Botswana	Rural and urban	1981	2.5
2. Côte d'Ivoire	Rural and urban	1985	2.1
3. Ethiopia	Urban	1984	3.6
4. Ghana	Rural and urban	1981	4.0
5. Kenya	Urban	1986	4.5
6. Madagascar	Rural and urban	1983	1.2
7. Malawi	Urban	1977	2.5
8. Mauritania	Rural and urban	1980	2.9
9. Mauritius	Rural and urban	1983	4.5
10. Nigeria	Rural and urban	1985	2.9
11. Seychelles	Rural and urban	1985	2.3
12. Sudan	Urban	1983	3.2
13. Togo	Rural and urban	1982	3.3
14. Zambia	Urban	1986	3.8
15. Zimbabwe	Urban	1987	5.2
Average			3.2

Source: Derived from ILO: *Yearbook of Labour Statistics* (various years), National labour force surveys and JASPA country studies.

supports both types of interpretation. On the one hand, they confirm that unemployment rates decline as one moves higher in the the age pyramid of the labour force. On the other hand, a closer look at the available data reveals that the newcomers are facing more than just transitory employment difficulties.

Evidence given in table 9 supports that first interpretation of the problem. Results of labour force surveys confirm that age and unemployment are negatively correlated. This supports the employability-gap thesis according to which youths are more vulnerable to unemployment because they lack sufficient work experience, social contacts and maturity to be competitive on the labour markets.[30] Youth unemployment is seen as part of their normal socialisation process.

However, a closer look at the available data reveals that the recruits are facing more than transitory difficulties. First, the duration of unemployment is usually longer than what is commonly believed. In Nigeria, for instance, 45 per cent of the urban unemployed in 1983 had been out of work for more than one year. A survey carried out three years later in urban Kenya revealed that as much as 61 per cent of the unemployed had been jobless for more than a year. Second, survey results confirm that the unemployed youth lower their reservation wage over time but remain unemployed for long periods. Third, most of the unemployed people in the region are actively looking for a job. The 1986 urban labour force survey in Kenya used two definitions of unemployment, depending on active and passive job search.[31] Based on active job search, the

Table 9. Unemployment rates by age in selected African countries

Age group	Urban Nigeria		Urban Kenya		Ghana	
	1974	1983	1978	1986	1960	1970
15-19	20.7	47.2	26.6	36.2	21.2	24.9
20-24	11.4	28.0	18.5	29.2	9.4	13.1
25-29	4.9	2.7	4.8	8.6	4.9	5.2
30-34	1.8	2.2	2.0	3.7	3.2	2.6
35-39	1.4	1.7	1.8	2.1	2.6	1.8
40-44	3.0	0.8	0.7	0.7	2.1	1.3
45-49	1.2	0.0	1.1	2.0	2.1	1.1
50-54	0.9	1.3	1.4	0.9	2.0	0.9
55-59	0.0	2.7	1.5	4.1	2.1	0.9
60-64	0.0	–	3.2	–	2.0	0.7
65+	0.0	–	2.2	–	2.2	0.5
All	6.2	7.3	6.7	9.7	6.0	6.0

Source: National labour force surveys.

survey found an unemployment rate of 14.8 per cent, while the inclusion of passive job search yielded an unemployment rate of 16.2 per cent. Hence, only a small proportion of the unemployed were passively looking for a job. Fourth, women are particularly vulnerable to unemployment, which reflects a structural imbalance on the labour market. Their unemployment rate is usually twice as high as men's.

Table 10. Unemployment rates by level of education in selected African countries

Level of education	Côte d'Ivoire Total 1985	Ethiopia Addis Ababa 1984	Kenya Urban 1986	Mauritius Total 1983	Nigeria Urban 1985
None	1.0	9.2	13.5	13.5	2.5
Primary	5.2	7.3	–	28.8	5.2
Lower level	–	–	14.5	–	–
Upper level	–	–	15.6	–	–
Secondary	–	–	–	36.8	30.5
Lower level	21.7	8.4	22.2	–	–
Upper level	11.7	20.8	8.2	–	–
University	13.7	4.4	5.4	13.2	5.2
Total	3.7	10.5	16.2	22.8	8.3

Source: National labour force surveys or population censuses.

Table 11. Composition of the unemployed by level of education

Level of education	Urban Kenya		Nigeria	
	1978	1986	1974	1985
None	23.6	8.7	22.6	22.6
Primary	43.1	34.2	53.1	23.5
Secondary	29.8	54.5	24.0	50.6
University	3.5	2.6	0.3	3.3
Total	100.0	100.0	100.0	100.0

Source: National labour force surveys.

Fifth, and finally, the high and rising unemployment rates for educated youths reflect the seriousness of the problem. Contrary to the situation in the industrialised countries, where the lack of education and training constitutes the major characteristic of unemployed youths, educated youths in Africa are more prone to unemployment than uneducated youths. Unemployment seems to be positively correlated with the level of education. Typically, the unemployment rate by level of education follows an inverted U-shape. Evidence from sub-Saharan African countries indicates that the unemployment rate is relatively low for the workforce without any formal education, increases for those with primary education, peaks for those with lower secondary education, and declines for upper secondary and university graduates. Table 10 provides support for this inverted U-curve pattern.

Secondary-school leavers constitute the labour force category for which unemployment is increasing fastest. Table 11 indicates that they have borne a disproportionate share of the growing unemployment problem. Their share in the total number of unemployed doubled between the mid-1970s and the mid-1980s. In urban Kenya, about 55 per cent of the unemployed had completed secondary education in 1986, compared to 30 per cent in 1977-78. In Nigeria, the proportion of the unemployed with secondary education increased from 24 to 51 per cent between 1974 and 1985.

Furthermore, results from recent labour force surveys contradict the thesis according to which educated people are unemployed, not because they are educated but because they are young. The cross-classification of unemployment by age and level of education, based on the results of the Botswana and Kenya labour force surveys, is summarised in table 12. The data show that the relative vulnerability of youths to unemployment is positively related to the level of education. Youth unemployment rate by level of education follows the same inverted U-curve noted earlier. Moreover, the ratio of youth to adult unemployment suggests that it is not only age which determines the degree of unemployment.

Table 12. Unemployment rates by age group and level of education

Level of education	Botswana (1985-85)			Urban Kenya (1986)		
	Youth	Adults	Ratio	Youth	Adults	Ratio
None	31.1	20.2	1.54	22.6	12.5	1.81
Lower primary	30.2	22.8	1.32	39.5	9.4	4.20
Upper primary	42.0	24.0	1.75	36.3	7.5	4.84
Lower secondary	44.0	15.3	2.88	49.3	10.9	4.52
Upper secondary	16.4	7.7	2.13	23.5	4.2	5.60
University	5.6	3.3	1.70	20.7	3.9	5.31
Total	37.8	20.7	1.83	41.0	9.0	4.54

Source: National labour force surveys.

A final point worth mentioning is that unemployment is gradually creeping up the educational ladder. In the 1970s, the primary-school leavers constituted the bulk of the unemployed, as was clearly demonstrated by the 1972 Kenya Report. Evidence provided in tables 10 and 11 indicates that secondary-school leavers became the majority of the unemployed during the 1980s. It is not unlikely that unemployment among graduates of higher education will skyrocket during the 1990s. Recent surveys show that graduates are experiencing growing difficulties on the labour markets in the region. A longitudinal tracer study of Kenyan university graduates,[32] spanning the period 1970-83, did not find evidence of a major unemployment problem, mainly because of the guaranteed employment policy which was pursued by the Government during this period. However, the results of the survey clearly indicate that their employment prospects are worsening over time. The growing length of job search, the increased reliance on government employment, the rise in temporary employment and the reduced utilisation of acquired skills all suggest that their labour market situation has deteriorated since the late 1970s. A 1986 tracer study of university and polytechnic graduates in Nigeria revealed that the situation had further deteriorated, with only 58 per cent of graduates in full-time employment 18 months after leaving the National Youth Service Corps.[33] Moreover, nearly 80 per cent of employed graduates in both countries had been recruited by the public sector. With the abandonment of the policy of guaranteed employment for university graduates in most sub-Saharan African countries, the number of unemployed graduates is bound to increase many times over during the next decade. University graduates in several countries are already encountering growing labour market difficulties. As a first reaction, most countries are putting the brake on the rate of expansion of university enrolment. Some countries such as Côte d'Ivoire, Guinea, Madagascar, Mali, Senegal and the United Republic of Tanzania have even reduced their university population in absolute numbers.

Saturation of the informal and agricultural labour sponges

Despite the overwhelming evidence that open unemployment in Africa is on the rise, it does not mean that those who fail to secure a job in the modern sector all join the ranks of the unemployed. On the contrary, the large majority of the labour force recruits have found employment despite the crisis, albeit at strongly reduced wages and incomes. The two major labour sponges are the informal and agricultural sectors of the economy.

It is not a coincidence that the informal sector was first "discovered" in an African country. The measurement of the sector's importance in terms of employment is fraught with difficulties, both conceptually and quantitatively. Estimates of informal sector employment are normally based on ad hoc surveys which have a limited geographical and/or sectoral coverage. Therefore, they tend to understate the importance of informal sector employment. The methodology whereby informal sector employment is estimated residually is likely to provide a better estimate. In table 13, we attempt to estimate residually the importance of informal sector employment in sub-Saharan Africa for the years 1980 and 1985.[34] The results indicate that informal employment has increased by a respectable 6.7 per cent per annum between 1980 and 1985, far above the urban labour force growth and the labour absorption in the modern sector. By 1985, the informal sector employed about 60 per cent of the urban labour force, or 15 per cent of the total labour force in the region. Table 13 also indicates that the informal sector created some 6 million new jobs on the urban labour market between 1980 and 1985, while the modern sector added only 0.5 million new jobs in the same period. The modern sector absorbed a mere 6 per cent of new labour force recruits, whereas almost three-quarters of them were absorbed in the informal sector.

Although government attitudes in the region have changed in favour of the informal sector, there are signs that the sector is encountering growing difficulties in coping with the tide of rural-urban migrants. Romanticising the informal sector as a labour sponge that has virtually no saturation point could be misleading. As output growth has generally not kept pace with the rate of labour absorption, the informal sector is primarily creating low productivity jobs and promoting precarious forms of employment. Hence, the sector is increasingly operating as a refuge which eases the extent of unemployment by converting it into underemployment.

Since the primary sector remains the backbone of most economies in the region, a healthy small-scale agricultural sector will be crucial for economic recovery and sustained development. Recent economic policy reforms have been relatively favourable to the rural sector, and the urban bias in development strategies has been reduced in many countries. Of late, the enabling environment for agricultural development has improved markedly. Agricultural producer prices in particular have increased more rapidly than wages and prices in general. Consequently, the long-term decline in the domestic terms of trade has been halted in most countries and reversed in some. This has

Table 13. Urban employment in sub-Saharan Africa, 1980 and 1985 (millions)

Indicator	1980	1985	Increase 1980-85	Annual change
Urban labour force	28.1	36.3	8.2	5.3
Urban wage employment	9.6	10.1	0.5	1.0
Urban employment	2.8	4.5	1.7	10.0
Informal sector employment	15.7	21.7	6.0	6.7

Source: Tables 6 and 7, UN population estimates, ILO labour force estimates and own estimations.

undoubtedly improved the employment and earnings prospects in the rural sector. It has also led to a narrowing of the urban-rural income gap, although rural income inequality has increased.[35] However, the slump in agricultural commodity prices on world markets has undone most of the progress made in recent years, for the internal terms of trade are dependent on the international terms of trade in primary commodity-exporting countries. Producer prices for coffee and cocoa have recently been halved in some member countries of the Communauté Financière Africaine (CFA) and it will be increasingly difficult to protect the real producer prices for these tradeables in non-CFA countries through continued devaluation.

The agricultural sector alone, however, is unlikely to absorb productively all new labour force recruits in the rural areas, particularly in land-scarce countries. Hence, rural non-farm activities will have to play a lead role in the creation of new jobs in the region. The importance of rural non-farm activities in terms of employment in Africa is difficult to quantify because they are usually carried out as a secondary occupation. But it can be safely assumed that their importance has been increasing over time. Table 14 gives the composition of rural household income in some countries. It clearly shows that rural households obtain a significant and growing proportion of their income from sources other than farming.

The increased importance of non-farm activities as a source of employment and income in rural areas stems from the combination of three factors, namely higher agricultural output and incomes, a shift in the structure of consumption in favour of informal sector goods and services, and the growing population pressure on arable lands.[36]

Conclusions and areas for future research

This paper has shown how the 1980s have witnessed a process of informalisation of labour markets in sub-Saharan Africa. Labour market informalisation has taken two different forms. First, the production structure has been informalised in the sense that an increased proportion of economic

Table 14. Composition of rural household income (selected countries, percentages)

Source of income	Kenya		Sudan 1978-80	Lesotho 1986	Ghana 1988
	1974-75	1981-82			
Farming	57.0	48.1	47.7	24.8	69
Non-farm activities	9.7	16.9		6.0	16
Salary and wages	22.4	21.3	52.3	10.0	11
Remittances and gifts	10.9	13.7		59.2	4
Total	100.0	100.0	100.0	100.0	100

Source: National household budget surveys.

activity is taking place outside the formal sector. At present, formal wage employment represents merely 8 per cent of the regional labour force. The second type of informalisation concerns the conditions of employment in the formal sector. Modern sector labour standards have gradually been informalised. Money wages have declined in some countries, while real wages have been remarkably flexible downward in most countries, both in absolute and relative terms. The high wage levels that prevailed until the early 1970s have been replaced by near-starvation wages in the 1980s, especially in the public sector. Wage and salary payments have become irregular and/or belated. The extent of casualisation of employment has increased and retrenchment has reduced employment security.

From the reviewed evidence on trends in real wages, compression in wage structure, and reallocation of labour to the traditional and informal sectors, one could conjecture that sub-Saharan labour markets are functioning relatively well and have been subject to market forces. However, the precipitous fall in real wages and the compression of the wage structure have been policy-induced, not market-induced. Moreover, the trends are far from presenting a basis for sustained growth and development in the future. The observed adjustments are little more than a search for survival in the context of severe economic contraction and social regression. Widespread "work-sharing" has taken place through which the burden of the crisis and adjustment has been shouldered by the majority of the labour force. Work-sharing has made it possible for most newcomers to find employment despite the crisis, albeit at much reduced wages and incomes.

The employment outlook for sub-Saharan Africa remains gloomy. The 1989 World Development Report projected an economic growth rate of just over 3 per cent per annum during 1988-95,[37] implying that per capita income would, at best, stagnate at the depressed level. However, economic growth in recent years has been below the target of 3 per cent. Indeed, economic growth in Africa averaged only 2.4 and 2.9 per cent in 1988 and 1989, respectively.[38]

**Table 15. Employment estimates and projections for sub-Saharan Africa
(millions)**

Sector	1980	1990	Projected growth rates (%)			2000
			Output	Produc-tivity	Employ-ment	
Rural	102	123	3	1	2	150
Informal	16	30	4	1	3	40
Modern	14	15	3	1	2	18
Unemployed	4	8	–	–	–	26
Total	136	176	3.2	1	2.2	234

Source: African employment report 1988 (Addis Ababa, JASPA, 1989); *Economically active
population 1950-2025* (Geneva, ILO, 1986); *World development report 1989* (Washington, DC,
World Bank, 1989); own estimations.

The hesitant recovery was driven by good weather conditions, indicating that
economic performance continues to be extremely vulnerable to external conditions. The policy reforms undertaken in the context of structural adjustment
programmes have yet to show any strong impact.

Our employment projections for the 1990s are based on the most
optimistic scenario of the World Development Report of 1989, namely that the
sub-Saharan economies will grow by 3.2 per cent a year. The sectoral growth
rates are estimated to be 3 per cent for the modern and rural (farm and
non-farm) sectors, and 4 per cent for the informal sector. Assuming a 1 per cent
increase in labour productivity overall, one can project sectoral employment
growth for the next decade. The indicative figures are given in table 15. Overall,
productive employment will increase by 2.2 per cent per annum while the
regional labour force is projected to expand by 2.9 per cent. Hence, the
employment situation will deteriorate further. The unemployed population is
expected to increase by over 10 per cent a year over the next decade. Consequently, the unemployment rate will more than double from 5 to 11 per cent.
Of course, most of it will be converted into underemployment through continued work-sharing, which will inevitably aggravate the poverty situation. The
two most important labour sponges during the 1990s will continue to be the
rural and informal sectors, generating 68 and 25 per cent, respectively, of all
productive new jobs. The modern sector is unlikely to generate more than 5
per cent of the number of jobs required in the future.

The consensus is growing that standard adjustment and recovery programmes will not be sufficient to tackle the employment problem in an adequate manner. Directive adjustment programmes oriented towards social
adjustment will be required if the region is to meet its major development
challenge. The development challenge facing sub-Saharan African countries is
essentially twofold: (i) the search for renewed economic growth[39] and (ii) the

translation of economic growth into increased employment opportunities to ensure that the majority of the people will reap the benefits from growth. In the past, the pattern of economic growth was such that the majority of the people hardly participated in the process of economic growth and, hence, did not benefit from it.

The implications for policy research are far-reaching. The link between labour market policies and adjustment and recovery programmes is clear. If labour market behaviour and institutions are such that they prevent labour moving between sectors, or wages adjusting, or productivity increasing, the adverse impact of structural adjustment programmes that assume short-term labour mobility and wage flexibility will be magnified, which will jeopardise the political commitment to necessary adjustments. Enhanced knowledge of the structure of employment and labour market behaviour will allow policy-makers to improve the design of recovery and adjustment programmes by incorporating country-specific historical, social and institutional labour market developments. It will be important for social adjustment programmes to avoid simplistic and doctrinaire prescriptions. Therefore, research on labour markets should be enhanced and could focus on the following issues.

Public sector employment and privatisation

Retrenchment and privatisation have played catalytic roles in sensitising African governments and donors to the social consequences of adjustment. The issue of public sector employment has been tackled in stages. At first, wage freezes were introduced, followed by a stricter enforcement of the legal retirement age. The next step consisted of an elimination of "ghost" workers and the lay-off of temporary workers. Then came the recruitment freeze. It was only when the final step of dismissal of public sector workers became inescapable that the employment and social consequences of adjustment were given attention. Indeed, it is surprising that projects like SDA (Social Dimension of Adjustment), PAMSCAD (Ghana), PASAGE (Madagascar) and PAPSCA (Uganda) have been launched many years after the first adjustment programmes were introduced in Africa. Their timing, i.e. once the issue of retrenchment became acute, shows that the employment problem in the region is still perceived as primarily a modern sector wage employment problem. As the public sector is an important wage employer in most African countries, it is not surprising that public sector employment has received priority in the employment debate.

Excessive recruitment by the civil service, especially at the lower echelons, is forcing more governments to retrench thousands of workers. Today, numerous countries are implementing redeployment exercises to create a leaner but better remunerated, trained and motivated civil service. However, reducing the size of the civil service to improve the level of remuneration and motivation of the civil servants is not as straightforward as it may appear. The policy very often fails to achieve its stated objective because attractive sever-ance payments and costly compensatory measures represent a new financial burden for the government.[40] Attempts to reduce employment levels in the public sector are extremely difficult, both from a political and a financial point of view. Therefore, as Derek Robinson argues in his chapter, retrenchment on a voluntary basis is likely to be more effective than compulsory retrenchment. Without increased budgetary resources to cover the high redundancy payments and non-labour operating costs, it will be extremely difficult to improve the incentives structure in the civil service. None the less, orthodox adjustment programmes aim at both reducing budgetary expenditure and the share of the wage bill therein. Labour market research in Africa should, therefore, focus on more efficient and socially acceptable ways to improve the capacity of the civil service in carrying out essential economic and social development tasks.

The decay of African economies is perhaps best reflected in the dete-riorating quality of the civil service. There is a widespread view that civil services in Africa are "overstaffed bureaucracies afflicted by eroding salary scales, pervasive demoralisation, corruption, moonlighting and chronic absen-teeism".[41] However, overstaffing in the public sector should not become an article of faith. Overstaffing is an empirical question and should not be deter-mined by a prior reasoning. Moreover, the proposed reform packages still leave much to be desired. In particular, the short-term objective of fiscal balance invariably conflicts with the longer-term objective of increased capability and improved efficiency. But the former continues to receive priority attention in the existing reform programmes.

Wage policy

As a consequence of widespread work-sharing, the large decline in modern sector wages has not led to a significant reduction in the labour cost per unit of production, because labour productivity has remained dismally low. Morale and efficiency of wage earners have fallen in line with real wages. The generalised breakdown of the incentive system in the modern sector has resulted in increased inefficiencies, demoralisation, absenteeism and corrup-tion. The situation seems to be particularly grave in the public sector. There-fore, improvements in the level of remuneration for modern sector wage employees, especially in the civil service, are critically needed in many countries to raise labour productivity.[42] Moreover, any further compression in the wage structure will produce strong disincentives for motivation and work effort in the modern sector.

Although the reduction in occupational wage differentials has consid-erably narrowed the excessive wage ranges that most countries inherited from the colonial era, further unselective compression in the wage structure is likely to create a serious trade-off between equity and efficiency. Some countries will require a degree of decompression in the wage structure. At the country level, there is a need to examine the mechanism of wage formation with a view to restoring an adequate incentive system for modern sector wage earners. The effectiveness of minimum-wage fixing has to be re-examined. Not only have minimum wages fallen below the poverty level but there is also widespread non-compliance with the legislative provisions. The economic and social aspects of minimum-wage setting need to be revisited in the light of the gradual labour market informalisation that is taking place in the region. The linkage between wage setting in the organised and unorganised sectors has to be examined in more detail.

One important dimension of the urban labour market segmentation is still the public/private dichotomy. Very often, overall wage trends hide important differences between the public and private sectors. Since parastatal salaries and allowances are generally higher than those for the civil service, new parastatals have often been created for the sole purpose of improving the incentive system and efficiency level of the employees. Until recently, parastatals set their own salary scales, resulting in large wage disparities within the public sector. However, both the *raison d'être* of public enterprises and their salary scale have recently come under scrutiny in an increased number of countries, leading to severe employment and/or salary cuts. Therefore, future analysis of wages and salaries should provide disaggregated evidence on the differential trends between the civil service, public and private enterprises.[43] Wage trends in the tradeable and non-tradeable sectors should also be given more attention in future research.

Orthodox adjustment programmes consider unemployment as a relative price phenomenon, as John Weeks pointed out in his chapter. The basic assumption is that lower wages lead to more employment because of the downward-sloping demand curve for labour. However, the evidence is unconvincing. It was noted earlier that wages in Africa have been very flexible downward over the past 15 years. But despite the sharp falls in real wages, there are no signs of renewed employment growth. On the contrary, wage employment is stagnating. As a result, orthodox adjustment is imposing further wage cuts, although it has been admitted that "it is clear that some pieces of conventional wisdom have been unhelpful".[44] In many countries, wages have fallen to starvation levels but unemployment is mounting. The question is to know how far do wages have to fall further before the markets will clear? Do wages have to become negative before neoclassical propositions become true?

In a labour-surplus situation, the objective of reaching a market-clearing wage is inefficient and inappropriate, both from an economic and a social perspective. The decline in real wages in the civil service has led to widespread moonlighting and the disappearance of a committed and specialised workforce. This has eroded the efficiency of the civil service. The result is that essential development tasks of the government are being neglected. Orthodox adjustment programmes rightly call for an improved enabling environment and an appropriate incentive system in the product and capital markets. But the same is not urged for labour markets. A strategy built around the concept of human-centred development should not omit essential labour market considerations. From a social perspective, we need to search for a "just wage" or an "efficiency wage", a wage that gives due attention to the relation between the price and the quality of labour. Evidence suggests that the private sector in Africa has kept this relationship in perspective better than the public sector, because the latter's wage bill has too often been used as a major instrument in achieving macro-economic targets set by structural adjustment programmes.

Unemployment

Evidence indicates that unemployment is increasing, but the real meaning of the phenomenon remains unclear. Is it a transient or a structural problem? First, high unemployment among the educated workforce can be explained by the fact that the possession of a school certificate raises expectations, which makes youngsters withhold their labour while they queue for a white-collar job. Over time, however, they lower their job aspirations and reservation wage and eventually are absorbed into the labour market. Second, educated unemployment may result from a static urban labour market which is characterised by relatively high wage differentials on the combined primary and secondary labour markets, which make extended periods of job search an economically rational choice from the individual point of view. It is noteworthy that individual benefits stemming from education have diminished over the past decade through direct labour market intervention (recruitment freeze, declining salaries, compression in the wage structure, cuts in fringe benefits, etc.). Nevertheless, demand for white-collar jobs remains extremely high in African countries. Is it because social preferences are hard to change or is it because a job in the modern sector, however lowly paid it may be, still represents a profitable choice because of the access it gives to the secondary job market?

Before this question can be answered, additional research on the dynamics of labour markets at the household level should be undertaken. Extraordinary things are happening in the field of adjustment in Africa. According to official statistics, many African economies have collapsed. Mass starvation can be expected. Nevertheless, people survive and do so remarkably well in the circumstances. Hence, adjustment by people at the grass-roots level is taking place. We need to be informed about these experiences if we are to assess the impact of standard labour market policies.

Fusion of labour markets

This brings us to the issue of the fusion of labour markets discussed earlier. The question could be asked whether the fusion of labour markets is a new phenomenon and whether it has been increasing or decreasing over time.

Since the 1950s, complaints have been heard about excessive rates of turnover in the modern sector. Hence, market fusion could be a longstanding characteristic of African labour markets, as circular migration has always existed in response to low wages. Based on more recent evidence, Livingstone reports that circular migration in Kenya has given way to more permanent migration.[45] Would this mean that the extent of fusion is decreasing?

Even the relative size of the overlapping areas in figure 1 remains a point of discussion, primarily because of the lack of reliable quantitative information. The most important overlap is between the modern and informal sectors. Although this area has certainly been growing over time, its importance should not be exaggerated, because of certain conditions that need to exist before one can become an operator in the informal sector. Indeed, land, capital and skills are required before a modern sector employee can set up a micro-business. Therefore, the higher the income and/or skill level of the employee, the more likely he or she will obtain secondary income from informal sector activities.[46] Hence, the argument that widespread moonlighting will automatically cushion the social impact of wages and employment cuts is doubtful, because access to supplementary sources of income very often depends on the position one occupies in the modern sector. Fusion does not automatically mean that urban labour markets become more flexible. The generation of adequate information about the fusion of labour markets should form part of future labour market research in Africa.

Training for informal sector employment

Unemployment trends in Africa raise the issue of relevance of the education and training systems. Most countries are in the process of reforming primary education to make it more meaningful as a terminal programme. Vocational streams are being introduced and their length is being extended to eight or nine years. The implicit assumption is that it will facilitate the access of youngsters to self-employment in the urban informal or rural non-farm sectors. However, the widespread idea that labour force recruits can be settled easily into self-employment is largely based on an incorrect understanding of the functioning of informal labour markets. In most African countries, there exists a gap of at least 15 years between the moment the school leaver joins the labour market and the moment he or she becomes a micro-entrepreneur in the services or manufacturing sector. Youths face grave obstacles in gaining access to self-employment outside petty trading because they lack the necessary maturity, skills, experience and financial resources to start and run their own business. Indeed, the road to self-employment is long and tortuous. The gap is usually filled with periods of unemployment, apprenticeship, wage employment - often both formal and informal - and petty trading.

Another misconception about employment promotion in the informal sector is the implicit assumption that the majority of the urban labour force will be self-employed. Quantitative evidence contradicts this assumption. Labour force surveys confirm that the chief employment status in urban areas is wage employment. Rapid urbanisation of the labour force means that the importance of wage employment in the informal sector (either as paid worker, apprentice or unpaid family worker) will increase. It would not be realistic to expect that most newcomers to the urban labour market will become self-employed.

Therefore, the real education and training challenge facing the region is how to improve its outreach capacities to upgrade the skill level of the millions of youngsters who join the urban informal and rural non-farm sectors each year. Formal systems of learning are beyond the financial carrying capacity of most countries. One of the few feasible ways will be to improve upon apprenticeship targeted on the out-of-school youth. Hence, more work needs to be done on the modalities of such an expanded apprenticeship system (hiring conditions and remuneration, duration and type of training, trade testing, compensation of micro-entrepreneurs, access to tools and credit facilities, institutional aspects, etc.).

Special Employment Programmes

Apart from the required improvements in the overall enabling environment and incentives system, Special Employment Programmes (SEPs) represent one of the few instruments for employment promotion. In a period of extreme scarcity of resources, labour investment or labour accumulation take on increased importance. SEPs also have the advantage of yielding immediate results, whereas policy reforms take time before they have any measurable impact on employment. However, such schemes in Africa have tended to be uncoordinated, short-term and ad-hoc measures, initiated under heavy political pressure. In the future, SEPs will need to be better integrated into national development plans and human resource programmes to ensure a wider and lasting impact.

Existing SEPs in Africa have the following major characteristics. First, most are designed, financed and executed by the central government with little or no involvement of the local community. Second, they enrol males predominantly. The limited range of training and employment activities often lead to implicit discrimination against women workers, although their vulnerability to unemployment is often twice as high as men's. Third, the level of education of the participants is relatively high and rising over time, indicating that SEPs are inadequately targeted. Finally, most SEPs have a disappointing record with respect to the objective of employment creation.

Despite their many shortcomings, the challenge of the 1990s will be to formulate guide-lines for rapid expansion in the scope of employment-intensive programmes. In designing SEPs, attention should be paid to the following four considerations. First, as national resources for such programmes are limited, the cost-effectiveness of SEPs will be of crucial importance if they are to have an impact on the country's employment. Second, involvement of the local community should start from the initial phases of the project. A decentralised approach will avoid the usual pitfalls in the design of schemes, improve their integration in the local economy and make replicability easier. Third, the jobs created should be sufficiently long-lasting to allow participants to acquire on-the-job training and experience to enable them to settle into self-employment, either individually or in groups. Finally, SEPs should make an explicit distinction between male and female youths, because they often face very different situations in African labour markets.

Income distribution

Though many of Africa's economic woes can be blamed on external factors - in particular low commodity prices, high interest rates and inappropriate corrective adjustment programmes - governments must bear a share of the responsibility for their economic mismanagement, especially their failure to prevent the development of vast income inequalities. Indeed, there exists a link between equity and economic performance. Economic reforms are often impeded by social conflict which arises from excessive income disparities. The social conflict can both be active or passive (e.g. farmers withdrawing into subsistence agriculture or entrepreneurs hiding in the informal sector). In an environment of wide income discrepancies, economic policy-making becomes the battleground of competing interests among social groups, leading to ill-defined policies in the economic sphere. The pervasive lack of democracy, accountability and popular participation has had adverse implications on the decision-making process in Africa.[47]

During the 1970s, a considerable amount of research was undertaken on the issue of income distribution in the course of economic development.[48] In the 1980s however, the issue has fallen into oblivion, both in developed and developing countries. Only recently has it regained some importance due to UNICEF's initiative of Adjustment with a Human Face.[49] Additional research is required on the distributional impact of adjustment programmes, that goes beyond the social aspects and duly considers the linkages between income distribution and economic policy-making. It should be pointed out that employment creation represents one of the most effective ways of distributing incomes in developing countries.

In conclusion, an economic steering wheel is of crucial importance for achieving prosperity, because social development is not automatically a by-product of economic growth. However, without a democratic governance of the steering wheel, prosperity will remain illusory. Unfettered orthodox policies that ignore the linkage between income distribution and economic growth are inadequate and can be dangerous. Did David Ricardo not predict that the main problem in economics would be to explain the laws that govern the distribution of income?

Notes

[1] P. Lerner: *Economics of employment* (New York, McGraw-Hill, 1951), Chapter 1: "The economic steering wheel". By economic steering wheel was meant the set of Keynesian mechanisms for the maintenance and regulation of prosperity.

[2] Milton Friedman has coined the tide of free markets as the "Hayek-tide".

[3] World Bank: *Towards sustained development in sub-Saharan Africa* (Washington, DC, 1984).

[4] ILO: *The challenge of adjustment in Africa.* Background document to the Tripartite Symposium on Structural Adjustment and Employment in Africa, Nairobi, 16-19 October 1989.

[5] UN Economic Commission for Africa (ECA): *African alternative framework to structural adjustment programmes for socio-economic recovery and transformation* (AAF-SAP) ECA (Addis Ababa, 1989). V. Jamal (ed.): *The African crisis, food security and structural adjustment.* Special Issue of the *International Labour Review*, Vol. 127, No. 6, 1988.

[6] The recent attempt by the World Bank in World Bank: *Africa's adjustment and growth in the 1980s* (Washington, DC, 1989) to show that strongly reforming countries have performed better than non-adjusting ones actually demonstrates how the former group has had, through cross-conditionality, increased access to additional resource flows which have reduced the extent of import strangulation and investment cuts. In other words, the analysis indicates that strongly reforming countries have been allowed to "finance" their way out of the crisis. This calls into question the sustainability of reform programmes.

[7] These characteristics include poorly developed markets, a predominance of traditional and informal sectors, weak inter-sectoral linkages, a fragile ecology, a high degree of openness, extremely high concentration of government revenue and export earnings, and the hypertrophy of non-productive sectors.

[8] Moreover, the distinction of short and long-term objectives is usually based on the premise that the long term is merely a series of short terms.

[9] The call for increased donor assistance to Africa implicitly recognises this fundamental characteristic of financial imbalance.

[10] The useful distinction between these two approaches to structural adjustment is discussed in A. Chowdhury, I. Islam and C. Kirkpatrick: *Structural adjustment and human resource development in ASEAN* (New Delhi, ILO/ARTEP Working Paper, 1988).

[11] The World Bank's recent long-term perspective study on Africa admits that "(...)much more is needed. (...)They [the structural adjustment programmes] should evolve in order to take fuller account of the social impact of the reforms, of investment needs to accelerate growth, and of measures to ensure sustainability". World Bank: *Sub-Saharan Africa: From crisis to sustainable growth* (Washington, DC, 1989), p. 62.

[12] UNDP/World Bank: *African economic and financial data* (Washington, DC, 1989), tables 1-16 and 1-17, and preliminary data provided by the ECA Secretariat.

[13] UNESCO: *Statistical Yearbook 1989* (Paris, 1989), table 2.10. The decline stemmed primarily from an 8 per centage point fall in the male gross enrolment ratio (from 90 to 82), while the female gross enrolment ratio decreased by three percentage points (from 71 to 68). Recent cost-reduction mechanisms, however, seem to be reducing female enrolment more than male.

[14] National Commission for Development and Planning: *The new economic recovery programme* (Lusaka, 1987).

[15] ILO: *Recovery and employment.* Report of the Director-General to the 76th Session of the International Labour Conference (Geneva, 1989), p. 35.

[16] Diverging wage trends among African countries are likely to be related to their different types of economies, e.g. land-scarce vs. land-surplus economies, or the relative importance of the public sector.

[17] For example, trade unions in Ghana threatened a general strike in April 1986 in response to the Government's decision to abolish the leave allowance.

[18] D. Lindauer et al.: "Government wage policy in Africa: Some findings and policy issues", in *Research Observer,* Vol. 3, No. 1, 1988, pp. 1-25.

[19] D. Robinson: *Civil service pay in Africa* (Geneva, ILO, 1990).

[20] UNDP/World Bank: *African economic and financial data,* 1989, op. cit., table 4-24.

[21] This is confirmed by a World Bank study which concluded that "In many countries government workers have borne a larger then average share of the adjustment to deteriorating macroeconomic conditions". Lindauer et al., 1988, op. cit., p. 7.

[22] V. Jamal and J. Weeks: "The vanishing rural-urban gap in sub-Saharan Africa", in *International Labour Review,* Vol. 127, No. 3, 1988, pp. 271-92.

[23] A senior civil servant in the United Republic of Tanzania reported that he earns 25 times more through his small-scale poultry farm than through his monthly salary. Similar anecdotal evidence is available elsewhere.

[24] A survey of the registered unemployed in Mauritius in 1981 found that a third of them had worked at least one day in the two-week reference period. Moreover, this proportion was inversely correlated with the level of education, increasing from 5 per cent for those with a secondary-school certificate to 40 per cent for those who possessed a primary-school certificate or less.

[25] For a systematic documentation of the process of de-industrialisation, see W. van Ginneken and R. van der Hoeven: "Industrialisation, employment and earnings (1950-87): An international survey", in *International Labour Review,* Vol. 128, No. 5, 1989, pp. 571-599.

[26] P. Heller and A. Tait: *Government employment and pay: Some international comparisons.* IMF Occasional Paper No. 24 (Washington, DC, 1984). The data referred to the late 1970s and early 1980s.

[27] For instance, employment in the Ghanaian civil service expanded by 15 per cent per year between 1975 and 1982, whereas manufacturing employment declined by 2.3 per cent. In the Nigerian federal civil service, the number of employees expanded by 10 per cent per annum between 1970 and 1980.

[28] Moreover, recent evidence challenges the view that "... for what the available data is worth they show constancy in [unemployment] rates rather than any general tendency for rates to increase". D. Turnham: *The employment problem in less developed countries: A review of the evidence* (Paris, OECD, 1971).

[29] Even in the 1960s, the number of urban unemployed was estimated to be growing rapidly, often at more than 6 per cent per annum. A. Berry and R. Sabot: "Unemployment and economic development", in *Economic Development and Cultural Change,* Vol. 33, No. 1, Oct. 1984, pp. 99-116.

[30] JASPA: *Youth employment and youth employment programmes in Africa.* A comparative subregional study (Addis Ababa, 1986).

[31] Active job search included a direct approach to an employer, union hall or labour exchange, answering a newspaper advert, etc. Passive job search was defined to include "asking relatives or friends". Republic of Kenya: *Urban Labour Force Survey 1986,* Nairobi (Central Bureau of Statistics, 1988).

[32] R. Hughes: *Human capital: The wealth of nations or drain on resources.* IDS working paper No. 428, Nairobi (University of Nairobi, 1985).

[33] Federal Republic of Nigeria: *Report of graduate tracer study,* 1986. A follow-up study of 1984 University and Polytechnic Cohort. Manpower Studies No. 24, Lagos, National Manpower Board, Federal Ministry of National Planning, Government Printer, 1988.

[34] In line with estimates of the urban population, the urban labour force is assumed to have grown by 5.3 per cent per year in the first half of the 1980s. Table 7 indicates that modern sector wage employment accounted for 9.9 per cent of the regional labour force in 1980. Its urban share is reckoned to account for 75 per cent of total wage employment, the remainder consisting of plantation workers, teachers and other wage earners in rural areas. Table 6 shows that modern sector wage employment increased by 1 per cent per annum between 1980 and 1985. The 1980 benchmark for urban unemployment is estimated at 10 per cent, and the number of unemployed is assumed to have grown by 10 per cent per year during the quinquennium 1980-85, which is in line with the data given in the previous section. The residual (i.e. the urban labour force less urban wage employment and urban unemployment) gives an indication of urban informal sector employment trends.

[35] Jamal and Weeks, 1988, op. cit.

[36] Evidence from Rwanda and Kenya - two countries that are facing high population pressure on arable land - clearly shows that non-farm income is inversely correlated with the size of the holding. In Rwanda, the elasticity of non-farm income with respect to holding size was -0.26 ($R2=0.74$; $t=2.95$; $df=5$), while in rural Kenya the elasticity of wage income with respect to holding size was -0.35 ($R2=0.77$; $t=3.67$; $df=4$)

[37] World Bank: *World Development Report 1989* (Washington, DC, 1989), table 1.2.

[38] ECA: *Review of economic and social conditions in Africa 1988-1989.* Paper presented to the Sixth Session of the Joint Conference of African Planners, Statisticians and Demographers, Addis Ababa, 15-20 January 1990.

[39] One long-term perspective study of the World Bank stated that "If Africa is to avert hunger and provide its growing population with productive jobs and rising incomes, its economies will have to grow by at least 4 to 5 per cent a year. This must be the minimum target". World Bank: *Sub-Saharan Africa: From crisis to sustainable growth*, 1989, op. cit., p. 4.

[40] In Guinea, for instance, severance payments were equivalent to 5 years of salary. In Ghana, the Cocoa Marketing Board laid off about 20,000 workers at an average cost equivalent to 11 years of the individual's base salary. The heavy financial burden resulting from honouring the legal provisions has halted redeployment programmes in state-owned enterprises

[41] B. Numberg: *Public sector pay and employment reform.* Policy, planning and research, Working Paper No. 113 (Washington, DC, World Bank, 1988).

[42] R. Klitgaard: "Incentive myopia", in *World Development,* Vol. 17, No. 4, 1989, pp. 447-59.

[43] The degree to which aggregate wage data can be misleading is illustrated by the case of Côte d'Ivoire in V. Levy and J. Newman: "Wage rigidity: Micro and macro evidence

on labor market adjustment in the modern sector", in *The World Bank Economic Review,* Vol. 3, No. 1, 1989, pp. 97-117.

[44] Lindauer et al., 1988, op. cit., p. 22.

[45] I. Livingstone: *Rural development, employment and incomes in Kenya.* An ILO/JASPA study (Aldershot, Gower, 1986).

[46] The differential access to secondary labour markets may explain why the compression in the wage structure has met with so little resistance.

[47] ECA: AAF-SAP, 1989, op. cit.

[48] J. Lecaillon et al.: *Income distribution and economic development: An analytical survey* (Geneva, ILO, 1984).

[49] G. Cornia et al. (ed.): *Adjustment with a human face.* A study by UNICEF (Oxford, Clarendon Press, 1987).

4

The changing nature of informal employment: The case of Mexico

by Bryan Roberts *

Introduction

After decades in which labour rights have increased in terms of security of work, wages and conditions of work, a contrary trend is apparent throughout the world. This is occurring through government policies and through the increase of non-standard forms of labour (self-employment, part-time employment, casual employment) with less rights than the standard of full-time employment (Marshall, 1987; Michon, 1987; Standing, 1989).

This paper takes up the issue of the decline of labour rights with reference to urban informal employment, concentrating on the case of Mexico. In Latin America, informal employment has often been defined in terms of the absence of state regulation (Portes and Benton, 1984; Roberts, 1989; PREALC, 1976, 1978; Tokman in this volume).[1] The informal is that which escapes regulation and, consequently, contrasts with a formal sector regulated by observance of a labour code, by fiscal obligations and by whatever bureaucratic planning exists for its branch of economic activity. The absence of labour rights is, then, only one aspect of informal employment since, for instance, small-scale entrepreneurs or the self-employed may enjoy applicable labour rights (e.g. an income at or above the minimum salary, membership of trade associations), but are informal because they avoid state fiscal and planning regulation.

In advanced industrial countries, the issue of informality is usually identified with this second aspect, as researchers and policy-makers concentrate on assessing whether the freedom that the small-scale firm enjoys from bureaucratic regulation makes for enterprise and innovation. Employee rights are usually not the issue - in the United Kingdom, for example, informal employment has been reported to be negligible outside of illegal activities (Pahl, 1984). The current issue of labour rights in the United Kingdom is that of their erosion, not their non-observance by an informal sector of employers.

* Population Research Center, University of Texas at Austin.

This situation may well be changing, and in Italy, for instance, trade unions have been concerned with the absence of labour rights in small-scale enterprises.

In the developing world, the two aspects of informal employment - the enterprise one and the employee one - are equally present. A substantial part of the wage-earning population is still denied basic labour rights, though other workers enjoy them. At the same time, independent work, whether in small-scale enterprises or in self-employment, continues to generate a substantial part of urban employment.

The discussion of informal employment and of its policy implications in the developing world must take into account the heterogeneous nature of those who work informally. They include small-scale entrepreneurs, workers in medium and large-scale enterprises, workers in small-scale enterprises, the self-employed, family labour and, often, domestic out-working. These categories have different connotations attached to them, and the confusion of the different aspects of informal employment accounts for the wide disparity in attitudes towards the informal sector. The small-scale entrepreneurs of the informal sector have been viewed as possible sources of entrepreneurship and wealth creation whose potential for growth is hampered by excessive government regulation (De Soto, 1986). Policy recommendations for this category often includes providing credit, suitable technology and reducing red tape. For other commentators, the problem of the informal sector is not restriction of enterprise, however, but very low wages and lack of access to welfare (Márquez, 1988). The remedies proposed from this latter perspective involve government intervention to raise the minimum wage, enforce social security obligations, extend welfare benefits, and stimulate, through state purchasing and credit policies, the goods and services produced in the 'informal' sector (DGSPE/ PREALC, 1974).

I shall use the case of Mexico to explore these issues, examining the characteristics of those who are informally employed, the sectors of the economy in which such employment is mainly found, and the types of regions and cities in which it concentrates. Note that this informal-formal distinction is often more of a continuum than a contrast, as Tokman makes clear in his discussion in this volume. Even in the case of employment - where the distinction is sharper than in the case of firms - employees can be partially covered by existing labour rights, benefiting from a minimum wage, for example, but not from social security coverage. I will consider various possible explanations for the persistence and growth of informal employment, such as rural-urban migration, economic cycles and sectoral changes in the national economy, and will also examine the part played in the creation of informal employment by the strategies of entrepreneurs and workers. I also want to consider the changing significance of informal employment in the contemporary period compared with the 1960s and 1970s, when Mexico had high rates of economic growth and was making a rapid transition from an agriculturally based to an urban-industrial economy.

It will be argued that despite the positive role assigned to informality by observers and by the informally employed, there is little evidence that it makes any independent contribution to employment generation. Even in the best years of Mexico's growth, the incomes generated by informal employment represented a trickle down from formal sector enterprise and from the high incomes earned in that latter sector. The problem represented by informal employment is not excessive government regulation, but its ineffective nature. Informal employment has been a substitute for an inadequate state welfare system, and the growth of such employment is due to the pressures of an urban poverty made worse by the failure of both state and market to provide adequate housing and other urban amenities. The issue of labour rights has been sharpened by the present Mexican recession. The final section of the paper, will consider the changing nature of informal employment during the 1980s, when added to the absence of labour rights among the informally employed was an erosion of labour rights in formal employment arising, in part, from Mexico's changing position within the international economy.

The case of Mexico

The data for Mexico are unusually rich because of government-sponsored surveys of the informal economy, and the considerable amount of other empirical work and analysis that has been carried out on this topic.[2] Mexico is also an interesting case for comparative purposes. Like several Latin American countries in the 1960s and 1970s, it had one of the fastest rates of economic growth in the world, which transformed its economy from an agricultural to an urban one. By 1980, some 25 per cent of the Mexican population was employed in agriculture, and 65 per cent was classed as urban, with 47 per cent of that urban population living in the three metropoli of Mexico City, Guadalajara and Monterrey. The capacity of its urban economy to absorb the rapid increase in the labour force - both from agriculture and from new entrants to the labour market - was such that Gregory (1986) uses the Mexican case to argue for the success of the unregulated market in solving employment problems.

Mexico's pattern of economic development has begun to diverge, in recent years, from that of other fast urbanising Latin American countries such as Brazil, because of the greater importance of export-oriented industrialisation in Mexico, and because of its proximity to the United States. Extensive international labour migration has served to mitigate the scarcity of rural income opportunities through providing labour markets north of the border and remittances back home. The border region has become a favoured location for foreign investment, especially in assembly industries, seeking reduced labour costs.

Mexico has a long history of state regulation of the labour market, but is similar to other Latin American countries in that labour protection is more honoured in breach than in observance. As Marshall (1987) comments, the inflexibility of labour law in Latin America in providing blanket protection means that it is regularly avoided.

Minimum wage legislation was introduced in Mexico in 1934 and was designed to raise rapidly the incomes of urban workers; but substantial numbers of workers even in large-scale enterprises still earn below the minimum wage. The labour code, completely revised in 1970, provides extensive protection for all types of labour, including domestic servants and domestic out-work (Mexican Labour Law, 1974) - but even official publications have recognised that this protection is ineffective for such categories (DGSPE/PREALC, 1974). Casual labour contracts are prohibited in other than exceptional circumstances, and all classes of employees, irrespective of the size of enterprise, are given the protection of the minimum wage, social security and equal pay for equal work. With few exceptions, employees are entitled to participate in profit sharing and to receive housing benefits to which employers must contribute. Yet, constantly renewed (and thus illegal) "temporary" contracts which do not provide such benefits are common in large-scale industries in Mexico, even in those controlled by the Government such as the petroleum monopoly PEMEX.

Official tolerance of such practices, including the connivance of the trade unions, are good examples of what Standing (in this volume) calls "implicit de-regulation" and antedates by many years the present policy of explicit de-regulation. Implicit de-regulation has resulted from the compromises that have been part of Mexico's stable one-party rule, since the 1910 Mexican Revolution undermined the power of landowners and of the urban entrepreneurial classes. The extension of government control over a territory that, in the 1920s, was highly fragmented both politically and economically, has been achieved by co-opting locally powerful elites, including labour leaders, into what, until recently, has been a single-party system. The role of organised labour has been that of controlled participation (Zapata, 1987). In contrast to the Indian case described by Mukhopadhyay in this publication, organised workers have not received sharply higher rewards than have unorganised workers. The unions are centralised in national federations that are part of the governing party, and follow the policies determined by the Government in return for concessions over minimum salaries and other labour rights. The structure of control is from the top down, with little shop-floor participation, and many unions see their day-to-day activity as ensuring that labour keeps to the agreements reached nationally and regionally, with management and state authorities.

Up to 1980, the wage-earning population increased substantially as a proportion of the urban labour force, while self-employment and family employment declined. In 1940 some 37.9 per cent of the non-agricultural population were owners of small businesses, self-employed or family workers, whereas by 1980 the proportion was 23.2 per cent (Oliveira and Roberts, 1989). This decline occurred in a period in which there was a massive increase in the absolute numbers of non-agricultural labour, from approximately 2 million in 1940 to just over 10 million in 1980, representing an annual average growth in the urban economically active population of some 4.5 per cent. In the same period, the agricultural population grew absolutely, from just under 4 million to approximately 6 million, with high levels of rural-urban migration resulting in low annual growth rates of the agricultural workforce, especially from the 1950s onwards.

This growth appears to have taken place amidst a rise in the real average wages of workers and a substantial expansion of labour rights. The urban employed population covered by social security rose from 46.5 per cent of the total workforce in 1975 to 61.6 per cent in 1984 (INEGI, 1987, pp. 78-82). Union affiliation was 10.7 per cent of the total labour force in 1950; whereas it had risen to 18.9 per cent by 1970 with a 36.8 per cent rate of affiliation in manufacturing industry, 93.8 per cent in extractive industries and 84.5 per cent in transport and communications (Leal, 1985, table 3). The rise in real wages during this period was consistent and seems to have benefited all categories of urban workers, including domestic servants (Gregory, 1986).

The large-scale rural-urban migration of the period, concentrating in the large metropoli, does not appear to have produced a marginalised sector of people of rural origin. Migrants appear to have occupied much the same range of urban jobs as the city born and, in all three metropoli, a substantial proportion of the industrial proletariat that was formed in the 1960s and 1970s was of migrant origin (Muñoz, Oliveira and Stern, 1982; Balan, Browning and Jelin, 1974; Escobar, 1986).

The distribution of informal employment

Despite the extension of labour rights and the decline in family employment and self-employment, a substantial proportion of the urban labour force continued to be informally employed by the late 1970s. A 1976 government survey, covering two-thirds of Mexico's urban population, provides estimates of informal employment using minimum wage and benefits as its criteria (SPP, 1979).[3] The figures from this survey for the proportions of urban workers who are small-scale employers, self-employed or family workers are similar to those reported above from the 1980 census: 22.9 per cent compared with 23.2 per cent. However, the survey reported a much higher proportion informal by the wage/benefits criteria: 39.4 per cent of the total employed population was found to be informally employed. Approximately a third of wage workers were found to be informally employed, two-thirds of the self-employed and, by definition, all family workers (SPP, 1979, table 1d).

Though small-scale enterprises of under five people contributed about a third of overall (formal and informal) employment in 1977, most of those informally employed were not in entrepreneurial positions.[4] Unprotected employees made up 57 per cent of those recorded as informal in the 1977 survey, and family workers were a further 9 per cent. Just over half (56 per cent) of the unprotected employees work in small-scale enterprises of five or less people

(SPP, 1979, table 7). I estimate their employers to make up a further 11 per cent of the informally employed. The remainder (23 per cent) are self-employed workers, such as street vendors, seamstresses, repairmen etc., with little or no capital nor prospects of building up a business and creating employment.

The lowest percentage of informal employment (35.3 per cent) is found in Mexico City which in the period up to 1970 was not only Mexico's largest city by far, but its fastest growing city. The highest percentage of informality (46.8 per cent) was reported for the non-metropolitan cities. The suggestion is that informal employment is more characteristic of smaller urban places than of the largest urban centres.

The proportion of the 1980 economically active population not registered by the economic censuses will be used as an indicator of informality, and this issue will be further explored by looking at the state of Jalisco and its capital, Guadalajara.[5] In Jalisco, the small towns and rural areas of the region have higher proportions of informal employment than does Guadalajara, and the contrast is particularly pronounced in manufacturing. Guadalajara's informal employment in manufacturing is 31.2 per cent, compared to 41.2 per cent for the non-metropolitan municipalities. Even the casual traveller in the small towns and rural areas of Jalisco can identify one of the main components of this difference: the presence of considerable amounts of domestic out-work in garment making, shoemaking and other craft-type occupations. This type of essentially rural outworking is common elsewhere in Mexico, and is common in areas where male labour migration (mainly to the United States) and poor agricultural resources have created an abundant local supply of female labour eager to supplement household income (Arias 1988). Remember, however, that the absolute amounts of informal employment are much higher in Guadalajara - the high proportions of informal employment in the non-metropolitan areas are not due to the greater needs of rural, as opposed to urban, households to supplement their incomes, but to the scarcity of formal employment opportunities outside of agriculture.

Of the three major metropolitan centres, Guadalajara, Mexico's second largest city, had the highest levels of informality (41.5 per cent) in the 1976 survey, a finding corroborated by other studies of the three metropolitan areas which used an income measure of informality (DGSPE/PREALC, 1974). Guadalajara contrasted with both Mexico City and Monterrey by having an economic structure that is more "traditional" in its base (Roberts, 1989). In comparison with the other two cities, Guadalajara had, in 1980, a much higher proportion of its industrial production concentrated in basic consumer goods industries, mainly in textiles, garments and shoes (56.8 per cent of its industrial product compared with 27.3 per cent for Monterrey and 32.8 per cent for Mexico City). Small and medium-size enterprises abounded in Guadalajara, and the city had few of the giant enterprises found in Monterrey or Mexico City.

In the period up to 1980, informal employment in Mexico thus appeared to be associated with the unevenness of the transition from an agriculturally based economy to a modern urban-industrial one. It was most characteristic of those regions, places and activities heavily involved in providing basic goods and services for a local and low-income market. The 1976 survey shows that informal employment was most heavily concentrated in the basic consumer goods sector, in commerce and in personal services (57 per cent of informal employment as compared to 43 per cent of all employment). This concentration was most marked in those industrial branches which most lend themselves to small-scale enterprises: 30.8 per cent of informal employment in manufacturing was in the garment and shoemaking industries, although only 11.7 per cent of formal manufacturing employment was located there. A similar picture emerges from the services sector. Informal employment was most heavily concentrated in domestic services (42.9 per cent of total informal employment found in the services), followed by food and drink services (14.7). These two services contribute, in contrast, 15.9 per cent of formal employment in the services.

The decline in informal employment from the 1940s onwards is mainly produced by a shift in the industrial structure of the country, and in that of associated services. This shift consists in the increasing concentration of employment and production in intermediate, capital and consumer durable goods industries. These industries, in contrast to those of basic consumer goods, are less likely, it can be argued, to create opportunities for family labour or self-employment or to employ casual or unskilled labour. Increasing productivity in certain basic consumer goods industries, particularly the food industry, has also had negative consequences for the overall growth of employment in these industries, including informal employment. A further factor in the relative decline of informal employment has been the increasing modernity of Mexico's industrial structure, which requires and stimulates the growth of modern services: producer services; government services and, in commerce, concentration in supermarkets, chain stores and so on.

Though this account exaggerates the extent of genuine (productivity related) modernisation in Mexico's economic structure, there is clear evidence that between 1940 and 1980 Mexico's urban employment shifted from activities that lent themselves to informality to those that did not. The fastest-growing services in terms of overall employment were producer services and government services. In manufacturing, intermediate, capital and consumer durable goods accounted for 18.8 per cent of employment in 1940, and 51.1 per cent in 1980 (*Censos Industriales*, 1940 and 1980). Within manufacturing, there was a pronounced shift of employment towards, administrative, technical and managerial functions, from 11 per cent of the total employed in manufacturing in 1940 to 22 per cent in 1980. Furthermore, in 1940 owners of small-scale businesses were a much larger component of the managerial group than they were in 1980.

This process is evident in the Guadalajara region which, we noted, was the most traditional of Mexico's three main industrial regions. In 1970, 49 per cent of those working in manufacturing had been informally employed, compared with 31.2 per cent in 1980, and this shift is partly associated with the increasing importance of intermediate good and durable consumer good industries in the city in the 1970s. In this decade, Guadalajara expanded its importance as a commercial and service centre, acquiring some of the largest shopping areas in Mexico and, as the regional centre of western Mexico, experiencing a rapid expansion of employment in government and producer services.

Some of the dynamic of informal employment, as Benería and Roldan (1987) suggest, comes from the linkages between very large-scale enterprises, smaller firms that subcontract from them and their domestic out-workers (at least some of whom are classed as self-employed in the census). It would be a mistake to exaggerate the importance of these linkages for employment. They are most likely to be found in those branches of industry, such as garments and shoemaking, in which the production process can easily be broken-down into separate operations which do not require costly tools or machinery. Because of its industrial structure, Guadalajara does have hierarchies of subcontracting. In Guadalajara, 11 per cent of firms reported, when responding to an industrial survey in 1981, that they subcontracted work, with large firms making most use of it (Roberts, 1989).

The characteristics of the informally employed

By using the 1976 survey and various case studies carried out at about that date, we can obtain a reasonably good picture of the characteristics of the informally employed. The 1976 survey does not provide information on the migrant background of informal workers, but other studies (González de la Rocha, 1986; Escobar, 1986) suggest that the association between migrant status and informal employment is not strong. Rural migrants were disproportionately concentrated in construction activities, which seem to provide the "easiest" entry to urban employment for recent migrants, but in Guadalajara, at least, these migrants were not likely to be found in informal employment in manufacturing, probably because finding work in small shoemaking workshops and the like requires prior urban contacts. Informal employment requires less credentials than formal employment, and the best income opportunities within it are accessed through family and community networks.

The educational levels of the informally employed were lower than those of the formally employed: whereas 57.3 per cent of the informally employed had not completed primary education, the equivalent proportion for the formally employed was 26.2 per cent (SPP, 1979, table T.3.1). Since, as we shall see, the informally employed are younger than the formally employed and since educational levels in Mexico have risen sharply over time, the relative lack of schooling of the informally employed is undoubtedly greater than the above figures suggest.

Informal employment may be a life-time or a life stage phenomenon. Workers may enter informal employment and stay there, either through preference or because they are trapped by lack of the credentials needed to obtain formal employment. Conversely, informal employment may provide an easy entry, low-cost way of acquiring skills that can later be sold to formal enterprises. This life stage perspective can be pursued further to include the passage, at older ages, of workers from formal to informal employment. Older workers leave formal employment when they find the work-routine too exhausting, preferring the time-flexibility given by self-employment, or by establishing a small business of their own.

The informally employed are, in fact, disproportionately concentrated in both the younger and the older age ranges. Thus, in 1976, 42.1 per cent of the informally employed were 24 or younger compared with 25.2 per cent of the formally employed, and 7.5 per cent were 55 or older compared with 5.4 per cent of the formally employed (SPP, 1979, table T.2.1). Case studies suggest that in the 1970s and early 1980s, this age distribution was, to some extent, produced by the work careers outlined above. In the sample in Escobar (1986, table 12) of the industrial labour force in Guadalajara, 67 per cent of workers in firms with over 100 employees had begun their careers in small-scale and often informal enterprises. The small-scale enterprise thus provides a training ground for the larger and more formal firm, and is the aspiration of many workers in large scale enterprises as they grow older (Balan et al., 1974).

Women are more likely to be informally employed than men, but the difference is not great. In the 1976 government survey (SPP, 1979), women comprised 36.4 per cent of the informally employed, but only 27 per cent of the formally employed. In the Selby et al. (1990) study of ten Mexican cities in 1976, women were *less* likely to be employed informally than men, though their earnings were substantially lower than men's.[6] Part of the explanation for this difference with the government survey is the high proportion (46.7) of women who were formally employed as white collar workers, mainly as shop assistants, but on very low pay (and thus likely to be classed as informal in the 1976 government survey). These white-collar women were, on average, younger than other classes of worker, male or female.

Female informality appears to be even more markedly associated with life stage than is male informality. In the study by González de la Rocha (1986, table 5) women heads of household were almost entirely employed in the informal sector, as domestic servants, as domestic outworkers for a manufacturer or in informal trading activities.

Informal employment provides a convenient means for a household to supplement its income, because it is usually easier to combine with other tasks, notably domestic ones, than is formal employment, and permits the incorporation of other household members who are too young or too old to obtain formal work. Because of the importance of life stage factors and because the flexibility of informal employment may make it attractive as a supplementary income source, households are not segmented between formal and informal sector employment. The percentage of informal employment is not, in that respect, an accurate indicator of the extent to which families are covered by welfare benefits, particularly medical ones. In González de la Rocha's (1986) account, unmarried daughters are most likely to be employed in the formal sector as clerks, shop assistants or factory workers, whereas their mothers may supplement household income by attending to a small shop or by taking in sewing or cleaning. Likewise, unmarried males may begin by learning a trade through working informally, whereas when they get married they will seek formal work and the medical and other forms of protection it brings to a family. In the Selby et al. (1990, table 7.9) study, the mixed household category (including both registered and unregistered workers) was the largest among the categories of registered and unregistered multi-worker households.

In both the Selby et al. and González de la Rocha studies, reporting before the economic crisis, single worker households comprised the majority of households, and these, inevitably, were segmented between formal and informal employment. The moves between informal and formal occupations ensured, however, that over the household cycle such segmentation was less marked: few households among low-income families were likely to have all their members in formal employment throughout the household cycle.

The rewards of informality in an expanding economy

The characteristics of the informally employed lead Gregory (1986, p. 86) to argue that their low earnings result from their modest endowments of human capital, rather than the segmentation of the labour market. We have noted some evidence above to support that view, but the issue is complicated because of the heterogeneity of informal employment, and the evidence above that the market for formal employment is different from that of informal employment, being particularly attractive to workers at particular moments of the life cycle or who occupy particular household positions. The evidence for Mexico up to 1980 is similar to what Durston (1987) reports for Brazil - that informal employment offers income opportunities comparable to those of formal employment for people of similar characteristics.

Informal employment is often seen to be synonymous with low earnings, and many studies, such as the 1976 government survey, use low earnings as a criterion for informality. Low pay is, however, a general characteristic of the Mexican economy and, in this respect, the difference between the informal and formal workers is not substantial. All informal workers in the 1976 survey had, by definition, incomes at or below the minimum salary, but even 72 per cent of the formally employed were earning salaries that were at the minimum level or barely above it (SPP, 1979, T.6.1).[7] The proportions of men and women earning below the minimum salary in the 1976 survey - 26.2 per cent and 44.6 per cent - is similar to that of the sample from ten cities in the Selby et al. (1990) study. There, 40 per cent of female and 30 per cent of male workers earned less than the legal minimum. In the ten city study, informal workers earned, on average, less than formal workers; but when other variables were held constant, such as education, gender and age, the differences were about 8 per cent (Selby et al., 1990, figure 6.6).

Most of the effects of education on income are produced by those with primary schooling and above. The regression analysis of Selby et al. suggests that for those with primary education or less, especially women in the tertiary sector, informal employment can bring higher income than would similar credentials in the formal sector. This finding is similar to that of Durston (1987) in his comparisons of the incomes of formal and informal sector workers in Brazil.

Further support for the notion that these are not segmented labour markets, in which the earnings of those formally employed are increased relative to informal workers by excessive protection, is given by the finding in the Selby et al. (1990) study that the earnings distributions of informal and formal workers are similar. The opportunities for earning high (or low) incomes are almost as great for those informally employed in the services, the sector in which informal employment concentrates, as for those formally employed in the manufacturing sector, in which most workers are formally employed.

The suggestion is that up to 1980, informal employment offered relatively attractive income opportunities for certain categories of workers; that is, those without high credentials and who, because of domestic chores or age, needed the flexibility offered by informal employment. The case studies carried out in Guadalajara provide many examples of this (Escobar, 1986; González de la Rocha, 1986; Arias and Roberts, 1985). Skilled workers in the shoe industry, for instance, moved from large-scale factories to small, informal workshops, preferring flexible working hours and the fact that they could often earn more by piece rate in informal shops than by fixed wage in the factories.

The dynamism of informal employment owed more to the absence of an adequate urban welfare system, and to poor pay and conditions of work in the formal sector than to any entrepreneurial dynamic of its own. Even in 1982, male wages in the formal sector were insufficient to maintain a household adequately. They were also subsidised by the minimal expenditures on housing and utilities resulting from self-construction and making-do without adequate water supplies, electricity and so on. Faced by poor housing and a general lack of urban amenities such as piped water, sewage or child care facilities, many women had no alternative but to seek any work that they could combine with heavy domestic responsibilities. As the case studies of Benería and Roldan (1987) make clear, women might be paid a pittance for domestic outwork, but they still valued the small degree of financial independence it gave them.

For men the attraction of the benefits attached to formal employment were not considerable. Informants complained of poor medical services and the fact that their salaries were discounted for benefits, such as housing, that they were never likely to receive.

The informal/formal divide in employment is, then, a calculus of advantage made by both employers and employees. It is an unequal calculus since employers have greater power to enforce their preference, but there will be times when employees' preferences also affect outcomes. There are certain constants that enter into this calculus. It is affected by the monetary costs of formality to employers and employees as compared to the benefits received. For employees, the variable costs are their contributions to welfare benefits as compared to the benefits they receive, and the inflexibilities in earnings imposed by contracts as compared to the opportunities for earnings in informal employment. For employers, similar comparisons exist between the benefits and disadvantages of formality; for instance the extent of the benefits they received from the state discounted by the extent to which regulations are enforced, compared with the need to reduce overheads.

There are, however, also advantages to employers in respecting labour rights, as Standing argues in this volume. These are the benefits deriving from a stabilised and committed workforce, particularly in industries which need skilled labour and aim for high productivity. Employers also obtain substantial benefits from the state through formality. Access to credit, for instance, requires formality. Doing business with a formal enterprise by supplying products or services also requires formality since the formal enterprise demands receipts and so on for its own fiscal protection. These reasons for respecting labour rights do not disappear in the changed economic climate of the 1980s. The recession and the accompanying economic restructuring does, however, as we will see in the next sections, curtail the expansion of labour rights, as self-employment grows and informal employment becomes increasingly located in the non-dynamic sectors of the economy.

The crisis, adjustment policies and the changing structure of employment

From about 1982, the Mexican economy entered a deep recession. Though the recession was triggered by the fall in oil prices and the mounting burden of debt, it also marked a longer-term shift in Mexico's political economy (see Benería in this volume). The 1980s have been the decade in which Mexico decisively abandoned policies of import-substitution industrialisation, and lowered protection for domestic industry, reduced food subsidies and cut back wages and employment expansion in the state sector. These measures were part of the austerity package required for debt renegotiation. The accompanying severe drops in real wages for both blue- and white-collar workers, and in the relative costs of foodstuffs and other components of urban subsistence are similar to those reported elsewhere in Latin America (Canak 1989, Walton and Ragin, 1989; Benería in this volume).

At the same time, the Government undertook a vigorous policy of promoting export-led industrialisation and growth through free market policies, a strategy that has been intensified under the present administration of President Carlos Salinas de Gortari. Mexico has joined GATT, reduced tariffs more than required by the treaty, removed many of the restrictions on foreign investment, and is moving towards a substantial privatisation of state-owned enterprises. In its policy documents, the Government emphasises its respect for existing labour rights, and the need to work with the unions in a "stabilisation pact" which regulates both price and wage increases. In practice, government's relations with even the official unions are less cordial and less symmetrical than in the past: prominent union leaders have been displaced and their positions taken by people who have shown less independence of government policies; and ministers openly criticise restrictive practices by union members and favour deregulation.

These policies need to be set within the context of the changing world economy: an international division of labour in which production and service delivery are integrated across international boundaries; the location of the unskilled and labour-intensive parts of manufacturing in newly industrialising countries, making use of "new" forms of labour such as the increasing supply of female workers; and the increasing financial integration of the world economy, which severely restricts states opting for full employment policies.

This shift in economic policy, and in Mexico's pattern of insertion into the world economy, creates a markedly different context for informal employment from that which had existed. As the economy has changed, so have the relative advantages of informality for the actors involved. The "withdrawal" of the state has affected the various economic sectors unequally. Large-scale enterprises have benefitted from de-regulation and the drastic reduction in the real minimum wage. Small-scale firms have experienced a sharp reduction in the benefits of formality since debt repayment has severely reduced the amount of bank credit for small-scale enterprise, and there is less demand for their products or services from the larger enterprises. They also face competition from imported goods, particularly in the lines - low-cost shoes, garments and furniture - in which they had established a niche. Relative to the potential profits of their operation, even low levels of taxation may become more onerous, thus disposing them to informality. Employees, faced by increasing job competition in both formal and informal employment, accept even lower wages or benefits. The pressure on people to obtain any job in order to make ends meet is great.

We have already noted that Mexico, in common with other Latin American countries, had a substantial rise in informal employment in the 1980s. Data from the Economic Commission for Latin America and the Caribbean (ECLAC) indicate that between 1980 and 1986 informal employment rose by 16 per cent, state employment remained static, and employment in both small- and large-scale private enterprises declined (ECLAC, 1989). In two of the three major metropolitan regions, there was, between 1976 and 1987 a substantial proportional decline in manufacturing, and a rise in service employment (table 1). Though Guadalajara shows little change in the structure of its industrial employment, but, as a government analysis of 1974 (DGSPE/PREALC, 1976) suggested, Guadalajara's industry has always been characterised by a

Table 1. Change in employment structure of major metropolitan areas, 1976-87

	Mexico City		Guadalajara		Monterrey	
	1976	1987	1976	1987	1976	1987
Manufacturing	30.1	23.6	29.8	29.2	38.5	28.9
Construction	5.6	4.5	7.7	7.2	8.2	8.3
Utilities	1.0	0.7	0.2	0.6	0.5	0.6
Commerce	18.1	18.9	21.7	22.4	16.0	18.5
Transport	4.9	6.4	5.2	4.8	5.6	4.8
Personal services[1]	11.7	9.4	11.2	9.4	5.8	9.3
Repair services	1.7	5.0	1.8	4.4		4.8
Diverse services[2]	2.6	3.2	6.6	4.5	12.8	3.9
Business and professional services[3]	15.9	18.7	11.0	13.5	9.8	17.0
Administration	8.4	9.6	4.8	4.0	2.8	3.9
Total	100.0	100.0	100.0	100.0	100.0	100.0

[1] Personal services include domestic service, hotels, and food services. [2] Diverse services are unspecified, but are likely to be forms of either personal or repair services. This is probably the case for Monterrey in 1976, where no figures are given for hotels, restaurants or repair services. [3] Business and professional services include financial, educational, health and recreational services

Sources: INEGI: *Encuesta nacional de empleo urbano: Indicadores trimestrales de empleo* (enero-marzo de 1987) [National survey on urban employment: Quarterly employment indicators (January-March 1987)], for Guadalajara, Monterrey and Mexico City (Aguascalientes, 1988) and SPP 1979.

Table 2. Change in employment status in major metropolitan areas, 1976-87

	Mexico City		Guadalajara		Monterrey	
	1976	1987	1976	1987	1976	1987
Employees	79.8	77.6	79.3	71.8	80.9	78.0
Owners	2.8	3.5	3.2	5.5	2.0	3.4
Self-employed	14.1	14.2	13.4	15.9	14.5	14.8
Non-waged	3.3	4.7	4.1	6.8	2.6	3.8
Total	100.0	100.0	100.0	100.0	100.0	100.0

Sources: INEGI, 1988, op. cit. SPP, 1988, op. cit.

substantial craft-type production, including domestic outworking, which is compatible with the trend towards self-employment. Guadalajara had the sharpest increase of the three areas in self- and non-waged employment (table 2). In the Guadalajara case, male self-employment increased more sharply than that of females, and male employment in manufacturing industry declined relative to female (Alba and Roberts, 1990).

In the Guadalajara region, the economic crisis seems to have affected the small, often family-based firms most, driving them either out of business or into informality. Our field work indicates that it was this latter route that most have taken.[8] Thus, in the course of checking a sample of the high number of small firms - with five or fewer workers - that existed in 1981 but were no longer listed officially by 1985 (384 out of 604), it was found that many continued their activities but with fewer workers. Informants from both small-scale firms and large enterprises concurred in seeing the recession as having hit the small-scale firm hardest.

This is the conclusion of Escobar's (1988a) study of the effects of the crisis on small workshops in Guadalajara. Whereas before the crisis, he, like the studies reported by Tokman in this volume, had noted a certain formalisation of the workshops in terms of hiring paid workers and observing labour rights, after the crisis the workshops became more informal of their employment conditions and pay was drastically reduced. He found that the workshops were faced with rising prices of their raw materials and a diminishing market. The ones he studied became more dependent on middlemen for credit during the crisis than had been the case previously. One response to difficult times was to go clandestine by moving location. The real wages in the shops dropped 40 per cent between 1982 and 1985, compared with the drop in official minimum wages of 22.5 per cent.

The recession has produced a certain restructuring of the Mexican economy, polarising more sharply than previously different types of employment. A survey of manufacturing in Jalisco in 1989, found that large-scale firms, especially those exporting part of their product, were most optimistic about economic prospects, whereas small-scale firms were more pessimistic, and complained of the negative impact of the new trade liberalisation measures (Alba and Roberts, 1990). Turnover in these large-scale firms was high - higher than in the comparable sample of enterprises surveyed in 1981 - and employers complained of labour shortages, especially for skilled workers. These large-scale firms were hiring a slightly higher percentage of casual labour than their equivalents reported in a similar survey in 1981 (Alba and Roberts, 1990). The explanation of these trends is unclear. As a result of reductions in the real minimum wage and rising prices for certain types of services, skilled workers could often earn more as self-employed craftsmen, such as mechanics. Benería (in this volume) cites a similar claim by her Mexican City informants. Informants also claimed that skilled workers were mobile because of the attraction of jobs in the booming export sector located mainly in the border region. Whatever the explanation, these data give no support to the existence of a labour market segmentation resulting from an overly protected formal sector that prevents labour mobility.

Labour mobility is linked to changes brought by restructuring in the location and employment dynamics of different sectors of Mexican industry. In Guadalajara, the new high technology industries, particularly in electronics, are growing fastest, taking on new workers, while older industries, such as shoes, steel and engineering, are laying off workers. The growing industries in Guadalajara employ higher proportions of women than the older ones. The rise of female employment in manufacturing is a national trend, increasing from 21.2 per cent in 1980 to 25.7 per cent in 1986 (Standing, 1989a, table 4). However, the major increases in both female manufacturing employment, and in manufacturing employment in general, are taking place in the border region between the United States of America and Mexico.

Carillo's (1989) study of the restructuring of the Mexican automobile industry demonstrates how the change in industrial structure with export industrialisation alters the character of formal employment. Mexico increased its automobile production considerably until the crisis of the early 1980s, when there was a sharp drop in internal demand. The recovery of the industry in the 1980s has been based on exports which, by 1986, accounted for nearly 40 per cent of all cars produced. This export-oriented sector of the industry, which includes auto parts as well as automobiles, is mainly located in the border region. By 1987, Carillo (1989) noted 140 assembly plants for parts and vehicles in the north of Mexico, employing some 60,000 workers. The characteristics of employment in the north contrast sharply with those of the automobile factories in the centre of Mexico which produce mainly for the internal market. Women are a much higher percentage of the northern labour force, especially in autoparts production where they comprise the majority of the labour force. Union affiliation is lower in the north and the northern branches of the unions are, in general, less sensitive to the demands of their members. They have also not been as successful as their counterparts in the centre of Mexico, in negotiating collective contracts. A main consequence is that wages are much lower in the north than in the centre for similar positions within the industry, enabling the northern automobile companies to pay lower salaries than are current in south-east Asian industry.

Carillo (1989) makes the point that restructuring involves the introduction of the latest production technologies, including those of flexible production. Workers are expected to exercise greater initiative, but they are paid less than their equivalents in the centre of the country. The automobile unions had been successful in the 1960s and 1970s in winning advantageous collective contracts giving workers average salaries that were several times higher than the minimum. Their success reflected the compromises of the import-substitution period between state, labour and employers. In the new period, the urgency to obtain foreign exchange has been eroding these compromises, leading Government and unions to accept what amounts to deregulation of the conditions of work in the new formal sector.

Most of the increase in female manufacturing employment is in the export sector, generally known as the *maquiladora* sector.[9] In Gabayet's (1989) study of women workers in electronic plants in Guadalajara, she found that almost three-quarters of them were single, with an average age in the early twenties. In all the plants, women received at least the minimum wage, but other labour rights depended on the size of firm and the type of production. Thus the smaller firms, which were mainly Mexican owned and supplied parts to the larger ones, were the most likely to employ women on temporary contracts. The large multinationals, that had a final product and a more complex production process, were more likely to have women on permanent contracts and on higher salaries. However, these plants, unlike the smaller ones, only employed a minority of women and these had at least secondary education.

The maquiladora labour force has been heavily female, with males contributing only 28 per cent to the total labour force of 143,918 in 1983 (Carillo and Hernandez, 1987, p. 104). However, there are indications that male employment has been increasing proportionately, due to the lack of alternative employment possibilities. By 1988, men made up 38 per cent of the total *maquiladora* labour force of 325,400 (INEGI, 1989). In Wilson's (1989) study of *maquiladora* plants, the proportion of men ranged from 49 per cent in traditional manufacturing plants, to 37 per cent in assembly plants and 34 per cent in the new, computer-controlled production plants. The changing structure of industry has, then, implications for both the gender composition and the geographical distribution of formal employment. The formal employment opportunities that are growing fastest are ones in which female participation is high. They are concentrated in the border regions and in regions, such as the west of Mexico, which have also attracted recent foreign investment. The stagnation of traditional industry thus means both an absolute decline in formal job opportunities for men and the likelihood that this loss is geographically concentrated in the old centres of this industry, especially Mexico City. In the case of Monterrey, the loss of jobs in heavy manufacturing is partly compensated by the increase in *maquiladora* plants.

Informal employment and the crisis

We can obtain some information on the significance of informal employment in this context by looking at the results of a pilot survey of informal enterprises in Mexico City, carried out in 1987-88 (INEGI, 1989).[10] This survey took as its population all enterprises (including self-employment) with six or fewer people.[11] According to the third quarter urban occupational survey, the employment structure of these enterprises was the following 8.4 per cent were owners, 37.4 per cent were employees or unpaid labour, and 54.2 per cent were self-employed, though this latter category includes a range of labour categories, such as out-workers, independent craftsmen, street vendors working on consignment and so on.[12]

Enterprises were asked whether they fulfilled certain requirements: registration for fiscal purposes, registration with local government, registration with a relevant *Camara* (industrial association), payment of social security taxes and, where required, registration with the health inspectorate. The most frequently reported registration was the fiscal one, with which just over half the enterprises claimed they complied. However, only 15 per cent of enterprises legally bound to register with *Instituto Mexicano de Seguro Social* (Mexican Institute of Social Security) said that they did so. Among those who had not registered, though legally bound to, the most frequent reasons for not complying were not complaints about excessive regulation, but ignorance of the law.

The general picture that emerges from the survey is of a sector of employment with little economic dynamism and with few links to formal. Only a fraction of enterprises had any appreciable capital. Almost all the enterprises were self-financed, with friends and relatives being the only other appreciable source of funds, and hardly any had made any recent investments in the business. Comparing these enterprises with their equivalents in the 1983 income and consumption survey, the report claims evidence for a decline in investments.

Less than 1 per cent of the enterprises were using bank or other formal credits. Nor was there any significant evidence of subcontracting. Less than 1 per cent of enterprises reported that they subcontracted for others, and only 4.3 per cent said that they subcontract to others. Taxes of any kind were only 1 per cent of the outgoings of even the small businesses with employees. Wages were also a relatively minor outgoing, representing 12 per cent for businesses having employees. The major expense was raw materials for all classes of enterprise and all branches of activity. Indeed, when reporting on the difficulties they faced, entrepreneurs overwhelmingly stressed competition, lack of customers and the expense of materials. Neither the costs of labour nor bureaucratic regulation were cited by more than 6 per cent as important.

The levels of income reported bear out a picture of a depressed economic sector. Over 40 per cent of both the self-employed and employees claimed to earn less than the minimum salary, and this at a period when the minimum had already declined by approximately 50 per cent compared with 1980. Evidence from Guadalajara shows that workers in informal workshops in the shoe and garment trades experienced the most severe drop in real incomes between 1982 and 1987: from 50 to 60 per cent, compared with the 45-55 per cent drop in a large-scale shoe factory and the 15 per cent drop in a successfully exporting steel mill (Escobar and Roberts, 1989). In the Mexico City survey, only among the owners of small enterprises were earnings, on average, more than the minimum salary, and it is among this group that the distribution shows greater spread, with some earning four or more times the minimum.

Lack of economic dynamism is not associated, interestingly, with desperation. Though about 90 per cent of entrepreneurs in the Mexico City survey said that they had been negatively affected by the crisis, some 28 per cent claim that they hoped to expand their business in the future and only 8 per cent said they intended to give it up. Among the whole sample, including employees, the great majority said that they had taken their present job voluntarily, and not for lack of alternatives. Only a minority said that they would take a job in formal establishments if they had the chance. Most were satisfied with their current position, and those who wished to change mainly wished to change status in the informal economies (i.e. from employee to self-employed). It is hard to evaluate this "optimism", since conditions of work in informal employment have clearly worsened. It probably reflects a realistic assessment of possibilities in the context of the "de-industrialisation" of Mexico City noted earlier, and the declining proportion of formal sector jobs, new entrants to which are likely to be drawn from younger and better educated cohorts than are represented in the survey of the informally employed.

There are some indications that the age and educational distribution of the informally employed has become more similar to that of the formal sector. The levels of education of the sample were higher than those of informal workers in 1976. We found 62.3 per cent had completed primary schooling or higher levels of education. Though educational levels are increasing in Mexico, it is unlikely that this alone would account for the difference. The age distribution of informal workers in the Mexico City survey was also more "normal" than that of 1976, with 21.1 per cent of workers being 24 years of age and under, and close to that of the employed population in Mexico City in that year. Escobar (1988) reports similar findings when comparing informal workers in Guadalajara in 1985 with those he surveyed in 1981.

The nature of household strategies in face of the crisis provides further insight into the changing balance of formal and informal employment. First, households have more of their members in the labour market than was the case earlier. In the Selby et al. resurvey of the City of Oaxaca, between 1977 and 1987 the average number of workers per household had increased from 1.4 to 1.85. This increase was sharpest among the poorest families (1.4 to 1.9), but even among the 40 per cent of families earning the highest incomes the increase was from 1.3 workers per household to 1.6 workers. For the poorest families the result was only a modest drop overall in real household income during the same period. A similar finding both for income and for the increase in the number of household members working is obtained by González de la Rocha (1988), reporting her ongoing study of 100 families first studied in 1982. Unlike the Selby et al. study, this sample was not randomly chosen, but it has the advantage that we can follow the individual changes in labour market strategy. She reports that the largest increases in labour market participation from 1982 to 1985 (the year of their second resurvey of the households), had occurred among adult women (15 years or more) and young men of less than 15 years. This increasing participation was mainly in informal employment. For female heads of households who increased their participation by 20 per cent, five of the nine new jobs were concentrated in informal services, one in an informal workshop and three were in formal enterprises.

The González de la Rocha data indicate that this increasing household participation in the labour market is partly produced by the aggregation of new members: relatives move in and contribute their incomes or a daughter moves back with her children. Extra members only marginally increase household costs, but make a considerable contribution to budgets or, as in some of the cases reported, help with domestic chores, thus releasing other members to take on paid work. The impact on overall participation rates in Mexico is, consequently, unclear. There is likely to be an increase in participation in certain categories, particularly adult women, but increases will be offset by the declines that might otherwise be expected from rising levels of educational participation.

The suggestion is that the supply of labour in the urban labour market has, in these years, become a supply heavily orientated to informal work. The available jobs tend to be concentrated in the service sectors where the intense competition and the lowest wages prevail. The tendencies in the formal economy - the reduction in real wages and the feminisation of the labour force - reinforce this situation. Male heads of households are decreasingly likely to earn a wage sufficient to maintain the family - in the Guadalajara study, male heads of household actually contributed a minority of household income in 1985 - creating pressures towards other members supplementing household income, including children of school age.

The impact of these trends on the educational levels of poor families is clearly negative. This would mean increasing polarisation of the labour market. Poor families are unlikely to educate their children sufficiently to obtain jobs in the best sectors of employment. In the Gabayet study, for instance, the best paid and protected female workers had a *minimum* level of education of secondary schooling.

Conclusion

One significant implication that I derive from the above data is that policies towards informal employment must take into account the changes in the nature of that employment brought about by the economic restructuring of the 1980s. Up to the 1970s, informal employment in Mexico was relatively benign, and evidence from elsewhere in Latin America suggests the same conclusion. Within a context of rapid urbanisation and industrialisation, it served to complement the formal sector in helping households obtain an adequate income; provided the experience to obtain stable formal sector jobs; and generated incomes that allowed families to educate their children. Even in that period, however, the dynamism of informal employment was less a sign of the virtues of entrepreneurship than of the absence of a welfare-orientated state. Poor families had thrust upon them not only the task of generating incomes, but of creating the city, often quite literally. Restricting informal employment at this period would have been counter-productive and, in any event, labour rights were being extended to cover most of the population.

The new period is more worrying. As Mexico becomes more competitive economically and seeks to reduce its debt, existing labour rights are being eroded. The drop in formal sector wages makes it less likely that a household can be supported on the income of a single wage-earner, especially when formal employment is also being restructured to employ more women who are usually young and single. The niches open to small-scale enterprises in the present period are less than in that of import-substituting industrialisation - the purchasing power of their market has been severely reduced and they face the severest competition from cheap imported goods. Under these conditions, informal employment is likely to become synonymous with underemployment. As whole families become dependent upon informal employment, the circle of poverty and deprivation is likely to be more intense than in the past.

This situation, and it is a common one in Latin America, makes it urgent to bring the state back in. The policy agenda needs to consider extending basic welfare and labour rights to the entire working population, particularly unemployment insurance and health care. Existing legislation concerning health and safety precautions also needs to be enforced over a broad range of working situations, both formal and informal. The current preoccupation with deregulation is thus misplaced. What is needed is more effective regulation, meaning regulation that is realistic and is enforced consistently. This entails, to be sure, labour legislation that takes account of the variety of working situations and their constraints, distinguishing, for example, between part-time and full-time workers.

Mexico is more fortunate than most Latin American countries in that the structure for collective bargaining is already in place that could secure mutually beneficial agreements between employers, workers and Government. To date, the Stability Pact[13] has worked reasonably well in restricting wages and controlling inflation, while government expenditures on health and education rose sharply in 1989. So far, the economic difficulties faced by the population have not resulted in political instability. The fact, however, that the Government is giving as much public attention to political reform as to economic reform, including a loosening of the dominant party's hold on power, suggests that it is aware that successful economic modernisation will only be accomplished through some degree of national consensus.

Notes

[1] In my definition, informality is not a question of business organisation and rationality, but of whether the firm or individual is regulated by the state in terms of a labour code, fiscal obligations and so on.

[2] I will make extensive use of *La ocupación informal en areas urbanas 1976* [Informal employment in urban areas, 1976], a survey carried out in association with the three monthly employment surveys administered to all major urban areas. There is also the preliminary report of the pilot survey of informal employment that was carried out in 1987/88 in the metropolitan area of Mexico City and based on the sample used by the employment survey. Other relevant material is the 1977 *Instituto Nacional de Desarrollo Comunal* survey of household employment and consumption patterns in ten Mexican cities reported in Selby et al. (1990). This survey also focussed on the issue of informality and in 1987 a re-survey was carried out in the city of Oaxaca to assess the changes due to the recession. I shall also rely on data and analysis drawn from my association with a group of Guadalajara researchers who have been making a special study of urban poverty, the informal sector, and the impact of the recession since 1981. In particular, I am greatly indebted to the work of Mercedes González de la Rocha (1986, 1988), and Agustín Escobar Latapí (1986, 1988a, 1988b, 1989).

[3] The survey was applied simultaneously with the *Encuesta continua sobre ocupación* [Continuous employment survey], a quarterly survey of the Mexican urban labour force. Its geographical coverage was the three major metropolitan areas of Mexico (Mexico City, Guadalajara and Monterrey) and the forty municipalities with more than 100,000 people in 1970. The observation unit was the household and, within it, all employed people of 12 years or more. The criteria for classing workers as informally employed were: for employees, that their wages were at or below the minimum wage and that they lacked at least two of their legal entitlements: medical assistance, housing and profit-sharing benefits, employment protection and trade union affiliation. In the case of self-employed workers, the minimum wage criterion was also applied to measure informality along with the lack of at least two attributes: medical coverage, license, receipt of credit and affiliation to associations. All family workers were considered informal.

[4] This estimate is based on summing those employed in small-scale enterprises, their bosses and the self-employed.

[5] The Economic Censuses (Industry, Commerce and Services) of 1981 refer to 1980, whereas the Population Census refers to 1979. This proportion is a reasonable indicator of informality because the economic censuses only capture registered enterprises, leaving out of account non-registered enterprises and those which have no fixed address. I have tried to ensure that the percentages reported are based on the same universes, i.e. same branches of activity, in both population and economic censuses. Thus, in the services, transport is not included because its economic census has not been published.

[6] The Selby et al. (1990) study uses the term "unregistered" to refer to the informally employed. The unregistered are those who are not registered with social security.

[7] Since the survey uses at or below the minimum salary as one of its defining characteristics of informality, it is not useful in exploring the income heterogeneity of this sector.

[8] Together with my Mexican colleagues, Carlos Alba, Fernando Pozos and Fernando Salmeron, I am looking at the impact of the recession on the economic and industrial structure of the West of Mexico. We are undertaking a resurvey of a representative sample of all manufacturing industries in Jalisco, first surveyed by Alba in 1981 (Alba and Kruijt

1988). We have also been interviewing owners of small- and large-scale industries, and representatives of the banks and of the various industrial associations.

[9] The *Maquiladora* system was, originally, an in-bond system of industrial production for export in which parts and materials could be imported free of duty and the final product exported. Plants benefiting from *maquiladora* exemptions can sell part of their product on the Mexican market, and are encouraged to use Mexican suppliers of parts and other materials. With entry into GATT, the distinction between *maquiladora* plants and others producing for export and the internal market has lessened. The export manufacturing sector now includes a wide range of production processes, and is not just confined to assembly operations. In the car industry, the organisation of production is increasingly integrated with that of the north.

[10] The survey is meant as a pilot for a larger study of informal employment in urban Mexico. The results must thus be treated with caution, and the document reports only provisional findings. Like the 1977 survey, it uses the trimestral urban occupational survey to provide its sample, using a special questionnaire to explore informality. Unlike the 1977 survey, the focus is on informal enterprise and not on informal workers. Interviews are with entrepreneurs (owners and the self-employed), and not with workers.

[11] It is not clear whether enterprise size is five and less or six and less. Six and less is used in the tables to which I refer.

[12] These figures are not strictly comparable with those of the 1977 survey, when 38 per cent of Mexico City's labour force in small-scale enterprises was self-employed. The 1987/8 survey is confined to a sub-set of all small-scale enterprises, leaving out branches such as domestic service.

[13] The Stability Pact *(El Pacto para la Estabilidad y el Crecimiento Económico)*, established in 1988, consists of fiscal reforms, changes in the banking system, economic modernisation policies for infrastructure, agriculture and industry, some immediate attention to social priorities and a longer-term commitment to improving income distribution and employment.

References

Alba, C.; Kruijt, D.: *Los empresarios y la industria de Guadalajara* [Entrepreneurs and industry in Guadalajara]. Guadalajara, El Colegio de Jalisco, 1988.

Alba, C; Roberts, B.: *Crisis, adjustment and employment in Mexico:* Manufacturing industry in Jalisco. Working paper, Washington, DC, Commission for the Study of International Migration and Co-operative Economic Development, 1990.

Arias, P.: "La pequeña empresa en el occidente rural" [The small enterprise in the rural West], in *Estudios Sociologicos,* 1988, Vol. 6, No. 17, pp. 405-436.

Arias, P.; Roberts, B.R.: "The city in permanent transition: The consequences of a national system of industrial specialization", in Walton, J. (ed.): *Capital and labour in the urbanized world,* (Beverly Hills, California, Sage), 1985, pp. 149-175.

Balan, J.; Browning, H.; Jelin, E.: *The lives of men,* Austin, University of of Texas Press, 1974.

Benería, L.; Roldan, M.: *The crossroads of class and gender,* Chicago, University of Chicago Press, 1977.

Canak, W.: "Debt, austerity, and Latin America in the new international division of labor", in Canak, W. (ed.): *Lost promises: Debt, austerity and development in Latin America.* Boulder, Colorado, Westview Press, 1989, pp. 9-30.

Carillo, J.: *The restructuring of the automobile industry of Mexico: Adjustment policies and labor implications.* Texas papers on Mexico 89-07. Austin, Texas, Mexican Center, University of Texas at Austin, 1989.

Carillo, J.; Hernández, A.: *Mujeres fronterizas en la industria maquiladora* [Women living near the border and the Maquiladora industry]. Mexico, D.F., SEP/CEFNOMEX, 1985.

De Soto, H.: *El otro sendero* [The other path]. Lima, Editorial El Barranco, 1986.

Dirección General del Servicio Publico del Empleo (DGSPE); Programa Regional del Empleo para America Latina y el Caribe (PREALC): *Bases para una política de empleo hacia el sector informal o marginal urbano en Mexico* [Bases of an employment policy for the informal or marginal urban sector in Mexico]. Mexico, D.F., DGSPE/PREALC; 1976.

Durston, J.: *El subempleo revistado* [Underemployment reviewed]. Working document. Santiago, Cepal, 1987.

Economic Commission for Latin America and the Caribbean (ECLAC).: *The dynamics of social deterioration in Latin America and the Caribbean in the 1980s.* Reference Document LC/G. 1557, Santiago de Chile, ECLAC, May 1989.

Escobar, A.: *Con el sudor de tu frente: Mercado de trabajo y clase obrera en Guadalajara* [With your forehead's sweat: Labour market and working class in Guadalajara]. Guadalajara, El Colegio de Jalisco, 1986.

— —: "The rise and fall of an urban labour market: Economic crisis and the fate of small workshops in Guadalajara, Mexico", *in Bulletin of Latin American Research,* 1988a, Vol. 7, No. 2, pp. 183-205.

— —: *The manufacturing workshops of Guadalajara and their labour force: Crisis and reorganization (1982-85).* Texas Papers on Mexico, 88-05. Austin, Texas, Mexican Center, University of Texas at Austin, 1988b.

Escobar, A.; Roberts, B.: *Urban stratification, the middle classes, and economic change in Mexico.* Texas Papers on Mexico, Austin, Texas, Mexican Center, University of Texas at Austin, 1989.

Gabayet, L.: *Women in transnational industry: The case of the electronic industry in Guadalajara, Mexico. Texas Papers on Mexico,* 89-06. Austin, Texas, Mexican Center, University of Texas at Austin, 1989.

González de la Rocha, M.: *Los recursos de la pobreza: Familias de bajos ingresos de Guadalajara* [The resources of poverty: Low-income families of Guadalajara]. Guadalajara, El Colegio de Jalisco/CIESAS, 1986.

— —: "Economic crisis, domestic reorganization and women's work in Guadalajara, Mexico", in *Bulletin of Latin American Research,* 1988, Vol. 7, No. 2, pp. 207-223.

Gregory, P.: *The myth of market failure.* Baltimore, Johns Hopkins University Press for the World Bank, 1986.

INEGI (Instituto Nacional de Estadistica Geografia e Informatica): *10 años de indicadores ecónomicos y sociales de México* [10 years of economic and social indicators for Mexico]. Mexico, D.F., 1987.

— —: *Encuesta piloto sobre el sector informal: Documento metodologico, presentación de tabulados y breve analisis* [Pilot survey on the informal sector: Methodology document, presentation of tabulations and short analysis]. Mexico, D.F., mimeo., INEGI/ORSTOM, 1989.

Leal, J.: "Las estructuras sindicales" [The trade union structures], in Leal, J. et al.: *Organización y sindicalismo.* Mexico, D.F., Siglo Veintiuno, 1985.

Márquez, C.: *La ocupación informal urbana en México: Un enfoque regional* [Urban informal employment in Mexico: A regional focus]. Working documents. Mexico, D.F., Fundación Friedrich Ebert, 1988.

Marshall, A.: *Non-standard employment practices in Latin America.* ILO discussion papers, Labour Market Programme. Geneva, International Institute for Labour Studies, 1987.

Mexican Labor Law as of January 10, 1974. New York, Commerce Clearing House, 1974.

Michon, F.: *La segmentation 15 ans* après [Segmentation 15 years later]. Working Document. Paris, Université de Paris, Séminaire d'Economie du Travail, 1987.

Muñoz, H.; Oliveira, O.; Stern, C.: "Mexico City: Industrialization, migration and labor force, 1930-70", in *Selected Studies on the Dynamics of Migration,* 1982, Vol. 1, No. 46.

Oliveira, O.; Roberts, B.: "Los antecedentes de la crisis urbana: Urbanización y transformación ocupacional en América Latina: 1940-1980" [The antecedents of the urban crisis: Urbanisation and employment transformation in Latin America], in Lobardi, M.; Veiga, D. (eds.): *Crisis urbano en el cono sur* (Urban crisis in the southern Cone). Montevideo, Uruguay, 1989.

Pahl, R.: *Divisions of labor.* Oxford, Basil Blackwell, 1984.

Portes, A.; Benton, L.: "Industrial development and labor absorption: A reinterpretation", in *Population and Development Review,* 1984, No. 10, pp. 589-611.

PREALC (Regional Employment Programme for Latin America and the Caribbean): *The employment problem in Latin America.* Santiago, 1976.

PREALC: *Sector informal: Funcionamiento y políticas* [The informal sector: Its workings and policies]. Santiago, 1978.

Roberts, B.: "Employment structure, life cycle, and life chances: Formal and informal sectors in Guadalajara", in Portes, A.; Castells, M.; Benton, L. (eds): *The informal economy: Comparative studies in advanced and Third World countries.* Baltimore, Johns Hopkins Press, 1989, pp. 41-59.

SPP (Secretaría de Programación y Presupuesto): *La ocupación informal en* areas urbanas 1976 [Informal employment in urban areas, 1976]. Mexico, D.F., 1979.

Selby, H.; Murphy, A.; Lorenzen, S.: *Urban life in Mexico: Coping strategies of the poor majority.* Austin, Texas, University of Texas Press, 1990.

Standing, G.: "The 'British experiment': Structural adjustment or accelerated decline?", in Portes, A. et al. *The Informal Economy,* Baltimore, Johns Hopkins University Press, 1989, pp. 279-297.

Walton, J.; Ragin, C.: "Austerity and dissent: Social bases of popular struggle in Latin America", in Canak, W. (ed.). *Lost Promises,* Boulder, Colorado, Westview Press, 1989, pp. 216-232.

Wilson, P.: *The new Maquiladoras: Flexible production in low wage regions.* Texas Papers on Mexico 89-01. Austin, Texas, Mexican Center, University of Texas at Austin, 1989.

Zapata, F.: *Relaciones laborales y negociación colectiva en el sector público* mexicano [Labour relations and collective bargaining in the public sector in Mexico]. Working documents. Mexico, D.F., Centro de Estudios Sociologicos, El Colegio de Mexico, 1987.

5

The informal sector in Latin America: From underground to legality

by *Victor Tokman* *

Introduction

The idea that the informal sector operated in unregulated markets and constituted a clandestine activity, mostly performed outside the law and in some cases even against it, was one of the main factors considered in the pioneering work on the sector in Kenya, back in 1972. This factor, while recognised, was not allocated much significance, since the focus of the analytical innovation was to look at the working poor, defined as those performing low productivity activities. In fact, the many studies undertaken after 1972 mostly followed this form of production approach, distancing themselves somewhat from the initial mix between illegality and informality.

During the 1980s the situation changed. Today regulation in general, and legality in particular, have become key conceptual tools to analyse and to prescribe solutions for the informal sector. Two different approaches have contributed to this change.

The first conceptualises the informal sector as an outcome of the decentralisation and reorganisation of the production and work processes at the global level. In this approach, the existence of the informal sector is the result of the search for flexibility and of the need to reduce labour costs, which forces it to operate outside the regulatory framework. This allows the by-passing of laws and regulations, which are costly both in terms of financial costs and rigidities. Internally, the decentralisation of production and its effect on work arrangements provides a functional response to the need to increase profit margins by diminishing or avoiding trade union power and by allowing the transfer of the cost of demand fluctuations outside the firm. New technologies make this process technically feasible (Piore and Sabel, 1987; Gordon, Edwards and Reich, 1983).

* International Labour Office, Geneva. The author wishes to thank the collaboration received from Ricardo Lagos.

At the same time, increased international competition and the rapid penetration by the newly industrialised countries of world markets increased the emphasis on the reduction of costs, particularly labour costs, in order to retain both domestic and international markets (Portes, Castells and Barton, 1989). As a result, the informal sector, defined as comprising all activities performed beyond government regulation, becomes a universal feature of increasing dimensions, in developing as well as in developed countries.

The second variant follows a neo-liberal approach and is founded on the observation that informal activities are performed beyond the law in developing countries. This in turn is the result of inadequate legislation, excessive red-tape and inefficient bureaucracy. Informality and illegality became similar concepts, but this variant differs from the previous approach in that it is generated by the impossibility of complying with the existing regulatory apparatus and not by the need to lower costs or to increase flexibility. Laws, procedures and government are then targeted as responsible for the existence of a large and increasing share of employment in low productivity and badly remunerated jobs. It is further argued that regulations constitute a barrier preventing the development of informal activities, since access to resources and more dynamic markets can only be gained through the existing legal and institutional machinery (De Soto, 1986).

Our conceptualisation of the informal sector in Latin America is closer to the first interpretation, since in part the informal sector is being generated as a result of economic restructuring, which has led to production decentralisation. But these processes take place in a different structural context, the main characteristic of which is the existence of labour surplus. The result is a different informal sector. Decentralisation ensures, by its functionality, a more dynamic insertion in terms of links with markets, technological change and resources availability. This might well result in increased remuneration, at the cost of reduced protection and stability in relation to waged working arrangements. In developing countries, the competitive pressure of excess labour in the quest for survival pushes down incomes, and generates subsistence activities that are not dynamically linked to expanding modern sectors but cater for low-income markets, being excluded from access to capital, skills and technology. Average incomes are low and the informal sector becomes more heterogeneous, since it contains segments with different possibilities of expansion (Tokman, 1978, 1989b).

In spite of different interpretations, the three approaches share the conclusion that informal activities are performed beyond regulation because of functional requirements alone, or mixed with survival strategies, or simply because of the inadequate regulatory system. The observation could be common, but the diagnosis and hence the prescriptions differ. This opens a broad area for analysis. However, the objective of this paper is to concentrate on the common points, trying to test the validity of the conceptual distinction that identifies informality with illegality, and to examine the importance of the barrier presented by the regulatory framework, both in becoming legal and in operating within it. The paper will end with some general conclusions about regulations and working arrangements in the informal sector.

The paper is based on part of a co-operative research project co-ordinated by the author in Latin America. Sources will be duly identified in each case, but in general they refer to three types of analysis. One type is at a more aggregate level, undertaken in Bolivia and Mexico, in studies which explore the relations between informality and illegality. Another type is based on case studies of Bolivia, Brazil, Chile, Ecuador, Guatemala, Mexico, Uruguay and Venezuela, which analyse the effect of existing barriers in terms of mon-etary costs and time. The third type is found in a study made of the feasibility of providing social security coverage for all those working in the informal sector. While the conclusions are founded on this collective research base, they are not necessarily shared by the authors of each respective contribution, since they represent the author's personal reading of the results.

Illegality and informality: The predominance of grey areas

If to be legal means to comply with all existing regulations, and if illegality means the opposite, one must consider whether the informal sector operates beyond legality. For that purpose, it is necessary to differentiate at least two stages. One is the legal recognition which allows any business, firm or individual to become a full part of the regulated economy. This usually entails registration with local and national authorities. A second stage is to honour legality during the actual operation of the business activity, that is to comply with all established obligations.

Three types of legality can be distinguished according to prevailing systems. The first refers to legal recognition as a business activity, usually requiring registration and, in some cases, health and security inspections. A second sphere of legality is that relating to taxes, which implies registration for the purposes of identification as a potential contributor, but also generates a permanent commitment to pay the different taxes according to national legis-lation. Finally, a third aspect of legality refers to labour matters. This varies from registration as an employer and giving contracts to employees to ensuring non-wage benefits, like annual leave, and to such matters as working hours and social security contributions.

The main assumption derived from the conceptual discussion in its several variants suggests that informal activities are performed illegally, as opposed to formal ventures that comply with existing legal requirements. At the extreme, this should imply underground economic units. Reality, however, is different. Cases at either end of the continuum running from legality to illegality do not constitute the majority; most cases are usually found in the middle of the continuum. To sustain this conclusion we will review the available evidence.

First, the study for Mexico made by Elizondo (1988) shows that only 27 per cent of the cases studied are unregistered, while at the other extreme only 18 per cent can be considered fully legal, that is having fulfilled all registration requirements and permanently honouring commitments. Intermediate situations constitute the majority, nearly 55 per cent; the most prevalent case consisted of economic units that had made all the necessary registrations but that had not paid all their legal obligations (see table 1). In addition, it is interesting that unregistered informal units were only found in the industrial sector, mainly in home-based activities. Informal commercial activities are always located in the grey area between underground and legality.

A second source of information is provided by Casanovas (1988) for Bolivia. He reports that 49 per cent of the informal units of the country were registered in the taxpayer registry (Registro Unico de Contribuyentes). As in the case of Mexico, higher registration is found in commerce, around 95 per cent; while only 18 and 15 per cent of informal units in services and manufacturing, respectively, comply with this obligation. It is interesting to note that registration is even higher at the local level. In the city of La Paz, it is estimated that 65 per cent of all informal activities operate under a municipal licence. Legality shows an important reduction when effective tax contributions are examined. Only 19 per cent of those registered are paying. As in Mexico, the informal sector of Bolivia is, in terms of legal status, in an intermediate position. This should not, however, lead to the underestimation of the fiscal contribution made by the informal sector. Even in occupations like street sellers, which are usually considered as underground "par excellence", around 35 per cent of those located at La Paz are registered and contribute US$536,000 per year to the municipal budget.

Information from case studies confirms the predominance of intermediate status and allows the identification of distortions in what might appear to be legal situations. An interesting illustration, for example, is provided by Cartaya (1988) in her study of Venezuela. A business producing and selling cosmetics (depilation wax) is underground on the production side, while legal on the marketing side. This latter part of the business is split between the owner's home, where he keeps a small stock by which he justifies legal sales, and well-established premises that he rents in downtown Caracas for three hours a week. There he receives his clients and uses a business card with telephone numbers, telex and even fax of the firm from which he rents. This office also provides the informal operator with secretarial help and recording of messages. At home, the commercial activity is legal; but in a backroom he, in fact, produces the product. To legalise this part of his business requires many licences, since the handling of chemical inputs is subject to a variety of controls. Although his intention is to become fully legal and he has taken some steps in that direction, he meanwhile keeps a false licence, lent by a friend, just in case his operation is detected by the inspectors.

This example, rather than constituting an exception, is found systematically in most developing countries. In some, like Brazil, these situations have

Table 1. Mexico: Enterprises by legality status (in percentages)

Legality status[1]	Under-ground	Restricted illegality	Restricted legality	Legal	Total
Number of enterprises	27.3	18.2	36.4	18.2	100.0
Sector of activity					
Manufacturing industry	46.1	23.1	7.7	23.1	59.1
Commerce	–	25.0	75.0	–	18.2
Services	–	–	80.0	20.0	22.7
Location					
Shop	9.1	27.3	36.4	27.3	50.0
Home	55.6	11.1	22.2	11.1	40.9
Without fixed location	–	–	100.0	–	9.1

[1] *Underground:* without any registration; *restricted illegality:* with some registration of nul cost or which only requires a once for all payment; *restricted legality:* with all required registration but not contributing to some of them; *legal:* all requirements of inscription and contributions met.

Source: Elizondo (1988).

even become institutionalised. According to a study made by Looye (1988), a popular way to move in the real world of Brazilian legality is with the "jeitinho". This is a system by which the firm registers, but then uses different sorts of arrangements (jeitinhos) to diminish the cost of legality. These arrangements are diverse, including, for example underdeclaration of initial capital or declaration that the business is a new venture rather than an ongoing one, both make the business eligible to receive subsidies; registering only some of the activities, as in the previous example of Venezuela; use of legal bills only for part of the sales; underdeclaration of incomes; use of probationary contracts to avoid being the subject of labour law obligations; and underdeclaration of the number of workers and/or wages for social security purposes. Indeed, the use of some of these "jeitinhos" is not only made by informal units; rather they are a resource also used by economic units outside the informal sector. Illegality in this broader context then becomes a criterion which cannot be used to distinguish different segments of the economy.

The main question is why the most common situation is activities which operate in the grey area between underground and legality. It seems that such status offers a higher probability of obtaining average incomes. In the case of Mexico, underground activities can be found at both extremes of the income distribution, while legal firms tend to be concentrated in the above average incomes bracket (more than 3 minimum wages). The highest frequency of enterprises with average incomes between 1 and 3 minimum wages is found to be operating under restricted legality. This arrangement allows the informal enterprise to have access to benefits, to minimise risks and to reduce costs, particularly operational costs.

It allows for access to benefits, since in most cases it is sufficient to be registered to enable the business to start operations legally. This is a requirement which generally takes a short time and does not involve high costs, particularly when in most cases it is not necessary to complete all registrations. The first registration generally gives access to organised markets, since the informal shop can become visible and it is entitled to give legal bills for its sales. In addition, registration potentially permits a business to request credits. This, however, has not emerged in the cases studied as a determining factor, since collaterals constitute the main requirement.

Risks of sanctions are also minimised by partially legalising activities. That is the reason why businesses that are more exposed show a higher level of registration. Commerce activities, which need to be visible to attract their clientele, record proportionally more registration than industries which do not depend so heavily on direct sales to the public. The risk is also associated with the inspection capacity of government, which tends to be greater at the local level. This explains why in La Paz registration at that level is the highest.

It also allows for cost reductions by paying less taxes and/or diminishing labour costs. This is also the case of formal firms. The difference is perhaps one of degree, particularly in relation to labour costs. Informal units have a different arrangement of the work process, which is mostly organised on a family basis, with fluctuating hours and high turnover and hence, in most cases, not being subject to labour protection laws. The point is that this form of production is the result of survival strategies and production decentralisation, in an economic environment characterised by limited resources and insufficient job creation in modern sectors. In some cases more control of existing laws could enforce labour protection, but in the majority it is not economically feasible, either because the organisation of work is beyond the normative framework, or simply because the surplus generated by the economic unit is insufficient to absorb additional costs. This calls for new forms of regulation to be considered.

Barriers to becoming legal

In spite of the difficulties of defining what is underground or legal, it is important to estimate the cost of becoming legal. This requires a series of registrations, which involve financial costs and are time-consuming. The latter is, in turn, the result of the degree of complexity of the existing normative framework and of the efficiency of public agencies to process the applications or to undertake inspections when needed. The data available from the case studies, which are presented in table 2, give three interesting pieces of information.

The first refers to the time involved in filling all the registration requirements. These are highly variable between countries and even within countries. The range of time involved is from one month to one year, with the exception of Guatemala where it is close to two years. The upper limit coincides with the

Table 2. Costs of entry to legality

Country	Economic sector	Time (No. of working days)[1]	Financial costs			
			Without modifications		Required modifications	
			Amount (US$)	Percentage of annual profits	Amount (US$)	Percentage of annual profits
Bolivia	Commerce	15-30	14	2.8		
	Industry	15-30	13	0.25-1.6		
	Services	15-30	16	0.25-1.6		
Brazil	Commerce	31-60	44	3.5-7.5[1]		
	Industry	44	84	17.7[2]		
	Services	31	99	–		
Chile	Commerce	12	110	–	5 308	128.3
	Industry	65	222	2.8-5.4	11 135	147.8
Ecuador	Commerce	60-75	32	15.5	70	33.8
	Industry	180-240	239	23.4	70	6.8
Guatemala	Commerce	179	216	4.2		
	Industry	525	894	8.6		
Mexico	Commerce	83-240	210-368	–		
	Industry	83-240	210-368	–		
	Services	83-240	210-368	–		
Uruguay	Industry	75-90	337	159.5	613	290.5
	Services	75-90	405	6.1-13	613-675	19.7-10.2
Venezuela	Commerce	170-310		5.7		21.5
	Industry	170-310		23.5		181.5

[1] For Bolivia, Mexico and Venezuela, this refers to calendar days. The time required was the effective time spent in Bolivia, Brazil and Uruguay. The rest were estimated on the basis of time required for each specific legalisation step.   [2] As percentage of invested capital.

Sources: Bolivia: Escobar de Pabon (1988); Brazil: Looye (1988); Chile: Velasquez (1988); Ecuador: Placencia (1988); Guatemala: Saenz (1988); Uruguay: Quijano and Antia (1988); and Venezuela: Cartaya (1988).

results reported by De Soto (1986) about the time required to initiate activities in the clothing industry to be located in Lima (289 days). However, this is not the case in all countries. There are countries - like Ecuador, Guatemala, Mexico and Venezuela - which seem to be close to the upper limit, but in Bolivia, Brazil, Chile and Uruguay the time spent in the process varies between one and three months.

The second piece of information available is that financial costs of entry are also highly variable. They can vary from US$1 required by a street seller in La Paz to be able to operate legally, to US$1,080 paid by a small car repair shop in Uruguay. The proportion of costs, in relation to annual profits of the surveyed informal units, varies from less than 2 to almost 160 per cent (see table 2).

The third piece of evidence suggests that in most cases it is more costly to legalise activities in manufacturing than in commerce.

The date and the history of the cases studied also allows us to make two additional comments. The first is that a key factor in determining both the time and cost involved in entry to legality is whether or not the unit requesting registration needs to introduce changes in its premises. These can constitute requirements relating to health, security or other matters, and final approval of registration is usually conditional on fulfilling such requirements. An illustration of the increased cost is included in table 2, where it can be seen that they usually exceed the normal costs of legalisation by a considerable margin. The issue is then whether these additional requirements constitute unjustified constraints or whether they should be enforced to protect the more general interests of the population. Three of the cases studied are very illustrative of the conflict between the interests of the informal operator and other private and public interests. The additional request made by labour authorities in the case of an establishment in Ecuador was to build sanitary facilities on the premises given that three permanent workers were usually working for the firm. The cost of this construction amounted to 34 per cent of the annual profits and the total costs of legalisation increased to 50 per cent of annual profits. In spite of the additional cost, the regulation in this case is meant to protect the workers' rights to a minimum standard of working conditions, which should be beyond discussion in any civilised society.

A second example refers to the establishment in Uruguay of an enterprise to produce sandwiches. As this is a food-producing industry, there are construction requirements to ensure proper production conditions. In this case, the requirements were the installation of protection nets on the windows to keep out insects and of a spring attached to the washroom door to ensure that it closed automatically, and that the floor and the walls, up to a height of 1.80 metres, be covered with ceramic tiles. The additional cost amounted to US$500, making it impossible for the informal entrepreneur to comply with regulations because of lack of funds. The issue here, as in the previous example, is not that this is reason enough to de-regulate, since in this particular instance the norm has been introduced to protect minimum health standards, to avoid risks for the consumers. The financial inability of the informal producer cannot in this case be solved at the cost of endangering the consumers' health.

Finally, a third example where there are conflicts between private and public interests can be illustrated by the situation in the taxi markets. A comparative analysis made for Lima (Chavez, 1988) and Santiago (Scholnik, 1988) shows the importance of regulations. In Lima, regulations are not observed, nor is there any will or capacity on the part of the authorities to enforce them. As a result, the taxi service is performed in very poor conditions. No meters are required, so fares are bargained each time. Car inspections and insurance are not compulsory, so the security of neither the passenger nor the public in general is protected. In addition, as the entry to the market is open, competition generated by excess labour supply pushes down tariffs and hence net incomes are low, affecting the renewal and maintenance of cars. The case of Santiago illustrates the opposite situation. Consistent with the general policies followed in the country in recent years, de-regulation was also applied to the taxi market. There, however, all regulations to ensure that a public service (although performed by the private sector) maintains its standard were retained. Flexibility was introduced into the requirements for entry and on tariffs. The superiority of results in terms of the service available is evident for any visitor to these two cities. The general point is that norms and regulations are generally there to protect legitimate interests of other private groups or of the public in general. The proposals for de-regulation, even if justifiable in view of the private costs that regulations entail for informal producers, cannot be socially sustained.

A second observation that can be made on the basis of the information available is that country situations differ. A typology could be made including, at one end, those countries in which the case study analyses show that legalisation is not a costly process, either in terms of time or of financial costs. This is the case in Bolivia, Brazil and Chile. There is also an intermediate group, where the financial costs involved are not too high, but where legalisation is time consuming. At the other extreme, one can group countries such as Ecuador, Guatemala and Peru, where the process of becoming legal involves high financial costs and takes a long time.

This classification leads on to the question of causes. The first, obvious factor is the inadequacy of regulations and the inefficiency of the bureaucracy, a factor which applies to most countries, but particularly to the latter group. The number of administrative steps required shows that countries in the most time-consuming category do require the most steps (see table 3). However, the correlation is not high since, although Bolivia requires the fewest administrative requirements, this is not the case for Brazil and Chile which are similar to the countries in the intermediate group. The situation is different for a country that is highly centralised than for one in which there is decentralisation. This, in turn, is also related to the administrative organisation of the country. It is also linked to the efficiency of government in general, not only in processing registration permits. Chile is perhaps a good example of a traditionally efficient public administration, and hence it is not surprising that registration can be accomplished in a shorter period.

An additional factor is the adequacy of promotional regimes. The existence of such special regimes can help to ease the process or can constitute barriers that worsen the situation. Examples of the former can be found in Bolivia and Brazil, both of which are in our first group. A major tax reform was introduced in Bolivia in 1987 which aimed to simplify and consolidate the numerous taxes. This reform allowed for an automatic and inexpensive registration process which, as we have seen, resulted in almost half of the informal units being registered. In Brazil, a new statute for micro enterprises was introduced, accompanied by a system to help the informal producers in their registration process. This also resulted in increased legality. The opposite

Table 3. Administrative steps required for registration (numbers)

Country	Initial registration	Location	Health and security	Taxes	Labour	Total
Bolivia	4	–	–	1	–	5
Brazil	6	3	3	10	–	22
Chile	4	10	4	5	–	23
Ecuador	39[1]	–	5	7	9	60
Guatemala	4	–	–	22	5	31
Mexico	16	2	1	2	–	21
Uruguay	5	2	1	1	4	13
Venezuela	13	–	5	5	5	28

[1] Includes 34 steps required by promotion laws for classification.
Source: As for table 2.

situation can be seen in Ecuador, where the incentives law is old and the understanding of the prevailing regulatory framework is further complicated by the sanctioning of a new law which did not completely replace the previous one and in some cases, overlapped with it. As table 3 shows, Ecuador requires 60 administrative steps, out of which 34 are related to a cumbersome process of classification and skill recognition related to the promotion law.

This shows the importance of placing the discussion in the appropriate perspective, since the richness of information at the micro level should not be allowed to mislead those responsible for the diagnosis and the proposed solutions. On the contrary, they do contribute to raising specific issues in a context of what should be a more general discussion. Regulations should not be seen merely as obstacles to informal entrepreneurship development, but be analysed rather as instruments resulting from State organisation and policies, incentive systems, and the government responsibility to protect different groups and society as a whole.

The costs of being legal

To the costs of entering into legality must be added those involved in complying with legal requirements during the operation of the enterprise. They relate mostly to tax and labour obligations. The information available raises several issues of policy significance.

First, the costs of remaining legal permanently mostly affect those informal units with hired workers. They do not significantly affect the self-employed or those using unpaid family labour only since they are not subject to most of the legal obligations. Second, as in the case of entry costs, the situation varies according to country, the costs of remaining legal ranging from 17 to 70 per cent of annual profits. The incidence is, however, high in all cases, since they more than duplicate registration costs. In addition, there are cases like Bolivia where - although as a result of the tax reform the permanent costs are around 13 per cent of annual profits - they would represent, if paid, a reduction of around one third of family incomes.

Third, labour costs are the highest component in the permanency costs. Taxes do not have a heavy incidence, since income taxes and profits are insignificant at the prevailing level of profits in these units. Value added tax, which is the most significant cost in most countries, greatly diminishes its impact if properly calculated. Labour costs account for the largest share, ranging from 64 per cent of total costs of permanency to 90 to 93 per cent in the cases of Bolivia and Colombia (Caro and Acevedo, 1986). This would imply an increase in labour costs of around 20 per cent, absorbing what is estimated as average profit ratios for informal units (Tokman, 1988). The additional labour costs are divided more or less equally between two main components - (a) benefits, such as vacations and 13-month indemnities, and (b) contributions to social security.

Why is it that most informal units only partially observed these obligations? A first explanation is that they are unable to absorb the increased costs involved. This, in turn, is the result of the way in which the informal sector operates. Lack of access to resources and markets, in conjunction with surplus labour unable to find well remunerated jobs, lead to heavy competition at low levels of surplus. The inability is not then a matter of financial insufficiency or inadequacy of regulations; it is a structural constraint. A second explanation is that the work process is organised in a different manner within the informal units. Labour relations are not subject to contracts, there is flexibility of working hours and remuneration and there exist are ad hoc payment arrangements.

The studies also suggest two additional observations. The first, based on an analysis of the conditions for success in Bolivia (Larrazabal, 1988), is that the growth of the informal firm brings a progressive improvement in the observance of labour obligations. Three-quarters of the successful firms studied show that, as they expanded, vacations and 13-month payments were recognised. Part of the increased benefits is then distributed to the workers through this mechanism. However, none of the successful firms was making contributions to social security. This suggests that the subject of social security goes beyond the micro-level discussion, and should be dealt with by a systemic approach.

The other observation is that this semi-legal way of operation constitutes a non-conflictual working agreement. This arrangement is far removed from the class conflict environment, which historically has resulted in increased labour protection and social security. In some cases, paternalistic working relations tend to be developed in a context where family ties, apprenticeship relations and direct personal involvement of the owner of the informal unit prevail. No unions exist in such small-sized enterprises. In addition, the high instability associated with the sector leads workers to envisage these jobs as transitory employment. No career development is foreseen and hence the basis for contributing to social security, particularly in relation to potential retirement benefits, does not exist. This, together with the previous observation, indicates that if the incorporation of the informal units into the social security system is an objective, the process will not occur automatically since the basic assumptions upon which most of the systems are based are not relevant for this form of production.

Formalising the informal: The case of social security

If those working in the informal sector cannot have access to social security coverage given the characteristics of the sector, the question that should be asked is whether it is possible to ensure social security coverage by going in the opposite direction, that is that the social security system should be able to reach informal workers. This has been analysed in depth for four Latin American countries by Mesa-Lago (1989), who arrives at the conclusion that there is no single answer, since each country constitutes a special case.

There are several key parameters that determine the feasibility of reaching universal social security. The size of the informal sector is an important factor - the larger the employment share of the sector, the more difficult the task. Feasibility also depends on the prevailing system, particularly in relation to its present coverage, the type of benefits and its financial situation. These characteristics vary from country to country. In some countries, such as Jamaica, coverage is compulsory for all workers, including self-employed and domestic servants. In Peru, domestic servants are also supposed to be insured on a compulsory basis, but for the self-employed it is optional. The same happens for both categories of informal workers in Mexico and Costa Rica. There are also differences according to the coverage by type of benefits. Health is universally covered in most cases, whether outside the social security system through a national health service, as in Jamaica, or because the system guarantees access to hospital, medical care and maternity benefits to the whole population, as in Costa Rica. Finally, there are differences as regards pensions, since in some cases special support is envisaged for the most impoverished, while in others there is a requirement of previous contributions independently of the insured person's income level.

As health coverage is high in Latin America, the main issue is basically to analyse why only between 2 and 5 per cent of the self-employed, who are the largest group within the informal sector, have access to social security. Four factors help to explain this situation. First, the cost of the contribution is high. Required contributions of the self-employed are usually two to four times those of wage workers. In relation to incomes, the differences are smaller, since in some of the prevailing systems it is possible to contribute on the basis of a fraction of total income. The second factor is of an administrative nature, since there are problems of identification, registration and control of social security in general, but particularly in small units. The current levels of arrears and evasion are high. The third explanation is that pensions have deteriorated in real terms and hence incentives to join the system voluntarily are low. In Jamaica, for example, average pensions are one-fifth of per capita income, being clearly insufficient to ensure an adequate level of living. Finally, access to social security does not constitute a high priority for those working in the informal sector, mostly because of their uncertain occupational career. Political pressure from the potential beneficiaries is low or non-existent and this, as history has shown, has been one of the main factors behind increased social security coverage.

Possibilities of reaching those working in the informal sector differ according to country situations. Mesa Lago (1988) analysed the cases of Costa Rica, Jamaica, Mexico and Peru. Costa Rica constitutes a case where it is feasible to cover all informal workers with the present system. Present coverage is already high, the informal sector is relatively small and the financial position is sound, since operating surpluses are registered both in health and pensions. The aspect which requires attention is the high cost involved for the self-employed; perhaps a differential pension, lower than the minimum, could be introduced which would require a reduced contribution. The answer seems to be positive also in the case of Jamaica. In spite of a large informal sector, the system presents the advantage of being limited to pensions and of being of fairly recent origin. The ratio of pensioners to contributors is still very low and the expansion of the system can be absorbed given its favourable financial situation. Hence, both cases illustrate that universalisation from the system to the informal units is feasible.

The situation is different in the case of Mexico. Present coverage is low and the system registers operating deficits both in health and pensions. An expansion of the system cannot be absorbed financially under these conditions. There are, however, some proposals under consideration to enlarge the coverage by State participation in the contributions of the self-employed (providing one-third of the contributions) and offering a reduced package of services. The answer in Mexico seems to be a search for differentiation within the system.

The last country examined, Peru, clearly illustrates that the task is unfeasible. Low coverage is accompanied by an undercapitalised system with significant operational deficits, low quality of health services and insufficient pensions. If all the informal units were covered, the Peruvian Institute of Social Security would have to expand its coverage by 180 per cent and its health expenditure would have to increase by 88 per cent. This requires answers outside the system. The existing one needs to be drastically reformed to cover those already incorporated adequately. Protection for those outside the system can be improved by other solidarity arrangements on a private basis. Some interesting experiences of this type are already under way in Peru.

The answer provided by a systemic approach is not uniform. In some cases, like Costa Rica and Jamaica, it is feasible to provide universal protection, in which case what is required is to find ways to ensure that the cost involved is consistent with the absorptive capacity of those working in the informal sector. This is not just a financial problem, since working arrangements and job instability also constitute strong disincentives to join the system. Cost reduction measures would probably have to be accompanied by other changes to ensure portability of contributions or to shift from benefit-defined to contribution-defined systems. There are intermediate cases like Mexico, where it seems feasible to explore solutions within the system. This could imply differential benefits, but compared to the existing situation it could still result in increased equity. Finally, there are cases where the feasible way to improve protection of informal workers can be solidarity arrangements outside the State system. These arrangements can help to mitigate the situation, but do not constitute long-run alternatives to the necessary reform of the prevailing system.

Conclusions

This analysis leads us to four main conclusions. First, the informal sector operates between underground and legality. In doing so, the informal producer obtains access to what he or she evaluates as important, while minimising the risks associated with illegality. Non-observance of regulations, - a common feature attributed to informality according to all interpretations - becomes a relative matter.

Second, regulations in the context of the informal sector discussion have a much longer history than the present policy of diminishing government intervention in economic activity. These rules and procedures were introduced to protect the general interest of society or to safeguard absolute needs of those more vulnerable groups. When placed in this perspective, some of today's common prescriptions to promote the development of informal sector entre-preneurs are clearly unacceptable. There is, however, room for improvement. The studies show that a case in point is the special promotion laws, often well intentioned but usually ill conceived; the same is true of tax systems that are the result of hundreds of modifications adding new taxes or creating special cases that result in widespread evasion. Simple and semi-automatic promo-tional laws and tax structures have proved to be more efficient, and they can promote the regularisation of the informal sector in particular. In addition, they diminish bureaucratic interference, reducing the time and costs involved in becoming legal.

Third, there is the issue of labour legality. On this there are several comments that should be made. While in this paper we have defined the informal sector from the point of view of the productive unit, confusion arises between this concept and informal labour. The latter refers to non-permanent forms of labour use, which have sometimes evolved with small productive units, implying some overlap with the former definition. Although these new arrange-ments can be promoted voluntarily by some members of the labour force searching for work flexibility, the main impulse probably comes from the firm, both to reduce costs and to increase flexibility. This calls for new forms of regulation, since the existing standards devised for permanent workers become inapplicable. The boundaries for part-time or decentralised arrangements should include those small enterprises created exclusively for that purpose and depending on the parent firm for their survival. New or existing norms require additional enforcement capacity in this case.

Furthermore, many of those in the prevailing informal units are self-employed. In such units, the issue of labour standards becomes entangled with the subjective issue of self-exploitation. However, from a macro-level perspective, access to social security becomes an important area for policy reform, since the costs and incentives of prevailing systems discriminate against the self-employed. For wage-workers in informal units, estimated to make up between 10 and 20 per cent of total informal employment, the whole range of labour standards should in principle be applicable.

It could be useful to distinguish the type of labour regulations according to objectives, since some of them try to ensure current income and working conditions (minimum wage, vacations, working hours), while others are meant to protect employment security (hiring and firing regulations) and others cover loss of income due to accident or illness or retirement (social security). From the preceding analysis, it seems that the enforcement of the first set of standards improve with the growth of the informal unit. The second is generally not applicable because of the prevailing working arrangements, and the third is not considered because of financial incapacity and even lack of interest of the would-be beneficiaries.

One tactical approach could be to regulate the application of standards in order to increase the likelihood of enforcement. This could be done by diminishing the requirements or by allowing for progressive implementation. Partial solutions tend to be difficult to enforce, to perpetuate differences and to lower the standards of those already protected, since there is a downward pressure for equalisation. In this sense, if the needs are so strong, the preference should be for a systemic reform rather than "ad hoc" adaptation.

As we have seen, the answers in relation to social security will vary depending on the country concerned. In some countries, only a few mitigating measures outside the system can be envisaged. In others, the problems of cost of entry need to be confronted, but preferably avoiding increased differentiation if the prevailing system is benefit-defined. This would require government contributions or very efficient management of the system which might allow a more ambitious income redistribution. If this is not feasible, as is the case in many countries, it might be advisable to reconsider the whole system by, for instance, introducing a contribution-defined scheme accompanied by a minimum guaranteed income. This would introduce differentiation, but would also ensure basic coverage for all members of the labour force. The reform in this case, while probably solving the problem of access of the informal workers to social security, would surely have to be based on an evaluation of the situation of those already within the system.

The issue of hiring and firing regulations should also be approached systematically. If it were the case that present regulations introduce excessive rigidities, the problem would be to modify the general norm without taking the prevailing flexibility in the informal sector as a benchmark. The main objective should be, as in the case of social security, to improve the overall efficiency of regulation and, as a by-product, to facilitate its enforcement in the informal sector. That would be preferable to introducing special treatment, which would almost certainly result in lower labour standards for all.

Finally, although the paper has concentrated on regulations, this should not lead to the conclusion that they are the cause of informality. As we have argued in the introduction and elsewhere (Tokman, 1989a), operating beyond regulations represents a way to produce goods and services in a structural environment characterised by lack of well-remunerated job opportunities and by excess labour. For this reason, a policy encouraging regulation would help, but cannot constitute by itself a sound policy for supporting the informal sector.

References

Cartaya, V. 1988. *Costos de legalización de empresas informales, el caso de Venezuela* [Legalisation costs of informal enterprises, the case of Venezuela], unpublished paper. Santiago, PREALC, Regional Project Policies for the Informal Sector.

Caro, B.; Acevedo, J. 1986. *Análisis de la problemática de legalización de la microempresa* [Analysis of the problem of legalisation of the micro enterprise]. Bogotá, Colombia, SER Institute.

Casanovas, R. 1988. *Informalidad e ilegalidad: una falsa identidad* [Informality and illegality: A false identity], unpublished paper. Santiago, PREALC, Regional Project Policies for the Informal Sector.

Chavez, E. 1988. *Efectos del marco legal y su reglamentación en el mercado de taxis* [Effects of the legal frame and its regulations in the taxi market], unpublished paper. Santiago, PREALC, Regional Project Policies for the Informal Sector.

De Soto, H. 1986. *El otro sendero* [The other path]. Lima, Editorial El Barranco.

Gordon, D.; Edwards, R.; Reich, R. 1983. *Segmented work, divided workers: The historical transformation of labour in the United States.* Cambridge, Massachusetts, Cambridge University Press.

Elizondo, N. 1988. *La ilegalidad en el sector informal urbano de la Ciudad de México* [Illegality in the urban informal sector of Mexico City], unpublished paper. Santiago, PREALC, Regional Project Policies for the Informal Sector.

Escobar de Pabon, S. 1988. *Los estableciminetos informales ante la ley,* [Informal establishments and the law] unpublished paper. Santiago, PREALC, Regional Project Policies for the Informal Sector.

Larrazabal, H. 1988. *Legalidad ¿condición del éxito económico en el sector informal urbano?* [Legality, condition of economic success in the urban informal sector?], unpublished paper. Santiago, PREALC, Regional Project Policies for the Informal Sector.

Looye, J.W. 1988. *Real vs ideal and the Brazilian Jeitinho: A study of microenterprise registration under the new microenterprise statute,* unpublished paper. Santiago, PREALC, Regional Project Policies for the Informal Sector.

Mesa-Lago, C. 1989. *Protección del sector informal en América Latina y el Caribe por la seguridad social o medios alternativos* [Protection of the informal sector in Latin America and the Caribbean through social security or alternative means], unpublished paper. Santiago, PREALC, Regional Project Policies for the Informal Sector.

Piore, M.; Sabel, C. 1987. *The second industrial divide.* New York, Basic Books Inc.

Placencia, M.M. 1988. *Costos de legalización de las empresas informales en Ecuador* [Legalisation costs of informal enterprises in Ecuador], unpublished paper. Santiago, PREALC, Regional Project Policies for the Informal Sector.

Portes, A.; Castells, M.; Benton, L. 1989. *The informal economy.* Baltimore, Johns Hopkins University Press.

Quijano, J.; Antia, F. 1988. *Costos de legalización de microempresas del sector informal* [Legalisation costs of informal sector micro enterprises], unpublished paper. Santiago, PREALC, Regional Project Policies for the Informal Sector.

Saenz, L.F. 1988. *Costos de legalización del sector informal urbano en Guatemala* [Legalisation costs of the urban informal sector in Guatemala], unpublished paper. Santiago, PREALC, Regional Project Policies for the Informal Sector.

Scholnik, M. 1988. *El mercado de servicios de taxis: Políticas de regulación y liberalización, 1978-87* [The taxi service market: Regulation and liberalisation policies, 1978-87], unpublished paper. Santiago, PREALC, Regional Project Policies for the Informal Sector.

Tokman, V.E. 1978. "An exploration into the nature of the informal sector relationship", in *World Development,* Sep.-Oct. 1978, Vol. 6, pp. 1065-1075.

— —. 1988. "The informal sector: A policy proposal", in K. Haq and U. Kirdar (eds.): *Managing human development.* Islamabad, North-South Roundtable Publications, pp. 67-82.

— —. 1989a. "Economic development and labour market segmentation in the Latin American periphery", in *Journal of Inter-American Studies and World Affairs,* Vol. 31, Nos. 1-2, pp. 23-47.

— —. 1989b. "Policies of heterogeneous informal sector in Latin America", in *World Development,* Vol. 17, No. 7, pp. 1067-1076.

Velasquez, M. 1988. *Los costos de legalización del sector informal urbano: Chile, estudio de casos* [The legalisation costs of the urban informal sector: Chile, case study], unpublished paper. Santiago, PREALC, Regional Project Policies for the Informal Sector.

Labour market responses

Structural adjustment programmes induce individual worker responses, community responses and enterprise responses. These must, of course, help shape subsequent labour market, social and economic policies. The following papers helped focus consideration of each of these sets of issues. Lourdes Benería, who has long been involved in analyses of women's vulnerable labour market involvement, through sub-contracting and related flexible forms of employment, highlights how Mexican families have survived in the context of a structural adjustment programme by resorting to more intensive labour force participation by all or most household members. Her paper points to the need to develop social and family policies to reduce the adjustment burden placed on women.

Lucio Geller, drawing on his experience in PREALC, paints a picture of adaptation of employment and labour practices by firms in Latin America, which in turn points to where labour policy might intervene to facilitate more equitable adjustment practices by firms. It also argues cogently for direct involvement by unions in raising productivity in the context of structural adjustment programmes, enabling the process to be less costly in social terms and in enlisting worker acceptance of change. Lucio Geller's paper raises questions that need to be addressed in every case of macro-economic adjustment, and indeed those were being addressed in enterprise-level flexibility surveys being conducted at the time this book was published.

Finally, Christoph Colclough returns to the awful reality of wage labour market responses in Africa in the 1980s. His analysis shows how far real wages in Africa fell in the period, and indeed how in the supposedly rigid public sector "protected" wages and salaries fell incredibly, much of the fall reflecting the conditionality clauses of structural adjustment agreements.

6

Structural adjustment, the labour market and the household: The case of Mexico*

by Lourdes Benería **

"... I warned Santander that the good that we could do for the nation would be worthless if we accepted the debt, because we would continue paying interest for century after century: the debt will defeat us in the end." (Simon Bolivar, as written by Gabriel García Márquez in *The General in his labyrinth*)

Introduction

Much has been said about the negative impact of structural adjustment policies (SAP) on the lives of a large proportion of the population in the countries where they have been implemented. At the time the research for this paper was initiated, in the summer of 1988, UNICEF had pioneered a series of studies documenting the devastating effects of SAP on the poor in Latin America and Africa (Cornia et al., 1987). Other studies on this subject have followed. Some of them have focused on the macroeconomic aspects of SAP and their effects on different economic sectors and population groups, particularly the most vulnerable (Pinstrup-Andersen, forthcoming). Others have focused on the significance of these changes for the labour market and labour policies as well as on the responses generated at the level of the firm, employment, labour supply and working conditions (Standing; and Roberts; both in this volume). A different set of studies has analysed coping strategies at the household level (Cornia, 1987). Finally, the gender dimensions in these adjustment processes have been emphasised through an analysis of aggregate data as well as by using more specific information at the level of the labour market and the household (Barbieri and Oliveira, 1987; Benería and Feldman, forthcoming).

* I would like to thank M.A. Díaz González for her research assistance, A. Bottum, E. Harber and A. Lind for their help with computer work, and W. Goldsmith, P. Olpadwala and G. Standing for their useful comments on the original draft of the paper. A closely related paper is included in L. Benería and S. Feldman (eds.): *Crises, households and women's work,* forthcoming.
** Cornell University, Ithaca, New York State.

One of the questions often posed by those concerned is how the poor survive the austerity programmes brought about by SAP during the 1980s. Given the already precarious conditions under which the poor lived before the debt crisis erupted, how have they managed to cope with the new situation? What are their survival strategies, or do the poor have any choice among them?[1] What kind of labour market adjustments have followed? Have collective strategies to deal with daily survival emerged? How is the crisis lived within a specific household and how does it affect different household members? Does it have a differentiated impact by gender and age? How has it affected women?

These were the initial questions behind the research done for this paper. Its objective was to document, in more detail than had been done in previous studies, the effects of SAP on daily life, including labour market strategies and other types of adjustment registered at the household level in Mexico City. The paper has two parts. The first summarises the main aspects of Mexico's adjustment policies designed to deal with the debt crisis, with particular emphasis given to policies that have had an impact on the distribution of resources and living standards. The second part deals more specifically with the coping mechanisms that have been followed at the household level, with special emphasis given to those relevant for the functioning of the labour market. The empirical study used for this analysis provides the basis for the main argument of the paper, namely that the profound restructuring of the Mexican economy has been accompanied by a parallel reorganisation of daily life in the area of reproductive as well as productive activities, with important implications for the participation of different household members in the labour market.

The debt crisis and adjustment policies

The most salient facts about the Mexican debt crisis are well known: an outstanding debt of $108 billion in 1989, seven years after its severity surfaced in the summer of 1982 when the IMF and the United States Government "rescued" Mexico from international insolvency with loans of $3.5 and $1.8 billion respectively; the fact that this is the second largest debt in Latin America after Brazil; a public debt service ratio of about 37 per cent (and of over 45 per cent for public and private debt combined); one of the heaviest long-term debt service ratios taken as a percentage of exports; a burden of debt payments for foreign and domestic debt that, on average, has represented close to 60 per cent of the federal budget; and a declining economic performance that saw a decrease of 3.1 per cent in real GNP during the 1982-88 period and in a debt/GNP ratio of over 95.

Yet Mexico is viewed by the American Government and the international financial community as a showcase of debt management and restructuring. It was for this reason that it was the first country to benefit from debt reduction and renegotiation through an agreement announced in July 1989 as a result of the Brady initiative. To back up this programme of debt reduction, Mexico received new loans of $3.6 and $1.5 billion from the IMF and the World Bank, respectively, during the spring of 1989. By the time the final result of debt negotiations was announced on February 1990, the estimated debt had been reduced to $80 billion, the first debt reduction negotiated under the Brady plan.

This expression of support from the international financial community represents the seal of approval for the very orthodox adjustment policies initiated with the August 1982 "rescue" and which has continued to the present. These IMF-type adjustment policies also launched Mexico into a process of economic restructuring that has had a profound effect on Mexico's economic landscape. The following are among the key features of this process.

1. Devaluation

An initial devaluation of the peso in 1982 was followed by a corresponding process of price increases and continuous depreciation of the currency throughout the period; thus, the exchange rate for the Mexican peso shifted from 23 pesos to US$1 in the summer of 1982 to 2,500 pesos to US$1 in the summer of 1989. The subsequent price increases have resulted in a rapid deterioration of real wages; during the 1981-88 period, the urban real minimum wage decreased by 46.4 per cent, the largest decrease (together with Ecuador) in Latin America during that period.

2. Austerity programme

Belt-tightening policies and drastic cuts in government spending and subsidies rapidly decreased the amount and quality of government services to severe minimum limits in areas such as health, education and social security. Thus, per capita public expenditure on education in 1984 had already been reduced to 66 per cent of that for 1982, while the corresponding reductions for health and social security were to 70 and 75 per cent of the 1982 figures, respectively (Lustig, 1987). This resulted in unemployment among previously well-paid government employees, with a corresponding impact on other sectors. For those still employed, real wages over the period have fallen to unprecedented low levels. Such has been the case for teachers, over half a million of whom joined a wildcat strike in April 1989 to ask for a 100 per cent wage increase.

3. *Privatisation, liberalisation and globalisation*

A process of economic restructuring, often called "modernización" in Mexico, has been a fundamental part of the adjustment since 1982. It has been strongly supported by Salinas de Gortari, as current President of Mexico and previously as Secretary of the Department of Planning and Budget (SPP) under the previous presidency of Miguel de la Madrid (Salinas de Gortari, 1987). The process has been intensified since 1987 as a result of the dramatic shifts in economic policy that were introduced together with the Pacto de Solidaridad Económica, and which have generated profound changes in the Mexican economy. The Pacto, the only unorthodox measure in Mexico's adjustment programme adopted before the 1988 election, was an agreement between the Government, businesses and unions, based on a wage and price freeze (including exchange rate stability) which reduced wage increases to practically zero and inflation from a level of 200 per cent in 1987 to about 20 per cent in 1988.

"Modernisation" has been shaped by a variety of policies, including fiscal and monetary tightening and a series of structural changes at different levels. First, a very extensive process of privatisation has been undertaken. It has placed previously state-controlled industries in private hands and reduced public investment dramatically. Estimates of the number of firms controlled by the Government show a decrease from close to 1,200 in 1982 to 237 in 1988 (Salinas de Gortari, 1987; Olave, 1988). Some industries have been privatised *completely*, such as automobiles and some branches of the chemical industry, textiles and various sectors of the construction industry like cement. In others, such as tourism and entertainment, the Government has substantially reduced its participation. Second, the economy has been opened up to international competition by such means as the liberalisation of imports, the promotion of foreign investment, and an aggressive policy of export promotion.

Thus, the average import tariff was reduced from about 100 per cent in 1982 to 35 per cent by 1987 and, during this period, 70 per cent of imports were liberalised (Olave, 1988).[2] The result has been a considerable rise in imports of consumer as well as capital goods. Likewise, government estimates show that direct foreign investment has increased gradually - reaching, for example, an annual growth rate of 69.4 per cent in 1987 (Olave, 1988). The old policy which restricted foreign ownership to a maximum of 49 per cent of invested capital has been lifted, and foreigners can now manage Mexican firms if they get immigrant status. Finally, the Mexican economy has been reoriented towards the export sector, as a means of financing the debt, with the use of a wide range of incentives that have resulted in a considerable increase in exports in recent years, after a drop in the mid-1980s.[3] Large multinational firms and the "maquiladora" industries, whose growth has been considerable during the crisis period, can be counted among those that have been the most dynamic exporters and have benefited most from export promotion policies.[4]

4. Productivity and competitiveness

The above measures have been accompanied by policies intended to rationalise and reorganise the public sector, including the trimming of government bureaucracies and waste. Together with the push to introduce and update modern technologies in the public and private sectors, this is part of the effort to increase productivity and competitiveness throughout the economic system. It is also part of the IMF-inspired international shift towards greater reliance on the market mechanism to allocate resources and influence decision-making.

Taken together, it is clear that these policies have initiated a new period of restructuring and globalisation of the Mexican economy similar to that undergone by other countries during the past decade. In this way, debt-related adjustment policies have been used to shift Mexican capitalism to a new stage of higher integration with the global economy. As Rendón and Salas (1988) have argued, these changes amount to a shift from a model of accumulation based on the domestic market and import substitution to one oriented towards the international market.

The success in the export sector, together with the orthodoxy with which the IMF-style adjustment policies have been followed, account for the extent to which Mexico is viewed - by the international financial community and the American Government - as the model that other countries should follow in dealing with their own debt crises. It also accounts for the American Government's interest in seeing Mexico as the first country to reduce its debt. As Martin Feldstein put it, at a conference on world economic restructuring held in Mexico City in 1987, "current changes in Mexico are part of a process of economic restructuring that will modify and wake up the entire world" (Feldstein, 1987).

The social costs of adjustment

Typically, the Mexican SAP have been implemented at high cost and devastating consequences for a large proportion of the Mexican population. Rising unemployment, price increases, the reduction of services, and the reorientation of the economy away from the domestic market have resulted in a persistent deterioration of living standards, particularly for those whose living depends on fixed wages and salaries. This is what some authors have referred to as the "crushing of labour", as the relative share of GNP going to wages has fallen drastically.[5] The disparity between price and salary increases has affected most social classes, as we will see, although it is clear that the poorer groups are the most vulnerable given that their subsistence is severely threatened.

To illustrate, according to a study released in August 1988, a standardised basket of 28 products considered absolutely indispensable for survival (Canasta Obrera Indispensable or COI), was estimated to cost 12,924 pesos per person daily, almost 5,000 pesos above the daily minimum wage.[6] Many poor households, of course, do not even have anybody earning a minimum wage; as will be seen, their survival depends upon the pooling of income among household members.

To be sure, severe poverty problems existed in Mexico before the debt crisis erupted. The poor have traditionally included peasants and agricultural workers as well as urban households outside the formal economy (Lustig, 1980; Benería and Roldán, 1987). It is well known that, despite its relatively good economic performance during the post-Second World War decades, Mexico has maintained a very skewed distribution of income and resources, which has often resulted in welfare indicators below those of other countries with a similar per capita income. This is the case in the area of health, nutrition, education, as well as housing (Lustig, 1987).

All indicators seem to suggest that the redistribution of resources generated by the debt crisis and the adjustment policies that have followed have intensified these inequalities. In particular, the diminishing proportion of income going to wages and salaries and the drastic cuts in government expenditures have contributed to this trend.[7] First, as the modernisation process and cost reduction policies designed to meet international competition continue, the pressure to reduce wages and weaken unions has intensified. This has affected a section of the working population that previously had enjoyed relatively high wages and stable employment, namely the stable working class and middle class, whose relative position has deteriorated. One study shows that real income for some of these sections decreased very drastically during the 1985-88 period, while that of the poorest families seems to have increased (Insituto Nacional del Consumidor, 1989). As will be argued, this might be a reflection of the enormous effort made by the poorest households to survive at a subsistence level, while those at higher income levels had a greater "margin of subsistence".

Second, income distribution seems to have deteriorated overall. Rudiger Dornbusch (1988), for example, has stated that "there is little doubt that distribution has worsened over the 1980s". Official statistics for 1977 show that the richest 20 per cent of the population controlled 54.4 per cent of the income, whereas the poorest 2 per cent received only 2.9 per cent. More recent private surveys suggest that the subsequent tendency has been towards even higher inequality (Quick, 1989). At the same time, some sectors of the business class have benefited considerably from the economic changes associated with the restructuring of the economy, particularly those connected with the export sector, the internationalisation of the Mexican economy, and the deregulation of economic activity. The financial sector is one of them. Thus, the Mexican stock exchange, like others in other countries during this period, had been booming before the Wall Street crisis of October 1987, and it has recovered since then. As an illustration, one brokerage house (casa de bolsa) reported net profits of 88.4 per cent of capital in 1987 and an average of 53.1 per cent for the 1986-88 period (Lissakers and Zamora, 1989). Although a portion of the professional middle class has also benefited from the stock market and has used its boom to compensate for falling real wages,[8] the great beneficiaries are those connected with financial capital associated with "modernisation" and the new model of export-led accumulation.

For other sections of the population, drastic reductions in living standards have been well documented. However, the details of this reduction are still a matter of controversy. Lustig (1987), for example, argues that, regarding basic food consumption, "it is possible to say that the crisis has not resulted in problems of food availability, nor has it resulted in a clear deterioration of the average daily diet" (p. 245). On the other hand, as Lustig herself also points out, average aggregate figures can be very misleading. In fact most indications suggest that, at least for the poor, the deterioration in food consumption has been drastic.

Social indicators also point towards diminishing health and educational standards as well as towards a deterioration of the quality of life - as suggested by an increase in the crime rate and by the dramatic deterioration of public transport and pollution standards (Lustig, 1987; Rohter, 1989). In addition, some negative consequences of economic restructuring have been felt with particular intensity in specific areas and sectors - as illustrated by the retrenchment under way in steel towns affected by government divestiture and the pressure of "modernisation".[9]

It is no wonder, therefore, that many of these changes have resulted in progressively more open public discontent and have generated drastic political changes - such as the appearance of "Cardenismo", i.e., the appearance of a new populism around the figure of Cárdenas, and the decrease in political support for the governing party. As a journalist put it, the significance of the large number of votes that went to Cárdenas in the 1988 election amounts to a "non-violent revolution" in a way that "Mexico will never be the same again". The political significance of that election, which threatened the long domination of Mexican politics by the governing party, cannot be underestimated. It explains the United States' continuous interest in making Mexico a showcase of debt renegotiation and forgiveness, and may also be at the root of the recently announced plans to begin official talks towards a joint common market for the North American countries. In what follows, we will examine in more detail the basis for this discontent, by analysing the ways in which SAP have affected the daily life of different households, their organisation and modes of survival.

A sample of Mexico City households

The research on which this paper is based was carried out in Mexico City in the summer of 1988. In addition to posing the questions listed earlier in this paper, the study responded to a very concrete interest, namely how some of the households that we had visited during a study of industrial home work carried out in 1981-82 (Benería and Roldán, 1987) had survived under the

Table 1. Bi-weekly income categories, 1988 (Mexican pesos)[1] (N=55)

Socio-economic category	Mean income ('000)	% of households	Average household size
1. Extreme poverty	114	38.2	5.9
2. Subsistence	210	14.5	6.2
3. Poor	299	27.2	5.8
4. Lower middle class	626	9.1	4.6
5. Middle class	1 111	10.9	5.0
Total	338	100.0	5.7

[1] 2,300 pesos to US$1 (summer, 1988).

severe burden of the crisis. Fieldwork began at the time when many Mexicans were still questioning the results of the presidential election of July 1988 in which Salinas de Gortari had been declared the winner. The political truce between the Government, business and workers created by the Pacto de Solidaridad during the pre-election period was starting to wear thin, and Mexicans seemed to be caught up between the massive demonstrations in which Cárdenas became the central figure and symbol of the opposition, and the expectations created by the new presidential term.

The analysis that follows is based on interviews with members of 55 households derived from a larger sample of 140 households engaged in home work during the 1981-82 period and scattered in different areas of Mexico City.[10] Generalisations from this non-random sample must be viewed with caution, although there is no reason to believe that the sample is not representative and therefore indicative of the changes and struggles that have characterised Mexican households during this period. The interviews which took place, with only two exceptions, within the homes of those interviewed, were carried out in a variety of "colonias" or neighbourhoods.[11] In most cases, the questions were answered by women - usually by the housewife/mother but occasionally by others such as a grandmother, sisters and daughters - although, in the few cases in which the husband/father was present, he often took an active role in the exchange.

The average household size for the sample was 5.72, slightly lower than that reported by studies carried out in the early 1980s (Benería and Roldán, 1987). Variations by income category are reported in table 1 and suggest a negative correlation between household size and income. Nuclear family households represented the large majority in the sample, with only 12.7 per cent classified as extended families, and 14.5 per cent of all households headed by women. Average bi-weekly income was of 338,712 Mexican pesos or about US$147. As expected, practically all households had more than one income earner - the average being 2.3 - while 50.3 per cent of those working for an income did so in some form of job in the informal sector.

Figure 1. Housing categories, 1988 (percentages)

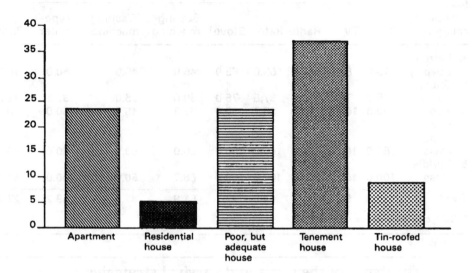

The breakdown of households by income categories included in table 1 was estimated with reference to the minimum wage and baskets of consumer goods standardised during the time of the study.[12] As can be seen from the table, two-fifths of households in the sample were poor, with more than half extremely poor or at bare subsistence levels.

A similar picture is given by sample data on housing: the great majority of these households were living in very poor conditions. As figure 1 shows, nearly half (46.3 per cent) of them lived in dwellings with tin roofs and tenements while almost one-quarter (24.1 per cent) lived in poor but adequate dwellings. The rest of the households (close to 30 per cent) lived either in residential one-family homes or in apartments which corresponded to lower-middle-class or middle-class standards.

Other indicators of consumption standards are presented in table 2, which shows the proportion of households owning different consumption goods, by income category. The figures indicate that the possession of a telephone and car was the most visible sign of a middle-class standard. On the other hand, a high proportion of poor households owned radio and television sets, even though, as will be seen, the crisis had probably made many of them useless, for lack of repair.

Table 2. Consumption indicators by income category, 1988 (N=51)

Socio-economic category	Percentage of households that have:								
	Car	TV	Radio	Refr.	Stove[1]	Sewing machine	Washing machine	Type-writer	Phone
1. Extreme poverty	15.0	85.0	90.0	55.0	65.0	45.0	40.0	50.0	10.0
2. Subsistence	25.0	75.0	100.0	37.5	75.0	50.0	25.0	37.5	12.5
3. Poor	20.0	100.0	80.0	66.7	80.0	53.3	45.7	60.0	26.7
4. Lower middle class	80.0	100.0	100.0	100.0	100.0	60.0	60.0	80.0	80.0
5. Middle class	100.0	100.0	100.0	100.0	100.0	66.7	50.0	100.0	66.7
Total	33.3	90.7	90.7	64.8	77.7	51.8	42.5	59.2	27.7

[1] Refers to large stove with oven.

The depth of the crisis and survival strategies

Although our sample does not include upper middle-class and wealthy households, for the categories included the effects of the crisis were felt strongly by all households, despite some differences across income levels. As table 3 illustrates, "great difficulties" in making ends meet were perceived by a large proportion of the households; although that proportion was lower for the middle-class households, it still represented half of them. This implied that they had been forced to make drastic adjustments in their budgets and consumption habits. Even those who did not fall into this category reported that they had "some difficulties", and had therefore made "important adjustments" in their expenditures. Unemployment, housing and debt were also among the problems causing great difficulties, although the proportion of households reporting them were significantly lower (and zero in the case of debt for lower middle-class and middle-class households). However, unemployment and debt were often reported as having caused "some difficulties" by households in all income categories - the proportion ranging between 17 per cent and 40 per cent for unemployment and between 33 per cent and 62 per cent for debt. Belt-tightening therefore has been felt deeply across households and socio-economic categories.

Interestingly, very few households complained about the availability of food or other basic goods. Only a few mentioned occasional difficulties finding some products in the market. During the time of fieldwork, long and very tense queues developed in some "colonias" in front of shops that distributed government-subsidised food ("Canasta Básica") at lower prices.[13] However, the same products for which women stood in line were readily available, often in the same

Table 3. The depth of the crisis, by income categories (N=55)

Socio-economic category	Percentage of households reporting "great difficulties" in:			
	Budget	Unemployment	Housing	Debt
1. Extreme poverty	86	19	10	19
2. Subsistence	87	13	12	13
3. Poor	67	7	21	13
4. Lower middle class	80	20	–	–
5. Middle class	50	17	17	–

shop, at higher prices. The "great difficulties" mentioned in many households therefore were not caused by food scarcity or deficiency in distribution, but by insufficient household earnings to buy it. As one of the women interviewed, a young and energetic mother of 23 years with two children of her own and three more from her husband's previous marriage, put it: "When our income cannot pay for what I need to buy every day, I feel desperate and I ask myself whether we can survive this situation."

In all cases the depth of the crisis was felt in a way that escapes statistics and analytical quantification. To illustrate with one of the households classified under "extreme poverty", there were no chairs to sit on, the children did not wear shoes, the roof was leaking, the floor was not tiled, the inside walls were extremely dirty, the house had only three small rooms (kitchen, dining-room and a bedroom) for a family of seven, while extra space was rented to another family for very little money. Job insecurity for the father and only occasional paid work for the mother was a constant source of anxiety and even despair. Yet despair was not exclusive to extremely poor households. Tension and anguish about making ends meet was found among better-off households as well.

What kind of adjustments had been made to deal with the effects of the crisis? One of the overwhelming impressions during fieldwork came from the observation that, in the absence of a welfare State and of collective efforts to ensure daily survival at the neighbourhood and community level, it is at the level of the household where the fierce struggle is centred. The majority of households were surviving, even if at a very high cost. Our data show that there were two types of families. A small proportion (just over 5 per cent of our sample) were practically disintegrating under what seemed to be insurmountable problems: unemployment, inability to generate the income necessary for bare survival, domestic violence, housing needs, absence of any community support, abandonment and so on. These were cases often associated with a drunken husband, prostitution, drugs or some other forms of criminal behaviour; the economic crisis probably intensified rather than created these problems.

The majority of households, however, had reorganised their lives to deal with the problems brought about by the crisis and had succeeded in various degrees. In what follows, the different coping mechanisms observed are classified under three basic categories: (a) labour market adjustments; (b) budget changes; and (c) restructuring of daily life.

(a) Labour market adjustments

A common response to the crisis had been the increase in the number of household members participating in the labour market, in order to contribute to family income. As reported in table 4, the proportion of affected households was highest for the middle income categories; the lower proportion for the poorest group is likely to reflect the already high number of family members earning an income before 1982. Two groups of people in our sample were the most affected by this response. One was the population of teenagers among the non-middle-class income categories who, under the pressures of participating in the paid labour force, had to discontinue their education, particularly by not moving to higher levels of schooling. This was found to be common among teenagers finishing secondary public education. Given the duration of the crisis, this interruption in schooling was likely to be permanent, therefore leaving a lasting negative impact on the educational and skill level of those affected. For a country like Mexico, much in need of a more skilled labour force to increase productivity, this schooling effect is likely to have a long-term economic and social impact.

Women constitute the second group affected across income categories; their initially lower involvement in the labour force, particularly among mothers, made them part of the labour pool from which to draw at a time of crisis. Studies on the effect of SAP on women's employment show a remarkable increase in their participation rate (Oliveira, 1988). Interestingly enough, we found that, although increased labour force participation was typically the case for women without children, mothers with husbands or a male partner were still the last household members to enter the paid labour force and still worked at home to an unexpected degree (34 per cent in our sample).[14]

There seem to be three main reasons for this. One is the prevalent division of labour which assigns to the mother the primary task of child care and domestic work, i.e. the main responsibility for reproductive activities. This division of labour, with the notion that the mother should stay at home, particularly if children are small, is still deeply ingrained in the Mexican family. Related to this is the still rather prevalent opposition of the husband or male companion to the mother's paid work. This explains, for example, the case of women who, despite serious financial difficulties and their desire to earn an income, were not in the paid labour force because the husband "would feel humiliated" or "would not let her work outside of home". Finally, women tend to be the least schooled members of the household, making them less able to

Table 4. Some coping strategies, by income category

Socio-economic category	Proportion of households % that resorted *regularly* to:			
	New HH members in LF	Buy less food and clothes	Change in purchasing habits	Decrease in visits to family
1. Extreme poverty	38	76	76	57
2. Subsistence	62	75	63	62
3. Poor[1]	64	67	73	40
4. Middle class	17	50	50	33

[1] The lower middle-class category is not reported, due to incomplete data.

find formal employment or even to perform tasks that require some skill in the informal labour market.

Still the large majority (almost 66 per cent) of the mothers with a male partner earned some income, two-thirds of them working in the informal sector either continuously or sporadically. That is, less than one-third had jobs in the formal sector, and this was confined particularly to middle-class women. The rest worked either sporadically or continuously under conditions associated with the informal sector. The importance of this sector for women's earnings is therefore obvious and due to at least two reasons. The main reason was the difficulty for poor women to find employment either full time or with any degree of job security. A second reason was their preference for work that could be done either in the home (as in the case of industrial home work) or in the surrounding community (as street vendors for example) in order to better integrate it with domestic work and the care of children. This preference, however, was determined by the lack of alternatives to deal with child care and domestic work.

Women's high involvement with the informal economy is linked to the typical precariousness of work in this sector, a subject that has been analysed extensively and is not the focus of this paper. Although it was clearly the main source of women's earnings in our sample, the insecurity and low earnings associated with it were also a source of anxiety. To illustrate, less than one-fourth of the women who had been engaged in industrial home work six years earlier had continued doing it, either because it was no longer available or because it was too sporadic and insecure to rely on it. As a result, they had been forced to look for other sources of income.

An alternative labour market strategy was found among those who worked overtime or had more than one job. This normally involved the more "established" workers in the formal sector such as, for example, nurses, carpenters and other construction workers. However, the precariousness of employment conditions had made it difficult for them to find extra work in the formal market. As a result, some skilled workers had become self-employed;

given the possibility of increasing prices for their services, they were among those who could cope best with the crisis.

A clear conclusion to be drawn from this information is that, despite the effort at increasing the participation of diverse family members in paid production, there remains a good proportion of untapped labour that is under-employed or working at the margins: men and women workers that cannot find a full-time job and others working very long hours but always looking for better job opportunities or working conditions. The informal sector absorbs a portion of this labour reserve but, as Bryan Roberts argues in this volume, under deteriorating working conditions as a result of the crisis. For employers, this means that labour can be found at any time, in any amount, and under any conditions, representing a slight improvement over the precariousness in which many workers find themselves. If anything, the debt crisis has intensified the problem of labour absorption, thereby further facilitating the process of labour flexibilisation, a very important component in Mexico's economic restructuring and export-led growth.

(b) Household budget changes

It is probably no exaggeration to say that austerity policies have altered the budgets of practically all Mexican households. Budget adjustments have been drastic for a large proportion of the population. In our sample, 69.4 per cent of the households regularly bought less food, clothing, shoes and other daily expenses such as transport, drinks and snacks than in the pre-1982 period. Table 4 shows the high proportion of households that had regularly been purchasing less food and clothes - the lowest being 50 per cent for the middle-class group.

What exactly had been cut, however, varied according to household income and social background. Thus, although practically all households had curtailed meat consumption, poor families had eliminated it from their diet. Similarly, the poor had completely eliminated other products, such as canned foods and a rather large number of fruits and basic foods, such as milk, unless they were subsidised.[15] Most poor households were no longer buying *new* clothes and shoes, nor could they afford any new household equipment.

Middle-class families had a thicker cushion to start with. Their budget cuts concentrated on non-essential goods such as restaurant eating, coffee and drinks outside of the home, imported goods such as olives and wine, photography-related expenses, gifts, domestic service, clothing, trips, particularly trips abroad, and parties. For many, this appeared as a shift down the social ladder which in some cases seemed to be a source of great anxiety.

For households in extreme poverty, or around the bare subsistence level, the pressure to concentrate on the most urgent needs implied a continuous neglect of others such as home unkeep. Unpainted walls, unpaved floors, leaking roofs and broken tables and chairs were a common sight not just in the poorest homes, but in others that had regularly taken care of these tasks. We found several homes with a variety of items (refrigerators, television sets, washing machines, radios and mixers) that could not be used because the household could not afford any repair. As one mother with five school-age children put it: "Our priority is to buy the minimum of school supplies that we can afford and to postpone repairs". The significance of such processes should be emphasised, since they imply that a negative investment in the infrastructure of households had been taking place. In turn, this is likely to lead to an underestimation of the negative impact of the crisis.

(c)   The restructuring of daily life

Budget adjustments have generated many changes in the way households organise themselves and live their daily lives. The following are typical of these readjustments.

Changes in purchasing habits

Close to 73 per cent of the households in our sample stated that they were shopping in cheaper markets, most of them regularly. For poor families, this often meant buying daily supplies from street vendors whose products tend to be of lower quality than those in regular shops. The tightness of budgets reinforced this tendency, since only small quantities could be bought at a time, therefore often making shopping a daily chore. Shopping on a daily basis was reinforced by other factors, such as unrepaired refrigerators in which food could not be preserved, with the corresponding intensification of time spent in this aspect of domestic work. Among households that could afford weekly shopping, trips to the large central market in Mexico City were common in order to obtain better food at lower prices. Given the size of Mexico City, this could be done only with a car or by organising several family members to help with the shopping, usually on Saturday; the latter required an effort that only a few households could manage. In any case, changes in purchasing habits had taken place through income categories - the lowest proportion (50 per cent of the households) again corresponding to the middle-class group.

For middle-class families, the search for lower prices often meant shopping in markets away from their neighbourhoods. In some cases, it also meant the co-ordination of shopping with other family members, including the use of extended family networks. As explained by a middle-class woman who had married in 1985: "My aunts know where the bargains are, so I see my aunts and my mother more than I ever did." In any case, the greater availability of private transport, and also of cash, for middle-class families made it easier for them to benefit from shopping in large quantities and in the less expensive markets outside their communities.

A different type of adjustment resulted from the need to save on transport and other daily expenses. Thus, almost 51 per cent of the households in our sample had decreased or eliminated trips to visit relatives and friends, and the attendance at family parties and religious holidays. This applied to intra-city visits as well as to traditional annual or semi-annual trips to other parts of Mexico, such as for those associated with Christmas, vacations and other family gatherings. Recent immigrants to Mexico City complained bitterly of their inability to return to their home towns "as they used to before the crisis". Others pointed out that, as new immigrants to Mexico City, they had not been able to fulfil the promise of remittances to their ageing parents and other family members. For some sections of the middle class, the curtailment of travel abroad as an important reduction in their expenses represented a drastic change in their living standards, and also a source of bitter complaints.

Social life had also been affected by the reduction or elimination of expenses associated with parties and other social activities. The traditional and important "fiesta" organised for the fifteenth birthday of daughters in Mexico could no longer be afforded by many families. In one neighbourhood, at least one of the churches had begun to organise parties to honour several 15-year-olds at the same time. This was one of the few coping mechanisms encountered that represented a semi-collective form of dealing with the crisis. Finally, the need to reduce expenses had changed the way different household members organised leisure time. For example, some parents of teenagers said that on Sundays they no longer went anywhere outside their neighbourhood, and preferred to let their children go out ("weekend movies have been cut to a minimum").

The role of the family

During our fieldwork, the Mexico City daily *El Excelsior* published an article emphasising the role of the Mexican family as the main pillar in efforts to deal with the crisis. Our study supports this thesis. The "culture of ingenuity" around which daily life is being organised for that purpose is indeed centred on the family. There has been a major gathering of forces at the household level, which corresponds to a *privatisation* of the struggle; in the absence of a welfare State and in the face of the decrease in governmental services and subsidies, the family has become the only source of support and of alternative strategies.

An initial objective of our research was to investigate the extent to which collective efforts had been developed, as has been the case with Peru's "comedores populares" or soup kitchens and with Bolivia's "olla comun" or common pot (Lafosse, 1986; Cornia, 1987). Despite the fact that much collective organising at other levels had developed in Mexico,[16] the virtual absence of such efforts *at the level of daily life* provided a sharp contrast at the time of our fieldwork.[17] The private household, therefore, was left facing the crisis alone, with some help received only from the extended family. However, given the nuclear character of the urban household in Mexico City, this help was found to be minimal - the most common in our sample being the grandmother's help in domestic work and child care so as to allow the mother to participate in the labour market.

To be sure, this privatisation of the struggle was devastating for the few families that were disintegrating. For the large majority of the households, however, the gathering of forces and pooling of resources represented a heroic effort, described by some of our interviewees as resulting from greater family unity ("We are more united now because we cannot risk fighting among ourselves") and ability to plan ("We have to plan everything and our level of communication has increased"). No family member could evade this effort, particularly in poor households. This is not to say that tensions did not develop within the family, but that a conscious effort was made to avoid them in order to deal with the most pressing issues.

Tensions in fact did develop, since this unity and resourcefulness came at a cost. First, the continuous struggle of each household to survive seemed to be accompanied by mistrust and hostility towards outsiders. Thus, interviewees often complained about their neighbours and community members for their behaviour ("They stole chicken from our backyard", "We cannot rely on them for help", etc.). Likewise, feelings of frustration were often expressed as aggression towards outsiders ("When I am upset, I don't want to take it out on my sister, so I push people when I get on the bus").

Second, tensions resulted from the unequal distribution of the burden of survival among family members. The crisis had resulted in an intensification of domestic work - from daily shopping due to more restrictive budgets, to the need for increased cleaning and tidying when spaces are reduced, to more cooking, fixing, mending and sewing at home. Although all family members participated in these tasks, a large proportion of this work fell upon women, regardless of whether or not they were also working in the labour market. Thus, in 68.8 per cent of the households in which the crisis had generated changes in domestic work, it was perceived that women's work had increased. For some middle-class housewives, this had been accompanied by a reduction in domestic help, with the subsequent perception of isolation, loss of social status and downward social mobility.

In addition, the crisis had not visibly changed previous inequalities in income pooling and intra-household distribution of resources; although this was not the focus of our research, we found no clear change in previous patterns, by which women's income is totally used for household expenses, while men's is pooled only partially (Benería and Roldán, 1987). As in the earlier study, many women received an allowance from their husbands or male companions, often without knowing their total earnings. When the allowance was viewed as very small, or when it was sporadic and uncertain, it tended to be a source of bitterness and complaints. In households at the verge of collapse, the burden on the mother tended to be overwhelming; the usual problems of survival in this case were intensified by the tensions generated by domestic violence, inability to meet the family's needs, and the awareness of sinking into a world of despair.

For daughters employed in the labour market, the pressure to participate in domestic work had contributed to what seems to be a rising consciousness regarding a gender-based asymmetry in the division of labour, thus creating new tensions between them and, in particular, their brothers. Thus, in 53.1 per cent of the households in which the crisis had generated changes in domestic work, it was felt that daughters had to help more. Older daughters in particular felt this burden most intensely; even then they held a full-time job, they were expected to take up a great deal of responsibility in the home - responsibility not expected from their older brothers or fathers. In comparison with their mothers, the daughters' higher levels of skills made them more likely candidates for paid work outside of the home and raised expectations regarding their contribution to household income ("They expect that I can solve all their problems"). This is what I have called "the oldest daughter syndrome" (Benería, 1989), leading also to bitter complaints on the daughter's part.

In the case of households headed by women, the burden on the mother (or grandmother) depended on the age and composition of other family members; although the burden could be heavy if children were small, it was alleviated when they - and particularly daughters - were old enough to contribute some income and share responsibilities. The absence of an adult male income in any case explains why all women who headed a household were engaged in paid work; the choice was basically non-existent.

In sum, the crisis has intensified the contradictory forces within the family. On the one hand, it is the only source of protection for all members; there is nowhere else to turn to. The family is essential for survival, for fun and social activity, for warmth, love and protection. The degree to which these functions are exercised in the midst of such difficulties is indeed moving. The household represents the locus of this survival - realised through the interdependency of its members. On the other hand, this co-operation takes place within the context of a "forced" unity and existing tensions, which are intensified by the sheer weight of the struggle as well as from its unequal distribution among family members.

How long this "unity" can last will depend on different factors, including the duration of the crisis. Some of these tensions, in fact, might be at the root of future changes. For example, the pooling of work and income and, in particular, the responsibilities taken on by women, might lead some household members, unduly burdened by their contribution to the household, to break the unity by, for example, leaving it - depending upon available alternatives - to survive on their own.

Concluding comments

The debt crisis and corresponding SAP in Mexico have set up the framework in which the "supply-side" model of labour market policies (Standing, in this volume) has been applied. The drastic decrease in people's living standards and devastating deterioration of real wages has typically worsened the relative position of labour. Thus the profound restructuring of the economy has forced the restructuring of daily life, while the privatisation of the economy has had a parallel in the privatisation of survival centred around the mostly nuclear household. Most families so far have survived the crisis through an heroic effort, in which all members participate through new combinations of work for self-consumption and work for income. This has implied an increased involvement of various household members in market activities, but also an intensification of reproductive activities, often resulting in an unequal distribution of the burden within the household.

The Brady plan of debt reduction arrived at a point when, at least for the poor, resources had already been stretched to the utmost. It arrived precisely after the danger of bankruptcy on the part of the international commercial banks had disappeared, as a result of the severe austerity programmes implemented to repay the debt. For Mexico, the current debt reduction is likely to be too little and too late. For the middle class, the fall in the standard of living has been the source of a great deal of anxiety and frustration. The amount of debt renegotiated and reduced so far is unlikely to shift significantly the burden of austerity. In fact, the late arrival of the Brady plan and the difficulties of implementing it illustrate the impotency of many countries with policies at the mercy of international finance.

What are the alternatives facing Mexico? At best, its development might follow the Chilean model, with growth badly distributed through a dualistic economy of haves and have-nots. If the existing export-led "modernisation" based on cheap labour prevails, a "social adjustment" model (Standing, in this volume) could be introduced through high-productivity/high-wage policies. As Geller (in this volume) has argued, this would require the introduction of technological and organisational changes to increase productivity. An important ingredient in this policy would be the upgrading of skills and the training of the workforce for the requirements of the labour market. In particular, much can be done to implement these policies with regard to the informal market. A high-productivity/high-wage policy would facilitate the growth of the domestic market and the implementation of redistributive measures. If, instead, the present situation of low-wage policies with deteriorating working conditions continues, the impatience that has surfaced during the past few years is likely to intensify.

Notes

[1] As has been pointed out by other authors, the word "strategy" implies the possibility to choose among alternatives. However, the choices are very much reduced by the extreme scarcity of resources and precarious living conditions. In such cases, the use of the expression "survival strategies" is therefore not very appropriate.

[2] Previous to this trade liberalisation, Mexico had joined GATT in 1986 and negotiated trade regulations with the United States in 1987.

[3] These incentives range from export credits and tax reductions to trade agreements, the gradual devaluation of the peso, and the low-wage policies geared to increase the competitiveness of Mexican products in the international market.

[4] *El Financiero,* 6 Oct. 1987, p. 37.

[5] By 1982, this share represented 36 per cent of GNP (down from 40 per cent in 1976) and it has declined further throughout the decade (Edel and Edel, 1989).

[6] The basket of 28 products was selected from a larger basket of 118 products or *Canasta Obrera Básica* (COB), considered to be basic for an adequate working class standard of living (*Uno Mas Uno, 8 Aug.,* 1988).

[7] For example, the proportion of total income going to wages and salaries diminished from 42 per cent in 1982 to less than 30 per cent in 1987 (Lustig, 1988).

[8] The loss of about three-quarters of the stock market's value during the crash was in fact a severe blow for this group (Edel and Edel, 1989).

[9] Such is the case with the cities of Monterrey and Moncloa in the north-east which have been negatively affected by the Government's policies towards the steel industry. These policies have resulted in the loss of thousands of jobs, with their corresponding negative impact on the city's economy.

[10] Close to 50 per cent of the households interviewed were derived from the original list of 140. The rest were arrived at through a snowballing technique, which included middle-class households for comparative purposes.

[11] They concentrated in the following "colonias": Palmitas, San Rafael, San Andrés de Atoto, Lázaro Cárdenas, El Molinito, Moctezuma, Oriente, Cándido Aguilar, Narvarte, Coyoacán, and Portales.

[12] The breakdown in income categories was established as follows:

		Income range (Mexican pesos)
1. Extreme poverty:	below COI	<193,999
2. Subsistence:	COI-COB estimate*	194,000-224,999
3. Poor but adequate income		225,000-499,999
4. Lower middle class		500,000-999,999
5. Middle class		>1,000,000
* Twice the minimum wage.		

[13] The tension was due to the fact that shops often run out of the subsidised product and those in line (overwhelmingly women) were fighting to be as close as possible to the head of the line.

[14] This is a conclusion reached by other observers as well (conversation with J.A. Alonso).

[15] Some families survived with a few basic staples, namely rice and beans, oil, tortillas, milk and some inexpensive fruits. During fieldwork, we encountered anxious housewives worrying about how they would pay for the beans and rice that they needed for the day.

[16] One example is the many groups that had developed around housing and other urban issues (Ramirez, 1986), while political mobilisation intensified around issues connected with the crisis. Municipal election campaigns, for example, were used to organise around basic needs and democratic rights. However, these efforts were carried out at the political level, not at the level of daily life around the household as was the case in other collective efforts in Latin America.

[17] Since then, different efforts seem to have emerged, particularly among women's groups, to organise such collective efforts around basic needs.

Bibliography

Barbieri, T.; Oliveira, O. 1987. *La presencia de las mujeres en America* Latina en una decada de crisis [The presence of women in Latin America in a decade of crisis]. Santo Domingo, Ediciones Populares Feministas.

Benería, L.; 1989. "The debt crisis in Mexico: Restructuring the economy and the household", in Benería and Feldman (eds.).

Benería, L.; Feldman, S. (eds.). *Crises, households and women's work.* Forthcoming.

Benería, L.; Roldán, M. 1987. *The crossroads of class and gender.* Industrial *home work, subcontracting and household dynamics in Mexico City.* Chicago, the University of Chicago Press.

Cornia, G.A. 1987. "Adjustment at the household level: Potentials and limitations of survival strategies", in Cornia et al below, Vol. 1, pp. 90-104.

Cornia, G.A.; Jolly, R.; Stewart, F. (eds.). 1987. *Adjustment with a human* face. *Protecting the vulnerable and promoting growth.* New York, Oxford University Press, two volumes.

Dornbusch, R. 1988. *Mexico: Stabilization, debt and growth.* Boston, Massachusetts, Massachusetts Institute of Technology. Unpublished paper.

Edel, M.; Edel, C.K. 1989. *Analyzing Mexico's accumulation crisis.* Paper presented at the Social Sciences Research workshop on "Issues in Mexico's security". Mexico City, 22-24 Feb.

Feldstein, M. 1987. "El curso probable de la economia en los proximos anos" [The probable economic course in the next years], in de la Madrid, M. et al. *Cambio Estructural en Mexico y en el Mundo.* Mexico City, Fondo de Cultura Economica/Secretaria de Programacion y Presupuesto.

Instituto Nacional del Consumidor. 1989. "El gasto alimentario de la poblacion de escasos recursos de la ciudad de Mexico" [The food expenditure of low budget people in the city of Mexico], in *Comercio Exterior,* Vol. 39, No. 1, pp. 52-58.

Lissakers, K.; Zamora, J. 1989. *The financial sector in Mexico's economic reform.* Paper presented at the conference on Mexico: "Contrasting visions". New York City, Apr.

Lustig, N. 1987. "Crisis económica y niveles de vida en Mexico: 1982-85" [Economic crisis and living standards in Mexico: 1982-85], in *Estudios Económicos,* Vol. 2, No. 2, July-Dec., pp. 227-49.

— —. 1988. "La desigualdad economica" [Economic inequality], in *Nexos*, Aug., pp. 8-12.

Nash, J. 1988. *The mobilization of women in the Bolivian debt crisis.* Unpublished manuscript.

Olave, P.C. 1988. "Apertura comercial y privatización: dos caras del proyecto del gran capital" [Trade opening and privatisation: two faces of the project of the big capital], in *Momento Economico,* Feb.-Mar., pp. 29-32.

Oliveira, O. 1988. *Empleo femenino en Mexico en tiempos de recesion* economica: *Tendencias recientes* [Female employment in Mexico, in times of economic recession: Recent trends]. Unpublished manuscript.

Pinstrup-Andersen, P. (ed.). 1990. *Macroeconomic policy reforms, poverty and nutrition: Analytical methodologies.* Ithaca, New York, Food and Nutrition Policy Program, Cornell University.

Quick, S.A. 1989. *Mexico's macroeconomic gamble*. Washington, DC, Joint Economic Committee, US Congress, Conference Paper No. 12.

Ramirez, S.; Manuel, J. 1986. *El movimiento urbano popular en Mexico* [The popular urban movement in Mexico]. Mexico City, Siglo Veintiuno Editores.

Rendon, T.; Salas, C. 1988. *Wages and employment in Mexico*. Paper presented at the URPE/ASSA meeting, Dec.

Rohter, L. 1989. "Mexico City's filthy air, world's worst, worsens", in *The New York Times*, 12 Apr.

Safa, H. Forthcoming. *Women and the debt crisis in the Caribbean*. Prepared for PACCA.

Salinas de Gortari, C. 1987. "Introducción", in de la Madrid, M. et al. *Cambio estructural en Mexico y en el mundo*, Mexico City, Fondo de Cultura Economica/Secretaria de Programacion Presupuesto, pp. 13-20.

Sara-Lafosse, V. 1987. "Communal kitchens and the low-income neighbourhoods in Lima", in Schmink, M.; Bruce, J. (eds.). *Learning about women and urban services in Latin America*. New York, The Population Council, pp. 90-204.

Scobie, G. 1987. *Macroeconomic stabilization and the poor: Toward a research strategy*. Report on a workshop at Cornell University, 30 June-2 July, 1987.

UNICEF. 1987. *The invisible adjustment*. The Americas and the Caribbean Regional Office.

7

Labour market adaptation: Towards an action agenda

by Lucio Geller *

Structural adjustment, labour market flexibility-adaptation strategies for productivity

The concept of *flexibility* has provoked serious reservations or resistance in Latin America among the trade unions. They tend to see it as a particular type of employer strategy, and prefer the concept of *adaptation* as a way of speaking about correcting the rigidities that affect the functioning of the labour market, but from the viewpoint of their interests. This has led us to use the compound noun *flexibility-adaptation.* This paper presents tentative conclusions on labour market flexibility derived from technical assistance activities in three countries of the region, carried out in the framework of the Regional Employment Programme for Latin America and the Caribbean (PREALC).

According to estimates available in the Regional Employment Programme for Latin America and the Caribbean (PREALC), the principal elements of the employment situation in seven of the major countries of the region (Argentina, Brazil, Chile, Colombia, Costa Rica, Mexico and Venezuela) are the following:

- In the whole decade of the 1980s, in the seven major countries combined, barely 30 million new jobs were created in non-agricultural branches of production. Only 15 million of these were in the formal sector (5 million in the public sector and 10 million in the private sector). The economically active population grew by 36 million during the same period.

- In 1990, the estimated underutilisation of the labour force (open unemployment and underemployment, the latter in terms of equivalent unemployment) was 33 to 35 million jobs.

- The economically active population is projected to grow by around 45 million during the 1990s.

---

* PREALC, Santiago.

- According to these data, even minimum goals of employment growth in the non-agricultural formal sector during this decade will be hard to attain. These goals should include absorbing the underutilised labour force and avoiding a growth of unemployment. These goals imply an effort during the 1990s to create some 20 million jobs in the non-agricultural formal sector - twice as many as were created during the 1980s. No doubt these goals will be difficult to accomplish. Any other objective over and above them constitutes an even greater challenge, considering the severe constraints of external resources that will continue to dominate the growth of the countries of the region in the 1990s. In reality, employment in the year 2000 will probably not reach these minimum goals, unless there were substantial changes in the rate of capital accumulation and skill formation.

Unemployment and underemployment levels in Latin America make it necessary to place labour market policies in the context of strategies for *economic growth*. However, the need to correct macroeconomic - fiscal and balance-of-payments - disequilibria has given priority to discussion about programmes and policies that flow from the concept of *structural adjustment*. Although this has been defined in many different ways, no great error will be committed if the following are recognised as components of the concept: macroeconomic reallocation of resources towards the production of tradeable goods and intrasectoral reallocation of resources in favour of more efficient enterprises ("productive reconversion"); transformations in the basic technology and organisation of plants ("productive modernisation"); modification of the relative roles of the public and private sectors in the accumulation process ("privatisation of public enterprises"); and adaptation of labour markets to the new conditions of labour supply and demand ("flexibility of the labour market").

It would be difficult today even to discuss, much less to elaborate, an employment policy that contradicts a *structural adjustment* process. No policy would be accepted by the dominant economic and social groups if its objectives and instruments made it impossible to correct macroeconomic disequilibria.

It must nevertheless be recognised that a *structural adjustment* policy will not necessarily generate enough jobs to cover the demographic growth of the labour force in the region. On the contrary, those policy initiatives that respond to "productive reconversion", "productive modernisation", and the "privatisation of state enterprises" could have immediate costs in terms of employment. These costs can often be high. Even when those components could produce compensating effects in the medium and long term, it is not certain that the net result for formal sector employment would be substantial.

There is no serious reason to conclude that greater flexibility of the labour market would substantially increase the number of formal sector jobs, even though there are not enough empirical studies on this point in the region. Although some of the evidence is strong, much is inconclusive, and many of the policy recommendations derive from historical experiences from outside the region.

To reinforce that point, it is important to note that some of the legal initiatives along these lines are said to be means to stimulate employment. However, their main objective is none other than to "normalise" the illegal flexibility that has occurred in the labour market, legitimising certain hiring practices, so protecting "precarious" workers from the need to preserve fair competition between employers, as discussed in the next section. Yet even if flexibility became an issue for negotiations between unions and employers, the results of the individual points involved (employment, income, job and work security) would not all be favourable for employment, even though it ranks as the unions' top priority (Standing, 1986).

In spite of the risks and uncertainties in the labour market that could come from structural adjustment programmes, many governments have proceeded with them more because of the failure of previous growth strategies than from any conviction about structural adjustment itself. For this reason, the economic measures aimed at promoting structural adjustment need to be accompanied by others designed to protect employment and income from their probable negative effects in the short term.

Of course, this last claim might be disputed by enthusiastic backers of structural adjustment, with the argument that successful implementation of that style of growth would make specific employment and income policies unnecessary. However, the time factor must be considered. An analysis must be made of how long it takes for the correction of macroeconomic imbalances to affect the growth of employment, income and productivity. Equity and efficiency can be jeopardised. If there were a considerable lapse of time between the attainment of macroeconomic equilibria and the appearance of positive effects on employment, income and productivity, then economic and social policies to bring cause and effect closer would be justified. This point has been recently stressed in an ILO report (ILO, 1989).

Moreover, some labour market problems that could arise from structural adjustment programmes predate the 1980s crisis. For example, employment problems for young people and women have been constant in the countries of the region. They are worse now because of the crisis, and also because of the constraint on resources that has persisted. Likewise, forms of precarious work figured prominently in public discussion during the 1980s, although clear evidence exists that those forms were already considerable in the 1970s in some countries (e.g. Orsatti, 1988, provided comparative figures for the 1970s and 1980s for precarious employment in Greater Buenos Aires). The solution to these problems in the 1990s without a doubt belongs to the domain of labour market flexibility.

Since structural adjustment is a far-reaching concept affecting a great number of people, the discussion of its nature and extent, and in particular the discussion of flexibility, could not be indifferent to political developments. Most countries of the region are reconstructing democracy. Some authoritarian governments in southern Latin American countries recently left power, leaving structural adjustment pending, or enforced some structural corrections at high social costs. The challenge is not only to correct inefficiency but also to construct new institutions that would allow a new consensus to emerge to deal with the present and future problems of the functioning of the labour market.

Structural adjustment means the application of a new set of "disciplinary" norms to which the behaviour of workers, employers and government officials would be subject, in substitution for less efficient, old "disciplinary" norms. *What* "disciplinary" norms are adequate in the new context and *how* they are elaborated, negotiated and implemented, are questions that divide workers and employers, make needed corrections of the labour market difficult, and jeopardise the democratic reconstruction process.

Governments are frequently pressured by macroeconomic imbalances and opt for ways of implementing structural adjustment that leave out consultation with and the participation of workers and employers through their organisations, even though the purpose of this process is to modify the behaviour of the economic and social actors. Some politicians and public officials believe that entrepreneurs' and workers' behaviours are so rigid that they cannot be modified without external pressures. But not only employers and unions are excluded from the decision-making process; most of the time the new "disciplinary" norms (rate of devaluation of exchange rates, reduction of tariffs, elimination of subsidies, guidelines for wage adjustments and other similar points) are elaborated exclusively by the corresponding ministries, sometimes in close collaboration with experts of (public and private) external financial institutions. The ministries very rarely engage in close consultation with the National Congresses.

It is certainly more difficult for enterprises to increase productivity as a *result* of changes (often unexpected) in the "disciplinary" norms elaborated by public agents, than to incorporate productivity programmes that *anticipate* the application of consensual "disciplinary" norms. The effects on employment are probably negative in the case of unanticipated exogenous changes and positive in the negotiated alternative as suggested by the "productivity paradox" (Skinner, 1987).

That paradox means that entrepreneurs' efforts to be competitive only by economising production expenses may lead to a loss of efficiency, if no attempt were made to incorporate more efficient technologies and changes in the labour process. The first strategy - as the experience of many countries of the region shows - is *defensive*, directed at lowering production costs in the short run, mainly the cost of manpower, and postponing investment projects. In contrast, the more efficient productivity programmes are those based on an increase in enterprises' expenditures, including investment, to diminish the unit cost of production in the medium term. Comparing strategies, the former has direct and indirect costs for workers in terms of wages and employment, while the latter might have better results considering the whole set of backward and forward linkages.

An exclusively defensive strategy draws the attention of executives to conventional efforts to lower costs, without significant results (professionals experienced in production normally hold that barely 20 per cent of a competitive advantage comes from reducing costs in a conventional manner). There is a risk of generating attitudes and aptitudes that take away the flexibility needed for introducing changes in products or for developing new products. Competitiveness not only comes from costs but also from the capacity of an enterprise to satisfy the tastes of its customers, in terms of quality and price.

Second, a productive strategy designed to reduce labour input per unit of product could be counterproductive: increased tiredness from work speed-ups could be incompatible with training and retraining needs required by changes in technology and work organisation.

Moreover, an adequate strategy for quality improvement and control can lower the unit costs of production, but the inverse proposition is not true: many cost-reduction strategies can lead to poorer quality, with a consequent loss of competitiveness.

This points to the need to distinguish between short-term production strategies (that is, cost reduction) and *dynamic* strategies for productivity (that is, programmes to increase competitiveness). The latter are those that make it possible to avoid "the paradox of productivity". The dynamic strategies - changes in the product, work processes and work organisation - are alternatives that could contribute to removing justified suspicions that structural adjustment processes affect employment negatively.

Similar reflections could be made regarding the theme of flexibility in the labour market. The situation is different in each of the countries of the region. Nevertheless, the common elements in the position of the social actors seem to be the following: a dominant (not exclusive) attitude among employers' organisations that the problems of flexibility-adaptation in the labour market should be solved by labour deregulation - or by increasing regulations that allow for a freer functioning of labour market forces; a dominant (not exclusive) attitude in workers' organisations that those problems should be dealt with in collective bargaining; lastly, a relative weakness in the ministries of labour, since the absence of *active* labour market policies, especially during the 1980s, has prevented the accumulation of experience that could lead to solutions to problems of flexibility.

The workers' and employers' positions with respect to flexibility are at times so far apart from each other that some official initiatives which did not have initial agreement from them could fail to obtain final approval or might generate social reactions that would make the overall functioning of the labour market inefficient. In contrast, these initiatives could have greater possibilities of being accepted if there were recognition beforehand of the need *to bring the positions of the two parties closer together* regarding specific themes (through programmes to disseminate flexibility-adaptation experiences in other contexts or to train employers and unions to negotiate successfully); the need to *establish appropriate mechanisms for negotiation* that would allow for settling specific questions (e.g. collective work agreements); the need to *define "measurable" goals for negotiation* to make it clear that greater flexibility is a means of reaching them.

Productivity strategies in different sectors and plants are the most adequate "measurable" goals for identifying flexibility needs. In that context, Bowey and Thorpe (1986), assess the relation between payment systems and productivity schemes. Unless productivity is taken as the basic issue, unions and entrepreneurs could be caught in rigid positions in which common ground for negotiations could not be easily identified. Selecting appropriate strategies depends, first, on identification of productivity profiles by sector and by enterprise that show the critical issues for the management of the enterprises. Based on that, conclusions can be drawn regarding technological and organisational innovations needed to raise overall productivity. Finally, the implementation of those innovations constitutes a context for placing actual and potential conflicts over conditions for hiring and firing, labour costs (including expenditures for training and payment-by-results schemes) and the modalities of internal occupational allocation of the workforce. Criteria would thus be identified for deciding on negotiable priorities and questions. The appropriate mechanism for discussing and solving questions of flexibility would be collective bargaining sessions where each side could obtain a net positive result if they engaged in productivity programmes.

Two major obstacles to the application of these recommendations are the *attitudes* of employers and unions, which reflect the underdevelopment of labour relations, and their *aptitudes,* in terms of their ability to make economic and social calculations needed for participating in the negotiation and implementation of solutions that relate both to sectoral and general interests. As the time needed to correct these attitudes and aptitudes could be prolonged, governments end up being tempted by more pressing commitments to solve questions of flexibility-adaptation by partial changes in labour legislation, which increase the uncertainty of unions and employers.

The remainder of this paper will provide examples of this diagnosis. However, if laudable employment goals are to be pursued in the 1990s, it must be realised that the structural adjustment strategy (and its component, labour market flexibility-adaptation) is inadequate for tackling employment and income problems. It is essential to incorporate former priorities, attention to which was postponed by the urgent needs arising from the crisis of the 1980s. This implies concern for the overall *strategy for economic development.*

First, the agricultural sector can still contribute greatly to employment growth and to correcting external disequilibria in many countries of the region. The possibilities of *expanding the agricultural frontier* in those countries would have to be reconsidered, particularly where the natural growth of the rural population and internal migration are considerable. The necessity of meeting basic needs, or self-sufficiency in food, could complement the concept of integrated systems of production based on comparative advantage, by putting more emphasis on agriculture when allocating investment.

Second, a strong concern for employment is related to the *size of the enterprise* in the economic growth strategy. The impact of the crisis, which so sharply increased labour underutilisation in the region, created a widespread desire to boost micro and small enterprises, because of their greater direct employment-product linkages, that is, the increase in employment associated with increased output. However, as was demonstrated for many Latin American countries (García and Marfán, 1987), those employment advantages tend to disappear when consideration is given to indirect employment effects associated with differential inputs, including labour force qualifications, consumption and the impact on the balance of payments. In addition, it has not been sufficiently demonstrated that a dynamic process of accumulation and satisfaction of fundamental needs can be based on the absolute and relative growth of small and micro-enterprises.

Another example can put this relation between employment and the size of enterprises in a different perspective. Some studies hold that an increase in work shifts would solve the sluggishness of production and employment growth, given the severe restriction of external resources (Flaño and Giménez, 1987; Ramos, 1978; Shydlowski, 1976 and 1980). But, as has been pointed out, in Latin America one difficulty in increasing shifts arises from the typical size of industrial enterprises. The family character of the micro and small enterprises frequently makes it preferable to meet an expected increase in sales by acquiring new equipment rather than by introducing more shifts. This latter alternative could make organisational changes necessary - for example, obliging the owner to hire professionals and delegate responsibilities - that are incompatible with the family structure of the enterprises. In contrast, medium and large enterprises with a non-family organisation could increase the number of shifts if they could first solve problems of internal flexibility and labour adaptation.

A third point concerns *appropriate technologies* and their impact on wages and employment. The desire to increase labour absorption in developing countries has produced an argument in favour of labour-intensive technologies. This position has resisted criticisms that objected to its static reasoning: if the choice of technologies were aimed at increasing the employment-product elasticity, it follows that their systematic application would lead in the medium term to an increase of average wages, making new productivity increases necessary. It should be noted that wage increases would come mainly from changes of demand and supply in the labour market.

Recent international conditions have undermined the appropriate technology view. Developing countries are competing more and more among themselves in the international market for manufactured products. Cost differences between countries frequently change by exogenous changes in circumstances, mainly due to abrupt devaluations of national currencies. An increasingly implemented view is that in an increasingly interdependent international context, export competitiveness has to be based on technological change that can support high and sustained productivity growth rates. Wage increases, in this view, would be backed up by productivity increases and by favourable effects in internal labour markets, especially to the benefit of highly skilled workers.

Given the force of these conflicting tendencies, one can anticipate heightened uncertainty regarding wages and employment in the medium and long term. With regard to the former, considering international competition, the rate of the average wage increase in each country would be limited not only by the relative increase of its average productivity, but also by the relative rate of increase of productivity and wages in the competing countries. Thus, the future trend in wages would not be directly related to the technological modernisation of each country.

The uncertainty with respect to employment is also considerable. The debate concerning the net direct and indirect employment effects of technological change in the production of *tradeable* goods has still not been resolved, because of the difficulty in separating theory from facts. For instance, to identify these effects more accurately, the impact on employment of monetary, fiscal, income distribution, foreign trade and labour market policies would have to be isolated. Even those who wish to take an optimistic view could scarcely conclude that the positive effects would be substantial.

The recognition that important technological changes are also needed in the production of *non-tradeable* goods leads to more uncertainty. Inefficiency in sectors that produce non-tradeable goods end up communicating to the tradeable goods sectors through channels connected with the circulation of inputs and productive factors. In these conditions, it needs to be reiterated that the rate of increase of productive jobs and wages will depend mainly on the growth of investment in equipment and human resources.

Some regional examples of flexibility-adaptation

The part-time work contract (Ecuador, 1989)

The first example of the procedural dilemmas in searches for greater labour flexibility or adaptation relates to recent attempts to increase employment flexibility in Ecuador. In 1989, the Ecuadorian Government drew up a draft law for a part-time work contract (PTWC) to make the labour market more flexible. This was conceived as a follow-up to a previous initiative submitted to the Ecuadorian National Congress in August 1984, which was not approved at that time. The second initiative modifies both the purposes and norms of its predecessor. For example, the first initiative made overt reference to illegal forms of labour market flexibility that had grown and sought to preserve fair competition between employers by protecting "precarious" workers. The second initiative stressed the need to facilitate the creation of jobs for a growing proportion of the unemployed and underemployed and the need to increase capacity utilisation of enterprises, reduce production costs and increase productivity. Both initiatives had the support of employers but were opposed by the labour organisations. The 1989 draft law, like its predecessor, never passed the legislative stage.

The PTWC project contemplated hiring workers for a whole or part of the day on Saturdays, Sundays and holidays. Salaries were to be freely negotiated between employer and employee, but could not be less than the regular salaries agreed by collective agreement, or the minimum wage if there were no collective agreements, according to the hours worked. Workers hired according to this system would have all the rights and guarantees of regular workers, in proportion to the hours worked. The only exception was the guarantee of employment security, which was not recognised for these workers.

Other clauses of the PTWC limited the employers' ability to enter into these contracts to cases where permanent workers did not wish to work on Saturdays, Sundays and holidays. Also, outside workers who had permanent jobs during the regular work-week could not apply for these part-time jobs.

There was no prior evaluation by the Government of the probable impact of this initiative on employment. The Ecuadorian system of statistics lacked a survey of establishments that could show the probable effects of any kind of economic or social policy on the labour market. Labour market information had been obtained very unsatisfactorily from household surveys.

Nor was there much basis for expecting that this supply-side policy would have a major impact on employment or unemployment. First, Latin American employers have frequently claimed that many measures aimed at stimulating labour market supply do not work, owing to market uncertainty. In Ecuador, this gave rise to demands that the Government produce complementary stimuli to domestic and external markets. Second, although the draft law was aimed at the unemployed, its articles provided for the possibility of hiring visibly underemployed workers (those who work less than five days in the week). As enterprises would be likely to prefer workers with qualifications or work experience, the positive effects of the PTWCs would be divided between the underemployed as well as the openly unemployed.

However, even though the project's effects on employment were not considerable, one of its merits would have been that, to the degree that employers had recourse to those legal norms if they planned to increase production and employment, the illegal hiring of workers (part-time or full-time) could have avoided becoming a chronic aspect of the Ecuadorian labour market. This objective should not be undervalued.

In all the countries of the region, illegal flexibility is known to have been common in modern sector labour contracts, and the Ecuadorian case is no exception in this respect. For example, according to data from the Permanent Household Survey on Employment, Unemployment and Underemployment carried out in November 1987 and published by the National Employment Institute in December 1988, 27 per cent of workers receiving wages in the modern sector were not affiliated with the Ecuadorian Social Security Institute. The outstanding example of illegality is the evasion of social contributions because of the absence of contracts, or because legal norms are manipulated to treat permanent work relationships as transitory. Consequently, there is a tendency in many countries to modify labour legislation in order to legitimise certain hiring practices by correcting their "precarious" character, without greatly affecting the implicit advantages for employers.

Ecuadorian employers regarded the 1989 legal initiative positively, arguing that productivity could be increased because equipment and installations would be used more. Unit costs of production were expected to be reduced, due to the effect of distributing fixed costs over greater production and because the greater number of hours worked would be partially composed of regular wages, even though the work would have been done on non-workdays. However, there would have been disadvantages, which together suggest that alternative ways of looking for part-time employment might be preferable.

First, it was probable that unemployed or underemployed workers incorporated into production through PTWCs would initially have had lower productivity than permanent workers. This difference would be difficult to correct because job discontinuities like those expected in PTWC would hardly improve workers' qualifications. Moreover, no specific training was planned that would have enabled the unemployed to compete with the underemployed for the jobs to be created.

Second, the increased operation of the machinery would occur during weekends and holidays, instead of adding production shifts during the normal work-week. Administration costs for both alternatives might have been similar, but this was not the case for some machinery-operating costs. Even optimum use of equipment during workdays entails idle times and additional energy expenditures that could be avoided if output growth was obtained by extending the number of hours worked by extra shifts.

Third, the law could have introduced frictions into labour relations, offsetting the planned advantages. Such would be the case if employers had used the law and transferred production normally done in overtime to non-workdays, in order to lower labour costs, which would cut some workers' total income. In technologically complex enterprises, the organisation of work on Saturdays, Sundays and holidays would probably call for permanent workers and PTWC workers to collaborate in production. While the former would be paid overtime, the latter would earn less than the regular wage. If the new ways of organising work meant that permanent and part-time workers performed the same functions, it could be claimed that the principle of "equal pay for equal work" would be undermined. This would be another source of tension between employers and unions, and between different groups of workers in the plants.

In fact, the unions opposed this initiative, arguing, among other points, that they were not consulted. The draft law stated that the PTWCs were not a matter for collective bargaining, but rather that they were to be individual contracts between workers and employers. This means that the labour rights and guarantees recognised for the workers hired under these contracts were those of the Labour Code, not those coming from collective bargaining (except for wages). In addition, by removing contracts of part-time workers from collective bargaining, those workers would have been denied the opportunity to join unions.

These reasons are sufficient to understand the unions' resistance. On the other hand, the employers' support for this initiative seemed less related to any hoped - for increase in employment, or to a reduction of unit costs of production, than to a weakening of employment security.

One of the most hotly debated points in Ecuador regarding the inflexibility of labour legislation is the cost of severance pay when firing workers. In the employers' judgement, collective agreements have increased the compensation payments for dismissal recognised by the Labour Code to the point of making them highly burdensome. Employers feel that they cannot increase employment to meet a *temporary* increase in demand, due to the severance pay contemplated in collective agreements. By contrast, the initiative did not provide severance pay for PTWC workers. Moreover, the employers argue, it is more economical to meet a permanent increase in demand with equipment that saves on manpower, given the high indirect costs involved in setting aside reserves for lay-offs.

As this initiative did not make it through the Ecuadorian Congress, one might be correct to conclude that measures to make the labour market more flexible are, to a large extent, problems of labour relations, reflecting attitudes and aptitudes of workers and employers in collective negotiation, and of productivity growth strategies.

In the first place, it is probable that the goals sought by the PTWC project could be reached through dialogue in negotiating practices. The nature of present labour relations in the countries of the region, and the lack of initiatives to improve them, prevent the labour market from functioning efficiently.

The question of employment security and its associated costs must be reconsidered in Ecuador soon, and there are good reasons for doing so. The problem is how to choose the appropriate procedure: changing the law or including the issue in collective bargaining. It is true that changing the law does not preclude a collectively bargained solution between those directly involved, which would then be accepted by other interests in society represented in the legislative branch of the Government. The difficulties are greatest when a legislative approach substitutes for collective agreement. Seeking solutions through collective bargaining guarantees that the interests of both parties be taken into account, and presents an additional advantage: it is likely to include other matters, such as consideration of the number of hours worked, the workers' right to consultation and to express themselves in the internal labour market that would exist in enterprises, worker-training programmes and internal worker mobility.

Second, questions of labour market flexibility-adaptation would be approached more effectively if they were part of the negotiation over productivity strategies. The unions and employers would know that the flexibility-adaptation measures would not be a zero sum game, but would be an appropriate way to divide the benefits of productivity growth.

The above comments justify the need to search for other formulae to increase production, productivity and employment. One formula to be explored was the introduction of more shifts during weekdays. This approach also supposed that the context of the discussion was collective bargaining, and that the Government should create incentives and conditions for such negotiations. The starting point was not zero, since some Ecuadorian enterprises already operate several production shifts per day. Positive experience gathered in this context could motivate legislative changes.

An increase in shifts presented more advantages than those provided by the PTWC project. For employers, these consisted of higher productivity from part-time workers, because of skills acquired in the more continuous exercise of their functions, and in lower operating costs for equipment. Advantages for PTWC workers were associated with better chances of acquiring skill and with the availability of jobs during weekdays. Unions could also benefit, provided they had a say in the negotiation process.

Indeed, the fact that the Ecuadorian legislative initiative was not successful, or that other perhaps more efficient approaches were not contemplated, is an indication that workers' and employers' organisations still do not have the ability to search for compromise solutions to employment problems. The discussion that followed the Government's initiative also teaches us that the procedures for reaching employment objectives are almost as important as the definition of objectives and mechanisms for reaching them.

Wages and productivity (Uruguay, 1988-89)

Another interesting case of the search for labour flexibility-adaptation comes from Uruguay, where it has been very difficult to make increases in real wages compatible with decreases in the rate of inflation. The wage policy that came into effect in 1985, with the return to democracy, has coexisted with a fairly stable level of inflation (table 1).

The new wage policy was preceded by a "democratic" commitment on the part of the social and political organisations in the aftermath of the military regime to promote a recovery of real wages. That goal of achieving "social peace", initially predominated over any consideration connected with productivity.

As for the wage recovery objective, there was never any agreement about which base-year should serve as a reference. Thus, for the organised workers, the real wages of reference were those in effect in the period immediately prior to the onset of the dictatorship in 1968. Employers and

Table 1. Consumer price in Uruguay, 1984-89

Year	Consumer price index (annual average growth rate)
1984	55.3
1985	72.2
1986	76.4
1987	63.6
1988	62.2
1989	82.2[1]

[1] From September 1988 to September 1989.

Source: Central Bank of Uruguay.

government officials preferred to use the 1981-82 real wages as the base, just before the debt crisis. So, for the latter, the wages have already recovered; for the former, there is still some way to go.

The political commitment to recover real wages ran into a structural obstacle from the outset: the high indexes of domestic and external indebtedness in the public and private sectors. Under these conditions, there has been increasing pressure on income distribution and the share of wages and profits in national income. In the late 1980s, the need to relate wage increases to productivity was increasingly emphasised by government officials, as a substitute for a policy of wage recovery and improving income distribution, in order to control inflationary pressures and external imbalances.

A review of the evolution of wages shows this combination of intentions and constraints (table 2). When the democratic Government first took over, wages increased rapidly in both the private and public sectors. Later, the growth of private sector wages tended to slow, while public sector wages remained stable. In real terms, the national minimum wage - which serves as a reference for social contributions, as well as severance pay in some circumstances, and other labour cost items - never recovered from its 1983 fall.

In 1985, at the beginning of the democratic Government, it was established that Wage Council negotiations would be held every four months and would be subject to the following official guideline: readjustment of group-specific minimum wages at a rate of 100 per cent of past inflation, with additional points to recover real wages. Enterprises could give higher increases as long as those were not transferred to prices. As table 1 shows, the inflation rate jumped in 1985.

Considering the first agreements and their impact on prices, the Government thought it pertinent not to convoke the Wage Councils each February and instead administratively to set the wage increases according to an anti-inflationary criterion. As a result, according to official estimates, the percentage wage increases that occurred in this second phase were half the sum of past and

Table 2. Real wages, Uruguay, 1981-88 (Base: December 1984 = 100; Annual averages)

Year	National average	Public	Private	National minimum	Rural
1981	130.33	134.66	125.66	101.23	109.13
1982	129.92	134.51	124.80	102.87	106.74
1983	102.98	105.42	100.25	87.68	87.67
1984	93.57	92.08	95.23	88.29	88.37
1985	106.80	105.04	109.40	92.27	94.10
1986	114.00	110.13	118.15	87.59	91.79
1987	119.37	110.67	127.53	89.38	96.27
1988	121.13	111.26	130.34	83.63	97.50

Source: Bureau of Statistics and Censuses of Uruguay.

expected inflation. However, as real inflation was always higher than expected inflation, this administrative approach was widely discredited.

Even though determining wages administratively meant only two opportunities a year for revising wages through bargaining between workers, employers and government, that frequency of negotiation exhausted the social actors at the end of three years. At the beginning of 1988, the Government proposed - and the employers and workers accepted - that the negotiations should cover longer periods (preferably two years) beginning in the following June. Official guidelines were issued to regulate these negotiations, justified on the grounds that the favourable external factors that had sustained the growth of the gross domestic product in Uruguay in the previous two years had disappeared.[1]

The guidelines included anti-inflationary objectives and flexibility criteria for wage increases, as follows:

(a) *adjustments* every four months of money wages below inflation (90 per cent),in order to weaken the indexing mechanism, except in the first four-month period in which there was to be an adjustment equivalent to 100 per cent of inflation. Additionally, different *corrections* of money wages were admitted in the first year of the guidelines to allow for the recovery of any real wage loss that might arise from non-fulfilment of official anti-inflationary goals. It was announced that these corrections were aimed at maintaining the real wage during the pre-electoral period (the presidential and legislative elections being held in November 1989) at the same level as at the time of the negotiations in June 1988, when the unions agreed to accept the guidelines. These adjustments and corrections could be transferred to prices;

(b) wage increments were also allowed in February 1989 and October 1989 according to the positive *rate of growth* of any of the following real indicators: GDP or sectoral product, sales, productivity or any other related indicator agreed by workers and employers. This increase was the flexibility criteria and, as such, was not transferable to prices;

(c)   any other upwards drift of wages by negotiated clauses between parties outside the official guidelines could be authorised by the Government, but that was also not transferable to prices. This disciplinary instruction was a warning addressed mainly to entrepreneurs to resist undue wage pressures.

A representative sample of the results of 12 Wage Councils, which accounted for 63 per cent of the workers covered by the negotiations in June 1988, shows interesting results. Table 3 was prepared by the professional staff of the labour federation of Uruguay, PIT-CNT.[2] But before analysing the results, one must appreciate the positions of the parties at the time of the negotiations in June 1988.

The Government would have preferred that the wage revisions be adjusted to more severe anti-inflationary criteria. The instructions finally issued were the outcome of frictions and negotiations within the Government, within the union organisations, and between them and the employers. Stabilisation goals ended up being tempered by political considerations. Nevertheless, once the instructions were made, the Government warned that it would not authorise any agreement that did not adhere to the guidelines, and that in those cases, it would proceed to fix wage increases by decree, as well as in other cases in which the parties could not reach any agreement whatsoever.

With a few exceptions, the unions had the political prudence to accept the guidelines for wage negotiations. This was because the positive international factors had disappeared and because the Government's argument that the external and regional situation was unfavourable for increased wages without output and productivity growth was acquiring more weight.

Second, in the practice of wage negotiations in Uruguay, agreements must be approved by decree of the Executive Power, so that its clauses be applicable to workers of all enterprises in the industrial sector. Such approval is considered indispensable by the unions, in spite of their ideological objections to the tripartite character of the negotiations, due to the weakness of control exercised by the employers' organisations over their members' implementation of the agreements.

As for the employers' organisations, they went to the Wage Councils more as an unavoidable fact corresponding to the stage of democracy, rather than because of any conviction that that was the best procedure for determining wages. Yet those Councils reflect their limit of negotiation, since the employers' organisations still have not decided to involve themselves in practices conducive to more advanced collective labour agreements. The employers' main argument for not progressing in collective bargaining is that the union leaders are not representative. Thus, there has been a stalemate.

In that context the results of the June 1988 negotiations were reflected in the following points summarised in table 3. First, the weighted increase in real wages, according to the sample of the Wage Councils, was around 1.33 per

Table 3. Final official results of 12 Wage Councils, Uruguay, June 1988

Sectors	Adjustment for inflation		Wage growth according to real variables	Wage increase variables					Number of workers covered by the agreement	Equivalence with regard to Consumer Price Index
	First fourth-month period	Second and third fourth-month period		Seniority bonus	Holiday pay	Transport ticket	Assistance bonus	Other clauses		
Commerce	O.G.[1]	O.G.	= GDPrg[2]	xx	x				113 000	CPI+1.00%
Interdepartmental transport	>O.G.	O.G.	>GDPrg	x					4 500	CPI+3.00%
Urban transport	>O.G.	O.G.	GDPrg	x					9 000	CPI+3.00%
Meat packing industry	>O.G.	O.G.	=AGPrg[3]	x					9 250	CPI+1.50%
Clothing	>O.G.	O.G.	GDPrg + Additional		x				10 000	CPI+0.00%
Clothing (minimum wage)	>O.G.	>O.G.	GDPrg + Additional "Estimated" sectoral productivity=5.5%						10 000	CPI+1.25%
Wood and cork	O.G.	O.G.	=GDPrg	x						
Tanning	O.G.	O.G.		x	x	x			3 000	CPI+1.25%
Flower mills and flower products	O.G.	O.G.				x	x		11 000	CPI+1.25%
Milk products	O.G.	O.G.				x		(difference between milk price increase and wage increase in milk products sector)	4 000	CPI+1.00%
Beverages		O.G.						(nominal sales) volume)	3 000	CPI+0.75%
Fishing industry	>O.G.	O.G.	=GOPrg		x	x	x		7 000	CPI+2.25%
Construction	>O.G.	O.G.				x		Clothes and tools	30 000	CPI+3.00%
Private health clinics	>O.G.	>O.G.							20 000	CPI+1.00%

Notes: [1] O.G.: official guidelines; >O.G.: higher increase than official guidelines. [2] GDPrg: equal to GDP rate of growth: >GDPrg: higher increase than GDP rate of growth. [3] AGP: agricultural gross product.

cent in the first year after the long-term agreements went into effect. Private sector workers obtained real wage increases that confirmed the slow-down of the past few years. Consequently, there was a relative adaptation of the average increase to the performance of the national economy.

Second, the effect of the indexation guidelines for nominal wage adjustment meant a cut of real wages of 3.2 per cent for the first 12 months of the agreements (June 1988 to May 1989). If there had been another wage increment in February 1989 equal to the GDP rate of growth at the time of adjustment (1.4 per cent between September 1987 and September 1988), the sum of *adjustment* and *growth* criteria from the official instructions would have meant a real wage depreciation of 2.8 per cent in the year. The gap between this and the negotiated wage growth, according to the data in the sample, is explained by the following three factors:

(a)   a fraction of the gap resulted from adjustments due to inflation agreed by the Wage Councils over and above those in the guidelines. The Government approved them for pragmatic reasons (the relative strength of the parties, the existence of depressed minimum wages in the textile sector, and recognition of other inherited situations that evidently needed correction);

(b)   another fraction of the gap is explained by the influence of clauses regarding different working conditions: seniority and attendance bonus, paid holidays, transportation, clothes and tools, vacations and other remunerations of that type;

(c)   finally, reference in the negotiated and approved agreements to the behaviour of real variables meant a novel development in many cases tolerated by workers, employers and government officials in order to "validate" wage changes not strictly adjusted to the guidelines' anti-inflationary spirit. There were cases in which both parties agreed to wage increases based on ex-ante, expected productivity growth, without allowing for later corrections or negotiated fixed wage variations in case productivity fell below some "acceptable" limits; or other subtleties of that type.

This last point is significant. The employers' and workers' organisations were not technically trained to negotiate a flexible relation between sectoral wages and productivity. There was confusion over the concept of productivity, and in practice it was replaced in negotiations by the concept of total production. The Government had not taken any initiative to train the negotiators and thereby facilitate negotiations. Official statistics on sectoral production and productivity had no strict correlation with the nomenclature of the Wage Councils. The employers were not inclined to give the workers the right to information that would have allowed them to substitute enterprise-level data for sectoral data. These obstacles meant that all parties opted to use indicators for productivity (or production) different from those corresponding to the sector, or simply evaded the instructions.

Other attitudes existed that were unfavourable to developing a relation between wages and productivity. The workers' organisations systematically rejected any attempt to link wage increases to productivity, on the grounds that they wished to recover real wages lost during the military regime. Some unions later developed a more flexible position, but by early 1990 that had still not been incorporated into the strategy of the PIT-CNT.

A strong reason held by the unions in Uruguay is common to unions throughout Latin America. Workers generally consider that programmes of productivity growth implemented in the enterprises are synonymous with greater exploitation. When circumstances oblige them to define policies regarding this matter, the anticipated actions remain outside the enterprise and are located preferably in political spheres, and affect social agents beyond those directly involved in wage negotiations.

Unions of the region resist productivity strategies at the plant or sector level because of what they expect to be negative effects on employment. An extreme position is that those strategies are the exclusive responsibility of employers. So, when considering productivity growth, those unions refer to the functioning of the global system, and advocate that policy-makers should expand the agricultural frontier, or solve the problem of the external debt, or lower profit margins in order to stimulate effective demand, production and productivity. The essence of these proposals is that the actions advocated by workers have been beyond the limits of the workplace, and beyond the immediate responsibility of workers or employers.

That was demonstrated in 1989 in negotiations in the Wage Councils in Uruguay. When the negotiators were obliged to choose an indicator to decide on the relation between wages and real variables, they went back to measures of GDP or agricultural product (confirming the confusion between production and productivity), or to differences between variations in production prices and wages in the relevant sector, or to any criterion except productivity increases in their enterprise or sector.

Meanwhile, the refusal of employers to countenance reform of labour relations, based on the claim that the union leaders were not representative, and their reticence to recognise the workers' right to information, are attitudes that reinforce the resistance of workers to discussions of and negotiations over payment-by-result schemes.

Another equally important reason is that the unions in Uruguay have taken as an important component of their strategies the reduction of wage differentials. Indeed, the tendency of Wage Council awards has been to narrow these differentials. The principal argument put forth for that position is the solidarity of the workers' organisations.

However, negotiations in some Wage Councils have also taken into account the special circumstances that affected enterprises that could not immediately afford the agreed wage increases, owing to the likely effects of wages on employment. Thus, exceptions were made to allow a delay in the implementation of agreements and for a temporary cut in the negotiated increases for enterprises in difficulty. This flexibile negotiation process shows that the unions know from experience that development is unequal between sectors and between enterprises in the same sector. But it is not the only possible flexibility. The negotiation of a flexible relation between wages and productivity could also lead to a differentiation in average wage adjustments by applying payment systems tied to performance. The unions prefer to operate with the first flexibility, allowing exceptions in negotiated wages rather than payment-by-result schemes.

Of course, such schemes could be an instrument of labour market policy. In conditions of structural adjustment that require mobility of workers from low-productivity sectors into higher-productivity sectors, wage differentiation is only one of the ways of encouraging mobility. An alternative is to rely on *active* labour market policies (Standing, 1988). In the Uruguay of today, the political alliances capable of governing for a prolonged period are not sympathetic to such *active* policies. Political sympathies lean more to market forces. And even though the institutional capability to design *active* employment policies exists to some degree, especially in the Ministry of Labour, it is still necessary to add to that capability in order to implement those policies and control their effects.

This situation gives rise to contradictory options for the unions. The workers prefer to make their employment and wage demands to the State, while the State is not inclined to meet them, precisely because the alliances in power exclude the labour movement and its related political parties. The unions could gain some autonomy vis-à-vis the State by opening negotiations with employers on productivity, wages and employment. For this to happen, however, they would have to accept existing wage differentials between sectors and enterprises.

This last option is not only the result of historical experience and present political considerations. It must also be recognised that workers are not trained to negotiate these matters, and that to do so, they would need support from technical staff. The employers' organisations also lack the attitudes and aptitudes needed to negotiate. If this diagnosis is correct, the State should promote the institutional redefinition of labour relations to include the comprehensive negotiation of wage and employment problems within the context of the domestic labour market.

The question is how to take the first step. That step remains the development of tripartite channels - initially informal, but aimed at becoming institutionalised - to debate the content, procedures and control of new forms of negotiation over wages and other working conditions, which would mean going well beyond the present Wage Councils.

Workers' attitudes towards flexibility-adaptation (Argentina, 1989)

A third example of the bargaining dilemma comes from Argentina. A pilot survey, sponsored by a training institute for workers headquartered in Argentina (INCASUR), was conducted in 1989 among a small number of workers from the metalworking sector. The immediate objective was to evaluate the merits of that instrument for identifying workers' attitudes with respect to the relation between productivity, wages and employment. The next objective was to apply that instrument on a larger scale as soon as possible.

A methodological warning should be given here. As the survey budget was insufficient to allow for interviewers, the questionnaires were completed by the workers themselves. Given that only 13 per cent of the workers had completed secondary schooling and that the survey asked about technical and organisational aspects in the plants, it was not surprising that there was a high percentage of invalid answers ("does not know - no answer") to the more demanding questions. For those reasons, the conclusions that follow are given as suggestions of what was important as perceived by the workers.

Ninety-two union leaders and plant workers answered the questionnaire from a total of 56 metalworking companies. All the workers had a permanent contract and most were aged between 21 and 44 years. With only one exception, those interviewed worked a full workday. The vast majority had been in the enterprise and in their section for more than three years. Most of the enterprises were owned by national private capital and were either small or medium sizes, as measured by the number of workers.

Seventy per cent of the workers recognised that there had been productivity increases in the enterprises. For the workers, those increases were associated almost equally with incorporation of new equipment (including "new technologies") and with an increase in the pace of work or in the duration of the workday (including overtime). The workers attributed rather less influence to improved labour relations.

The workers believed that the productivity increases corresponded to programmes for improving the quality of production and to programmes for economising on raw materials and fuel. Equipment maintenance and inventory reduction programmes were also mentioned, but to a lesser extent.

When the workers were asked about the principal causes of work stoppage and of lower productivity, they laid the responsibility on the shoulders of management (problems in the planning of production or a lack of maintenance of the equipment) or on external variables, such as weak demand. Less emphasis was given to the factors that directly involved the workers, such as conflicts with the enterprise or insufficient training.

Asked about the productivity programmes' effects on living standards and working conditions, the workers indicated that there were no salary increases with those programmes - wages remained the same or were lowered.

They produced a relative increase of fatigue, illness and accidents, while higher qualifications required by the productivity programmes were not accompanied by opportunities for training.

A different set of responses would certainly emerge from such questions posed to management of the enterprises. Nevertheless, the importance of the workers' answers is that they suggest some of the basis of their and their organisations' immediate *attitudes* with respect to production and productivity problems in the plants. To the degree that the workers do not admit, or minimise, their responsibilities for problems, there is less room for enterprise-level negotiation between workers and employers. Negotiation about productivity should be a give-and-take process, where the anticipated benefits for each side exceed their concessions.

This conclusion was reinforced by the responses workers gave to being asked which "mixed committees" they thought their representatives should participate in. As expected, the answers favoured those that deal with immediate realities: wages, health and safety, and training, in that order. Fewer demands were mnade for mixed committees dealing with productivity or technological change. Correspondingly, the workers gave lower priority to a reduction of the workday, less tiring or more creative work, and to the availability of more flexible schedules or more time for training. Such answers are surely partially the result of *aptitudes* not developed by the workers or their organisations to understand the overall production process.

In any case, what stands out is that the request for mixed committees shows the workers' desire to be involved in the problems of the plant. This intention contrasts with the immediate reality. The fact is that most of the answers to another set of questions showed that the workers had no participation in the enterprise, and when they had some, it was limited to being informed of management's decisions. When the workers were asked about what degree of participation they thought they should have in the mixed committees, most leaned toward the most intense participation according to the following scale, from less to more important: "information" → "consultation" → "take part in decision-making".

Better administered surveys and in-depth interviews might confirm the following assumption that arises from the workers' answers: their attitudes and aptitudes are favourable only for developing defensive strategies. Observing the order of importance the workers gave to both the causes that affect production and productivity and the mixed committees in which they would like to participate, it is clear that the effects of the relations of production in the plants were more important for them than the content of those relations.

This defensive character of the unions' strategies limits the questions that could be discussed and negotiated in order to adapt and make the labour markets more flexible. Even so, that defensive character still contains a broad range of questions that the unions could incorporate into their negotiations. The conditions for these strategies to be expressed is that the present authoritarian character of labour relations in the plants be replaced by some forms of participation, the space and intensity of which have to be in correspondence with the workers' aptitudes for negotiation. The development of training programmes to give workers the capacity to use economic calculations to negotiate strategies for productivity and technological change will necessarily increase the scope and intensity of participation.

It is important to emphasise that the workers' answers made it possible to detect other elements of flexibility in their disposition.

First, the majority of the answers pointed to a preference for improving their standard of living and working conditions through collective bargaining on the sectoral and plant level, in that order. Legal recourse received less support. This should not be interpreted as a willingness to accept less legal protection, but rather as evidence of a flexible attitude with respect to the conditions of the enterprise and the sector.

Second, a substantial proportion of the workers recognised the need for unemployment insurance. At the time the survey was conducted, there was a limit to severance pay for lay-offs. That protection could reconcile the employer demand for greater flexibility in hiring and firing with more stability in the displaced workers' incomes, if an acceptable solution could be found to the question as to who should bear the burden of the cost of that unemployment insurance or any other redundancy-payment alternative (ILO, 1989).

Third, fewer than half the workers accepted that a wage system should include performance-related incentives; a slight majority preferred a fixed wage system or one with incentives linked only to attendance at work. This should be interpreted in part as a reflection of the belief of most workers that they were not responsible for the solution of productivity problems in enterprises. The attitudes to performance pay schemes would probably be modified if the workers and, most of all, the employers, could be convinced of the need to define enterprise-level productivity strategies.

The preference for fixed wages, with bonuses for attendance, was also associated with the critical judgement made by the workers of actual payment-by-results schemes in enterprises. Some of the workers responded by the last section of the questionnaire to evaluate different systems of wage incentives. Examining those data, it is clear that most of payment-by-results schemes in the metalworking sector were individual, according to the workers' descriptions. Less frequent were systems tying payment to the performance of teams, sections or departments, or other collective schemes. This distribution corresponds appropriately to other answers where the workers recognised a relative autonomy in the performance of their productive functions.[3]

The answers to the set of questions on the payment-by-results schemes in the enterprises leads to the following suggestion. First, workers were dissatisfied with those schemes. A partial interpretation of that discontent is that the workers believed they had little participation in the selection and administration of the payment-by-results schemes. The answers also indicated that dissatisfaction over the wage-incentive schemes was more intense among production workers than among factory delegates or union leaders. This factor should be considered by unions, since involvement and acceptance by the rank-and-file could be necessary for implementation of an efficient payment-by-results scheme.

Second, the workers tended to favour a change of character in the schemes actually in effect. This was associated with the *negative* link that the workers saw between payment-by-results and the pace of work, accidents and illnesses, and competition between workers. This negative view predominated over any belief that salaries were associated *positively* with performance-related wage systems. In general, if a wage incentive scheme were applied in an enterprise, the workers were inclined to prefer a change to a more collective scheme, preferably tied to the profits of the enterprise.[4]

This is an issue that requires more detailed analysis than is possible here. Preference for profit-sharing can be a consequence of a desire for a simplified union strategy or the consequence of an ideological perspective. It might also reflect a lack of knowledge on the part of the workers about the income advantages or disadvantages and for worker participation in enterprise decision-making that could result from both productivity programmes and corresponding collective incentive schemes. This is an issue that needs to be discussed within and between unions and employers' organisations.

Third, according to the workers, management introduced payment-by-results schemes mainly to increase production or profits. There were very few who cited other reasons for existing schemes, and referred to specific programmes to increase productivity in the enterprise. In that respect, it would be valuable for evolving negotiating practices if comparable in-depth interviews were conducted with entrepreneurs, as well as workers, to evaluate whether productivity programmes are effectively applied, whether the workers know the contents well enough to commit themselves to their objectives, and whether their economic results are distributed acceptably between workers and employers. Among the anticipated conclusions, policy-makers could learn *what* training programmes on productivity, employment and wages are needed and to whom they should be offered.

Conclusions

Collective negotiations at the enterprise and sectoral levels should be preceded by discussions of productivity strategies to identify efficient technical and organisational changes, as well as priorities regarding flexibility-adaptation in terms of employment, wages and other working conditions. Those discussions would surely help enterprises to become more competitive *before* most structural adjustment policies are put into action, or would diminish the social and economic costs of accommodating to those policies if they were already implemented.

The context of labour relations needs to be improved, especially in relation to industrial and enterprise-level collective bargaining. These are the levels where the first initiatives for flexibility-adaptation should occur. Although there are too few empirical studies, their conclusions do not justify believing that changes in labour legislation - especially those dealing with conditions for laying off workers and for part-time work - have substantial effects on the level of employment. In contrast, collective bargaining would make it possible to attack simultaneously different problems in the domestic labour market. In doing so, it is the best procedure for reaching socially acceptable solutions.

A second conclusion of the preceding is that a much greater effort should be made to train union leaders and the technical staff of the unions, so that they can participate in collective bargaining with sufficient capabilities.

Finally, labour market statistics in Latin America must be improved by much greater application of establishment-level sample surveys, which have rarely been conducted. It is essential to provide appropriate information for identifying labour market rigidities that hinder productive and technological modernisation, and for monitoring and evaluating the effects of flexibility-adaptation policies.

Notes

[1] The percentage variations in GDP were 0.3 per cent in 1985, 7.5 per cent in 1986, 5.9 per cent in 1987, and about 0.5 per cent in 1988.

[2] PREALC provided technical assistance for the study, which was financed by the UNDP through Regional Project RLA/85/016.

[3] As is known, individual wage incentives are ineffective in process industries, where the autonomy of the workers is nil or minimal.

[4] This is contrary to the proposal made by Weitzman, 1984.

Bibliography

Bowey, A.; Thorpe, R. 1986. *Payment systems and productivity,* London, Macmillan.

Flaño, N.; Giménez, G. 1987. *Empleo, política económica y concertación. ¿Qué* opinan los empresarios? (Employment, economic policy, and concerted action. What is entrepreneurs' view?) Santiago, ICHEH.

García, N; Marfán, M. 1987. *Estructuras industriales y eslabonamientos de* empleo [Industrial structures and employment], México, Fondo de Cultura Económica.

ILO. 1989. *Labour market policies for structural adjustment,* Governing Body, GB.244/CE/4/3, 244th Session, Geneva, ILO.

Orsatti, A. 1988. "Entre costos laborales y escaso control", in *Informe* Especial [Between labour costs and little control], Buenos Aires, Centro de Estudios Laborales.

Ramos, J. 1978. *La ampliación de turnos en la indústria chilena: La factibilidad de una política de empleo productivo* [Shift increase in the Chilean industry. The feasibility of a policy of productive employment], Santiago, PREALC.

Schydlowsky, D.M. 1976. *Capital utilisation, growth, employment and balance of payments and price stabilisation,* Discussion Paper Series, Boston, Massachusetts, University of Boston.

— —. 1980. *The short run potential for employment generation on installed capacity in Latin America,* Discussion Paper Series, Boston, Massachusetts, University of Boston.

Skinner, W. 1987. "The productivity paradox", in *The McKinsey Quarterly,* Winter.

Standing, G. 1986. *Labour flexibility: Towards a research agenda,* Aspects of Labour Market Analysis Working Paper No. 3, Geneva, ILO.

— —. 1988. *Unemployment and labour market flexibility: Sweden,* Geneva, ILO.

Weitzman, M. 1984. *The share economy: Conquering stagflation,* Cambridge, Massachusetts, Harvard University Press.

8

Wage flexibility in sub-Saharan Africa: Trends and explanations

by Christopher Colclough *

The performance of real wages in Africa prior to 1970-75 was significantly different from that which followed. Between 1960 and 1970 (or 1975 in some countries) wages rose. Subsequently they fell. Why did this occur? Can one explain these contrasting experiences of workers in the formal sector primarily by pointing to changes in market conditions, by which is meant changes in the economic environment which led to substantial net changes in the demand and/or supply of workers to jobs? Or are there other changes, particularly in the area of public policy, which have had a dominant influence upon the apparent extent of wage declines in recent African circumstances?

In addressing these questions, this paper documents the extent of change in real wage outcomes since 1970. Changes to the structure of wages and salaries are also investigated for the public sector in a sample of countries in sub-Saharan Africa (sSA). Some differences between actual wage trends and those theory would predict are observed. The paper argues that these differences suggest that wage flexibility in Africa has been determined less by the nature of the labour market and its institutions *per se,* and rather more strongly by the extent to which labour can or cannot capture the patronage of public policy.

The record

Between 1960 and 1970/75 wages rose substantially in real terms in a majority of developing countries - usually much faster than agricultural output and per capita incomes.[1] Within the formal sector, wages and salaries grew fastest outside agriculture, implying growing gaps between what might loosely be termed rural and urban wage employees (table 1).

As indicated by the data in table 2, the growth in real average wages outside agriculture came to a halt during the 1970s - albeit with strongly different performance between different world regions. In Asia as a whole, real wages continued to rise, although this result was particularly influenced by the

* Institute of Development Studies, University of Sussex, United Kingdom.

Table 1. **Trends in average wages and salaries in agriculture compared with the rest of the economy, selected countries, selected periods, 1962-80**

Country	Period	Earnings ratio[1]	Period	Earnings ratio[1]
Ghana	1962-70	126.7		
Kenya	1962-66	106.0	1972-80	85.2
Malawi	1968-71	97.3	1972-80	113.4
Mauritius	1966-71	107.4	1972-80	136.8
Tanzania	1962-71	116.1	1972-78	101.0
Zambia	1962-71	111.0	1972-78	103.2
Botswana			1975-80	122.9
British Honduras	1962-70	97.0		
Cuba			1972-80	100.8
Sri Lanka	1962-71	104.7		
India	1962-70	130.1		
South Viet Nam	1962-70	174.3		
Fiji			1972-80	96.9

[1] Calculated by expressing average earnings per worker in the non-agricultural sectors as a proportion of average earnings in agriculture. The start of each period shown is set equal to 100.

Sources: Data for the 1960s are from Michael Lipton, 1977, table 5.3. Those for the 1970s have been calculated from ILO: *Yearbook of Labour Statistics* (Geneva, 1982), tables 16 and 21.

newly industrialising countries, and by China since 1979/80. In Latin America, real wages generally fell, although with differences between individual countries: Brazil, Argentina and Colombia registered significant gains in real wages over the period 1971-84, compared with sharp falls elsewhere. In sub-Saharan Africa, however, the situation was completely different. Wages fell in almost every country for which data are available, and in some cases (Ghana, Tanzania, Sierra Leone) the decline was dramatically sharp. In the countries shown, real wages fell by one-fifth over the 1970s and by a further one-third between 1979 and 1984. By consequence, wages in sub-Saharan Africa were typically halved between 1970 and 1985.

Thus, real wage flexibility seems to have been particularly pronounced in Africa. This conclusion invites investigation of the extent of change in the structure of wages and salaries that has attended their overall decline. This would allow examination of the extent to which the burden has been spread equally, and of whether the losses have been particularly shouldered by richer (or poorer) groups. Unfortunately, data showing the details of African pay structures are not generally available. Information on particular firms or organisations can be obtained, but these are not usually representative of the economy as a whole. Time-series data on average earnings by occupation, age, sex and education levels simply do not exist for most countries in sSA. On the other hand, information on public sector pay scales *is* available, on a time-series basis, for a good number of countries. Owing to the proportionate importance of the public sector in total formal employment, and to its influence upon levels

Table 2. **Average annual growth rates of real non-agricultural wages in selected developing countries, selected periods, 1971-86**

Region/ country	Period (1970s)	Average annual growth %	Period (1980s)	Average annual growth %
Sub-Saharan Africa				
Burundi	1973-79	− 2.4	1979-86	+ 2.3
Ghana	1971-79	− 13.4	1979-83	− 18.6
Kenya	1972-79	− 1.9	1979-86	− 3.3
Malawi	1971-79	− 1.9	1979-85	− 7.5
Mauritius	1971-79	+ 5.3	1979-86	− 3.6
Sierra Leone	1971-79	− 5.3	1979-86	− 14.3
Tanzania	1971-79	− 3.4	1979-83	− 17.3
Zambia	1972-79	− 4.7	1979-84	− 4.6
Zimbabwe	1971-79	+ 1.5	1979-84	+ 0.2
Mean[1]		(− 2.9)		(− 7.4)
Asia				
Bangladesh	1976-79	− 2.5	1979-84	− 0.5
China	1971-79	+ 2.7	1979-86	+ 4.4
Fiji	1971-79	+ 4.8	1979-84	− 1.8
Korea (Rep. of)	1971-79	+ 10.6	1979-86	+ 4.1
Myanmar	1971-79	− 7.8	1979-83	+ 1.1
Singapore	1971-79	+ 2.2	1979-85	+ 6.1
Thailand	1971-79	− 8.4	1979-84	− 2.9
Mean[1]		(+ 0.2)		(+ 1.5)
Latin America				
Argentina	1971-79	− 2.7	1979-84	+ 7.9
Brazil	1971-79	+ 4.2	1979-84	+ 1.5
Bolivia	1971-79	− 0.5	1979-84	− 10.4
Colombia	1971-79	+ 0.0	1979-84	+ 4.0
Costa Rica	1973-79	+ 3.8	1979-85	− 1.2
Ecuador	1971-79	+ 4.2	1979-83	− 0.9
Guatemala	1971-79	− 5.5	1979-83	+ 9.1
Mexico	1972-79	+ 1.5	1979-84	− 5.0
Paraguay	1971-79	− 2.0	1979-84	− 0.9
Peru	1971-79	− 3.7	1979-86	+ 0.8
Uruguay	1971-79	− 8.0	1979-84	− 5.0
Venezuela	1971-79	+ 2.3	1979-86	− 3.3
Mean[1]		(− 0.5)		(− 0.3)

[1] Simple unweighted arithemetic averages of the average annual growth rates for the countries in each region.

Sources: Data for 1970s from ILO, 1987a, table 5.1, p. 99. Data *for 1980s* mainly calculated from ILO, 1987b, tables 16 and 23. Otherwise, from ILO, 1987a.

of pay throughout the economy, examination of public sector wage trends is of both intrinsic and extrinsic interest.

Table 3. Public service real starting salaries by educational qualification, selected countries, selected years, 1970-87

	pcgnp	unsk	prim	msec	hsec	ugrad
Botswana						
1970	100	100	100	100	100	100
1974	206	192	109	112	105	96
1980	218	186	121	120	122	86
1983	316	192	125	n.a	n.a	89
Gambia						
1972	100	100	n.a	100	n.a	100
1976	119	104	n.a	111	n.a	82
1982	100	73	n.a	80	n.a	58
1986	85	31	n.a	33	n.a	24
Kenya						
1970	100	100	100	100	n.a	100
1975	99	114	80	73	n.a	65
1980	98	90	54	51	n.a	42
1985	78	66	45	36	n.a	28
1986	84	72	49	39	n.a	30
Sierra Leone						
1970	100	100	n.a	100	100	100
1975	95	126	n.a	91	91	85
1980	103	106	n.a	77	71	66
1985	36	23	n.a	16	14	13
1987	11	13	n.a	9	7	6
Zambia						
1970	100	100	100	100	100	100
1975	75	106	112	122	100	112
1980	61	67	68	66	51	66
1983	51	93	94	66	n.a	55

Note: pcgnp = per capita GNP; unsk = unskilled; prim = primary; mesc = middle secondary; hsec = high secondary; ugrad = university graduate.

Sources: (i) Salary indices deflated by consumer price indices as reported in IMF: *International Financial Statistics* (Washington, 1988), except for Botswana for which the CPI series was unavailable for the full period. In this case the gross domestic product deflator has been used, also from the same source.
　　　　(ii) Other sources: Appendix, table 2.

Time-series data on salaries at different levels of the public services of eight countries in sSA are shown in the Appendix. These allow investigation of the extent to which salary decline within the public sector has been shouldered by different groups. Table 3 examines the changing real value of starting salaries for those joining the public service with different levels of schooling. It shows, first, that at least until 1975 (and in two countries into the eighties) the real value of wages paid to unskilled workers requiring no schooling was preserved in all five countries for which data are available. This was not consistently so for entrants to the public service with higher levels of qualification. Second, although the value of the wage of unskilled workers subsequently fell, real wage cuts were far less - absolutely and proportionately - than those affecting more highly educated entrants to the service. Botswana is something of a special case among the countries shown in that it alone has enjoyed buoyant, and almost entirely sustained, growth over the past two decades. Yet here too graduate real salaries were reduced between 1970 and 1983, a period during which real wages of unskilled public employees almost doubled.

It follows that differentials in starting salaries between more and less educated recruits to the public sector in Africa have been much reduced over the last two decades.[2] Table 4 indicates the extent of such compression, showing that the reduction in differentials was in all cases proportionately greatest when comparing leavers from the top and the base of the school system. The average reduction in the salary differential between university graduates and the un-schooled was 46 per cent for the five countries and periods shown. Taking account of the different lengths of time covered by data for different countries, the average rate of decline of this differential was 3.1 per cent per year over the 1970s and early 1980s.

This picture is confirmed by the data in table 5, which show a narrowing of the differentials between the highest and least well paid civil service jobs for eight countries. Excluding Swaziland, where data for the 1980s are not shown, the average reduction in this differential was 45 per cent, which converts to an annual reduction of 3 per cent for the countries and years shown.

These trends indicate that the wage distribution within the public sector in sSA became more equal over 1970-85, assuming that employment structures within the civil service (i.e., the proportion of people at each level of seniority) did not change fundamentally over the period. Although this does not allow generalisation to the rest of the formal sector, it is likely that similar trends would have occurred in the private sector of these economies: in some cases incomes policies explicitly linked private and public sector pay norms (Botswana, Zambia); elsewhere private sectors were in any case small, and were influenced strongly by public sector salary policy.

It is not implied that income distribution in a broader sense was improved by these trends in public sector pay. This is partly because the documented real decline of wage and salary scales does not necessarily imply that the real earnings of their recipients declined by a similar amount. Increases in absenteeism, moonlighting, and corruption are widely reported to have increased in Africa in response to salary decline, while in some countries salary reductions have been partially compensated, for some groups, by accelerated promotion across salary scales and by increases in untaxed job-related allowances. These changes have not been random across all levels of the service: absenteeism, for example, mainly affects established posts, since daily-paid workers do not generally receive payment for absent days. Thus the net impact

Table 4. Public service salary differentials, by educational qualifications, selected countries, selected years, 1970-87

	ugrad/ pcgdp	ugrad/ unsk	ugrad/ prim	ugrad/ lsec	ugrad/ msec	ugrad/ hsec
Botswana						
1970	18.11	9.10	5.16		3.64	2.22
1974	8.46	4.57	4.57		3.14	2.03
1980	7.18	4.23	3.66		2.61	1.57
1983	5.11	4.22	3.66		n.a.	n.a.
% change 70-83	− 71.80	− 53.59	− 29.03		n.a.	n.a.
Gambia						
1972	17.86	4.85			4.44	
1976	12.30	3.85			3.28	
1982	10.33	3.87			3.25	
1986	4.92	3.73			3.15	
% change 72-86	− 72.45	− 23.13			− 29.04	
Kenya						
1970	22.00	14.15	8.18		4.38	
1975	14.40	8.08	6.62		3.88	
1980	9.40	6.60	6.43		3.62	
1985	7.80	5.98	5.07		3.38	
1986	7.80	5.93	5.04		3.38	
% change 70-86	− 64.55	− 58.11	− 38.40		− 22.76	
Sierra Leone						
1970	19.60	11.26			4.65	2.93
1975	17.50	7.62			4.33	2.73
1980	12.59	7.03			4.00	2.73
1985	6.89	6.24			3.62	2.73
1987	11.02	5.36			3.11	2.52
% change 70-87	− 43.79	− 52.44			− 33.16	− 13.87
Zambia						
1970	5.50	4.57	3.81	3.61	1.85	1.30
1975	8.19	4.82	3.81	2.31	1.70	1.47
1980	5.95	4.50	3.73	3.14	1.85	1.71
1983	5.96	2.72	2.25	2.01	1.56	n.a.
% change 70-83	8.36	− 40.53	− 40.84	− 44.25	− 15.84	

Note: ugrad = university graduate; pcgdp = per capita GDP; unsk = unskilled; prim = primary; lsec = low secondary; msec = middle secondary; hsec = high secondary.

Source: Calculated from data in Appendix, table 2.

of these phenomena will probably have kept the decline in earnings differentials within the public sector below the levels of decline for wage/salary scales documented in this paper. In addition, of course, and particularly during the 1980s, per capita incomes in many African countries have been falling. It is

Table 5. Public service salary differentials, by position in service, selected countries, selected years, 1970-87

	unsk	tos	tos/unsk	pcgnp	unsk/pcgnp
Botswana					
1970	211	5 580	26.45	106	2.00
1974	528	6 864	13.00	285	1.85
1980	1 082	16 320	15.08	637	1.70
1983	1 257	22 344	17.78	1 039	1.21
% change 70-83			− 32.78		− 39.42
Gambia					
1972	825	12 250	14.85	224	3.68
1976	1 644	16 080	9.78	515	3.19
1982	1 884	17 700	9.39	705	2.67
1986	1 980	17 796	8.99	1 500	1.32
% change 72-86			− 39.47		− 64.10
Kenya					
1970	78	2 275	29.17	50.15	1.56
1975	150	2 334	15.56	84.15	1.78
1980	219	2 712	12.38	152.9	1.43
1985	300	3 408	11.36	227.4	1.32
1986	339	3 672	10.83	255.45	1.33
% change 70-86			− 62.86		− 14.64
Malawi					
1970	70	2 800	40.00	59	1.19
1975	150	5 937	39.58	103	1.45
1980	225	9 648	42.88	153	1.47
1985	312	11 097	35.57	274	1.14
1987	396	18 084	45.67	367	1.08
% change 70-87			14.17		− 9.40
Nigeria					
1970	129	3 900	30.23	91	1.42
1975	720	12 696	17.63	318	2.26
1980	1 200	12 996	10.83	617	1.94
1985	1 500	13 812	9.21	685	2.19
% change 70-85			− 69.54		54.15
Sierra Leone					
1970	228	6 500	28.51	131	1.74
1975	432	7 670	17.75	188	2.30
1980	702	10124	14.42	392	1.79
1985	1 187	13 363	11.26	1 074	1.11
1987	3 324	28 397	8.54	1 616	2.06
% change 70-87			− 70.03		18.46

Table 5. Public service salary differentials, by position in service, selected countries, selected years, 1970-87 (continued)

	unsk	tos	tos/unsk	pcgnp	unsk/pcgnp
Swaziland					
1971	336	6 420	0.05	222	1.51
1978	660	10 000	0.07	610	1.08
% change 71-78			26.11		– 28.57
Zambia					
1970	360	6 760	18.78	299	1.21
1975	540	8 616	15.96	318	1.70
1980	696	8 748	12.57	526	1.32
1983	1 470	12 000	8.16	670	2.19
% change 70-83			– 56.53		81.97

Note: unsk = unskilled; tos = top salary paid in public sector; pcgnp = per capita GNP.

Source: See "Notes and sources for table 5 and for Appendix tables 1 and 2".

therefore an open, important question as to whether real wage reductions in the formal sector, and movements toward greater equality in the wage/salary distribution, have improved the distribution of income as a whole.

This question is highly complex, and its answers would be strongly sensitive to the structural characteristics of each country. These will not be attempted here. However, some proxy information of interest is shown in tables 4 and 5. These indicate, for example, that in Zambia, at least until 1983, the reductions in real public sector wages, and in differentials, were outpaced by the reductions in national income arising from the collapse in the copper price in the mid-1970s. It can be seen (table 5) that the ratio of unskilled wages in government to per capita GNP increased by 80 per cent between 1970 and 1983. Even university graduates' earnings in the public sector remained relatively favoured in comparison with other Zambian incomes. As shown in table 4, the graduate/per capita GDP ratio increased by more than 8 per cent over the period. Table 5 shows that the unskilled/per capita income ratio also increased during the 1970s and 1980s in both Sierra Leone and Nigeria, although this judgment is sensitive to which year is selected as a base. In these countries, as in Zambia, economic decline in the country more than kept pace with wage reduction at the base of the public service. During both prosperity and recession, the formal/informal earnings gap tended to increase.

In the four other countries shown in table 5, however, wage reduction and the compression of differentials exceeded the rate of economic decline. The differential between graduate salaries in the public sector and per capita incomes fell by more than two-thirds in Botswana, Gambia and Kenya by the mid-1980s. And that between unskilled wages and per capita income was cut by between 10 per cent and 15 per cent in Botswana, Gambia, Kenya and

Malawi. In these cases therefore, earnings gaps between the formal sector and other income-earning opportunities *may* have been reduced in recent years.

In summary, the following generalisations seem justified, on the basis of the above evidence:

(a)   real wages in sSA have fallen sharply since the early 1970s - more so than in other regions of the developing world;

(b)   changes to the wage and salary structure, as evidenced by the public sector, have been even more marked. The greatest proportional falls in real wages and salaries have been experienced by the more highly paid workers. There has been a sharp narrowing of wage and salary differentials measured according to both educational qualifications[3] and occupations at different levels of the service;

(c)   although real wage declines have been least for the unskilled and poorest workers, those not in receipt of wage/salary incomes (as proxied by per capita GDP) have sometimes (but not always) lost proportionately more than unskilled wage workers as a result of general economic decline. Thus, notwithstanding real wage decline and the narrowing of differentials within the wage structure, the implications of these trends for net changes in the distribution of income remain ambiguous in many cases.

Explanations and implications

The basic pattern of a rise in real wages to the mid-1970s followed by a pronounced and sustained fall would, at first sight, seem easily explained: the early years of independence in Africa were ones of strong growth in output and employment; the later period, following the oil crisis of 1973-74, was one of recession, rising levels of debt and economic contraction arising from the need to impose adjustment measures. Accordingly the wage trend seems to fit neatly into a demand-determined framework: wages rose when demand was rising, and they fell when demand went into reverse.

Such an explanation, however, does not take account of the pronounced imbalances between supply and demand which have traditionally characterised African labour markets. Three-quarters of the labour force still work in agriculture, mostly in self-employment or in work for their family, rather than being recipients of wages. Under these circumstances, the determinant of the unskilled urban wage was held to be average labour productivity in the rural sector, together with some margin to compensate for increased costs of urban living, and the costs of finding an urban job. This is the basic argument underlying "dual economy" growth models and models of rural-urban migration of the Lewis-Todaro type.

Thus, standard theory does not easily explain why wages at the minimum level initially increased rapidly during the early years of independence and in particular why they strongly outpaced the growth of per capita agricultural output. It predicts that minimum urban wages would be a little higher than rural incomes. The existence of a large and growing rural-urban income gap during the 1960s runs contrary to this - and indeed, to the idea that employers exhibit rational maximising behaviour. The phenomenon is equally problematic in the Marxian tradition, where labour power would not be expected to be remunerated at a level higher than the costs of own reproduction. The activities of unions cannot save the day for theorists in either tradition, since not only does the fact of endemic labour surplus make labour oligopoly more difficult, but union organisation is much weaker and less sophisticated in most countries of the South - and particularly so in sSA - than in more industrialised countries.

The most persuasive explanations for the phenomenon of rising unskilled wages in Africa after independence emphasise structural features of African economies, which influenced the nature of market-determined wage and employment outcomes in unexpected ways. Such explanations included the following observations: (a) in the sectors which are 'wage leaders', wage costs are often a small part of value added; (b) particularly but not exclusively in the extractive industries employers may value a stable and pliant labour force very highly, and the costs to them of labour disputes may be much higher than those associated with the peaceful (and generous) settlement of such disputes; (c) increases in productivity tend not to be passed on in terms of lower prices to the consumer; for individual producers (though not for all taken together) this is particularly true in export industries where the price of the product is fixed in foreign exchange, in such circumstances, the employer may be more willing to grant higher wages; (d) employers themselves benefit from increases in wage payments since they themselves draw salaries; and (e) in projects financed by foreign investment wages are substantially less than those in Western Europe; once the decision to invest has been made, and both risks and sunk costs have already been incurred, there may be a substantial margin within which wages can rise without undermining profitability relative to counterpart production in Europe.

Each of the above observations are part of the story and help to explain why private employers in developing countries have been prepared to pay employees substantially more than their minimum supply price, even in circumstances of endemic labour surplus. Nevertheless, for reasons set out below, we believe that the African State itself has had the dominant impact on the upward - and subsequently downward - movement of real wages over the past two decades.

The extreme imbalances between supply and demand in the African labour market (and those of other developing countries) have resulted in a more interventionist approach to wage determination on the part of the State than has been typical in more developed market economies. Although some analysts argued against the introduction of minimum wage legislation, on the grounds that the market could best determine the opportunity cost of unskilled labour by setting the wage at a level sufficient to ensure adequate labour supplies to the towns, others saw the need to protect the unskilled from exploitation. Not all workers faced a viable rural alternative, and in many countries it was argued that the market-determined urban wage would, for some groups, be well below the cash equivalent of average rural incomes. In most countries minimum wages were introduced with the explicit intention of guaranteeing a wage adequate to sustain the subsistence needs of a small family, yet not so great as to generate a gulf between average living standards in rural and urban areas. Unlike in industrialised countries these minimum rates governed the earnings of the majority of the formal sector labour force.

Higher up the employment structure, supply and demand conditions were usually very different. Instead of a labour surplus, there was often an extreme shortage of many categories of skilled and educated labour. In many ex-colonial countries of Africa the shortage of domestic skills (measured by the sum of vacancies plus expatriates employed) accounted for more than half the jobs requiring university qualifications, and more than one-third of those needing graduates from senior secondary schooling. Again, deficits of this size signified major, not marginal structural imbalances in the labour market, which could not be cleared by wage movements alone in reasonable time, and over a relevant range of wage movements. These shortages were not a product of inadequate earnings differentials, in the context of a perfectly elastic supply of facilities for education and training. Rather, they were the result of a historical lack of investment in education and training. By consequence, many countries in sSA were (and some remain) heavily dependent upon expatriates at the higher levels of the employment structure, particularly in technical jobs. Domestic salaries for workers with comparable skills were affected by expatriate remuneration, which was determined more by productivity levels in Western Europe and North America than by that in the host country. Even where expatriates were not preponderant, the shortage of local skilled workers allowed the latter to profit from scarcity rents, whereby their earnings were well above the levels which would hold in the absence of the shortage of domestic skills.

Accordingly, at these higher levels of the occupational hierarchy, where earnings were already 20 to 30 times unskilled rates, governments also adopted a policy of income restraint. Salaries had often been set by colonial governments, and bore little relation to domestic economic circumstances. The labour shortages at these levels aggravated these disparities, and it was clear that market-determined wages for the skilled and educated workers would continue to be higher than was compatible with an acceptable distribution of income for some years.

In these circumstances, which were typical of most ex-colonial countries in sSA during the 1960s and 1970s, many governments adopted an explicit policy on wages and salaries based upon two main principles: (a) minimum unskilled wages were to be linked to average standards of living in the rural areas; (b) wage and salary differentials within the formal sector were to be reduced. The adoption of these principles would, it was believed, ensure maximal labour absorption by the formal sector, minimise open unemployment and promote a more equal distribution of income. These principles can be found in incomes policy white papers - for example, in those for the United Republic of Tanzania, Kenya, Zambia, Botswana - and, where such policies were less formalised, in successive development plans, political speeches and budget papers for many developing countries. The "ethic" underlying these principles of incomes policy was primarily focused upon distributional concerns, in the sense that they were designed to achieve maximal formal sector labour absorption and minimal rural-urban income differentials.

In spite of the invective, the objective of wage moderation was initially not achieved, as we have seen. The reasons were basically political. First, the political power of unskilled labour in the formal sector is far greater than its numerical importance in the population. Minimum wages in the urban sector are perhaps the most important indicator of incomes to which rural migrants aspire. If unskilled wages rise, the potential rewards to aspirant jobseekers also rise, which increases the hopes and expectation of both rural and urban dwellers. Equally, increases in unskilled wages are a *tangible* benefit visible to all the population. Higher rates of labour absorption are not nearly so tangible. Thus, even if a trade-off between wages and employment growth is believed to exist by an administration, the temptation is often to opt for the more visible solution. Finally, many rural households are recipients of transfer incomes from migrants. In Botswana, for example, in 1977, two-thirds of rural households had received at least one such remittance from household members in the urban centres (Botswana, 1979). Thus, increases in urban wages bring *direct* benefits to the rural sector.[4] In these ways, it is easy for a government to cull political support among the direct and indirect beneficiaries of wage increases, while those made poorer by such a policy (or who are prevented from becoming richer by gaining access to the formal labour market) remain unaware of having lost out as a result of such policies.

The second category of reason is rather different: it is that those responsible for reviewing public sector salaries may often wrongly have believed that they were acting in the interests of the poorest sections of the population by granting generous increases in minimum wages.[5] To a casual empiricist, it appears - at each successive salaries review - that one should increase wages much more rapidly at the bottom than at the top of the distribution. This, after all, is likely to be a stated aim of policy towards formal sector wages. Rural incomes, it is realised, cannot be directly improved by this mechanism (except through the rather dubious mechanism of transfer payments mentioned above) but the government has *separate* policies for rural development, which it pursues in order to improve living standards in rural areas. This "urban-biased" viewpoint added to the pressures which led to the escalation of minimum wages relative to rural incomes in some African countries after independence.

This, then, amounts to saying that labour institutions, including trade unions, provided only a small part of the explanation for the escalation of real unskilled wages to the mid 1970s. The interests of employers often supported such trends. Governments found it against their own political interests to apply policies of wage restraint - even where such were their stated goals. Finally, state action often inadvertently added to these pressures, on the usually mistaken assumption that rapid real wage increases at unskilled levels were consistent with a policy of promoting a better distribution of income over time.[6]

One of the main ways in which the value of the real wage had been maintained in sSA was through the maintenance of nominal exchange rates, which became increasingly over-valued. This kept the price of both imports and exports, in terms of domestic currency, lower than they would otherwise have been, and thus enhanced the value of the real wage - particularly in comparison with agricultural incomes, which declined in per capita terms in most countries of sSA. By the same token, the reduction in real wages that has occurred since the mid-1970s is primarily a reflection of the change in policy towards exchange rates which occurred throughout the region - mainly in response to World Bank-IMF conditionality associated with loans to support balance of payments adjustment. This change in approach to exchange rate policy, combined with curbs on public spending which prevented the devaluation-imposed inflation being less than fully compensated by wage/salary increases, is the primary explanation for the downward flexibility of real wages that has occurred in sSA since the mid 1970s. Thus, as with the wage inflation that preceded it, the wage decline has been a policy-induced outcome representing a (perhaps temporary) triumph of international over domestic political forces.

The international institutions tend to see "policy reform" as primarily a technical matter. Calculations, for example, of the extent of required devaluation tend to remain couched in nominal terms - thereby assuming that domestic opposition, and attempts to neutralise devaluation by achieving compensatory wage increases, will have no force. This is both superficial and unwise. The political forces which maintain the longevity of African regimes may have changed in some countries in recent years. But in many they have patently not done so. Thus, to assume that this has generally happened, in the absence of corroborating evidence, is likely to be a mistake.

Our analysis of public sector wage and salary structures for a sample of countries in sSA has shown that, even during the years of decline, minimum wages have remained more protected than those associated with more senior posts, and that in some countries other income earners have lost out even more than those in the wage/salary sector. These two elements indicate some political continuity with the earlier period rather than a generalised and fundamental change. The onset of austerity did not necessarily change the relative bargaining power of previously privileged groups. The potential consequences of ignoring the power of politics - or of making incorrect political assumptions - are amply demonstrated by Zambia's food riots, which in 1987 led to the suspension of the IMF adjustment programme, and a reversion to the "national" development strategy (Colclough, 1989).

In conclusion, the demand-induced "market forces" explanation for recent changes in African real wages is an over-simplification. Both their rise and subsequent fall appear to have been determined more by policy-induced changes than by the operation of labour markets in the textbook sense. The decline of real wages since around 1975 has, it is true, reflected the market liberalisation of some African economies. To that extent labour *may* have lost the patronage of public policy in comparison with pre-1975. But there is evidence, from a number of countries, that earlier patterns of patronage remain. Thus, the relative deterioration of real wages may prove to be only temporary. Judgements about wage levels do not take place in a political vacuum. In particular country settings, the extent to which the cost of adjustment can be borne by wage and salary earners is likely to depend on how much is also borne by everyone else. Careful analysis of this question, and of conditions in the labour market more generally, thus become extremely important to securing the viability of externally imposed programmes of domestic policy reform.

Notes and sources for table 5 and for appendix tables 1 and 2

General

unsk – No educational qualification required and/or lowest salary or wage scale in public service.

prim – Entry point for those who have completed primary education.

lsec – Entry point for those who have completed lower secondary education.

msec – Entry point for those who have completed middle secondary or secondary education, e.g., "O" levels.

hsec – Entry point for those who have completed higher secondary education, e.g., "A" levels.

ugrad – Entry point for those who have completed tertiary education, e.g. university graduates.

For detailed explanation of these classifications refer to country notes below.

Country notes

Botswana

unsk – Industrial class group 6 in 1970; group 4 from 1974 onwards; salary on the basis of 264 working days a year: no formal qualification required.

prim – Clerical grade, C3 converts to GA6 in 1978; entry requirement: J.S.C.

msec – Clerical grade, C2 converts to GA5 in 1978; entry requirement: C.S.C.

hsec – Executive officer, E2 converts to E4 in 1974 and to GA4 in 1978; entry requirement: "A" levels or intermediate degree from university.

ugrad - Administrative officer, A3 converts to GA3 in 1978; entry point for graduates.

tos - Permanent secretary SII.

Sources:

(i) Report of the Commission on the Salaries and Conditions of Services of the Public Service and Teaching Service, July 1970.
(ii) Personnel Directive No. 5 of 1970, Sep. 1970.
(iii) Report of the Salaries Review Commission, 1974.
(iv) Report of the Salaries Review Commission, 1980.
(v) C. Colclough and P. Olsen: *Review of income policy in Botswana, 1972-83* (Gaborone, Ministry of Finance and Development Planning, 1984), p. 72, table 38.

Gambia

unsk – H1 converts to scale 3 in 1976; no qualifications.

msec – 3rd grade clerk, F1 converts to scale 4 in 1976; entry requirement: "O" levels.

ugrad – Assistant secretary B1 converts to scale 13 in 1976; entry point for graduates.

tos – Superscale 1 converts to scale 21 in 1976.

Sources:

(i) Sessional Paper No. 1 of 1970, Governmental Statement on the Report of the Salaries Commission on the Public Service of Gambia.
(ii) Estimates of recurrent expenditure, years corresponding to those reported in tables.

Remark:

(i) Units of currency changed from £ to dalasi in 1972, therefore source (i) has been used simply in order to match salary scale with educational qualification and job description. Salary comparisons therefore begin in 1972.

Ghana

unsk – Unskilled worker scale M1; no qualifications.
prim – "Recruit", scale M4; entry point for those who have completed primary education.
lsec – Scale M9; middle school graduate.
msec – Clerical officer, scale R17; entry requirement: "O" levels.
hsec – Executive officer, scale R24; entry requirement: "A" levels.
ugrad – Administrative officer, scale R49; entry point for graduates.
tos – Top administration, scale R100.

Sources:

(i) Report of the Salary Review Committee, July 1974, pp. 24, 25, 40-42, for educational qualifications.
(ii) Annual estimates, 1970-71 and 1974-75 (back covers), for salary scales in each year.

Kenya

unsk – Subordinate officer, Group A, no qualifications.
prim – Junior clerical officer, Group C; entry requirement: C.P.E.
msec – Clerical officer, Group D; entry requirement: E.A.C.E.
ugrad – Professional, Group J; entry point for graduates.
tos – Administrative superscale, Group M.

Sources:

(i) Report of the Commission of Inquiry (Ndegwa), 1970-71, pp. 322-369.
(ii) Report of the Civil Service Review Commission, 1979-80, pp. 148-156.
(iii) Estimates of recurrent expenditure, corresponding years.

Remark:

(i) Sources (i) and (ii) used to establish entry points corresponding to educational qualifications, while source (iii) used for salary scales in given years.

Malawi

unsk — Subordinate class, scale F4; no qualifications.
tos — Superscale group S1/P1.

Source:

(i) Estimates of revenue and expenditure for corresponding years.

Remark:

(i) Currency unit changed in 1971 from £ to kwacha, but this does not affect the table as it refers only to differentials within given years.

Nigeria

unsk — Watchman/gateman/cleaner, scale G1 converts to scale 1 in 1975; no qualifications.
tos — Permanent Secretary, scale SS3 converts to scale 17.

Source:

(i) Recurrent estimates of the Government of the Federal Republic of Nigeria, corresponding years.

Remarks:

(i) Cross comparability between old and new scales established by matching the latter with the job titles corresponding with the former.
(ii) Unit of currency changed from £ to naira in 1971, but table unaffected since it only refers to differentials within given years.

Sierra Leone

unsk — Lowest scale P1; less than "O" levels.
msec — Grade II officer, scale P4; "O" levels.
hsec — Grade I officer, scale P6; "A" levels.
ugrad — Senior officer, scale C(E)7; university graduate.
tos — Superscale A.

Sources:

(i) Report of the Commission of Inquiry into the Civil Service of Sierra Leone, 1970, pp. 105-119.
(ii) Estimates of Revenue and Expenditure, corresponding years.

Remark:

(i) Source (i) used to establish entry points by educational qualifications, source (ii) used for salary scales each year.

Swaziland

unsk – Messenger, scale E3 converts to scale 1 in 1976; no qualifications.
tos – Head of the Civil Service, scale SI converts to scale 17 in 1976.

Sources:

(i) Estimates 1971/72.
(ii) Establishments Circular No. 6 of 1976. Wamalwa Report: Salary Scales and Conditions of Service.
(iii) Establishments Register 1977/78.

Remark:

(i) Source (ii) used for cross comparability between sources (i) and (ii).

Zambia

unsk – Indoor servant, scale S21; no qualifications.
prim – Junior clerical officer, scale S19; entry requirement: Grade VII in school.
lsec – Clerical officer, scale S17; entry requirement: Form II/III in school.
msec – Clerical officer, scale 15; entry requirement: "O" levels.
hsec – Scale S15; entry requirements: "A" levels.
ugrad – Executive officer, scale S13; entry point for graduates.
tos – Senior administration, superscale S1.

Sources:

(i) Summary of the Main Recommendations of the Commission of Inquiry on the Salaries, Salary Structure and Conditions of Service, 1975, pp. 35-40.
(ii) Report of the Administrative Committee of Inquiry into the Salaries, Salary Structure and Conditions of Service, 1980, pp. 55-57.
(iii) Establishments Register 1970, 1981.
(iv) Personnel Circular No. 89 of 1980 and No. 83 of 1984 as in Meesook et al., 1986, Appendix table 8, p. 114.

Notes

[1] The evidence for this statement is less accessible than might be inferred from the strength and frequency with which it is asserted in the literature (see, for example, Turner, 1965; Jackson, 1971; Lipton, 1977). Nevertheless, it is usually confirmed by country-level analyses. For a recent assessment of the evidence for sub-Saharan Africa, see Jamal and Weeks 1990. They find that real (minimum, unskilled or average) wages peaked between 1970/75 in Uganda, Tanzania, Kenya, Liberia, Zambia, Ghana and Nigeria. Evidence for Zambia is also shown in Colclough, 1989.

[2] This generalisation is true also of salary *scales,* not just starting salaries. It continues a trend which became well established shortly after independence in most of the former British and French territories in Africa.

[3] By consequence, both private and social rates of return to schooling have fallen - particularly those associated with higher education. Estimates of the impact of these trends on private and social rates are given in Colclough, 1990.

[4] This phenomenon is often, incorrectly, used in support of a high wage policy. Where remittances are a small proportion of average urban incomes, there are much more efficient ways of increasing rural incomes than by granting urban wage increases. Additionally, the terms-of-trade effects of such measures are likely to reduce still further the incomes of the poorest rural sections who do *not* receive such remittances from urban workers.

[5] This view informed, for example, the Zambian Government's income policy of "narrowing the gaps" over the 1960s and early 1970s (Meesook et al., 1986).

[6] Such a policy *may*, of course, be so consistent - depending on what happens to salaries, profits, and agricultural production. We are merely arguing the contingent case that these developments did not have this effect in most of the countries concerned.

References

Botswana Government. 1979. *National migration study*. Gaborone, Central Statistical Office.

Colclough, C. 1989. *The labour market and economic stabilization in Zambia*, Working Paper No. 222. Washington, DC, Country Economics Department, World Bank.

— —. 1990. "Who should learn to pay? An assessment of neo-liberal approaches to education policy", in Colclough, C.; Manor, J. (eds.). *States or markets? Neoliberalism and the development policy debate*. Oxford, Oxford University Press.

ILO. 1982. *Yearbook of Labour Statistics*. Geneva.

— —. 1987a. *World Labour Report*. Oxford, Vol. 3.

— —. 1987b. *Yearbook of Labour Statistics*. Geneva.

IMF. 1988. *International Financial Statistics*. Washington, DC.

Jackson, D. 1971. "Economic development and income distribution in Eastern Africa", in *Journal of Modern African Studies*, Vol. 9, No. 4 (December), pp. 531-42.

Jamal, V.; Weeks, J. 1990. *Africa misunderstood, or whatever happened to the rural-urban gap?* Geneva, ILO.

Lipton, M. 1977. *Why poor people stay poor: Urban bias in world development*. London, Temple Smith.

Meesook, O. et al. 1986. *Wage policy and the structure of wages and employment in Zambia*, CDP Discussion Paper No. 1986-1, Washington, DC, World Bank.

Turner, H.A. 1965. *Wage trends, wage policies and collective bargaining: The problem for underdeveloped countries*, Occasional Paper, Cambridge, Department of Applied Economics, Cambridge University.

Table 1. Annual salaries paid in a sample of sub-Saharan African countries for posts at different levels of the civil service, selected years, 1970-87

	Lowest	Clerk	Executive officer	Administrative officer low	Administative officer high	Highest
Gambia (Dalasi)						
1972	825	900	2 625	4 000	7 250	12 250
1976	1 644	1 932	3 852	6 336	8 964	16 080
1982	1 884	2 244	4 524	7 284	9 996	17 700
1986	1 980	2 340	4 620	7 380	10 092	17 796
Kenya (Pounds)						
1970	78	252	414	1 104	1 398	2 275
1974	150	312	510	1 212	1 494	2 334
1976	183	369	594	1 350	1 614	2 514
1979	219	399	624	1 446	1 734	2 712
1982	300	531	834	1 794	2 154	3 408
1986	339	594	936	2 010	2 424	3 672
Malawi (Kwacha)						
1970	70	103	398	488	2 330	2 800
1974	150	222	1 038	1 038	4 944	5 937
1979	225	294	1 371	2 481	6 756	9 648
1982	261	312	1 578	2 856	7 770	11 097
1987	396	576	2 064	3 936	11 040	18 084
Nigeria (Naira)						
1970	129	198	621	1 700	2 292	3 900
1975	720	1 164	2 496	5 460	7 104	12 696
1980	1 200	1 500	2 832	5 760	7 404	12 996
1983	1 500	1 752	3 174	6 282	8 034	13 812
Sierra Leone (Leones)						
1970	228	552	1 692	2 568	3 200	6 500
1975	432	759	2 221	3 290	3 936	7 670
1980	702	1 234	3 331	4 935	5 755	10 124
1985	1 187	2 045	4 996	7 403	8 450	13 363
1986	1 662	2 863	6 495	9 624	10 850	16 704
1987	3 324	5 726	12 016	17 805	20 263	28 397
Swaziland (Emalangeni)						
1971	336	480	1 554	3 204	3 840	6 420
1975	587	665	1 440	2 453	3 307	
1978	660	792	1 620	2 760	3 720	10 000
Zambia (Kwacha)						
1970	360	888	1 644	1 944	3 300	6 760
1974	396	1 212	2 052	2 592	3 528	8 200
1975	540	1 536	2 604	3288	4 248	8 616
1980	696	1 692	3 132	3 444	4 404	8 748
1981	984	2 400	3 852	4 692	5 160	12 000

Table 2. Starting salaries (annual) for new entrants to the civil service in a sample of sub-Saharan African countries, by level of qualifications held, selected years, 1970-87

	unsk	prim	1sec	msec	hsec	ugrad
Botswana (Pula)						
1970	211	372	n.a.	528	864	1 920
1974	528	528	n.a.	768	1 188	2 412
1980	1 082	1 248	n.a.	1 752	2 904	4 572
1983	1 257	1 449	n.a.	n.a.	n.a.	5 308
Gambia (Dalasi)						
1972	825	n.a.	n.a.	900	n.a.	4 000
1976	1 644	n.a.	n.a.	1 932	n.a.	6 336
1982	1 884	n.a.	n.a.	2 244	n.a.	7 284
1986	1 980	n.a.	n.a.	2 340	n.a.	7 380
Kenya (Pounds)						
1970	78	135	n.a.	252	n.a.	1 104
1975	150	183	n.a.	312	n.a.	1 212
1980	219	225	n.a.	399	n.a.	1 446
1985	300	354	n.a.	531	n.a.	1 794
1986	339	399	n.a.	594	n.a.	2 010
Sierra Leone (Leones)						
1970	228	n.a.	n.a.	552	876	2 568
1975	432	n.a.	n.a.	759	1 205	3 290
1980	702	n.a.	n.a.	1 234	1 808	4 935
1985	1 187	n.a.	n.a.	2 045	2 713	7 403
1987	3 324	n.a.	n.a.	5 726	7 052	17 805
Zambia (Kwacha)						
1970	360	432	456	888	1 260	1 644
1975	540	684	1 128	1 536	1 776	2 604
1980	696	840	996	1 692	1 836	3 132
1983	1 470	1 773	1 986	2 562	n.a.	3 992

Labour market regulations

Many of the preceding papers touched on labour market regulations and policies, but the following four papers assess the role of labour laws more directly. Werner Sengenberger gives what might be called the standard, or even ILO, view of the rationale in favour of labour regulations, defending them even in circumstances of increased emphasis on competitiveness and arguing that it is perhaps in those circumstances that they are most needed. Christoph Büchtemann gives more force to those arguments by analysing the very specific and topical case of the impact of a specific form of "deregulation", as it was carried out in the Federal Republic of Germany in the 1980s. The question is whether the supply-side view is valid that employment protection regulations impede adjustment and thus employment growth. Büchtemann's response is unequivocal.

At first sight, Swapna Mukhopadhyay's paper on Indian labour laws might seem out of place. But we decided to include it because it is a subtle advocacy for regulation from below as the only realistic way of ensuring a reasonable degree of social protection and economic dynamism. The issues raised in the Indian context are especially relevant in other countries where adjustment programmes have been launched without any apparent regard for the creation of institutional mechanisms to protect those most vulnerable to poverty and labour market marginalisation as a short-term or longer-term consequence.

Gus Edgren and Rashid Amjad summarise developments in Asian labour markets, arguing that in general they have responded well to the needs of adjustment in recent years, and that the regulatory framework has not impeded the process. They go further, in arguing for a human resource development strategy as a crucial element for any successful programme of structural adjustment.

9

The role of labour market regulation in industrial restructuring

by Werner Sengenberger [*]

Introduction

Stemming from major social and economic changes that included greater cyclical fluctuations, the internationalisation of markets, shifts in consumer demand and various demographic trends, the 1970s and 1980s were decades of pervasive industrial restructuring.

Restructuring implies a shift in economic activity, i.e., the cessation of activities that are no longer profitable, the switching to new or better products and processes and the search for new markets. It may thus be said to encompass adjustments in both production and consumption.

A broad range of approaches to such adjustments can be observed (for a typology, see the paper by Guy Standing), some of which are more consonant with labour standards than others. Some have undermined labour institutions. The collective labour market organisations, especially the trade unions, but also to some extent the employers' organisations, have as a result been severely weakened, while the regulation of wages and terms of employment has been diluted. This is mainly the case where competitiveness has been sought through a reduction in labour costs, be it by means of lower wages, greater differentiation in pay or employment norms, or through the exemption from regulation of categories of firms and groups of workers.

Yet in some countries we also find attempts to cope with the challenges without relaxing labour standards, and there are even instances where labour institutions and labour standards have been extended or strengthened in the course of adjustment.

The wide variation of approaches to adjustment invites comparison of both their processes and outcomes. We can thus examine which measures are more compatible with the goals of stable and sustained economic development. In addition - and this is the major object of this paper - we can draw lessons

[*] International Institute for Labour Studies, ILO, Geneva.

235

concerning the requirements and preconditions for the proper functioning of labour standards, and the circumstances under which their full beneficial effects on the economy will unfold.

In assessing the economic and social implications of the various approaches, it is essential to adopt a comprehensive and long-term perspective. The "cheaper" means of adjustment, such as wage concessions, reduced safety standards or more casual employment, may turn out in the end to be the most expensive if one takes into account the costs incurred elsewhere in the economy, or the debt of costs and risks imposed on future generations. In fact, one would achieve flexibility or reap efficiency gains at the expense of other groups of workers, firms, regions or countries. The function of labour standards is to avert this "social pollution" that it is likely to violate the objective of stable and sustained development. Approaches coping with adaptation "internally" appear preferable and, as will be shown, labour market institutions and labour market regulation have a crucial role in both inducing and supporting this route to adjustment.

A clarification of the relationship between labour institutions and restructuring appears particularly desirable. Labour institutions and labour standards have become controversial; they are regarded as "rigidities" and "obstacles" for development by some, while others emphasise their social advantages. There are signs that where industrial restructuring is both economically and socially successful, it is built on forms of social consensus, participation and co-operation between the main actors, rather than on a purely competitive basis. Experience suggests that it is not the volume of economic and technological resources as such, nor their cost and price framework that are crucial for the economic outcome, but rather how effectively these resources are deployed. And the effective use of resources appears to depend on the relations between the key groups involved in restructuring, especially on their readiness and ability to co-operate. This places stable employment relations and security in a new context.

Links between flexibility and labour standards

Labour standards and flexibility are interdependent. This, at least, holds if we talk about functional flexibility and forms of flexibility not just for the individual firm but for the labour market and the economy as a whole.

Firms require flexibility to be able to observe and maintain labour standards. They need to have the capacity to adjust to a changing economic and social environment, without their wages, safety standards and other terms of employment being adversely affected. This implies above all that they have access to resources. As restructuring is a resource-consuming process, the question arises as to how resources can be generated, who bears the costs and risks and who reaps the benefits. Unless they enjoy some kind of monopoly, individual enterprises are normally in a poor position to mobilise resources that are not enterprise-specific, unless labour market competition is in some way regulated. For example, to produce polyvalent worker skills that are not specific to a particular job or to particular activities in one plant, but which can be marketed and utilised more generally in the labour market, some social accord is normally required that provides a generally-accepted formula for the sharing of training costs and the distribution of the risks of loss of returns arising from worker quits. Without this arrangement, individual employers are unlikely to pay for skill formation, out of fear of losing the workers after training. In other words, firms have not only to understand that worker qualification may be beneficial to restructuring, but also that they share this interest with other firms and that the joint generation and utilisation of skills can produce superior results beneficial to all of them. Collective solutions of this kind make collective organisation in the labour market imperative. They presuppose institutions that engage in the setting, implementation and control of rules and regulations.

Collective agreement on the content, cost and risk distribution of restructuring by no means implies that labour market competition is eliminated. It means, instead, a channelling of competition in "socially desirable directions", restricting certain avenues of adjustment that are held to be socially unacceptable and becoming the basis for standards of *protection* in a labour code. It requires, furthermore, the specification of "acceptable" actions and, consequently, institutional support for them. In resolving their adjustment problems, firms can only meet social obligations if they are *able* to adopt "profitable" solutions. To envisage such solutions and to make them economically attractive, labour institutions must not merely tell firms "what they shouldn't do", but also suggest suitable paths of development and promote them. *Promotion* is, thus, vital to make protection feasible and manageable. To make both protection and promotion effective, *participation* of the key groups, including management and labour, at the various levels of decision-making is indispensable. It is this aspect of labour institutions and labour standards, seen as a coherent "package" of regulations, which is central to their having a positive impact on the process of change. The subject of evaluation should therefore be the totality of interventions into the labour market rather than each individual rule taken separately.

It can be demonstrated that where labour standards are violated, it is usually the insufficient development of one or the other of these three basic ingredients of a social solution to the adjustment problem - participation, protection and promotion - which is to blame, rather than the prescription of labour standards as such. This perspective can help us to understand why during the past decade labour organisations and the regulation of the labour market have come to be so heavily criticised, both in intellectual debate and in the policy-making arena, and why they have been accused of pushing up labour costs, generating inefficiency and stifling competition. From observing the malfunctioning of one or the other rule, people have jumped to the conclusion that labour standards generally engender labour market rigidities. While there may have been instances of cumbersome rules, they are not due to the existence of regulation per se, but to the insufficient support of these rules and procedures by other, complementary measures that allow enterprises to seek more dynamic outcomes. Frequently, protective regulation could not be maintained and has been weakened by repeated violation or by a relaxation of legislation. Due to a lack of participative and promotive arrangements, there have been no feasible or effective alternative courses of restructuring that could have enabled the observance of these rules. This will be demonstrated with regard to employment protection.

A preliminary conclusion from an analysis of the role and functioning of labour institutions in the course of recent restructuring in Western market economies is the following: *where labour organisations and labour market regulation have appeared to conflict with adjustment requirements or, more specifically, where labour market flexibility has been felt to be restricted by the existing labour code, this was not so much a function of the excessive development of labour institutions as of their insufficient development.* There was too little institutional support to enable a viable outcome in line with existing social standards.

I feel encouraged to take this view because it has not been in those countries, industries or regions with extensive and comprehensive labour market institutions and labour market regulation that existing regulation has been most challenged, but where labour institutions and collective bargaining were comparatively weak and regulation fragmentary. In other words, deregulation occurred where at least one of the three vital components, participation, protection and promotion, was underdeveloped or non-existent.

Opportunities for socially adequate restructuring are limited most where insufficient and unbalanced development of labour market organisations and regulation exists and where intervention and support are restricted to the firm or industry level, or to action on the national plane. This observation applies, for instance, to the remarkable international divergence in the ability of trade unions to cope with the challenges posed by restructuring. Waning influence and falling membership of trade unions have been particularly striking in countries where union representation focusses merely on the firm, or where it is altogether absent from the firm, existing perhaps only at the national level. Conversely, trade unions whose organisation and methods of representation and operation span both central and local levels have tended to remain intact (Kjellberg, 1983; Visser, 1988). It follows that during the 1980s unions in weakly unionised countries, for example France, the United States of America, the Netherlands and Japan, have been weakened further, whereas those in highly unionised countries such as Sweden, Denmark, Finland, Iceland and Norway, have withstood the crisis much better. In these countries, union membership and density actually increased. There are nevertheless some exceptions to this pattern, such as the United Kingdom and Italy, where unions throughout the 1980s have faced heavy losses.

The interdependence of labour institutions and adjustment capacity: The case of employment protection

Firms need dynamic flexibility to be able to maintain labour standards, and they achieve this flexibility only with effective and comprehensive labour market regulation. This key proposition can be illustrated by examining the effects of employment protection in industrialised countries.

(a) No effective employment protection without flexibility

To shield workers from loss of employment, skill, income and other hazards in the case of business downturns or in relation to the installing of new methods or organisation of work, various legal and contractual arrangements were introduced or consolidated in the course of the 1960s and 1970s. Foremost among them were: advance notice in case of dismissal; the requirement of public authorisation of mass dismissal; the application of social criteria for selecting workers to be made redundant, so as to cushion the adverse effects of redundancy; forms of indemnity for redundant workers; and the requirement to use means of adjustment short of dismissal, such as overtime reduction, lower labour input, etc. These stipulations had the effect of either restricting legally the termination of employment contracts or of making redundancies more expensive, inducing employers to smooth workforce adjustment and thereby generate employment continuity in the course of cyclical fluctuations of labour demand and the rationalisation of production.

Whether these labour norms could be practised and employment stabilised, hinged on the firm's ability to prevent redundancies, or at least reduce the number by resorting to other means of resolving the problem of excess labour. If such means did not exist, inevitably the labour standard would be violated or ignored.

Take, for example, a piece of legislation for employment protection in place in France until 1986. Enterprises wanting to make workers redundant had to obtain authorisation from a factory inspector, who assessed the economic rationale given by the firm and social aspects before approving dismissals. In practice, however, redundancies were more easily permitted than in the Federal Republic of Germany or Sweden, where the authorisation requirements were far less rigorous. In addition, for fear of not being able to lay off workers when they no longer needed them, employers were reluctant to take them. Contrary to intentions, then, the requirement of public authorisation in France failed to stabilise employment (Brunhes, 1989, p. 27). In 1986, following strong pressure from employers' organisations, the authorisation procedure was relaxed considerably and it is now easier for private firms in France to lay workers off than in the Federal Republic of Germany or in Sweden.

One conclusion would be that collective standards merely curb flexibility, restrict competitiveness and are thus, in the end, futile. Another explanation is that protection cannot work as long as there are no effective alternative ways of handling the excess labour other than dismissal. Indeed there was, as many studies of the French labour market tell us, insufficient intra-firm numerical flexibility to deal with the redundancy problem. There were, for example, no provisions for publicly financed short-time working that would have permitted enterprises to maintain their labour force until labour demand picked up. Functional flexibility, involving switching to new products and processes, was also somewhat unfeasible. Due to rigid internal rules of labour allocation and exacerbated by insufficient training facilities, the scope for adjustment by way of internal conversion to new activities proved rather limited. There was little tradition of vocational worker training in France, and the French trade unions had comparatively little power at the enterprise level, which could have been used to push for positive solutions. There were, to use the above language, few institutions that could have encouraged "participation" and "promotion" to stem dismissals. This was recognised in a Parliamentary Bill introduced in May 1989, following discussions with unions and employers, to strengthen measures against redundancies. The draft Bill sought to introduce more joint union-employer control over workforce reduction; it foresaw "social plans" in the case of redundancies and the right of worker involvement in the execution of those plans.

In examining the experience of other countries with employment security provisions, one notices that norms for the protection of workers from dismissal were not the only labour standards undermined in the era of restructuring. We have seen almost everywhere the spread of irregular and a-typical forms of employment, such as fixed-term employment and casual work, which as a rule provide considerably less protection and less social security than the conventional standard employment contract. Moreover, a frequent response to adjustment was the reduction of wages or fringe benefits, through so-called "concession bargaining". These arrangements implied temporary or permanent cuts in worker pay in order to "save" existing employment or make future jobs more "competitive". Other serious encroachments into labour standards come from a relaxation of de facto health and safety standards by delaying or decreasing investments in safer equipment.

Frequently, such concessions are justified by arguing, "better a poor job than no job at all". This line of thinking implies that labour standards such as employment security, contract wages or safety standards are a sort of "luxury" affordable in prosperous periods, but which must be compromised when the going gets rough. While I do not wish to defend labour regulation in all circumstances, I would nevertheless argue that in most cases it would be short-sighted to perceive labour standards and adjustment as being in conflict with each other. That view disregards the adverse effects which a squeezing of labour can generate later in the same plant, firm or area, as well as in other establishments. Lower safety standards, for example, are likely to reduce the firm's effective labour supply, both through higher accident rates and through the reduced ability of the firm to attract qualified labour. This in turn may mean losses in productivity and the cancelling of the initial cost advantage. So, cutting labour costs in this fashion may turn out to be a Pyrrhic victory, actually proving more expensive for the firm in the long run.

Seeking competitive advantages through cutting standards may also engender "social pollution" by affecting demand or supply conditions elsewhere in the economy. Thus the widespread practice of wage concessions to restore or maintain competitiveness, or the lowering of social security levies, may mean reduced national income and weaker domestic demand. Moreover, it may contribute to poverty and induce a vicious circle of low wage employment and high social security costs.

The function of labour standards is precisely to stem the short-sighted, parochial economic rationality of the "here and now", a logic pertaining only to the individual firm and one that disregards negative external effects and long-term implications. Standards exist to avert competitive behaviour built on cheap labour, in the place of which they encourage competition based on innovation and increasing productivity. This in turn can enhance the level of qualification and adaptive capacity of the workforce, which may then facilitate future restructuring.

(b) Functional flexibility and restructuring

Instead of seeking to adapt through wage cuts, by lowering the quality of employment or otherwise reducing worker standards, restructuring may be accomplished through what has been termed "functional flexibility" - the conversion of the economic base to new and more competitive activities, with the ability to switch flexibly between them. This transformation may occur inside or outside a plant or enterprise, and as such we may distinguish between "internal" and "external" reconversion (Sengenberger, 1990).

Internal reconversion implies a shift in the firm's spectrum of products and/or production processes, coupled with the internal redeployment of the workforce in new tasks and functions. The latter normally entails retraining and possibly skill upgrading for the incumbent workforce, which is generally easier to accomplish if the qualification level is high initially. In most instances, internal reconversion means not only that a firm will engage itself in other activities, but also that it will undertake a wider production range. Such *diversification* makes the firm less vulnerable to the business cycle of particular products or to particular product cycles which, in the course of the past two decades, have tended to become shorter (Loveman, 1989). It also permits the firm to be less dependent on particular customers or suppliers. This is an important consideration for small- and medium-sized firms, which ordinarily have a limited range of products and services. Being able to respond quickly to new customers or new markets helps the firm to escape pressures from particular clients and from being constrained within particular price schedules and delivery terms. Diversification provides alternatives; it endows the firm with versatility in both the product and labour markets.

Internal restructuring through diversification was successfully practised among supplier and subcontractor firms in the German automobile industry when they saw themselves acting increasingly as buffers to the fluctuating business volume of big automobile companies in the 1970s. By adding new or related products to the production programme, they managed to manipulate in their favour a business relationship otherwise potentially characterised by subordination and dependency. In the meantime, large companies have begun to appreciate the benefits of suppliers with multiple clients and more broadly structured activities. They have learned that this stimulates higher quality, faster responses and better adaptibility to changing requirements. One may now even find customer firms insisting that they receive from any one of their subcontractors no more than 30 per cent of its total output so as to induce a regime of diversified business relations.

Diversification was also achieved in the German steel industry over the past twenty years in response to declining demand for basic iron and steel products. Under the system of worker co-determination, it proved particularly difficult to dismiss workers, and management was compelled to utilise the workforce in a different manner. Practically all steel companies started to extend their activities to iron and steel processing, engineering and trading. Today, there is no steel company retaining more than 45 per cent of its production in the iron and steel sector. Internal restructuring permitted the retension and redevelopment of capital and human resources in the same area, a factor of vital importance for endogenous economic development.

In some quarters, however, industrial decline was so rapid and pervasive that intra-enterprise reconversion proved impossible. This was especially true where the economic base of a whole industry collapsed or was eroded, as occurred for example in shipbuilding. Under these circumstances, "external" reconversion to entirely new activities became imperative, and it is interesting to study how the problem of massive production redundancy was resolved in various countries. By any measure, Sweden provides the best case studies of this type of restructuring. With a share of 10 per cent of world production, up to the early 1970s the Swedish shipbuilding industry was second only to Japan. Today there is not a single large shipyard left in Sweden. Within little more than a decade, an industry with around 25,000 employees had to be retrenched because of declining demand and was converted to entirely different economic use in the same region, partly through bringing in new industry and partly through the creation of public employment. While the transition was not totally devoid of social tension, it was comparatively smooth and at no point did the unemployment rate in the area exceed 3.5 per cent. Clearly, no single company could have shouldered the restructuring independently. The adjustment was made possible only by following a tri-partite approach involving the concerted efforts of employers, trade unions and government at local, regional and national levels.

According to Strath (1989), who documented the case, the following conditions were essential in assuring the adaptation: a strong and unified labour movement; union readiness not to defend unprofitable business but to support the development of new activities; the augmentation of industrial relations legislation in the early 1970s, extending the rights of worker co-determination in the event of operational changes; the existence of a national industrial policy facilitating restructuring across industries and regions; and finally, active labour market policy that permitted massive retraining of the redundant shipbuilding labour force.

This case illustrates the adaptive strength that can be derived from the collaboration, on various organisational levels, of the major interest groups, and from a coherent industrial policy linked to active labour market policy. It vividly demonstrates that protective standards need to be complemented and underpinned by institutions that afford worker promotion and participation. Lessons drawn from Europe with regard to the role of active, supportive public policy are consistent with experience in developing countries, where the absence of such policies and the corresponding lack of models have hindered the elaboration of solutions to the question of flexible adaptation (see also Geller, third volume).

Labour market regulation and type of competition

The creation of collective labour market organisations and the setting of norms and procedures to regulate competition will not eliminate competition, but will change its nature. The degree of transformation depends in part on the universality of standards, their effective control, and on the degree of differentiation found in regulated wages and other terms of employment.

(a)   Downward-directed labour market competition

Orthodox labour market theory starts from the idea of resource allocation based on factor prices. Disequilibrium in the labour market indicated by the over-use, the under-use, or non-use of labour is resolved more or less automatically through adaptations in the wage levels and changes in the price structure, i.e. wage differentials and other terms of employment. The belief that lower wages generate more jobs continues to preoccupy the minds of economists in spite of evidence to the contrary. To mention just one instance, repeated programmes in Europe to cheapen labour for the firm through wage cost subsidies, whereby employers hiring unemployed persons are subsidised for up to 90 per cent of the wage cost, have rarely led to the creation of substantially more employment opportunities.

Labour standards, it is argued from this perspective, impair the adjustment mechanism, the more universal they are, the more effective they are in fixing the terms of employment and the more they compress differentials across occupations, type of firm, size of plant, industry and territory. Setting an effective minimum floor for wages, fringe benefits, hours of work, social security, employment protection, health and safety, etc., and fixing the differentials between these terms, create "rigidities" in the utilisation of labour, which prevent the market from clearing.

Following this understanding of how the labour market works or should work, various initiatives have been taken to "deregulate", with the aim of rendering more flexible the labour market and labour utilisation, while bringing labour cost schedules of individual firms in line with their productivity. In many instances this change in regulation amounted to a greater differentiation in pay and other terms of employment, either within firms, as a result of increased differentials between skill levels, or between firms. As far as the latter is concerned, it was argued that regional imbalances in employment would be eliminated by larger wage differentials, that sectoral change across industries and between industries could be spurred by accentuated sectoral differentiation, and that growth of small firm employment could be encouraged by lowering the direct labour cost or by exempting this sector from various kinds of social protection enforcements and obligations. Although not explicitly argued in these terms, these measures amounted to injecting further inequalities into the labour market to improve flexibility.

While I do not wish to deny the relevance of labour costs, or appear to speak against any kind of differential for labour market adjustment, I would like to emphasise the detrimental impact of greater inequality on the restructuring process, and to direct attention to the role of standards in improving productivity. To the extent that the firm is allowed more freedom to compete through lower wages and other labour cost reductions, one not only discourages it from investing in human resource development, but in addition, one also removes the incentives for it to seek more dynamic paths to competitiveness, such as process innovation to gain higher productivity, product innovation or diversification. Removing institutional barriers to make labour cheaper carries the risk of entering a vicious circle of low cost, low productivity and low rates of innovation. This *downward-directed type of competition* is more likely, the more forcefully the more extensive the relaxation of standards and the more decentralised the wage-setting process. Given pervasive internationalisation of markets, it is questionable whether a low-wage strategy of competition can succeed in improving competitiveness. On the contrary, it pushes national industries into a fierce price and wage competition for the same standard good.

If it turns out that a particular industry or nation does not meet these competitive pressures, it is likely that further calls for wage moderation or even wage cuts will be provoked, initiating a new cycle of poor compensation, low productivity and declining international competitiveness.

It has been demonstrated that countries with large inter-sectoral wage differentials or large wage disparities by size of firm also have large productivity differentials. Thus, the United States, Japan and the United Kingdom stand out as countries with above average wage differentiation by industry, the first two also ranking top with regard to enterprise-size related pay differentials. The Nordic counties and the continental European countries, on the other hand, show comparatively minor wage gaps. This is reflected in their respective productivity differentials: they are moderate in Europe, enormous in Japan (Sengenberger, 1987).

This nexus between dispersion of wages and dispersion of productivity is easy to understand. Large pay differentials between enterprises or plants of various size go hand in hand with large productivity gaps. Conversely, in a system of wage determination that imposes uniformity in wage structure according to firm size or sector, productivity will also have to differ less, since firms with poor efficiency will not be able to meet the wage standard and will be squeezed out of the market.

A widening of wage differentials by firm size or the exemption of small firms from security arrangements, worker rights or social obligations is unlikely to yield competitive advantages to this sector, as orthodox economic theory asserts. Rather, the supposed advantages may turn out to be counter-productive for small firm performance. The inferior rewards in small firms will make it more difficult to recruit and retain skilled labour. Qualified and versatile manpower, however, is a crucial asset for many small enterprises in implementing a strategy of differentiated high quality production and for quick adjustment in the product market. Low wages often induce a drain of managerial talent and worker competence from the small firm sector, which will consequently threaten the competitiveness and survival of small enterprises. Moreover, widened labour-cost differentials constitute an incentive for large firms to use small firms as "buffers" against fluctuating demand and to step up their subcontracting and outsourcing, since small firms can produce more cheaply. While this may engender a shift of employment from large to small units, it merely amounts to a displacement of existing employment rather than additional jobs, and will not improve the overall level of efficiency (for details, see Sengenberger and Loveman, 1987; Sengenberger, 1988).

(b) Upward-directed competition

What viable alternative can be proposed that is compatible with labour standards? An appropriate strategy might set out to ban downward-directed wage price competition both by setting an effective floor to wage rates and other conditions of employment and by limiting differentials in these terms. This would make it unattractive for firms to survive or gain new competitive power simply by retreating to low wage areas, union-free zones or smaller plants with lower wages and less security, etc. It would guide the entrepreneur or manager towards alternative products, new markets and better technology in order to stay in business; it would spur, in other words, more dynamic competition and functional flexibility. If downward wage competition is barred and employers cannot eschew the labour standards there will be a likelihood of upward-directed wage competition. Yet, as long as that competition engenders productivity growth, wage improvements need not translate into higher unit labour costs and need not cause wage costs to fuel inflation. Indeed, considering OECD countries, it would be difficult to pretend that those with comprehensive collective wage-setting arrangements have had the poorest records of unit labour cost development.

It should nevertheless be recognised that setting a floor in the terms of employment is a necessary but not a sufficient condition for attaining dynamic efficiency. What, then, are the other conditions?

First of all, dynamic restructuring requires a more or less continuous re-adjustment of the labour force in terms of skill and qualification. It demands extensive investment in general training and retraining, which is of value to more than a single employer. This is more likely if the skill formation process is not left to the individual firm, but is part of a collective arrangement under which employers understand that they have a common interest in nurturing a versatile, adaptable labour force, and under which they share the cost and the risk of losing the return in the event of labour turnover.

Second, after resolving the "social" problem of skill formation skills must be utilised as fully as possible. This means providing jobs with a sufficiently broad skill content, as well as easy paths of internal job change with scope for additional learning and the opportunity to apply the skills acquired. Workers need to be granted employment security for, as has been shown by Thurow (1975), unless they can be reasonably sure that passing on their knowledge and operational skills will not be detrimental to their employment and income status, individual worker co-operation is unlikely. Instead, the insecure workers will tend to monopolise their competence.

There is another collective dimension to worker co-operation in industrial restructuring. As we know from numerous case studies, workers will accept and collaborate in innovation and modernisation only as far as the potential labour saving effects of restructuring do not threaten their employment. Loss of particular jobs is acceptable as long as others with equivalent pay and status are available. Again, in convincing the worker that such a quid-pro-quo can actually work, collaborative industrial relations are indispensable.

Finally, mutual trust is required when it comes to fostering inter-firm co-operation in order to achieve larger economies of scale and scope in the innovation process. Firms can attain substantial collective efficiency from the joint development of resources (e.g. through joint R & D; product design; joint resource utilisation; sharing of technology and equipment, etc.). In eliciting such inter-firm co-operation, purely individual opportunistic logic would prove a barrier. Firms need to arrive at an understanding of the areas in which they are to compete with each other and recognise of those steps considered unacceptable in gaining competitive advantages. Labour utilisation often plays an important role in this arrangement. Bonds of collaboration can easily be strained or destroyed if firms "cheat" on that front, by undercutting going rates of pay and social security standards, for example. Codified, enforcible and controllable standards thus have a vital function in building and maintaining trust, both in the labour market and the product market.

Labour standards as input or output to economic development

In advocating what has been termed here "dynamic upward-directed restructuring", or what in a wider perspective is named a "social adjustment approach", one can be sure of encountering sooner or later the objection that this concept may be appropriate for the advanced industrialised countries but ill-suited for developing nations. The appropriateness of this model for the latter is said to hinge, at least for some time to come, on their particular characteristics, namely lower wages and lesser protection.

Referring to the economic theory of comparative advantage (elaborated in Servais, 1989, p. 428), it is often argued that while technology and capital are cheaper in the industrialised countries, an abundant supply of low-cost labour is one of the labour market advantages of low-income countries. In view of this division, it is suggested that a trading arrangement beneficial to both "North" and "South" could be forged. It is assumed that the cost advantages of developing countries would gradually strengthen their position in international trade and thus permit them eventually to catch up with the more industrially advanced countries.

The implication of this position for labour standards is that one should abstain from improving standards in the developing world because it would eradicate the cost advantage. The same arguments are used today, incidentally, to warn against minimum wages and "upward harmonisation" of wage and working conditions within the European Communities. Efficiency levels in the poorer countries would first have to be raised and employment expanded before one could think about bringing wages and social standards closer to each other (Layard, 1989). But what, in fact, suggests that competitiveness built on lower cost levels will enable a country to catch up with the more advanced countries, and why should this lead to the higher labour productivity levels which seem indispensable for development?

Another way of characterising the point would be to say that there are two conflicting views as to how to raise labour standards. One regards standards as an outcome or an *output* of economic development, so that economic performance must improve before standards become feasible or practicable. This comes close to viewing labour standards as a luxury good, afforded only by the affluent. The counter-position would be to argue that labour standards are a necessary *input* to any comprehensive and sustainable economic progress, thus standards must precede development. While it is obvious that wage levels in developing countries cannot be lifted quickly, it remains paramount to create and observe basic worker rights and to set an agenda for the reduction of the social gap. In particular, it would seem essential to change relative wages and income distribution in order to eliminate the low wage sector and hence curb the opportunities for firms to compete on the basis of cheaper labour. This holds regardless of the average wage in the country concerned.

As long as low wages prevail, there is little incentive for employers to make the necessary investments to make human resources more productive and hence more "valuable". More productive labour, much more than advanced technology or the capacity for exporting, appears to be the crucial variable for effective development. Low wages also contribute to the persistence of labour surplus, because they force more people to enter the labour market in order to attain a subsistence income. An extensive labour surplus and low wages reinforce each other. They render effective labour standards almost impossible as long as workers are forced to compete unconditionally. Only in the course of establishing minimum rights and standards on a broad front can this circle be effectively intercepted (Polanyi, 1978). Only then can people begin to liberate themselves from coercive behaviour in the labour market and begin to acquire something resembling the individual choice, which economists emphasise as a precondition for a free and efficient labour market.

There is in this respect no difference between the "developed" and "developing" countries. Labour standards are indivisible by region. Countries that permit a large sector of low-paid and unregulated labour perpetuate downward-directed competition, which stifles comprehensive development. So-called developed countries do show pockets of "underdevelopment" - some more than others - and the difference between these and the poorer countries is one of degree rather than one of fundamental qualitative difference.

Summary and conclusions

In the face of greater volatility, qualitatively altered demands in product markets in recent years and the correspondingly increased or accelerated need for industrial restructuring, various philosophies and approaches have been adopted to cope with the challenges.

One such approach placed the onus of adjustment on the labour market. Assuming that labour market regulation creates "rigidities" and thus constitutes an impediment to adjustment, a scaling down or revision of rules and regulations was advocated and implemented, as well as a relaxation of norms and procedures, to make labour more flexible. The effect of a good deal of the measures taken has been to generate further inequality and insecurity in employment. In some instances, the level of pay was lowered in order to maintain competitivity.

This "low road" to restructuring has not produced the expected superior results. Those industrial sectors or countries that followed the "high road" to restructuring succeeded in maintaining comprehensive systems of industrial relations and collective bargaining, in keeping a well-developed welfare state and in avoiding massive deregulation, while accomplishing much better structural adaptation - as indicated by their international trade balance and other measures of economic performance.

The decisive factor accounting for the superior performance of economies that respected labour standards is the premium of adjustment power provided by a more productive and versatile workforce, which affords greater scope and more options to competitive strategies. Labour standards, when observed, prevent management from seeking an easy way out to the adjustment problem by resorting to cheap labour and price competition. While advantages derived from labour cost cutting cannot entirely be overlooked, they mostly turn out to be illusory and short-lived in the measure that they fail to improve productive capacity. To accomplish such improvements it seems indispensable to find innovative ways to compete in the product market, through the creation of better products and processes. By barring "cheap" solutions, labour standards can pave the way to such dynamic competition rather than stifling it.

Nevertheless, for this climate of "constructive" competition to unfold, it seems essential that "protective" standards, which forestall undesirable, downward-directed paths of adjustment be complemented by standards of "promotion", which help enterprises to implement desirable measures. Also necessary are standards of "participation", which are vital for fully exploiting know-how in the workforce and for assuring an equitable distribution of the costs and risks of adjustment. Where any one of these mutually reinforcing elements is missing, socially unsatisfactory outcomes are likely. The implication is that labour standards should not be watered down but should be more fully developed, so that they can bring to bear their beneficial impact on industrial reorganisation.

The critical role of labour standards is to overcome the misguided preoccupation with cost cutting, instead redirecting attention to the strengthening of productive power. Making human labour more productive and versatile is the most important consideration. Labour standards - to the extent that they restrain any opportunistic practice which seeks to gain advantage through the substandard utilisation of labour - can help to build relations of trust between firms, a vital precondition for the co-operation so essential for competitiveness.

References

Brunhes, B. 1989. "Labour flexibility in enterprises: A comparison of firms in four European Countries", in OECD (ed.). *Labour market flexibility - Trends in enterprises.* Paris pp. 11-36.

Deakin, S.; Wilkinson, F. 1989. *Labour law, social security, and economic inequality.* Unpublished paper. Cambridge, United Kingdom, Department of Applied Economics, University of Cambridge.

Kjellberg, A. 1983. *Tackling organisering; tolv länder.* Lund, University of Lund.

Layard, R. 1989. "A cautionary tale of North and South", in *Financial Times,* 22 Nov. 1989.

Loveman, G. 1989. "Changes in the organisation of production and skill composition of employment". Doctoral Disseration. Cambridge, Massachusetts, Massachusetts Institute of Technology.

Polanyi, K. 1978. *The great transformation.* Frankfurt, Campus-Verlag.

Sengenberger, W. 1988. "Economic and social perspectives of small enterprises", in *Labour and Society,* Vol. 13, No. 3, July 1988, pp. 249-259.

Sengenberger, W.; Loveman, G. 1987. *Smaller units of employment: A synthesis report on industrial reorganisation in industrialised countries.* Geneva, International Institute for Labour Studies.

Sengenberger, W. 1987. *Struktur und Funktionsweise von Arbeitsmarktes - Die Bundesrepublik Deutschland im internationalen Vergleich* [Structure and function of the labour market - The Federal Republic of Germany in international comparison]. Frankfurt/New York, Campus-Verlag.

Sengenberger, W. 1990. "Flexibility in the labour market - internal versus external adjustments in international comparison", in Schettkat, R.; Appelbaum, E. (eds.). *Labour market adjustment to structural change and technological progress.* New York, Praeger Publishers.

Servais, J.M. 1989. "The social clause in trade agreements. Wishful thinking or an instrument of social progress?", in *International Labour Review,* Vol. 128, No. 4, 1989, pp. 423-432.

Strath, B. 1989. "Industrial restructuring in the Swedish shipbuilding industry", in *Labour and Society,* Vol. 14, No. 2, Apr. 1989, pp. 105-120.

Thurow, L. 1975. *Generating inequality.* New York, Basic Books.

Visser, J. 1988. "Trade unionism in Western Europe: Present situation and prospects", in *Labour and Society,* Vol. 13, No. 2, Apr. 1988, pp. 125-182.

Visser, J. 1990. *Elements of a historial sociology of union growth.* Unpublished paper. Trento, Italy.

10

Does (de-)regulation matter? Employment protection and temporary work in the Federal Republic of Germany

by Christoph Büchtemann [*]

Introduction: "De-regulating" labour relations

De-regulation has become a major issue within the Western European debate on the labour market and employment policy. Under the impact of persistently high unemployment, heavy job losses in industrial core sectors and slow employment growth in the economic upswings following the recessions of the mid-1970s and early 1980s, the institutional infrastructure of labour markets that evolved in most countries during the 1960s and 1970s has been called into doubt, with respect to allocative efficiency and capacity to adjust to socio-economic and technological change. Whereas during the 1970s labour market disequilibria were largely regarded as crises in the labour market, the prevailing diagnosis has shifted towards that of a crisis of the labour market itself and its institutional infrastructure. Institutional arrangements of wage setting, working time regimes, job security, employment stability and shop-floor industrial relations that may have been efficient and even increased adjustment flexibility during periods of sustained economic growth and full employment based on the expansion of industrial ("Fordist") mass production have come to be seen as "rigidities" hampering adjustment to enhanced competitive pressures and increasing economic uncertainties. Consequently, increasing labour market flexibility through institutional "de-regulation" and a revitalisation of regulation through market mechanisms became the principal employment policy of the 1980s.

De-regulation of this type has been implemented in various ways by many Western European governments during the past decade. Labour standards have been reduced gradually, for example in the areas of working time and protective regulations; and in such fields as employment security, standards have been selectively suspended or abolished for certain types of jobs or

[*] *Wissenschaftszentrum Berlin für Sozialforschung* [Social Science Research Centre, Berlin], Berlin.

workers. Collective bargaining has shown a tendency towards decentralisation from industry level to the level of individual firms. In the Federal Republic of Germany, de-regulation of labour relations by legislative changes in the institutional framework of the labour market has been rather modest as compared with other European countries such as France or the United Kingdom. De-regulation has been largely restricted to minor modifications in labour law, such as a relaxation of working time regulations for apprenticeship training, the introduction of a six-month waiting period for employment protection of disabled workers, a modest reduction of the range of legal employment protection in small firms, and the legal facilitation of the use of temporary work (Buechtemann and Neumann, 1989).

However, from an analytical perspective, the concept of de-regulation covers more than just the active reduction of labour standards and the abolition of protective regulations through direct legislative changes and institutional modifications of the system of industrial relations. Apart from active or direct de-regulation, which has been in the focus of the recent political debate, there is also a process of passive or indirect de-regulation[1] resulting from structural changes on both the demand and the supply side of labour markets, and the non-adjustment of the institutional framework of labour markets to these developments. Thus the increase in "non-standard" or "atypical" forms of labour, such as self-employment, marginal part-time work and casual or temporary employment, frequently promoted through government programmes, has resulted in a growing part of the labour force being more or less excluded from protective regulations and social security standards applying to jobs conforming to the socially protected "standard employment relationship". Likewise, the growth of employment in small firms has led to a reduction of the range of legal employment protection regulations, collective representation at firm level and collectively negotiated benefits.

Whereas "indirect" de-regulation via the expansion of small firms and the increase in "non-standard" forms of employment has been intensively researched,[2] measures of "active" de-regulation in terms of a direct reduction or partial abolition of labour standards, though highly controversial in public debates on employment policy, have hardly been evaluated with respect to their impact on firms' manpower policies and job creation.

"Eurosclerosis", employment protection and temporary work

In debates about labour market flexibility and "institutional rigidities" supposedly reducing labour market efficiency, much attention has been given to employment protection and job security (OECD, 1986; OECD, 1989). Under the heading of "Eurosclerosis", legal employment protection regulations as well as collectively bargained employment security provisions, introduced and expanded during the 1960s and early 1970s, have come to be widely regarded as hampering employment adjustment, increasing labour costs, and thus accounting at least in part for persistently high unemployment in many Western European countries:

- by slowing down workforce reductions in times of declining labour demand, lay-off restraints such as legally imposed prenotification periods, redundancy procedures, and collectively bargained severance payments have been assumed to reduce firms' willingness to hire additional workers when the economy recovers, thus having a depressing effect on the level of employment over the cycle;

- by imposing restraints on individual dismissals, employment protection regulations are said to induce firms to increase selectivity and intensify worker screening when filling vacancies, thus promoting tendencies towards a segmentation between "outsiders" and "insiders" in the labour market, as manifested in the relative growth in long-term unemployment in most Western European countries;[3]

- as a way of evading legal and collectively bargained dismissal restraints, firms are assumed to recur to temporary staff and subcontracting instead ofadditional regular employees, thus promoting the growth of an "unprotected sector" which may result in a "two-tier society", "one with rigid job security requirements covering high-paid, senior full-time workers in large firms, the other more flexible, with part-time, low-paid, insecure workers in small businesses" (Hamermesh, 1988, p. 22).

Consequently, a relaxation, if not partial abolition, of employment protection regulations has gained high priority on the agenda of direct deregulation of labour relations as a way of stimulating employment and combating unemployment. The attention these have received from academics and policy-makers, however, contrasts with the absence of evidence to support them. Recent reviews, indeed, have concluded that "the empirical evidence on the impact of job security policies is fragmentary at best" (OECD, 1986, p. 92) and that it is best to "remain agnostic on this question" (Layard and Nickell, 1985; also Gennard, 1986; and Franz, 1989).[4]

Despite, this many Western European governments (for example, the United Kingdom, Federal Republic of Germany, France, Italy and Spain) have relaxed legal standards in the area of redundancy and dismissal protection and/or widened "loopholes" within systems of employment protection, e.g. by facilitating fixed-term contracts or reducing restrictions on the use of temporary workers from agencies (Emerson, 1988).

In the Federal Republic of Germany, the federal Government in 1985 passed the Employment Promotion Act 1985 *(Beschäftigungsförderungsgesetz 1985)* [5] which - apart from introducing new regulations for part-time work and job sharing - relaxed employment protection regulations for newly established small enterprises,[6] prolonged maximum periods for the use of agency workers,[7] and reduced legal restraints on fixed-term contracts. Among these innovations, the relaxation of legal restraints on fixed-term contracts has been the most important as well as most controversial new regulation enacted by the EPA. By this measure, initially designed to be in force for a limited period (1985-90) only, but prolonged until the end of 1995, the Government hoped to exert a positive impact on firms' hiring decisions in the face of persisting uncertainty over future labour demand. The spread of fixed-term contracts by the EPA can be regarded as a political compromise between the supporters of more thorough "de-regulation" of employment protection and the opponents of "de-regulation", headed by the unions, who wish to maintain a high degree of protection for the employed. In anticipation of the ending of the new regulations on temporary work in 1990, the Government in 1987 commissioned the Social Science Research Centre (WZB) to carry out a comprehensive evaluation of their impact on hiring decisions and job creation.[8]

Some of the main results are discussed in the following pages. After a brief outline of key characteristics of the regulatory context of the EPA some of the main findings on the use of temporary job arrangements and the new regulations will be summarised. In the concluding part these findings are discussed with regard to the more general question if "de-regulative" changes within the institutional framework of the labour market are likely to modify essential parameters of the "job generation process" and thus can be expected to boost employment.

The regulatory context: Employment protection and legal regulation of temporary work in the Federal Republic of Germany

Both the legislative changes brought about by the EPA and their impact on firms' manpower policies have to be seen in the wider context of the institutional framework of the Federal German labour market and the system of legal and collective employment protection.

Employment protection regulations

From an international perspective the Federal Republic of Germany certainly belongs to those countries with an elaborate system of employment protection. This is reflected by the results of a survey conducted by the International Organisation of Employers (IOE, 1985), according to which the Federal Republic of Germany ranked second after France among those countries in which legal obstacles to the termination of employment contracts are classified as "fundamental" (Emerson, 1988, p. 791).

Employment protection is regulated by law, court decisions and collective agreements, and covers the vast majority of the workforce.[9] Apart from seniority-based advance notification periods laid down by the Civil Code *(Bürgerliches Gesetzbuch)* and extended by collective agreements,[10] statutory employment protection has been regulated by the Federal German Dismissal Protection Act *(Kündigungsschutzgesetz)* of 1951 as amended in 1969, which covers all workers regularly employed for more than six months in establishments with at least six employees (excluding apprentices), i.e. roughly 80 per cent of the total dependent workforce. The regulations of the Act require all dismissals to be justified by "just cause";[11] with dismissals for economic reasons, "just cause" implies that redundancies cannot be prevented through work sharing *(Kurzarbeit)*, retraining or reassignment of the workers affected. For collective redundancies the law also requires the redundant workers to be selected according to "social criteria", such as seniority, personal economic situation and individual employment prospects. The labour courts have also established strict rules concerning individual dismissals for personal reasons, especially on grounds of bad health and/or frequent absenteeism. As a rule, both law and court decisions require the employer to undertake all reasonable efforts to avoid job terminations. In case of unjustified dismissals or violations of procedural rules prescribed by the Act, the worker may sue for reinstatement through the labour court, which has been shown in most cases to result in monetary compensation rather than in actual reinstatement (Falke et al., 1981).

Apart from this, employment protection also has a strong collective component. Under the Works Council Act *(Betriebsverfassungsgesetz)* as amended in 1972, all dismissals have to be approved by the works council; in case of disapproval the employment relationship automatically continues until a labour court has decided on the justification of the dismissal; the range of this rule is illustrated by the fact that in 1987/88 over two-thirds (68 per cent) of all workers were employed in establishments with an elected works council. In cases of major workforce reductions, the works councils are further authorised to demand a "social plan" designed to minimise social and economic hardships for the workers affected, e.g. by setting up early retirement schemes or granting seniority-graded severance payments - an institution which has been the focus of recent criticism of the system of employment protection in the Federal Republic of Germany. Finally, if unavoidable redundancies exceed a certain proportion of the firms' total workforce,[12] they must be announced to the local labour office, which may delay them for up to one month.

These restrictions on lay-offs and dismissals have been complemented by special laws and collective agreements that for certain groups exclude ordinary dismissals altogether. These apply to pregnant women and employees on parental leave, elected members of the works council, disabled persons and drafted employees during their military service. Collective master agreements *(Manteltarifverträge)* in some industries exclude ordinary dismissals for older workers after reaching a minimum tenure (15 or 20 years); since the beginning of the 1980s such agreements have been in force in industries representing 55 to 60 per cent of all dependently employed workers (Warnken and Ronning, 1989). In total, in 1985 ordinary dismissal was excluded through collective agreements for more than 2.5 million workers and employees (excluding public servants[13]) or more than 13 per cent of the total dependent labour force.[14]

The picture, however, would be incomplete without mentioning the country's relatively generous, insurance-based work-sharing scheme *(Kurzarbeit)*, which is an important public subsidy for firms' labour hoarding. Its range is illustrated by the fact that even during the rather "prosperous" two-year period from May 1985 to April 1987 more than 11 per cent of all private sector firms, representing roughly 20 per cent of all workers in private industry, had temporarily introduced "short-time working" for economic reasons. Finally, it has to be taken into account that the various publicly financed early retirement schemes have created selective "outlets" offering a way round the employment protection regulations applying to the majority of older workers. The range of these schemes can be seen by the fact that about one-third of all persons entering retirement at the age of 55 or older do so through special early retirement schemes ("59-rule" or *Vorruhestandsgesetz*).

Legal regulation of temporary work contracts prior to and since the EPA

So, both labour law and collective agreements have imposed substantial restrictions on firms' freedom to dismiss workers for economic as well as non-economic reasons. From the point of view of supply-side economics, it is logical to infer that temporary and fixed-term employment arrangements would be attractive to firms as a way of evading dismissal restraints applying to permanent work contracts (Walter, 1989; Lazear, 1988). Employment security regulations, in consequence, have been assumed to favour the growth of an "unprotected sector", promoting a "two-tier" labour market.

This notion seems to support the fears expressed by unions that the easing of temporary employment arrangements by the EPA would induce employers to resort to "hire-and-fire" strategies. It has also been the assumption underlying rulings on temporary work by the Federal Labour Court *(Bundesarbeitsgericht)*, which - in the absence of any explicit legislative regulation of temporary work - has developed since the early 1960s a comprehensive set of norms and standards for the conclusion of fixed-term employment contracts, with the aim of preventing an evasion of statutory employment protection regulations. Thus court decisions have restricted the establishment of fixed-term contracts for periods exceeding six months to a set of clearly defined "legitimate" cases, such as seasonal work, replacement of temporarily absent permanent employees, temporary help in periods of peak demand, carrying out of special tasks which are temporary in nature, and employment in trainee programmes or public job creation schemes; on the other hand, the

Federal Labour Court ruled out economic uncertainty about future labour demand as a legitimate "reason" for hiring workers on a temporary basis; in such cases fixed-term contracts would be treated as permanent, i.e. involving all legal obligations concerning protection from unfair dismissal and redundancy.[15]

By the regulations of the EPA, these judicial restrictions to fixed-term contracts were largely suspended. By abolishing the requirement of a legitimate "reason" for the establishment of fixed-term contracts up to a maximum duration of 18 months,[16] the Government legalised fixed-term contracts in case of uncertainty over future labour demand, hoping that firms would thereby be induced to substitute newly hired workers for overtime hours of their core workforces. In fact, the abolition of the requirement of a legitimate "reason" amounts to a *carte blanche* for all kinds of uses of fixed-term contracts which would have been considered illegal prior to the EPA (e.g., prolonged probation beyond legal probationary periods).

Given the restrictiveness both of German employment protection and of the rules set up for temporary employment contracts by the Federal Labour Court prior to the EPA, one might expect the EPA's regulations to have had an enormous impact on firms' hiring and personnel practices - a widely shared expectation which (ironically) underlies both the hopes of its proponents and the fears of its critics.

Empirical results: Impact of the Employment Promotion Act on hiring strategies and on employment

Scope and evolution of fixed-term employment

Despite the fears of the unions, that the EPA would cause a break in the "dam" of the protected "standard employment relationship", the overwhelming majority (92 per cent), of the German workforce are still employed in more or less long-term, permanent jobs. In 1987/88 less than 8 per cent (1,450,000)[17] were employed on a fixed-term basis.[18] However, fixed-term employment, as in most other West European countries, has considerably increased in both absolute and relative terms. Between 1984 and 1988 the number employed on a fixed-term contract grew by more than 350,000, or 46 per cent, whereas the number of permanent employees increased at a much slower pace (442,000, or 2.4 per cent). In other words, more than 44 per cent of the overall increase in dependent employment over the period 1984-88 consisted of temporary, i.e. fixed-term, jobs. But as shown in table 1, this increase in fixed-term employment largely took place between 1984 and 1985, i.e. before the EPA came into force, indicating that the increase in temporary work has been influenced by factors other than changes in the regulatory framework, such as cyclical variations in labour demand as well as medium-

Table 1. Workers on fixed-term contracts in the Federal Republic of Germany, 1984-88 (in thousands and percentage distribution)

	1984 (EEC-LFSS)	1985 (MZ)	1986 (MZ)	1987 (MZ)	1988 (MZ)
Workers and employees total[1]	19 375.1[2]	19 577.6	19 979.8	19 948.7	20 389.9[3]
thereof:					
– on permanent working contract (including 80,000 agency workers)	18 461.8[2]	18 224.0	18 423.3	18 612.2	18 903.7[3]
%	95.3	93.2	92.2	93.3	92.7
– on fixed-term contract (including on public job creation programmes)	765.8[2]	1 080.8	1 230.2	1 105.0	1 119.2[3]
%	4.0[4]	5.6[4]	6.3[4]	5.6[4]	5.6[4]
– type of employment contract not specified	148.5	272.8	326.3	231.5	367.0
%	0.8	1.4	1.6	1.2	1.8

[1] Excluding public servants, apprentices and persons on compulsory military/community service. [2] Estimated. [3] Preliminary data. [4] Proportion of fixed-term among all workers with specification of type of employment.

Source: Federal Statistical office, EEC-Labour Force Sample Survey 1984; Mikrozensus (MZ) 1985, 1986, 1987, 1988, special tabulations on behalf of WZB/LMP.
(c) Wissenschaftszentrum Berlin für Sozialforschung/AMB, 1989.

term structural changes of both labour supply and labour demand. The implications of this trend for labour market dynamics become apparent when the perspective is shifted from stocks to flows in the labour market. Under present labour market conditions, roughly 45 per cent of all newly hired workers (36 per cent) in private industry and more than 50 per cent in the public sector) start their job with a fixed-term employment contract; likewise, about one out of five job terminations is due to the end of a fixed-term employment contract.[19]

Firms' use of fixed-term contracts

Despite the large proportion of fixed-term engagements among all new jobs, fixed-term employment is still concentrated within a small proportion of all firms in the private sector.[20] In fact, two out of three (67 per cent) private sector firms had made no use of fixed-term contracts during the first two years after the EPA had come into force (although the majority of these - 80 per cent - had hired workers during the observation period). This group of non-users consisted largely of small- and medium-sized firms (employing on average 23 workers) with a rather skilled workforce, little fluctuations in product demand and low worker turnover. The main reason for not using temporary work contracts given by these firms was that they were "exclusively interested in stable, long-term employment relationships". While other reasons were hardly mentioned at all, this was given by 83 per cent of the non-users, representing not less than 50 per cent of all firms and accounting for roughly one-third of the total labour force in the private sector.

The remaining third (33 per cent) that did make use of fixed-term contracts have to be divided into two contrasting groups according to the intensity of their use of fixed-term contracts:

- more than half of these firms (or 19 per cent of all firms in the private sector) could be classified as selective or moderate users of fixed-term contracts, i.e. the large majority (74 per cent) of their recruits were hired on a permanent basis. This group consists mainly of medium-sized and larger manufacturing firms employing on average 121 workers and accounting for roughly 40 per cent of all new hires in private industry; these firms are characterised by relatively skilled workforces, which on average showed an expansionary trend over the period 1985-87;

- the other half of the user-firms were intensive users, hiring on average more than 74 per cent of their new recruits on fixed-term contracts. This group, by contrast, consists largely of smaller firms[21] subject to relatively strong fluctuations in demand due to irregular orders[22] and high worker turnover, and is further characterised by both a relatively high share of wage costs in total production costs and a negative employment performance between 1985 and 1987. Altogether these firms make up only 17 per cent of all private sector firms, but accounted for no less than 32 per cent of all new hires and 70 per cent of all fixed-term contracts concluded in private industry since 1985.

So, fixed-term contracts are highly concentrated in a small group of firms making substantial use of them. Moreover, they are concentrated not only within a small segment of firms in the private sector, but also in certain job categories. As to be expected from notions of human capital theory (Abraham, 1988), a majority of temporary jobs in the private sector, indeed, require neither vocational skills nor any on-the-job training; in fact, more than 70 per cent of all workers hired on fixed-term contracts are unskilled, who under present labour market conditions have a less than 50 per cent chance of being hired on a permanent basis; by contrast, skilled workers are still in most cases (80 per cent) hired on permanent contracts, reflecting their interest in keeping these workers for longer periods and avoiding premature (voluntary) quits.

Change in firms' recruitment behaviour since 1985

With regard to the evaluation of the EPA, our research concentrated on the question of how and to what extent firms have modified their recruitment behaviour and use of fixed-term contracts since the EPA regulations came into effect. The majority (78 per cent) of user-firms had actually intensified their use of fixed-term hires (26 per cent) or had used fixed-term contracts for the first time (52 per cent) since 1985. The large part of the increase in fixed-term employment, however, came in those firms that had already used fixed-term contracts before 1985. Still, it would be erroneous to conclude that this change in recruitment practice was mainly due to the regulations introduced by the EPA. Rather, our evidence shows that the intensified or first use of fixed-term job arrangements was due to a whole array of factors, such as cyclical demand for temporary help, new working time regimes, greater variations in business activity due to a reduction in product stores and increase in production by order. The legal extension of fixed-term contracts through the EPA, if at all, played only a subordinate role.

The relevance of cyclical and structural rather than regulatory factors in accounting for the increase in temporary jobs is further affirmed by the type of fixed-term contracts concluded in the private sector. In fact, 93 per cent of all fixed-term contracts concluded by firms were found to conform to the rules and criteria set up for fixed-term contracts by the Federal Labour Court long before the EPA came into force; most fixed-term contracts concluded were covered by one of the legitimate "reasons" defined by the rulings of the labour courts (85 per cent) and/or did not exceed six months in duration (70 per cent) up to which there have never been restrictions. In total, only 7 per cent of all fixed-term hires (or less than 2 per cent of all new hires) in the private sector did not conform to these criteria and thus have to be considered as "genuine" contracts under the new regulations. These contracts were concentrated in less than 4 per cent of all firms, employing hardly 10 per cent of all workers in private industry. In contrast to the majority using (traditional) fixed-term contracts, these firms consisted largely of medium-sized and larger enterprises in rather low-skilled distributive and service industries[23] reporting a high degree of uncertainty about future labour demand; on average, more than 60 per cent of these firms' new recruits were hired on fixed-term contracts.

The evidence presented so far suggests that apparently firms' flexibility needs with respect to temporary job arrangements have been met mostly by rules set up by the judiciary previous to the EPA. Only at first sight is this conclusion contradicted by the finding that few (26 per cent) of all fixed-term employment contracts in the private sector were formally established with "explicit reference" to the new regulations. Even in those firms that hired personnel on a fixed-term basis with explicit reference to the EPA, 90 per cent of all fixed-term appointments were covered by one of the traditionally accepted "legitimate reasons" and/or did not exceed six months in duration, i.e. conformed with the regulations in force prior to the EPA. The reason why firms nevertheless referred to the EPA when entering "traditional" fixed-term contracts must be the resultant simplification of contractual procedures (no requirement of a "legitimate reason" to be mentioned in the contract) and the ensuing reduction in judicial uncertainty (arbitration risk).

Firms' motives for using fixed-term employment contracts

Firms were also asked to report their motives for using fixed-term contracts and the new regulations. The answers show that firms' prime motive for using the EPA was the possibility of optimising on-the-job screening of workers without facing dismissal restrictions in the case of lack of ability or misconduct. This motive was classified as "very important" by one-third of firms making "explicit" use of the new regulations. This supports the argument put forward by Flanagan (1988) that, in the presence of "rigid" employment protection regulations, the combination of uncertainty about labour demand and uncertainty about the potential productivity of job applicants may explain both European employers' general hesitancy towards hiring additional staff and their intensified screening endeavours when hiring.[24]

Only secondly did firms mention the motive of a more flexible adaptation of labour to variations in business activity due to the absence of employment protection; this was considered "very important" by a quarter of all firms that had made "explicit" use of the new regulations, representing 4.8 per cent of all private sector firms. The popular notion that firms would use the regulations to resort to a "hire-and-fire" strategy appears to have little basis.[25] This conclusion is strongly supported by the finding that a substantial proportion (65 per cent) of all workers initially hired under the new regulations were subsequently taken into permanent employment. This allows us to conclude that factors other than dismissal protection legislation alone account for the prevalence of long-term employment relationships, and for German firms' renunciation of employment adjustment through high worker turnover.

Even less frequently, firms mentioned the motive of substituting additional hires from the external labour market for overtime work of the core workforce; this was classified as "very important" by only 15 per cent of the user-firms or 2.5 per cent of all firms in the private sector. The corridor within which firms were willing and able to substitute additional workers for hours seems rather narrow.[26] This finding, of course, has far-reaching implications for the employment effects attributable to the EPA.

Employment impact of the EPA

To assess the immediate employment impact of the EPA regulations we focused on those 7 per cent of all fixed-term contracts in the private sector that would not have been legal under the previous rulings of the Federal Labour Court ("genuine EPA contracts"). Of these, only about one in five (21.7 per cent) were classified as "additional" hires that would not have occurred without the new regulations. Additional fixed-term hires due to the EPA thus accounted for only 1.5 per cent of all fixed-term contracts in private firms, or 0.5 per cent of all new hires. In line with our other findings, the facilitation of fixed-term contracts apparently had hardly any effect on employers' willingness to take on additional staff. Most of the remaining 80 per cent of fixed-term contracts made under the new regulations must be considered as "substitution effects", i.e. the workers hired on a fixed-term basis probably would otherwise have been given a permanent contract from the outset. Substitution effects of the new regulations were three times the volume of direct (gross) employment effect, in the sense of hirings which, according to the firms, would not have occurred without the EPA. Of course, compared to the hopes and fears expressed in the debate on the EPA, both effects were rather marginal due to the fact that the actual use of the new possibilities has been restricted to a small number of cases (2 per cent of all new hires) and a small minority (4 per cent) of all private sector firms.

If there has been a small number of additional hires attributable to the EPA, the modest (gross) employment effects resulting are largely offset by an increased speed of workforce adjustment in periods of slack demand, which arise from the EPA's substitution effects. With fixed-term contracts, firms adjusted employment more rapidly to declining demand than with permanent employment contracts to which dismissal protection applied. This is illustrated by the results of our representative company survey. Whereas on average two-thirds of all workers hired under the EPA were subsequently taken into permanent employment by their firms, this amounted to 20 per cent in firms with a declining workforce over the observation period: this was reaffirmed not only by interviews with personnel managers in 30 manufacturing firms, but also by the results of our panel survey of newly hired workers. All other things being equal, fixed-term employment arrangements were found to imply much higher (involuntary) separation rates than for workers hired on a permanent work contract. Taking both positive and negative employment impacts into consideration, the net employment impact of the EPA regulations has been negligible despite the positive economic conditions since 1985. In the medium or long term, especially in major economic downturns, the marginal positive net employment effect may well be reversed into a negative one because of the observed substitution effects and the associated risk of job loss for the workers affected. Our findings support the conclusion from other studies, such as that by Bentoilila and Bertola (1988, p. 22), that "a mere reduction in firing costs does not increase a firm's marginal propensity to hire while it strongly raises their willingness to fire". Similar conclusions were drawn by Elbaum et al. (1986) for France, by Burgess (1988) for the United Kingdom, by Bayar et al. (1987) for Belgium, and by Bjoerklund and Holmlund (1987) for Sweden.

Employment promotion through less employment protection?

The evidence has shown that the assumption that a reduction in employment protection through a legal sanction of temporary contracts will result in more employment is ill founded, at least in the Federal Republic of Germany. Moreover, the expectation that firms' "liberation" from employment protection regulations through the "loophole" created by the EPA would have a strong genuine impact on hiring decisions, seems unjustified. Evidently, most (German) firms do not share the notion put forward by supply-side economists that an increase in external labour turnover will increase adjustment efficiency. Our findings also challenge the EPA's underlying "diagnosis" that by restricting lay-offs and individual dismissals employment protection regulations have a strong deterrent impact on firms' manpower strategies and hiring decisions.

The question remains, what kind of positive lesson can be learned from the experiment of the Employment Promotion Act with respect to the impact of (de-)regulation on labour markets and job generation? A preliminary answer can be given by taking a closer look at the reasons for the failure of the EPA to modify firms' employment decisions as intended by the Government. These can be analysed at two levels: (a) from a theoretical institutionalist perspective, and (b) from the empirical micro-perspective on firms' employment and labour market behaviour.

Reasons for the failure of the EPA from an institutionalist (macro-)perspective

A general conclusion is that focusing on single institutions such as employment protection, and neglecting the historical as well as economic setting in which institutions and regulations are embedded, is likely to result in misleading conclusions about the functioning of "real" labour markets.

There is no need to emphasise that from a comparative perspective the Federal Republic of Germany has a regulated system of labour relations whose foundations were laid before the Second World War and which was restored, complemented and expanded from the 1950s to the early 1970s. This was an extended period of economic growth accompanied by an enormous increase of both labour supply and demand during the 1950s, and then by a period of nearly uninterrupted full employment and rapid industrial growth from the beginning of the 1960s until the early 1970s (Lutz, 1987). The institutional "pillars" of this system were:

(1)   a "dual system of collective representation" with its complementary components of: (a) centralised wage bargaining at sectoral level, covering all workers employed by an industry, and (b) decentralised co-determination on recruitment, dismissals, internal mobility and work organisation at plant and enterprise level, through elected works councils;

(2)   a "dual training system" (apprenticeship) involving alternating "training-on-the-job" and attendance at vocational schools, the standards and curricula of which are regulated and continuously updated by both the State and the social partners, and which has provided a large proportion of the workforce with broad general as well as professional skills;

(3)   a fairly elaborate system of federal labour law and social security legislation which - apart from setting the regulatory framework for collective bargaining and workplace representation - also guarantees a relatively high level of employment protection and income security to the vast majority of the dependently employed.

Together with the traditionally strong export orientation of German industry this "triangular" institutional framework of the Federal Republic's labour market largely explains the particular "mode of adjustment" frequently referred to as the "German model": centralised wage bargaining at industry level, which allows only limited inter-industry wage dispersion in combination with a federally-regulated insurance-based social security system, has contributed to making the Federal Republic of Germany a high-wage economy ranking near the top of industrialised countries in terms of labour costs. Moreover, the development and spread of internal labour markets was favoured by the combination of a strong trend towards mass production and persistent labour shortages during the 1960s and early 1970s, and the expansion of a seniority-based system of legal and collectively bargained safeguards against redundancy and unfair dismissal and the strengthening of firm-level co-determination rights of works councils in the late 1960s and the early 1970s (Lutz, 1987, pp. 185 ff.). This growth of internal labour markets manifests itself in the prevalence of long-term job attachments and comparatively low turnover rates among the German labour force (see Bellmann and Schasse, 1988).

Within this framework of high labour costs, little wage dispersion and internal labour markets, German enterprises in export-oriented manufacturing sectors have been forced to maintain competitiveness through productivity increases, product quality and continuous product innovation (Streeck, 1989). That has had various spill-over effects on other sectors of the economy. This adjustment strategy has so far proved successful, partly because German enterprises have been able to rely on a relatively well trained labour force as well as ample skill reserves provided through both the dual training system and the expansion of the educational system. It has further been supported by the considerable expansion of vocational training and retraining measures within the system of "active labour market policy" and the provision of generous early retirement schemes, which have facilitated external workforce adjustments within socially acceptable boundaries.

It is against this background and the associated "logic" of adjustment that the Employment Promotion Act and its failure to modify firms' manpower strategies should be seen. The EPA, with its "philosophy" of employment promotion through facilitating external labour market adjustment, can be seen as a measure running counter to the predominant "logic" of internal adjustment characterising most of the German economy. In terms of systems theory, minor external impulses alien to its own functional "logic" tend to be ignored or absorbed by the economic system (Teubner, 1985). In terms of our evidence, this can be illustrated as follows:

- the majority of private sector firms made no use of fixed-term contracts, contending that they were "exclusively interested in long-term employment relationships"; these firms evidently have ignored the "message" of the EPA;

- of the remaining firms, a large majority used fixed-term contracts either for "traditional" reasons, such as temporary help, replacement of temporarily absent employees, etc., or to optimise "on-the-job screening" of candidates for integration into the core workforce, the latter being expressed by the high proportion of fixed-term workers taken into permanent employment at the end of their term;[27] these firms, too, apparently in most cases[28] ignored the impulse intended by the EPA;

- only a very small minority of all private sector firms have actually made use of the new possibilities introduced by the EPA, in most cases, though, without hiring more workers. From the information we have on their characteristics, these firms adhered to an external rather than internal mode of workforce adjustment long before the EPA came into effect; the majority merely absorbed the impulse given by the EPA without hiring additional staff in the way intended.

The EPA thus seems to provide a good example of policy failure due to what Teubner (1987, pp. 19 ff.) has termed an unsuccessful "structural coupling" of policy, law and the sphere of economic action.

Reasons for the failure of the EPA from the micro perspective of the firm

The failure of the EPA to achieve its designated goal has been explained by the assumption that its impulse - easing of external manpower adjustment - runs counter to the historical "logic" of internal adjustment characteristic of large parts of the German economy. This interpretation is strongly supported by a confrontation of the EPA's "philosophy" about firms' labour market behaviour with the micro-evidence collected at firm level.

First, our evidence supports the EPA's underlying notion of a widespread and growing reluctance of employers to take on additional staff. Thus, an overwhelming majority (74 per cent) of all placement officers in the public employment agencies asserted that firms had become more hesitant towards increasing their workforces during the past years (1983-88). This was reaffirmed by interviews with personnel managers in private companies: three out of five managers declared that as a rule hiring additional staff was taken into consideration after all other measures of coping with the workload (overtime work, temporary help, contracting out, etc.) had been exhausted (50 per cent), or that their firms were exercising a total hiring stop due to (current or expected) excess capacities (10 per cent).

However, our findings raise doubts as to whether this widespread reluctance to hire can be attributed to "deterrent" effects of existing employment security provisions and dismissal restraints. The vast majority (77 per cent) of personnel managers contended that they had been able to realise (almost) all intended dismissals without incurring major legal difficulties or dismissal costs. Accordingly, only a small minority (27 per cent) of personnel managers, most of whom reported ongoing major workforce reductions, attributed some impact on their firms' hiring decisions to employment protection regulations. However, in most cases they referred to the quality of recruits, i.e. a more careful productivity-oriented selection and screening of job candidates, rather than to the overall quantity of new hires. The finding that firms do not perceive employment protection regulations as serious obstacles to job terminations was found all the more true with respect to short-lived employment relationships of less than 18 months, as referred to by the regulations of the EPA. According to 88 per cent of the managers, the termination of such short-term jobs did not cause any legal or financial problems. This is why the evasion of legal dismissal restraints was hardly ever mentioned as a motive for firms' use of the new regulations.

The micro-evidence also raises serious doubts as to the legislator's assumption of a substitutability of fixed-term hires for (overtime) hours of the stably employed workforce. In fact, two out of three personnel managers reported significant amounts of overtime in their firms. But apart from cost and flexbility advantages associated with overtime as compared to hiring more workers, the large majority of personnel managers did not see any possibility of substituting additional workers for overtime hours of their workforce, the main obstacles to a reduction of overtime being limitations of space and capital equipment, problems in finding skilled workers from the external labour market, prolonged periods for on-the-job training of newly hired workers, and a high degree of irregularity of excess workloads across time as well as across work areas within the firm. As most overtime hours were worked by the skilled workforce, additional hirings on fixed-term contracts could hardly function as a viable alternative to overtime. Apart from a reported strong reluctance of skilled workers to accept fixed-term contracts, firms, especially when hiring skilled labour, tend to be exclusively interested in long-term (i.e. open-ended, permanent) job attachments, reflecting the high search and training costs usually involved.[29] Consequently, firms reducing or planning to reduce overtime in most cases did so by rationalisation and productivity increases rather than by hiring additional workers. This is why the reduction of overtime has not been an important motive for using temporary job arrangements, and why the easing of fixed-term contracts through the EPA has hardly created any additional labour demand.

There are also good reasons to doubt the assumption underlying the EPA that fixed-term contracts, aside from satisfying firms' flexibility needs in "traditional" cases of temporary demand, will increase firms' ability to cope with uncertainty about future labour demand. Fixed-term contracts by definition require the duration or date of termination to be fixed in advance; with premature terminations prior to the date of expiration, German law requires formal notice, involving all procedures and obligations applying to permanent work contracts; likewise, the renewal of fixed-term contracts for reasons of economic uncertainty is prohibited under the EPA. For the firm, therefore, it is rational to fix the duration of fixed-term contracts to the date to which labour demand can be anticipated at the time of the establishment of the contract. Usually, this "horizon" is defined by the time range of orders, which in German manufacturing amounted to, on average, 2.8 months during the period 1985-88, i.e. well below the threshold of six months beyond which the establishment of fixed-term contracts has been facilitated by the EPA. This largely explains the fact that most (70 per cent) fixed-term contracts in the private sector do not exceed six months and are thus beyond the potential range of the EPA regulations.

Finally, it should be noted that even in those exceptional cases in which firms acted according to the hopes and assumptions of the legislator (i.e. took on additional workers under the EPA), most personnel managers were not capable of clearly separating the various factors influencing their firms' hiring decisions and thus of assessing the genuine impact of the regulations. As far as firms modified their recruitment practices as a result of the EPA, this probably reflected the overall constellation of influences, such as the positive economic climate since 1985, increased labour demand due to working time reductions, and medium-term changes in employment practices, rather than to the impact of the new regulations alone.

Employment protection reconsidered: Reviewing the evidence

Contrary to widespread notions in the debate on "labour market flexibility" and to conclusions drawn from looking merely at the elaborate German system of employment protection from a neo-classical point of view, the evidence presented above tends to refute the view that employment security provisions have played a major part in accounting for firms' hesitancy towards increasing their workforces and thus have contributed to persistent high unemployment. Conversely, our firm-level evidence shows that legal and collectively bargained lay-off and dismissal restraints are not perceived as obstacles to job terminations by the overwhelming majority of private sector firms. This finding, which casts doubt also on the view that employment security by preventing lay-offs and slowing workforce reductions will have a genuine positive impact on the level of employment,[30] supports earlier research on the impact of employment security provisions.

In a company survey conducted in 1979-80 (Falke et al., 1981, pp. 151 ff.), the overwhelming majority of personnel managers declared that their firms had been able to realise almost all intended lay-offs and dismissals without major difficulties. Only a small minority (15 per cent) reported major difficulties due to employment protection legislation. This was supported by the finding that only 3.3 per cent of dismissals in the private sector (8 per cent of all intended dismissals in firms with a works council) were rejected by the works council.[31] Likewise, only a small proportion (7.9 per cent) of all dismissals ended up in a labour court; and in very few was the worker finally reinstated in his job,[32] most successful suits resulting in financial compensation for job loss.[33] The picture from this evidence was supported by a later survey of 186 medium-sized firms in late 1983, i.e. at the peak of the OPEC II recession, which found that most firms attributed to employment protection laws no influence on company decisions (Kayser and Friede, 1984, p. 38). In line with our findings, the evidence from such studies suggests that the genuine impact of employment protection regulations on firms' firing decisions has been exaggerated in the debate on labour market flexibility.[34]

The evidence also suggests that employment security regulations are unlikely to account for the low job separation and lay-off rates found in the Federal Republic compared with other industrialised countries. Studies in the 1970s and early 1980s unanimously showed a tendency of German firms to avoid redundancies as long as possible and to exhaust all other measures of "soft" workforce adjustment (hours, short-time working, natural attrition, early retirement schemes, etc.) before workers were laid off (Hotz-Hart, 1989). Involuntary separations were frequently grounded on personal (health, personal misconduct, etc.) rather than on economic reasons and strongly concentrated within specific sectors of the economy (small establishments with high worker turnover) as well as among low-skill and low-seniority workers (Falke et al., 1981).

Our data further show that - just like fixed-term arrangements - lay-offs and dismissals are also concentrated in a small minority of firms adhering to an intensive "firing-and-hiring" strategy: during the period May 1985 to April 1987, almost 70 per cent of all lay-offs and dismissals[35] were accounted for by 13 per cent of all private sector firms. In the same period, these "hire-and-fire" firms on average laid off or dismissed almost half (46 per cent) of those employed at the outset, implying an annual involuntary separation rate of almost 25 per cent.[36] This group consisted largely of small establishments (with on average 22 workers at the time of the survey) concentrated in the construction and low-skill service industries[37] (these two alone accounting for almost 50 per cent of the firms),[38] a high proportion of unskilled and semi-skilled workers (close to 50 per cent of all workers employed by these firms),[39] a high share of labour costs (exceeding 50 per cent of total turnover in more than a quarter of these firms),[40] and strong demand fluctuations (73 per cent reporting regularly recurring variations in capacity utilisation). Not only firms with declining workforces adhered to a pattern of adjustment through massive lay-offs and dismissals. Over half (55 per cent) of these "firing" firms had stable (18 per cent) or even increasing (37 per cent) workforces over the two-year period.[41] Firms adhering to an intensive "firing" policy also more frequently (59 per cent) reported difficulty in filling vacancies than other firms (30.6 per cent), indicating that massive external labour turnover does not necessarily imply adjustment efficiency.[42] Regardless of efficiency considerations, the mere existence of a small group adhering to "hiring-and-firing" strategy again raises doubt as to whether employment protection regulations have put a strong restraint on the freedom to dismiss and lay off workers.

With respect to employment protection, these findings also suggest that it is industry and firm-specific manpower options rather than the (universal) effect of job security regulations that account for the high degree of employment stability in the Federal Republic of Germany. This conclusion is in line with studies showing that labour hoarding in German manufacturing during recessions was motivated primarily by firms' interest in maintaining their qualified workforce and avoiding high search and training costs in the following upswing rather than by legal and collectively bargained lay-off restraints (Nerb et al., 1977).

Combined with our research, this evidence can be summarised as a partial congruence of lay-off and dismissal restraints imposed by regulations and collective agreements and the economic interest of the majority of firms in avoiding lay-offs and restricting dismissals to certain categories of workers. This interpretation casts serious doubts as to whether employment protection regulations are a genuine deterrent to firms' hiring behaviour. Company surveys have shown that it is primarily lack in demand that has kept German manufacturing firms from taking on more workers during the last economic upswing, whereas "insufficient flexibility in hiring and firing"[43] played at most a subordinate role (Nerb, 1986; Koenig and Zimmermann, 1985).

Conclusions

De-regulation of labour relations through facilitating temporary job arrangements, thereby suspending employment protection for newly hired workers, does not appear to be a successful policy for stimulating employment growth in economies like the Federal Republic of Germany. Of course, the question remains whether or not the failure of the EPA to modify hiring and employment decisions could be attributed to the insufficiency of the EPA incentive to hire more workers, i.e. that a stronger dose of "de-regulation" of employment protection and security standards would have induced more employers to give up their hesitancy about hiring more workers (see, for example, Nerb, 1986). This view, however, is contested by the findings reported above that most firms did not regard employment protection regulations as impediments to workforce adjustments. Indeed, recent studies have shown those industries with a high degree of employment protection through collective bargaining agreements have fared better not only in terms of employment performance but also in terms of innovative activities than industries with a lower level of institutional employment security (Warnken and Ronning, 1989).

Notes

[1] Standing uses the distinction between "explicit" and "implicit" de-regulation in this context: see Standing, 1986.

[2] For example, Sengenberger and Loveman, 1987; Rodgers and Rodgers, 1989; for the Federal Republic of Germany see: Buechtemann and Quack, 1989.

[3] For an overview of the theoretical assumptions underlying these arguments, see: Ehrenberg, 1985; Lazear, 1988; Flanagan, 1988. In the Federal Republic of Germany this type of argument has been recently put forward by both economists (e.g. Schellhaass, 1989; Siebert, 1989) and lawyers (e.g. Reuter, 1985).

[4] Ironically, the European debate on the allegedly detrimental effects of employment security has been conducted with a strong reference to the "American jobs miracle"; this is contrasted by the debate in the United States, where policy advisers have emphasised the beneficial effects of employment protection on worker productivity and on adjustment to technological change, and, consequently, have advocated the introduction of basic employment security provisions such as advance notification periods for plant closings: see for example Rosow and Zager, 1984; Ehrenberg and Jakubson, 1989. Recent developments in American legislation, court decisions and collective bargaining have in fact introduced significant deviations from the (still) prevailing doctrine of "employment at will": see Gould, 1987; Dertouzos, 1988; Mendelsohn, 1989.

[5] Henceforth referred to as "Employment Promotion Act" or "EPA".

[6] By partly exempting such enterprises from the obligation to set up a "social plan" in the case of major workforce reductions or production reorganisations and by changing the mode of calculation of the minimum number of employees required for the application of protection against dismissal under the Dismissal Protection Act (Kündigungsschutzgesetz) of 1951.

[7] The maximum period for individual missions under the Agency Workers Act (Arbeitnehmerüberlassungsgesetz) was extended from three to six months.

[8] The study, completed in May 1989, is based on: (a) a representative mail-survey of 2,392 firms in the private sector; (b) a representative (telephone) panel survey of 4,930 employed workers and 1,539 unemployed jobseekers; (c) a mail-survey of 1,968 placement officers of the Federal Employment Agency; and (d) 30 in-depth case studies in 30

enterprises of the metal-processing and engineering industries; empirical data were collected for the whole period from the enactment of the EPA in May 1985 to November 1988. For a detailed description of design and results, see the final report Buechtemann and Hoeland, 1989.

[9] For a more detailed description, see Oechsler, 1988.

[10] According to a survey of dismissed workers, prenotification periods lasted on average 24 days for blue-collar and 83 days for white-collar workers. Falke et al., 1981.

[11] Legitimate reasons for ordinary dismissals under the Act are misconduct (unsatisfactory performance, unjustified absence from work, violation of safety regulations, etc.), lack of personal capability or bad health involving high absenteeism and economic necessity (due to lack of demand or technological reorganisation). Personal misconduct may also justify "extraordinary" dismissal, in which case legal prenotification periods do not apply.

[12] More than five workers in companies with 21 to 59 employees, 10 per cent or at least 25 workers in companies with 60 to 499 employees, and at least 30 employees within companies with 500 or more employees (Work Promotion Act/*Arbeitsförderungsgesetz* of 1969).

[13] In the Federal Republic of Germany public servants in principle enjoy lifetime employment guarantees and, therefore, cannot be dismissed (except in case of serious offences). In 1987-88 the total number of lifetime public servants (excluding military personnel) amounted to about 1.6 million or almost 7 per cent of the dependent workforce.

[14] If one adds tenured public servants, the number of workers enjoying absolute protection against ordinary dismissals rises to 4.2 million or more than 20 per cent of the total dependent workforce.

[15] In addition to court rulings there exists a range of norms in collective master agreements relating to specific aspects of temporary work, i.e. maximum probation periods, etc., Buechtemann and Hoeland, 1989.

[16] Or 24 months in the case of new enterprises employing fewer than 20 workers.

[17] Due to an under-representation of workers with marginal workforce attachment in the official population surveys *(Mikrozensus)* of the Federal Statistical Office *(Statistisches Bundesamt)*, the numbers shown for 1988 in table 1 are significantly lower than those found in our survey.

[18] Temporary work in the sense of workers supplied by agencies has played but a minor role in the German labour market: at its peak in 1988, the total number of persons hired from temporary work agencies did not exceed 88,000 or 0.37 per cent of the total dependent labour force.

[19] The difference in the proportion of fixed-term "entries" and "exits" is because a considerable proportion (32 per cent) of workers initially hired on fixed-term contracts are subsequently taken over into permanent employment.

[20] The following results relate to the use of fixed-term contracts in the private sector only (excluding agriculture and forestry).

[21] 90 per cent of them not employing more than 50 workers at the time of the survey; on average these firms employed 69 workers and employees at the time of the survey.

[22] Seasonal workload was mentioned by only a minority of these firms as a reason for fluctuations in business activity.

[23] This category includes retail, hotels, catering, transportation, cleaning, body care and personal services other than health care and education.

[24] That employers have intensified their screening endeavours with respect to occupational skills as well as social qualifications of job candidates was reaffirmed by the answers given by the 1,968 placement officers surveyed in the context of our study, see Buechtemann, 1989.

[25] For a similar conclusion with respect to the prolongation of the initial waiting period for protection against unfair dismissal in the United Kingdom, see Evans et al., 1985, p. 62.

[26] This finding is in line with more general reasoning put forward by Ehrenberg and Schumann, 1982, pp. 37 ff.

[27] Workers hired on a fixed term by firms that classified the motive of prolonged probation of newly hired workers as "very important" in their decision to use the EPA regulations were subsequently taken into permanent employment significantly more frequently than fixed-term workers in firms considering the "screening" motive as secondary or unimportant.

[28] Some of these firms made formal use of the EPA regulations but merely for the technical facilitation of fixed-term contracts effected by the EPA (i.e. no "legitimate" reason to be given in the contract with all the legal uncertainties involved for the firms). This reaction might be termed "absorption" of the EPA's impulse, although firms did not make use of the additional options for concluding fixed-term contracts provided by the EPA; for a more detailed discussion of this, see Buechtemann and Hoeland, 1989, pp. 239 ff.

[29] Studies have found firms refraining from hiring skilled workers unless full utilisation is foreseeable for at least six to 24 months, Nerb et al., 1977, pp. 303 f.

[30] Macroeconomic studies have shown aggregate employment elasticity in the Federal Republic of Germany to be almost the same as in the United States and to be higher than in other Western European countries: see Blanchard et al., 1986, pp. 106 f.; see also Maurau and Oudinet, 1988; Auer and Buechtemann, 1989.

[31] Two-thirds of all dismissals were explicitly consented to by the Works Council: see Falke et al., 1981, pp. 184 ff.

[32] In 1979 this was true of only 0.7 per cent of all dismissed workers: Falke et al., 1981, pp. 959 ff.

[33] The average compensation decided upon by the parties being 0.56 per cent of monthly gross wages per year of seniority, i.e. in the case of a worker with a gross monthly salary of DM4,000 and ten years of tenure, DM22,400: see Falke et al., 1981.

[34] With respect to older workers this conclusion was reaffirmed by Warnken and Ronning, 1989.

[35] Excluding voluntary quits and separations due to the ending of fixed-term employment or training contracts.

[36] For the remaining 87 per cent this annual separation rate amounted to 0.8 per cent.

[37] This category includes hotels, catering transportation, cleaning, body care and personal services other than health care and education.

[38] Compared to 29.7 per cent of all private sector firms.

[39] Compared to 38.4 per cent of all workers employed in the private sector.

[40] Compared to 16.5 per cent among all private sector firms.

[41] Compared to 64 per cent of all firms in the private sector: only 45 per cent of these firms reported a net decline in employment as compared to 35 per cent among all firms in the private sector.

42 It should be mentioned that intensive use of lay-offs and dismissals seems to be inversely correlated with the use of fixed-term job arrangements; this casts more doubt on the common expectation that fixed-term contracts would be welcomed by firms as an efficient means of evading the "rigidities" allegedly inherent in permanent employment contracts.

43 Thus the suggestive wording of a question in a representative company survey undertaken by the EC in ten Member States in 1985. The results show that the item "insufficient flexibility in hiring and firing" ranked only in fifth place (after "lack of demand", "foreign competition"; "skill shortages"; "high non-wage labour costs") among reasons given by German firms for not hiring more personnel in the upswing (as compared to France and Italy where firing and hiring restrictions ranked first): Nerb, 1986, pp. 71 ff.

References

Abraham, K.G. 1988. "Flexible staffing arrangements and employers' short-term adjustment strategies", in R.A. Hart (ed.): *Employment, unemployment and labour utilization.* London, Unwin & Hyman, pp. 288-322.

Auer, P.; Büchtemann, C.F. 1989. "Arbeitsrechtliche" 'De-Regulierung durch Erleichterung befristeter Arbeitsverträge: Erfahrungen in der Bundesrepublik Deutschland und in Frankreich [Labour law "deregulation" through facilitating fixed-term contracts: Experiences in the Federal Republic of Germany and in France], in *Internationale Chronik zur Arbeitsmarktpolitik,* 38-1989, pp. 3-7.

Bayar, A. 1987. "Labour market flexibility: An approach based on a macro-sectoral model for Belgium", in *Labour and Society,* Vol. 12, No. 1, 1987, pp. 37-53.

Bellmann, L; Schasse, U. 1988. *Employment tenure in the United States and in the Federal Republic of Germany,* Fachbereich Wirtschaftswissenschaften, Discussion Paper No. 123, Hanover, Universität Hannover.

Bentolila, S.; Bertola, G. 1988. *Firing costs and labour demand: How bad is Eurosclerosis?,* Dec. 1988, mimeo.

Bjoerklund, A.; Holmlund, B. 1987. *Worker displacement in Sweden, facts and* policies. Paper presented at the December 1987 American Economic Association Meetings, Stockholm, mimeo.

Blanchard, O. et al. 1987. "Employment and growth in Europe: A two-handed approach", in O. Blanchard et al. (eds.): *Restoring Europe's prosperity: Macroeconomic papers from the Center for European Policy Studies,* Cambridge, Massachusetts, MIT Press, pp. 95-123.

Büchtemann, C.F. 1989. "Beschäftigungsförderung durch Erleichterung befristeter Arbeitsverträge: Arbeitsmarktwirkungen des Beschäftigungs-förderungsgesetzes aus der Sicht der Arbeitsvermittlung" [Promoting employment through facilitating fixed-term contracts: The labour market impact of the Employment Promotion Act from the viewpoint of the employment office], in *Arbeit und Beruf,* Vol. 40, No. 12, Dec. 1989, pp. 379-385.

Büchtemann, C.F.; Hoeland, A. 1989. *Befristete Arbeitsverträge nach dem Beschäftigungsfoerderungsgesetz 1985 (BeschFG 1985). Ergebnisse einer empirischen Untersuchung i.A. des Bundesministers fuer Arbeit und Sozialordnung (BMA)* [Fixed-term work contracts after the Employment Promotion Act, 1985. Results of an empirical research for the Federal Ministry of Labour and Social Order]. Bonn, BMA.

Büchtemann, C.F.; Quack, S. 1989. "How 'precarious' is non-standard employment? Evidence for West Germany", in *Cambridge Journal of Economics,* Vol. 14, No. 2, Sep. 1990, pp. 315-330.

Büchtemann, C.F.; Neumann, H. (eds.): 1989. *Mehr Arbeit durch weniger Recht? Chancen und Risiken der Arbeitsmarktflexibilisierung* [More work through less law? Opportunities and risks of greater labour market flexibility]. Berlin, Sigma, 1990.

Burgess, S.M. 1988. "Employment adjustment in UK manufacturing", in *The Economic Journal,* 98-1988, pp. 81-103.

Dertouzos, J.N. 1988. *The end of employment-at-will: Legal and economic costs.* Santa Monica, The Rand Corporation, mimeo.

Dickens, L. et al. 1985. *Dismissed. A study of unfair dismissal and the* industrial *tribunal system.* Oxford, Basil Blackwell.

Ehrenberg, R.G. 1985. *Workers rights: Rethinking protective labor* legislation, London, National Bureau of Economic Research (NBER), Oct. 1985, mimeo.

Ehrenberg, R.G.; Jakubson, G.H. 1989. "Advance notification of plantclosing: Does it matter?", in *Industrial Relations,* Vol. 28, No. 1, Winter 1989, pp. 60-71.

Ehrenberg, R.G.; Schumann, P.L. 1982. *Longer hours or more jobs? An* investigation *of amending hours legislation to create employment,* Cornell Studies in Industrial Relations, Ithaca, New York, Cornell University.

Elbaum, M. 1988. "Les attentes des entreprises vis-à-vis de la flexibilitéont jusqu'ici peu influé sur l'emploi" [Enterprises' flexibility expectations have so far had little influence on employment], in *Economie et Statistique,* 1-1988, pp. 13-31.

Emerson, M. 1988. "Regulation or deregulation of the labour market: Policyregimes for the recruitment and dismissal of employees in the industrial countries", in *European Economic Review* 32, 1988, pp. 775-817.

Evans, S. et al. 1985. *Unfair dismissal law and employment practice in the* 1980s. London, Department of Employment Research Paper 53-1985.

Falke, J. et al. 1981. *Kündigungspraxis und Kündigungsschutz in der Bundesrepublik Deutschland* [Dismissal practice and dismissal protection in the Federal Republic of Germany]. Bonn, BMA.

Flanagan, R.J. 1988. "Unemployment as a hiring problem", in *OECD Economic Studies No. 11,* Autumn 1988, pp. 124-154.

Franz, W. 1989. "Beschäftigungsprobleme aufgrund von Inflexibilitäten au Arbeitsmärkten?" [Employment problems stemming from labour market inflexibilities?], in H. Scherf (ed.): *Beschäftigungsprobleme hochentwickelter Volkswirtschaften,* Schriften des Vereins für Socialpolitik NF, Bd. 178. Berlin, Duncker & Humboldt, pp. 303-340.

Gennard, J. 1986. *Job security: Redundancy arrangements and practices in* selected *OECD countries.* Paris, OECD, mimeo.

Gould, W.B. 1987. "Stemming the wrongful discharge tide: A case for arbitration", in *Employment Relations Law Journal,* Vol. 13, Winter 1987, pp. 404-425.

Hamermesh, D.S. 1988. "The demand for workers and hours and the effects of job security policies: Theories and evidence", in R.A. Hart (ed.): *Employment, Unemployment and Labor Utilization.* London, Unwin & Hyman, pp. 9-32.

Hotz-Hart, B. 1989. *Modernisierung von Unternehmen und Industrien bei unterschiedlichen industriellen Beziehungen* [The modernisation of enterprises and industries with different industrial relations]. Berne/Stuttgart, Paul Haupt Verlag.

International Organization of Employers (ed.). 1985. *Adapting the labour market.* Geneva.

Kayser, G.; Friede, C. 1984. *Wirkungsanalyse der Sozialgesetzgebung, Institüt für Mittelstandsforschung* [Analysis of the impact of social legislation]. Bonn, Dec. 1984, mimeo.

Koenig, H.; Zimmermann, K.F. 1985. *Determinants of employment policy of German manufacturing firms: A survey-based evaluation.* Mannheim, Institüt für Volkswirtschaftslehre und Statistik der Universität Mannheim, Discussion paper No. 302.

Kronberger Kreis (W. Engels et al.), (ed.). 1986. *Mehr Markt im Arbeitsrecht* [More market in labour law], Schriftenreihe des Kronberger Kreises, Bd. 10. Bad Homburg.

Layard, R.; Nickell, S. 1985. *The causes of British unemployment.* London, Centre for Labour Economics, London School of Economics, Discussion Paper No. 204, Feb. 1985.

Lazear, E.P. 1988. "Employment-at-will, job security, and work incentives", in R.A. Hart (ed.). *Employment, unemployment, and labor utilization.* London, Unwin & Hyman, pp. 39-61.

Lutz, B. 1987. *Arbeitsmarktstruktur und betriebliche Arbeitskräftestrategie. Eine theoretisch-historische Skizze zur Entstehung betriebszentrierter Arbeitsmarktsegmentation* [Labour market structure and industrial labour force strategy. A theoretical-historical sketch of the origin of industrial labour market segmentation]. Frankfurt, Campus Verlag.

Maurau, G.; Oudinet, J. 1988. "Précarité et flexibilité: Un essai de comparaison des industries Européennes" [Precariousness and flexibility: An attempt to compare European industries], in *La note de l'IRES,* No. 18-4-1988, pp. 5-17.

Mendelsohn, S.R. 1989. *Wrongful termination litigation in the US and its effect on the employment relationship,* OECD working party on industrial relations, Paris, OECD, Jan. 1989, mimeo.

Nerb, G. 1986. "Employment problems: Views of businessmen and the workforce - results of an employee and employer survey on labour market issues in the member states", in *European Economy,* No. 27, Mar. 1986, pp. 13-110.

Nerb, G. et al. 1977. "Struktur, Entwicklung und Bestimmungsgrössen der Beschäftigung in Industrie und Bauwirtschaft auf mittlere Sicht" [Structure, development and projected size of employment in industry and construction in the middle term], in *Mitteilungen aus der Arbeitsmarkt- und Berufsforschung (MittAB),* 2-1977, pp. 291-310.

OECD (ed.). 1984. *Employment outlook 1984.* Paris.

OECD (ed.). 1986. *Flexibility in the labour market: The current debate. A technical report.* Paris.

OECD (ed.). 1988. *Employment outlook 1988.* Paris.

OECD (ed.). 1989. *Economies in transition: Structural adjustment in OECD countries.* Paris.

Oeschsler, W.A. 1988. "Employee-severance - regulations and procedures", in G. Dlugos et al. (eds.): *Management under differing labour market and employment systems.* Berlin/New York, de Gruyter, pp. 397-410.

Reuter, D. 1985. "Die Rolle des Arbeitsrechts im marktwirtschaftlichen System - Eine Skizze" [The role of labour law in the market economy - a sketch], in *ORDO,* 36-1985, pp. 51-88.

Rodgers, G.; Rodgers, J. (eds.). 1989. *Precarious jobs in labour market regulation: The growth of atypical employment in western Europe,* Geneva, International Institute of Labour Studies and Free University of Brussels.

Rosow, J.M.; Zager, R. 1984. *Employment security in a free society.* New York, Pergamon Press.

Schellhaas, H.-M. 1989. "Das Arbeitsrecht als Beschäftigungshemmnis? Referat für die Tagung 'Mehr Arbeit durch weniger Recht?" [Labour law as an obstacle to employment? Report for the session "More work through less law?"], in C.F. Buechtemann; H. Neumann (eds.): *Mehr Arbeit durch weniger Recht? - Chancen und Risiken der Arbeitsmarktflexibilisierung.* Berlin, Sigma, 1989 (forthcoming).

Sengenberger, W.; Loveman, G. 1987. *Smaller units of employment. A synthesis report on industrial reorganisation in industrialised countries.* Geneva, ILO.

Siebert, H. 1989. "Kündigungsschutz und Sozialplanpflicht - Optimale Allokation von Risiken oder Ursache der Arbeitslosigkeit" [Dismissal protection and duty of the social plan - optimal allocation of risks or causes of unemployment], in H. Scherf (ed.): *Beschäftigungsprobleme hochentwickelter Volkswirtschaften.* Schriften des Vereins für Socialpolitik NF Vol. 178. Berlin, Duncker & Humblodt, pp. 267-286.

Standing, G. 1986. *Labour market flexibility: Cause or cure to unemployment?* Public Lecture Series No. 25, Geneva, International Institute for Labour Studies.

Streeck, W. 1989. *On the social and political conditions of diversified quality production.* Paper presented at the WZB/LME conference "No Ways to Full Employment?" Berlin, Wissenschaftszentrum Berlin, July 1989, mimeo.

Teubner, G. 1985. "After legal instrumentalism? Strategic models of post-regulatory law", in G. Teubner (ed.): *Dilemmas of Law in the Welfare State.* Berlin/New York, de Gruyter, pp. 299-326.

Teubner, G. 1987. "Juridification: Concepts, aspects, limits, solutions", in G. Teubner (ed.): *Juridification of social spheres: A comparative analysis in the areas of labor, corporate, antitrust and social welfare law.* Berlin/New York, de Gruyter, pp. 3-48.

Walter, N. 1989. "The inflexibility of Labour Market Related institutions - some observations for Germany", in G. Dlugos et al. (eds.): *Management under differing labour market and employment systems.* Berlin/New York, de Gruyter, pp. 133-142.

Warnken, J; Ronning, G. 1989. "Technischer Wandel und Beschäftigungs-strukturen" [Technical change and employment structure], in R. Schettkat; M. Wagner (eds.): *Technologischer Wandel und Beschäftigung: Fakten, Analysen, Trends.* Berlin, de Gruyter, pp. 225-277.

Figure 1. Range of employment protection provisions in the Federal Republic of Germany, 1987-88

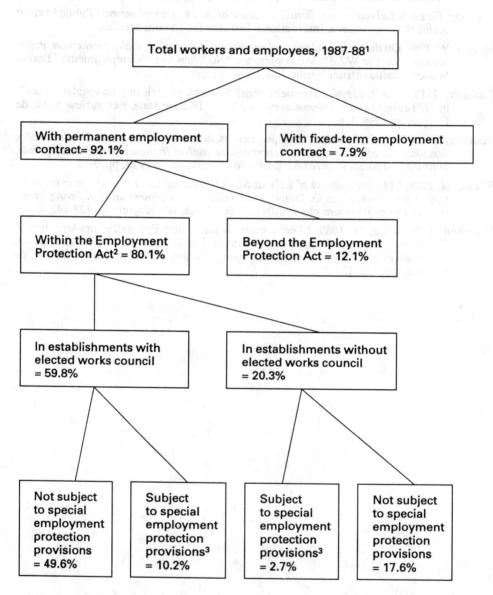

Total workers and employees, 1987-88[1]

With permanent employment contract= 92.1%

With fixed-term employment contract = 7.9%

Within the Employment Protection Act[2] = 80.1%

Beyond the Employment Protection Act = 12.1%

In establishments with elected works council = 59.8%

In establishments without elected works council = 20.3%

Not subject to special employment protection provisions = 49.6%

Subject to special employment protection provisions[3] = 10.2%

Subject to special employment protection provisions[3] = 2.7%

Not subject to special employment protection provisions = 17.6%

[1] Excluding public servants, military personnel and apprentices (n = 4,930).   [2] i.e. in establishments employing at least six workers on a regular basis and with tenure exceeding six months.
[3] Aged 45 years or older and with at least 20 years of tenure with present employer or disabled under the Disabled Workers Act *(Schwerbehindertengesetz)*.

Source: Representative telephone survey, 1987-88.
(c) Wissenschaftszentrum Berlin für Sozialforschung/AMB, 1989.

11

Social sanctions, labour laws and labour market flexibility: The Indian experience*

*by Swapna Mukhopadhyay***

Introduction

A fair amount of evidence has accumulated, the world over, on increased flexibility in the labour market and the consequent rise in worker vulnerability. As in many other developing countries, the urban labour market in India is characterised by a large pool of ill-paid workers in insecure employment who are *de facto* unprotected by law, coexisting with a small unionised segment holding relatively secure, career-oriented jobs. It has often been suggested that in a situation of surplus labour, stringent provisions of labour laws and the power of the trade unions together are to be blamed for the effort on the part of employers to avoid hiring regular employees and (to the extent possible) to have the work done through subcontracting or by casual workers - efficiency wage theories notwithstanding. Available Indian data in recent times do indeed show a rise in such insecure employment, both in absolute and in relative terms, although it may be difficult *a priori* to ascribe any specific portion of that rise to the factors mentioned above.

While quantification of such effects is useful, it is equally important to decipher whether such phenomena, to the extent they do exist, are socially acceptable, if not on moral at least on pragmatic grounds. For if they indeed are acceptable, enacting laws alone will not amount to much. The issue has to be analysed in the context of the complex pattern of inter-linkages between the social and political foundations of labour legislation in the country as well as its moral and ethical roots, the manner in which public opinion is moulded in matters of what is ethical and what is practicable, and the connections between

* I am very grateful to Dr. Chatrapati Singh of the Indian Law Institute for helpful discussions on labour laws and Mr. A.K. Ray Choudhury, Joint Adviser, Bureau of Public Enterprises, Ministry of Industry, Government of India, for allowing me access to some source material. Thanks are also due to T.N. Madan and Kanchan Chopra, my colleagues at the Institute of Economic Growth, who read and commented on an earlier draft. The author bears sole responsibility for the views expressed in the paper.

** Institute of Economic Growth, New Dehli.

the two in popular belief, the linkages between social sanction and judicial decisions, and the actual operation of labour laws in the context of a highly fragmented labour market. This paper is a preliminary attempt to chart out these inter-linkages with reference to the Indian situation as it exists today. The following section provides a very brief overview of the employment and earnings situation in urban India. The next section after that looks into the historical and philosophical roots of labour legislation in India, another section outlines the links between law and public opinion, and the final section derives some conclusion.

Wages, earnings and terms of employment in urban India

The labour market in urban India is highly stratified. As of 1983 total employment in urban India was of the order of 57.84 million,[1] of which 24.21 million is said to have been within the organised sector; 16.87 million in the public sector and 7.34 million in the organised private sector.[2] Thus at least three out of five urban workers were in the unorganised sector. This is only the lower bound, because a number of workers who are employed by large units may have been working as casual or contract workers.[3] In absolute and in relative terms, worker vulnerability has been high and may in fact have been rising in recent years.

There are a number of macroeconomic indicators of this increased vulnerability. Between 1973 and 1983, the number of casual wage labourers in Indian cities and towns rose from 4.8 million to over 10 million. In 1983, over two-fifths of the total male workforce and nearly half of the female were self-employed. A large majority of these self-employed people were in low-productivity, low-income services and trading activities. This is corroborated by the 1980 Economic Census data, which show that of all those working in urban enterprises nearly one-third were in own-account units, namely very small establishments that are run, predominantly, with the help of unpaid family workers and not even one hired person on a regular basis. A large number of the remaining two-thirds were employed by small establishments outside the purview of the Factories Act, at precarious pay and terms of employment.[4]

However, a small group of workers, especially those in the public sector, and a yet smaller number in the organised private sector have been in a rather enviable position. For various reasons, employment in the latter has been stagnant at times even declining in recent years. But employment in the public sector, especially at the state level, has been growing at a reasonable rate. Official documents define a public sector establishment as one that is owned, controlled or managed by:

(i) the Government or a department of the Government;

(ii) a government company, as defined in section 617 of the Companies Act of 1956;

The employment breakdown in different branches of the public sector in recent years is as follows:

Branch	Employment as of 31 March (100,000s)		Percentage change	
	1984	1985	1985/84	1984/83
Central govt.	33.11	33.29	+ 0.5	+ 1.4
State govt.	61.54	62.80	+ 2.0	+ 1.9
Quasi govt.[1] (central)	31.58	33.08	+ 4.7	+ 5.0
Quasi govt.[1] (state)	21.16	21.88	+ 3.4	+ 4.0
Local bodies	21.30	21.64	+ 1.6	+ 0.9
Total	168.69	172.69	+ 2.4	+ 2.5

[1] Quasi government comprises agencies financed, usually to the full extent, by the Government.

Source: *Employment Review 1984-85* (New Delhi, Ministry of Labour, Directorate General of Employment and Training), 1988, table 4, p. 3.

(iii) a corporation or a co-operative society established by a central or state Act and which is owned, controlled or managed by the Government; or

(iv) a local authority.

While terms and conditions of employment vary quite a bit between different branches of the public sector, regular employees in all branches of the public sector enjoy full employment security. Since profits are not supposedly the guiding principle of operation in public sector concerns engaged in production of goods and services, accountability for poor performance is low, so much so that the popular image of public sector enterprises (PSEs) is one of *de facto* non-accountability for inefficiency. Employees of PSEs under the central government, like the Steel Authority of India Ltd. or Coal India Ltd., totalling about 2 million workers, enjoy constitutional guarantees in line with those enjoyed by government civil servants in the various administrative departments of the central government. At the same time, they enjoy a number of benefits available to industrial workers which are not available to the latter. To cite an example, they are entitled to a dearness allowance (DA) or cost-of-living neutralisation formula, fixed at Rs.1.65 per point rise in the Consumer Price Index (CPI), whereas the corresponding figure applicable to central government employees under the rulings of the Fourth Pay Commission is Rs.1.23. The figure of Rs.1.65 for PSEs was fixed in 1985, with effect from 1983. Currently negotiations are in progress for a further rise in the DA formula. The workers' unions are demanding Rs.2.50 per point rise in the CPI. If past experience is any indication, the rate will indeed be raised upwards. Such revisions take place once about every four years for employees in PSEs, which is about three times as often as central government employees can hope for.

Strong union pressures have resulted in a steady upward trend in the pay and allowances of public sector employees. The average emoluments of employees in central PSEs went up from Rs.5,470 in 1970-71 to Rs.24,300 in 1984-85, registering an increase of about 344 per cent; while during the same period, the CPI had increased by about 270 per cent.[5] All this happened during a period of low or negative profits and dwindling productivity in many of these under-takings. Clearly, productivity or ability to pay of the undertaking have not been criteria in pay fixation. A regular unskilled worker in central public sector concern earns about Rs.50 a day, while a miner, covered by the Minimum Wages Act, is paid Rs.12 a day, and in most parts of the country an agricultural labourer, also covered by the Minimum Wages Act, can hope to make at most Rs.11 a day, and that in the rare cases where the letter of the law is followed. While degrees vary, the story is similar in most branches of the public sector, as well as in administrative departments, whether at the central or state level.

This is not to suggest that the entire problem of inefficiency and stagnation in public sector undertakings is one of workers' overpay, and that efficiency and productivity in these concerns would automatically go up if one could by some device contain their workers' demands for pay increases. The point that is being highlighted here is simply that emoluments and conditions of work vary enormously across different groups of workers, well beyond what is warranted by differences in skills or productivity. Moreover, paradoxically enough, the heterogeneity is sustained, among other things, by the selectivity of labour laws, as applicable to specific groups of workers.

Foundations of labour legislation in India

Almost in line with the fragmented nature of the labour market, the set of labour laws, consisting of legal statutes and case material, currently in existence in the country, can be looked upon as falling into two broad modal categories - one for formal sector employees and the other for unorganised sector workers, although one can find a number of instances where they do cut across both categories. In broad terms again, the evolution of these two kinds of law can be traced to somewhat different sets of factors.

Much of the legal structure and legal philosophy in India is inherited from the British and is rooted in the doctrines of common law. The statutory rights of collective bargaining as conferred by the Trade Unions Act of 1926 was more a reflection of similar legislation enacted in the United Kingdom rather than a result of an indigenous labour movement (Aggarwal, 1967). Here, as elsewhere, such legislation was instituted as a counter to the prevailing common law doctrine of criminal conspiracy which suggests that the concerted action of an organised group may affect society in a different and far stronger manner than if the same act were committed by individuals. Similarly, the Workmen's Compensation Act of 1923 was enacted to counter the common law doctrine of criminal negligence. Clearly statutes that purport to invest workers as a group with various rights, including the right of association, could not have derived their major sustenance from tenets of moral philosophy which have a strong individualistic bias. Thus, the guiding principles behind such legislation may be traced not so much to the prevailing libertarian theories of justice, but more to such factors as the international socialist and working class movements, changing notions of social justice, as embodied in the concept of the welfare state, the success of the Russian Revolution and the founding of the ILO in 1919, to which India was a signatory.

It is important to realise that these and most other pieces of post-independence labour legislation dealing with industrial relations, like the Industrial Disputes Act of 1948 and some of the social legislation measures like the Employees' State Insurance Act of 1948 or the Employees' Provident Fund Act of 1952, are meant to protect the rights of and confer benefits on only regular workers in the organised sector. Under the Industrial Disputes Act, ad hoc or casual workers are not entitled to any compensation in the event of a lay-off. They and others of their kind in smaller establishments are not covered by the Employees' State Insurance Act, nor are they entitled to provident fund benefits. There are some special Acts covering specific groups of workers, for instance the Plantations Labour Act of 1951, the Dock Workers (Regulation of Employment) Act of 1948 and the Motor Transport Workers Act of 1961 or the Mines Act of 1952, which have some provisions covering workers in such establishments. Provisions vary from case to case, depending on the size of the establishment, the nature of the industry concerned and the status of employment. In any event, for a large majority of workers the benefits conferred by such legislation are negligible, or even non-existent.

However, there is another set of statutory measures, by and large of a fairly recent origin, which invokes certain fundamental rights and principles laid out in the Constitution of India, and which are targeted mainly towards unorganised sector workers. According to a ruling of the Supreme Court of India, the fundamental rights conferred on the citizens of India in the Constitution of the country, along with the Preamble and the Directive Principles of State Policy (Part IV) constitute the core of the Constitution, which is not subject to amendment by Parliament.[6] The Indian Constitution confers a number of fundamental rights to all citizens irrespective of caste, creed, religion or sex. The Directive Principles of the Constitution provide for such constitutional goals as the right to work (article 41), just and humane conditions of work (article 42) and a living wage for all (article 43). Time and again such constitutional provisions have been invoked to enact fresh labour laws. Examples of such statutes in recent years are the Child Labour Act of 1987, the Inter-State Migrant Workers (Regulation of Employment and Conditions of Service) Act of 1979, the Equal Remuneration Act of 1976 and the Contract Labour (Regulation and Abolition) Act of 1970.

Such statutory laws, aimed at achieving constitutional goals, form an integral part of the labour law of the country. The Preamble to the Indian Constitution upholds the principles of liberty and equality. It abrogates discrimination on grounds of sex, creed or religion and preaches equality in the eyes of law for all. The links between such principles and the received tenets in the liberal theories of justice are reasonably direct and straightforward, even when one takes later day versions of such theories as expounded by Rawls (1971) or Barry (1973). There might be some disagreement on the question as to whether a similar statement can be made about the provision of preferential treatment of disadvantaged groups, like members of the scheduled castes and scheduled tribes as specified in the Constitution. The principle of equality is subject to a lot of inner tensions. Nevertheless, one could invoke the tenet of procedural justice to uphold such constitutional provisions. In fact, the Rawlsian Second Principle of Justice has been used to support the Affirmative Action Programmes in the United States of America (Goodman, 1979),[7] and similar arguments can be invoked to establish the principle of reservations for disadvantaged classes in the Indian Constitution as well (Anand, 1987). While elaboration of these linkages is beyond the scope of this paper, one can perhaps make the statement that the philosophical basis of such constitutional provisions, and through them of labour laws that have been enacted invoking such provisions, can be traced not so much to group-based working-class movements, but to prevailing individualistic theories of justice and human rights.

If the foregoing interpretation of the social foundations of labour legislation in India has an element of truth, then the implications of it are somewhat paradoxical. To the extent the worker has certain legal guarantees invoked by individualistic notions of justice, the violation of such law puts him or her as an individual against an immeasurably more powerful opponent: namely the employer. Given the prohibitively high transactions cost of legal disputes and the enormous difference in the economic, political and organisational power of the two parties involved, such individual rights have no cutting edge and are virtually non-justiciable.[8]

Thus the distinction between the first kind of labour laws and the second is not merely in terms of their historical and philosophical roots, but also in terms of their implementability. In the case of the first set of regulations, which apply to organised sector workers, the workers are unionised and are generally well aware of their rights and privileges, while the Government can have good control on implementation of the letter of the law. For the second group, implementation of laws is an administratively difficult if not an infeasible proposition, while workers themselves are either unaware of their legal rights or powerless to enforce their enactment. Thus the dichotomy in labour law persists alongside fragmentation in the labour market.

Law and public opinion

The linkages between labour laws on the one hand, and social sanction and public opinion on the other, cut both ways. At one level, one can argue that to the extent the Constitution of the country reflects the goals and aspirations of the polity, all statutes that seek to codify constitutional provisions have social sanction behind them. At a less abstract level, all laws, including labour laws, have to be passed by a Parliament which consists of elected representatives of the people and, hence, by some kind of transitivity argument, cannot grossly violate the prevailing majority opinion. Case law, which forms an integral part of the legal structure, reflects the prevailing values and norms of social justice as embedded in the social and moral philosophical thinking of the court, sometimes invoking principles that go beyond the strict wording of the law.[9] Finally, in a democracy, that part of statutory law that embodies the public policy of the executive also cannot run grossly counter to prevailing public opinion.

However, laws do not operate in a vacuum. The legal process evolves in conjunction with the prevailing economic system, public policy and the mode of functioning of the executive. For instance, what has emerged as the most important statutory provision on industrial relations in India, i.e. the Industrial Disputes Act of 1948, has very little to say on collective bargaining as a method of settling industrial disputes. Its main emphasis is on tripartite arbitration as a conflict resolution mechanism with the third party, that is the State, as the single most important repository of power. This is in sharp contrast to the experience of the United States of America on the United Kingdom until recent times, where official policy has been to foster the growth of healthy and responsible collective bargaining practices pretty nearly overshadowing the role of the legal process in industrial disputes (Kahn-Freund, 1969; Commons, 1950).

Contrary to this, the official policy in India since the early 1950s has been systematically biased against a healthy development of collective bargaining practices on the twin plea that the unions are not strong enough to face the employers across the bargaining table without the support of the State, and that unmitigated industrial disputes will hamper productivity and slow down economic growth. As a result, since the beginning of the fifties, the official stance has almost always been towards maintaining industrial peace through compulsory tripartite arbitration (Ramaswamy, 1984; Aggarwal, 1966).[10] The large trade unions in the country have come to depend on the state machinery as a crutch for support, and the State has been a ubiquitous presence in all kinds of wage negotiations and industrial disputes. In the process, these unions have not merely developed a dependent and greedy mentality with little sense of responsibility, but have also become irrevocably politicised. The large unions in India operate more as labour wings of the major political parties. The rights without responsibilities approach of the big Indian trade unions has resulted in the emergence of what the Planning Commission has termed as "high wage islands"[11] in a sea of low earnings. The continuous growth of the public sector in India has come to be seen not as a necessity spurred by economic logic, but as a means of patronage distribution in return for political support.[12] Under the Industrial Disputes Act, economically non-viable large private sector units cannot close down easily - a provision meant to assure employment security to organised sector workers. Once such units are declared sick, they are taken over by the Government. The policy is favoured both by inept management who can write off their losses with impunity and by workers' unions who become entitled to greater benefits in the process. The perverse logic of the situation does nothing to promote industrial efficiency in the country. Similarly, nationalisation of industrial units has generally found favour with workers' unions. It is difficult to discern how much of the enthusiasm for public take-overs can be explained in terms of pecuniary gains to interested parties and how much by adherence to socialist ideals.

At the other end of the spectrum are the large masses of unprotected workers who can derive little solace from the fact that the Directive Principles of the Constitution of the country guarantee them "a decent standard of life".[13] Their reservation price is low and, lacking any kind of organisation, they are not in a position to demand decent wages or secure employment. Nor does the economic rationale work in their favour, for if the public image of formal sector labour is one of less efficient and less responsible labour, it may even seem only fair that small-scale employers will strive to retain their small-scale stamp by restricting the number of regular workers to below the magic mark of ten employees with power or twenty without,[14] while getting into all kinds of flexible work arrangements with unattached labour for extra work. Pareto optimality dies hard: if both parties benefit by such arrangements, then why not?

The only problem with such arguments is that, apart from the fact that Pareto optimality is an inadequate criterion for social justice (Sen, 1987), they are also patently illogical. Income security for workers need not necessarily breed inefficiency, except under very special circumstances. The seeming unaccountability of a large section of public sector employees is the product of the manner in which growth of responsible "norm"-based collective bargaining practices has been thwarted in India, and the virtual absence of any productivity related incentive structure in public sector concerns. Employees in most such concerns now receive bonus payments as a matter of routine - shorn of any indicator of productivity or profitability of the concern. One must not also forget that the entire system functions in a highly politicised atmosphere, where economic decisions are taken regularly on grounds of partisan politics, so that it would be patently unfair to single out the workers' unions as the sole agents responsible for the poor performance of this sector.

However, in popular belief the step from positive statements to normative pre-conceptions is only a small one.[15] If unionised workers have in some situations been seen to act irresponsibly, the verdict may well be that it is sensible to switch to unorganised workers, so long as that option is open. It is little wonder that regular employment in the organised private sector has been virtually stagnant for many years now. The numerous ploys used by employers to restrict the number of regular workers on their payrolls are well known. It is easy to confuse issues, and by-passing the letter of the law may even come to gain a measure of sanctity in the public eye if it can be backed by evidence of irresponsible use of it by sections of the "other party". Meanwhile, given the overall direction of developmental strategy in the country, the constitutional provision of ensuring "a living wage to all workers - agricultural, industrial or otherwise" (article 43), continues to have very little cutting edge in terms of the prevailing economic reality. Thus laws that invoke such constitutional provisions also tend to end up as paper tigers. They come to be seen as no more than pious pronouncements or at best, goals to be achieved by society in some distant future.

Concluding remarks

While all this does lead up to the question of how to ensure a measure of responsibility and accountability in the functioning of the workers' unions, that is only a secondary issue. The major problem relates to the question of empowerment of the less fortunate majority of the Indian workforce which is outside the organised sector. Organisation is certainly one option, if not the most feasible one under the current situation. But even that is not likely to succeed too well without some economic back-up. Such back-up could be ensured by the State if the Government decided to direct public policy towards provision of employment guarantees, and hence a guaranteed minimum income for all persons willing to work, so that at least the worst forms of economic deprivation are taken care of and the worker is assured of a decent reservation price. The actual operationalisation of such programmes needs to be worked out. Some employment-generating schemes have been operative in rural India for some years, but their coverage is as yet very thin.[16] Similar schemes could be implemented in urban India as well. If the political will exists, resources need not be a binding constraint. Compared to the rising and enormous amounts that are paid out to public sector employees, or the massive subsidies provided to various pressure groups, the cost of such a scheme should not prove too prohibitive. Implementing the new dearness allowance rates that workers' unions in public sector undertakings are asking for alone would amount to an *additional* cost of Rs.800 crores for 2 million workers, a sum which is less than a third of what they have already been receiving as cost-of-living neutralisation allowance over and above pay and other allowances. This extra amount by itself could provide 200 days of employment a year at Rs.20 a day for two million unorganised sector workers. From the point of view of society, it would be a case of money better spent. This could also be the beginning of the process by which one could hope to bring the constitutional goal of securing "a living wage" for one and all within sight, apart from ensuring the constitutional guarantee of the right to work.

Notes

[1] Rough estimates calculated on the basis of the National Sample Survey (NSS), 38th round. Usual status figures are for 1983. Report 341 (New Delhi, Department of Statistics, Ministry of Planning, Government of India, Nov. 1987.)

[2] *Employment Review, 1984-85* (New Delhi, Ministry of Labour, Directorate General of Employment and Training, 1988). The figures relate to the financial year 1 April 1983 to 21 March 1984, and hence do not correspond strictly to the calendar year 1983 of the estimates for the NSS, 38th round. The break-up of private sector employment in 1983-84 was 6.53 million in larger firms (at least 50 workers) and 0.82 million in smaller units (10-49 workers).

[3] This is clear also from the fact that the NSS estimates for regular wage and salaried employees come to about 23.35 million in 1983, which is *less* than the Labour Bureau's figure for total organised sector employment in 1983-84 of 24.21 million. Even allowing for the discrepancy that may have arisen due to the mismatching of the periods concerned, this leaves little room for *any* regular wage and salaried employment in units employing less than 10 workers. The reason for this is clearly the incidence of casual employment in the organised sector. Also, the Labour Bureau's coverage of "small", "organised" private sector establishments, i.e. those employing between 10 and 24 workers being voluntary, is only partial.

[4] See S. Mukhopadhyay: *Urban labour markets in India*, World Employment Programme Research, Labour Market Analysis and Employment Planning, Working Paper No. 32 (Geneva, ILO, June 1989).

[5] *Report of the Fourth Pay Commission* (New Delhi, Government of India, 1986).

[6] Keshavanand Bharti versus the State of Kerala, *All India Reporter*, 1973. Supreme Court, 1961. See Galanter (1984), p. 481.

[7] The two principles of justice enunciated by Rawls are as follows:

First principle: Each person is to have an equal right to the most extensive total system of equal basic liberties compatible with a similar system of liberty for all.

Second principle: Social and economic inequalities are to be arranged so that they are both: (a) to the greatest benefit of the most disadvantaged, consistent with the just savings principle, and (b) attached to offices and positions open to all under conditions of fair equality of opportunity. (Rawls 1971, p. 302.)

The second principle, according to Rawls, is to have priority over the first. See Barry (1973) for a critical evaluation of the Rawlsian theory of justice from a left liberal viewpoint and Nozick (1974) from a right conservative one.

[8] It may be mentioned here that by the 42nd Amendment to the Indian Constitution, with effect from January 1977, the following subclause was inserted in the 39th article: Article 39A: *Equal justice and free legal aid* - "The State shall secure that the operation of the legal system promotes justice, on a basis of equal opportunity, and shall in particular, provide free legal aid, by suitable legislation or schemes or in any other way, to ensure that opportunities for securing justice are not denied to any citizen by reason of economic or other disabilities."

It may be worth noting that the deliverance of justice in India is an enormously protracted affair, and the time foregone could turn out to be as important an element of cost as actual legal expenses, if not more, especially for the poor, who have little savings to fall back upon.

[9] As Justice Krishna Iyer puts it: "Law including constitutional law can no longer "do it alone" but must be illumined by ethics and allied fields of knowledge". Judgement delivered in the State of Kerala, V.N.M. Thomas, *All India Reporter,* 1976, Supreme Court 490, 525.

[10] A striking exception to this broad trend was witnessed in the early fifties when Shri V.V. Giri, the Union Labour Minister, expressed his firm commitment to the goal of developing health, strong, yet responsible collective bargaining practices in the country. For a brief critical review of the growth of the trade unions in the post-independence era, see Ramaswamy (1984), Chapters 2, 5 and 6. See also the *Report of the National Commission on Labour* (New Delhi, Government of India, 1969), where the Commission notes the role of the Government in stifling the growth of collective bargaining.

[11] "In recent years, certain sectors have emerged as high wage islands, where white-collar employees predominate. They have, by using pressures, pushed up wages to levels that are much out of line with the general level of wages. It is necessary to resist this trend in a determined way. Or else, there will be heavy inroads into the estimated resources for the Plan and the country will be pushed into inflation and stagnation." *Approach paper to the Fifth Five-Year Plan,* Jan. 1973, Chapter 9, p. 52, para. 13.

[12] Dhar (1989), pp. 23-25.

[13] Article 43, Constitution of India.

[14] The criterion demarcates units covered by the Factories Act from those that are not, roughly corresponding to a popularly accepted demarcation between "formal" and "informal" sector establishments. See Mukhopadhyay (1989), endnote 7.

[15] The classic statement of this position, although in an altogether different context, can be found in Milton Friedman's *Methodology of Positive Economics*, Friedman (1953).

[16] These are the National Rural Employment Programme, the Rural Labour Employment Guarantee Programme and the erstwhile Food for Work Programmes of the 1970s, all of which have been subsumed as of early 1989 under the Jawahar Rojgar Yojana Programme of the central government. The aim of this programme has been to provide employment to at least one member of all families living below the poverty line. For a short review see Mukhopadhyay (1987), Section IV.

References

Anand, C.L. 1987. *Equity, justice and reverse discrimination.* Delhi, Mittal Publications.

Aggarwal, A.P. 1966. *Indian and American labour legislation and practices: A comparative study.* New Delhi, Asia Publishing House.

Barry, B. 1973. *The liberal theory of justice.* Oxford, Clarendon Press.

Coates, D. 1983. "The question of trade union power", in Coates, D. and Johnson, G. (eds.): *Socialist arguments.* Oxford, Oxford University Press.

Commons, J.R. 1950. *The economics of collective action.* New York, Macmillan.

The Constitution of India, New Delhi, Government of India.

Dawson, W.A. 1967. *An introductory guide to central labour legislation.* New Delhi, Asia Publishing House.

Dhar, P.N. 1989. *Constraints on growth: Reflections on the Indian experience.* Fourth V.T. Krishnamachari Memorial Lecture, 6 Oct. 1989, New Delhi, Institute of Economic Growth.

Friedman, M. 1953. *Essays in positive economics.* Chicago, University of Chicago Press.

Galanter, M. 1984. *Competing equalities: Law and the backward classes in India.* New Delhi, Oxford University Press.

Goodman, A. H. 1979. *Justice and reverse discrimination.* Princeton, New Jersey, Princeton University Press.

Hahn, F., Hollis, M. (eds.) 1979. *Philosophy and economic theory.* Oxford Readings in Philosophy Series, Oxford, Oxford University Press.

Harris, D. 1987. *Justifying state welfare: The new right versus the old left.* Oxford, Basil Blackwell.

Marshall, L.C. 1918. *Readings in industrial society.* Chicago, University of Chicago Press.

Millar, D. 1980. "Social justice and the principle of need", in Friedman, M. and Robertson, D. (eds.): *The Frontiers of Political Theory.* Brighton, Harvester Press.

Mukhopadhyay, S. 1987. *Intra-rural labour circulation in India: An analysis.* New Delhi, ILO/ARTEP (Asian Regional Team for Employment Promotion).

— —: 1989. *Urban labour markets in India.* Labour Market Analysis and Employment Planning, World Employment Programme Research, Working Paper No. 32, Geneva, ILO, June.

Kahn-Freund, O. 1979. *Labour relations: Heritage and adjustment.* Oxford, Oxford University Press.

Nozick, R. 1974. *Anarchy, state and Utopia.* Oxford, Basil Blackwell.

Ramaswamy, E.A. 1984. *Power and justice: The state in industrial relations.* Oxford, Oxford University Press.

Rawls, J. 1971. *A theory of justice.* Cambridge, Massachusetts, Harvard University Press.

Sen, A. 1987. *On ethics and economics.* Oxford, Basil Blackwell.

Seth, B.R. 1978. *Introduction to labour laws in India.* New Delhi, National Productivity Council.

Taylor, R. 1980. *The fifth estate.* London, Pan Books.

Teller, L. 1947, 1949. *Law governing labour disputes and collective bargaining.* New York, Baker, Voorkis and Co. Inc., 3 volumes.

Vaid, K.N. 1965. *State and labour in India.* New Delhi, Asia Publishing House.

12

The role of labour markets in employment generation and human resources development in Asian countries

by Rashid Amjad and Gus Edgren [*]

Introduction[1]

The Asian experience in recent years displays strong evidence that macro policies, in terms of an appropriate incentive structure and economic growth have been key determinants of employment performance. An important question which this paper addresses is the role that Asian labour markets play in this process of realising the potential of a favourable macro environment. If the interaction of demand and supply of skills and knowledge is to play an important role in economic development, it is important that they interact efficiently, or else human resources will be underutilised, and may even draw monopoly rents at the expense of the others. There has indeed been quite a debate in Asia as to whether labour markets are "flexible" in the sense of responding quickly to changing demand and supply conditions.

What is of considerable significance to employment planners is an understanding of how and under what conditions rapid economic growth translates itself into a rapid creation of jobs. This becomes especially important as the potential for direct employment creation by the large-scale manufacturing, and indeed entire formal or organised, sector is limited in relation to the growth of labour supply in almost all Asian countries. Most additional employment is created in the small-scale and informal sector comprising micro-enterprises and the self-employed. The links between macro policies, growth of the formal sector and the small-scale and informal sector is of considerable significance during periods of either rapid growth or recession or when the economy is subject to strong structural adjustments and macro-stabilisation policies under an IMF-World Bank adjustment programme. In analysing this

* ILO-ARTEP (Asian Regional Team for Employment Promotion), New Delhi, and United Nations Development Programme (UNDP), New York.

process it is crucial to consider not just the functioning of labour markets in terms of aggregate supply and demand adjustments but of labour processes at the micro-level through which employment, productivity and changes in income distribution take place.

The other important issue in employment planning in the Asian region is the moving away from a sole emphasis on employment generation through increasing labour absorption towards a more integrated approach to human resource development that emphasises links between investment in education and skill development (the supply side) and the creation of productive employment opportunities (the demand side). In the Asian NIEs (newly industrialising economies) and the potential or second line of NIEs, increasing emphasis is placed on a human resource driven strategy in which the competitive edge of the economy is neither commodities nor low wage labour, but skill and entrepreneurship development and research. For the South Asian economies the real challenge is to increase labour productivity and efficiency in the face of increasing pressures to open up their economies to international competitiveness.

Flexibility of labour markets: The Asian experience

The macroeconomic management of economic growth and stabilisation policies cannot be effective without a better understanding of the behaviour of enterprises, workers and consumers in the various markets which make the economy work. In this context the labour market is of major importance. Its ability to respond to changes in demand and to price incentives influences the effectiveness of the economy in making use of opportunities which open up in world markets and minimising losses flowing from past mistakes.

To varying degrees, the ability of labour markets to adjust to changes in demand and supply is influenced by the industrial relations system. It is customary in economic analysis of trade liberalisation and adjustment to treat trade unions and collective bargaining machineries as institutional obstacles to labour market flexibility. It has, therefore, been argued that the relatively smooth adjustment of Asian labour markets to external shocks in the 1970s and 1980s was facilitated by the relative weakness of trade unions or to the absence of restrictive legislation on hiring and firing in many Asian countries, particularly in East and South-East Asia. Conversely, it has been suggested that the relatively poor performance of the South Asian economies is partly due to the stricter regulations of employers' rights to hire and fire, and to granting unions wider scope for bargaining than the ASEAN and East Asian countries.[2]

While it is difficult to generalise on the basis of selected case studies of some industries, ARTEP's work suggests that the institutional bargaining machinery cannot be seen in isolation from the changing conditions in the domestic economy. This is especially true of the trade regime. In South Asia, oligopolistic privileges were given to certain enterprises when the need arose to develop indigenous industries. Part of those privileges were passed on to trade unions through high wages, trade union security (in some cases closed shop agreements) etc., privileges rare in industries exposed to harder competition because of ease of entry or less protection against imports. ARTEP is presently studying cases in India where the competitive situation in an industry changed through the admission of new entrants or liberalisation of imports. Preliminary results indicate that the unions' mode of operation, in some cases even their structure, as well as the industrial relations machinery tend to change in cases where there has been a drastic change in the trade regime.

In South-East Asia there are no prohibitions against going out of business and the only country in which permission is required for lay-offs is Indonesia. Here too permission is normally granted in all bonafide cases of retrenchment for reasons of restructuring, albeit with some delay. In the Philippines, the employers' right to declare workers redundant is explicitly granted in the Labour Code, while in Malaysia, Thailand and Singapore, it is implicit. Large-scale redundancies occurred in the Philippines during the 1983-85 crisis - particularly in the sugar industry - and in the Malaysian semi-conductor industry in 1984-85. The only ASEAN parallel to the Indian agreements on restructuring through gradual redeployment may be cases where public sector enterprises have been privatised. In most export processing zones (EPZs) of South-East Asia, trade unions and collective bargaining have had little impact. Foreign investors have naturally pressed for maximum "flexibility", as in the case of investment laws, taxes, etc. Government authorities have gone to great lengths to restrict strikes and promote company unions as opposed to industrial or general unions. During the 1980s, however, the general tendency in South-East Asia has been that industrial relations systems and practices in EPZs have gradually become more similar to conditions existing in non-EPZ manufacturing industries.[3]

Wages and adjustment

Wages represent the biggest component in labour costs and are an important factor in restructuring. Wage movements over the recent past suggest (figures 1 and 2 and table 1) the following:

(i) In the short term, wage adjustment is slower than employment adjustment. Nominal wages are normally changed in direct or indirect relationship to collective agreements or government decrees, which are adjusted at intervals lasting at least a year, sometimes several years. In addition, collective agreements and government pay scales provide for automatic seniority increments, which raise the average pay level even when no general wage increases are awarded. This means that in a recession, nominal wages may continue to rise even if the industrial parties agree on a pay freeze.[4] Real wages may fall due to price increases, but it often takes considerable time before an individual enterprise can compensate cost increases through increased prices. We have very little micro-level data on this process, but the macro data indicate that recessions affect employment faster than real wages.[5] The same appears to be true in the upswings, when lingering unemployment dampens the recovery of wage trends.

(ii) The data, although rough and not always reliable, tend to corroborate the impression that real wages adjust to changes in prices and productivity, with important differences in both time lags and strength of association. In the labour surplus South Asian economies there is a weak association between wages and productivity increases, which reflects a market-related advantage to the employers. But productivity decreases tend to be compensated more quickly by measures that reduce employment, particularly when they are related to a fall in capacity utilisation. In economies with emerging labour shortages, like the North Asian NIEs, Singapore and, in the early 1980s, Malaysia, productivity increases are more closely associated with wage increases, while price shocks are not strongly reflected in real wage trends.

(iii) In labour-intensive and highly competitive industries, like garments and electronic assembly, wages were an important determinant of factory location for multinationals. Rising wage levels in East Asia pushed labour-intensive industries further south to the ASEAN during the late 1960s and early 1970s, and some of the foot-loose industries have continued further to South Asia, where wages are even lower. This sensitivity to relative wage changes fell during the 1980s, as a result of technical and organisational factors affecting the multinationals, as well as by the fact that labour costs are no longer as significant for competition.[6]

In drawing conclusions on labour market flexibility and the role of industrial relations it is important to bear in mind that membership strength is rather unimpressive in most Asian countries, particularly in relation to the labour force as a whole. Total trade union membership in India is 6 million, from a labour force of some 300 million. However, as the number of members relates to 25 million workers in the organised sector and as union membership is concentrated in relatively large-scale enterprises in certain industries, one can see that, although limited, unions have a power base that is economically important. The situation is roughly similar in other South Asian countries, with Sri Lanka having a higher percentage of around one-third of organised sector employees. Among South-East Asian countries, membership is highest in the Philippines, accounting for 25 per cent of modern employees, with Singapore second at 15 per cent and Malaysia third at around 10 per cent. In Indonesia and Thailand union membership is estimated to be between 4 and 5 per cent of total employment in the organised labour market. In some public sector enterprises in Thailand, however, membership strength is quite significant, even though the overall figures are very low.

While it is difficult to draw firm conclusions, the main findings emerging from ARTEP studies are:

(i)   In a situation with excess supply of labour the enforcement of protective labour legislation is difficult to guarantee. This is especially true in South Asia. There is evidence from India of strict regulations on hiring and firing being modified by collective agreements to enable enterprises to adjust to external shocks or technology changes, an example being the rationalisation agreements reached in the steel industry. Also there are many cases where protective legislation has been circumvented by unilateral action from the employers' side through voluntary "retirement schemes" or even less favourable agreements by making it clear to the workers that their rights according to law cannot be guaranteed. There are, however, also cases like the Bombay textile industry in the early 1980s when the employers' restructuring proposals were met with a prolonged strike, and when more jobs were lost than was necessary. However, in India and other South Asian countries both unions and employers have by and large managed to reconcile their different interests and have agreed on how to handle redeployment, lay-offs and work reorganisation.

(ii)   In South-East Asia governments have gone to great lengths to restrict strikes and promote company unions as opposed to industrial unions. It is very difficult, however, to show that collective bargaining for wages and employment conditions have in any way led to disadvantages for the enterprises or to loss of employment. Where wage increases have reduced competitiveness, as in Singapore, this has been caused by labour shortages rather than by unions. In competitive industries like labour-intensive export manufacturing, it is unlikely that trade unions and collective bargaining will affect the level of remuneration to an extent that will negatively affect employment, except when there is tightening labour market.

(iii) While there has been considerable discussion on how sensitive international investors (in particular Japanese) are to the granting of bargaining rights to trade unions, the evidence suggests that foreign investors do not regard protective labour laws as obstacles and are far more concerned about political stability and regulations of capital movements than about labour laws or industrial relations.

(iv) What is of considerable concern is that in some Asian countries enforcement of protective labour legislation and a tightening of employment securit for permanent workers appear to lead to a worsening of conditions of casual and contract labourers working on the fringes of the organised labour markets. In Pakistan, for example, a recent ARTEP survey showed that almost 30 per cent of workers in the organised manufacturing sector were working as casual labour and that a large portion of the increase in employment took this form.[7] "Casualisation" as a phenomenon appears to be sensitive to protective labour legislation, but it is not clear just how sensitive it is. The tendency towards casualisation and subcontracting noticeable in the subcontinent also exists in countries with very few regulations on hiring and firing. An ongoing ARTEP study of manufacturing enterprises in the Philippines indicates that the use of casual or subcontracted labour varies considerably between industries, being highest in garment manufacturing, where only 35 per cent of the labour force are permanent employees. In this case it appears that the trend towards casualisation and subcontracting is not driven primarily by restrictions on hiring and firing, but by technological factors as well as by attempts by employers to reduce their risks by shifting more of the adjustment burden to the workers.

(v)   In sum, Asian labour markets have functioned fairly smoothly in terms of both employment and wage adjustments. It is difficult to argue that labour market adjustments have been seriously constrained by the strength of trade unions and restrictive legislation on hiring and firing in most Asian countries. This is especially true in a situation when new investment and growth opportunities have opened up to either domestic or foreign investors.

Labour processes and employment generation in urban areas

Besides the importance of the industrial relations system in determining the functioning of labour markets, there is need to analyse carefully the main characteristics of employment growth and features of urban labour markets in Asian economies in order to evaluate their importance in employment planning and policy formulation. Some of these characteristics are:

(i)   Micro-enterprises including the self-employed have contributed between a half and two-thirds of total employment in the major urban Asian centres.[8] The data also indicate that the importance of this sector has increased in almost all cities for which data are available.[9]

(ii) The main reason for that increase is that the direct employment-generating capability of large-scale formal firms, especially large-scale manufacturing, is limited.[10] Indeed the overwhelming evidence from most Asian countries is that, even under a more "favourable" economic environment, its contribution to solving the overall employment problem will fall in all subsectors. In most countries too, the potential for increasing employment in public services, excluding the social sectors, has been reduced by lack of finance.

(iii) The pressures on employment in urban areas in Asian countries have been further accentuated by the process of structural adjustment and macro-stabilisation to which the economies have been subjected. While the Asian economies adjusted more quickly and with less pain to the external shocks of the 1970s, with the exception of the Philippines, most countries are going through a process of structural adjustment related primarily to increasing international competitiveness and efficiency of their domestic economies. In China, for instance, the major urban centres are facing serious unemployment ("increasing job-waiting rate") as firms shed "surplus" workers and new job opportunities are diminished. In 1989, for example, in Beijing, with an urban labour force of 4.1 million, of the 280,000 waiting to receive employment 150,000 were "surplus" labour from existing enterprises. In Pakistan, industrial growth fell sharply in 1988-89, partly due to a severe credit squeeze imposed as a result of IMF credit ceilings as part of a structural adjustment package. This had an unfavourable impact on employment especially in the city of Karachi where a large part of Pakistan's industry is located in the Philippines, Thailand and Indonesia. During the recession from the early to the mid-1980s, Metro Manila and to a lesser extent Bangkok and Jakarta were adversely affected by the slow down in economic activity. In Metro Manila, the unemployment rate rose from 8.6 to 10.8 per cent between 1977 and 1983 and underemployment from 18.7 to 35 per cent. The Metro Manila Commission reported that more than two-thirds of the lay-offs in manufacturing that took place nation-wide in 1984 were in Metro Manila.

(iv) Labour markets are subject to imperfections and segmentation.[11] For identical occupations, there are likely to exist large wage differentials within the same city. There is discrimination on the basis of sex, age, ethnic origin and there exist many barriers to entry to jobs in the formal sector. This segmentation is more prominent in the Indian subcontinent than in South-East Asia. It is also noteworthy that segmentation is affected by technologies and incentive structures that are themselves subject to change in a longer term perspective. As Sing (1989, p. 29) emphasises and our review of Asian labour markets confirms, this means that "although the labour markets in the developing countries may be subject to segmentations and imperfections in the static sense, dynamically, they may be working reasonably well". There is evidence that education gives better access to job opportunities and to higher incomes. It is also shown, however, that education is more likely to be used as a screening device by employers rather than as an accurate reflection of the productivity level of workers.

A case study illustrating this problem has been undertaken by the Thailand Development Research Institute (TDRI) in Thailand.[12] A model for income and employment behaviour in the formal and informal sectors was worked out, which assumed that educated youths would rather queue for well-paid jobs in the formal sector than go into available low-income opportunities in the informal sector. The study shows that this behaviour is rational with respect to income expectations for educated youths and that the excess supply of insufficiently educated entrants to the urban informal sector will continue to depress earnings for many years to come, while there will be a shortage of skilled workers, technicians and engineers, that will further widen educational wage differentials in Thailand. This model has relevance to other South-East Asian labour markets, particularly Indonesia and the Philippines.

Each of these aspects of urban employment have been the subject of considerable research, much of which has been carried out by ARTEP, other Regional Employment Teams and the World Employment Programme. This is especially true of work on micro-enterprises, on the informal sector in Latin America and on urban labour markets. This work has also closely examined the impact of changes in economic activity, both during recession and high growth, on employment in the small-scale and informal sector.

What perhaps has not been given adequate attention is how the process of structural adjustment in terms of the opening up of the domestic economy to increased international competition will affect the various sectors and segments of urban employment. This has become especially important as some Asian economies, especially in South Asia, are being subject to such adjustment as part of the IMF-World Bank structural adjustment programmes. The primary focus of these programmes is on import liberalisation and reduction in tariff protection, which the manufacturing sector presently enjoys. However, the employment implications of these proposed changes are rarely worked out. There is a need to incorporate employment as a priority goal and systematically analyse the impact of the reform package on employment. This would make it possible to focus on and accelerate reforms in those fields where the employment impact would be maximum.

Also implementing trade policy reform especially the rationalisation of tariffs to provide a more uniform and lower protective structure, replacing import controls by tariffs and removing duty concessions as suggested by the World Bank adjustment programmes, is extremely difficult for many South Asian countries, at least in the short and even the medium term. One reason is that protection and import leakages (both formal and informal, e.g. smuggling) has fostered an inconsistent structure of protection with indeterminate and continuously changing effects on incentives for industrial investment. A sequential approach in the implementation of trade policy reforms would be more pragmatic, for it would allow devising packages which would help in the adjustment process.

To identify industries whose efficiency and growth could be stimulated by trade policy reform policy-makers and researchers need to give priority to their employment impact, both direct and through linkages with other industries and sectors. Working out the employment links between macro-policy reforms, their impact on the large-scale, small-scale and informal sectors and the required adjustments at the firm level could play a major part in identifying such industries. That information would also be vital for macro-planners, especially in making foreign exchange and credit allocations to different sectors. It would bring out the importance of meeting the credit and infrastructure needs of the small-scale and informal sectors and could play an important part in making employment planning more operational.

From labour absorption towards integrated human resource development (HRD)

Manpower planning is an exercise in mechanistic projections of detailed occupation/skill needs of the economy within a specific time frame is finally being dispensed with in most Asian countries after a short-lived revival in the late 1970s and early 1980s. The focus is shifting towards viewing manpower planning as providing an analytical framework for deciding appropriate investment in education, training and manpower development based on an analysis of labour market processes involved in the acquisition and utilisation of skills. Also investments in education and skill development are being linked with the growth and structural changes in the economy so as to integrate the supply aspects of human resource development with changes and shifts in demand, thereby ensuring more effective utilisation of human resources. Finally, there is increasing concern over the high costs of technical education, especially that imparted by public sector institutions, and the need for alternative cost-effective programmes for skill development with a major role for the private sector.

In the Asian region a major challenge of the 1990s is to shift the focus of policy-making from economic growth and employment generation to human resources development. The conventional approach to employment strategies in Asia has been to promote rapid economic growth in production lines which can productively absorb a lot of labour. This approach provides better long-term development prospects than a commodity-based development strategy, which leaves the economy open to the fluctuations in demand and prices in world commodity markets and lays the main emphasis on revenues rather than on jobs. But the labour absorption strategy is based on utilising unskilled workers. In the global division of labour maintained by trade and multinational enterprises, export-oriented Asian economies have assumed the role of supplying low-cost and efficient routine labour. This strategy leads to employment creation but is vulnerable to technology and organisational changes within the multinationals. It is also sensitive to changes in relative wage levels between the Asian economies. Even more importantly it leads to a form of dependent industrialisation, which is driven from outside and has very little dynamic and innovative strength to choose its own path.

In a human-resource driven strategy, the competitive edge of the economy is neither commodities nor low-wage labour, but skills, entrepreneurship and research. What has happened in the first tier of NIEs in Asia, in the Republic of Korea, Singapore, Hong Kong and Taiwan, China, is that these economies have shifted from labour-based lines of production to more skill- and entrepreneurship-intensive technologies. The extent to which they can be called HRD-driven strategies varies, but it is quite clear that the shift towards skills and innovation is one of the explanations for these economies having continued to grow so fast in spite of emerging labour shortages and rising real wage levels. The proof of the HRD-based development strategy is that the structural transformation of the economy is facilitated by a rising quality of labour supply and not primarily by overseas demand factors.

What are the implications of a human resource driven strategy for the rest of the Asian economies who still have surplus labour? For the next tier of NIEs, there is an urgent need to anticipate the transformation by stepping up the pace of education and training, thereby attracting industries that require those skills. For the South Asian economies, the primary objective is the upgrading of labour skills so as to be able to face up to increased competition, primarily as a result of increased import competitiveness and the increasing export penetration in the world economy.

Some of the important conclusions that have emerged based on Asian and other country experiences in terms of role and timing of different inputs in an HRD strategy are as follows:

(i) Primary education is the single most important element in any HRD strategy. It has a direct bearing on the rate of economic growth, it provides an essential base for further development of education and skills, and it has important indirect links with social factors that are part of the quality of life aspects of an HRD strategy, particularly health and nutrition. What must be emphasised, however, is that not only enrolments matter, but also the quality of primary education. In this regard, many Asian countries still have an inadequate base of primary education. Most Asian countries have done well in expanding primary education, with the exceptions of Pakistan and Bangladesh where enrolment, especially female, continues to be very low. The major shortcomings, however, relate to the quality of education in some countries, and to the unequal development of rural and urban schools. The quality problems of rural schools are most serious in the South Asian subcontinent and in China, but even in parts of South-East Asia they have been an obstacle for rural youths aspiring to higher levels of learning or skills. It is particularly mathematics and in some cases language education that have been insufficiently developed.

(ii) Secondary education is becoming a serious bottleneck to the continued expansion of some South-East Asian economies, especially Thailand.

(iii) It is difficult to judge to what extent enrolments in tertiary education and the addition of new graduates correspond to the requirements of economic transformation. A very large proportion of the output from universities in the region has an administrative and humanistic orientation, for which there is insufficient demand in the labour market. These problems have been especially acute in South Asia and the Philippines, but are also now emerging as serious in Thailand and Malaysia. While the oversupply of arts graduates is primarily a mismatch of supply and demand, the problem is more complicated than simply changing the academic streams from arts to science. While there is no shortage of science graduates, in economies with rapid industrial growth there is a shortage of experienced graduates and technicians. It seems that the labour market does not fill vacancies by retraining unemployed arts graduates, but by upgrading technicians and by increasing salaries in unfilled jobs. If we want to eliminate this so-called mismatch and adjust the supply of high-level manpower to the needs of a growing economy, it will be necessary to review not only the size and curricula of academic streams, but the salary structure and recruitment policies. Also there remains, even in countries like Singapore and Malaysia, a bias by private enterprises for engaging university graduates for technical, scientific or sales jobs in manufacturing and services. If industries are to develop new products and find other markets than those given by the multinationals, they will require more intensive use of high-level manpower in the private sector. Hence, both the demand and supply will have to be adjusted to eliminate the mismatch.

(iv) Major problems exist in the market for skilled workers and technicians. Institutional training has been criticised as being too expensive and even redundant, as private firms prefer to develop skills through their own training programmes. It has been argued that the public sector should concentrate on general education, especially primary education on which enterprise-based training can be more easily built. This case has been reinforced by evidence of high levels and periods of unemployment of vocationally trained graduates, who when hired by private firms find that their previous training does not earn them much in terms of pay or promotion.

(v)   There is clearly a need for improving the present performance of public vocational training institutions. Presently they have a tendency to over-emphasise a few standard training courses for which there exists a social demand.[13] The type of courses which would give the best results in terms of productivity and earnings might be more closely tailored to the require-ments of industry, with a broader theoretical base and on-the-job practice interchanged with institutional training. It is also necessary to study through surveys the effectiveness of vocational training programmes from the point of view of career development and earnings of the graduates compared to those given institutional training.

(vi) There is a need for a greater role by the private sector, not only in being directly associated with the running of public sector training institutions but for greater on-the-job training facilities, apprenticeship programmes and even the establishment and management of vocational training in-stitutions. The private sector has come forward in this field, especially in response to meeting demand for skilled manpower from abroad (espe-cially during the Middle-East boom). The Government may provide support for the establishment of such training facilities as well as assist-ance in curriculum development and certification.

(vii) While the need for universal primary education is a pre-condition for future growth and development, especially in some South Asian econ-omies, the development of primary education must not be seen as a substitute for technical training. While a concerted effort is required to improve enrolment in and quality of primary education, the supply of technically trained manpower to meet the needs of industrial growth, higher productivity and the adoption and absorption of modern technology are equally pressing. Even when resources are constrained, the choice must not be seen in terms of either primary or technical education but of diverting resources from unproductive sectors towards primary and technical education/vocational training.

(viii) One must also visualise vocational training as meeting not only an immediate market demand but as responding to the need for a long-term change in the technological level of the economy. The need for trained manpower may not always be manifest or explicitly shown in the job market. The shortage of skilled manpower may result in market adjustments that involve acceptance of less efficient methods and lower quality. Protection to industry also provides protection to this low technical competence trap. Those supposed to demand trained manpower can afford to exist with less qualified and inefficient manpower, as higher costs and lower quality products are passed on to the domestic consumers who have little else to choose from. However, as economies especially in South Asia are subject to increasing international competition it has become extremely important to initiate action to remove such negative influences on competitive strength arising from a low-level and improperly trained workforce. In such cases the private and public sectors have an even more important role to play in increasing the supply and quality of trained manpower. The public sector may be especially important in assimilating and spreading modern production technologies, especially in the application of electronics, computers and production systems.

(ix) Finally, one pressing problem is how to design cost-effective trainingprogrammes to raise productivity in informal sector enterprises. So far, the informal sector has offered few career opportunities for young skilled workers, and it seems that this will only come when the enterprise grows from micro- to small-scale level.

Conclusions

Policies to achieve appropriate incentive structures and macroeconomic performance have emerged as key determinants of job creation in the Asian region. However, to realise the potential of these policies it is crucial to develop an understanding of how labour markets operate, both in the formal and informal sectors. The evidence from case studies conducted by ARTEP suggests that by and large Asian labour markets have functioned fairly smoothly in terms of both employment and wage adjustments. Labour market adjustments have not been seriously constrained by trade unions or restrictive legislation on hiring and firing in most Asian countries. The paper also suggests that to make employment planning more operational there is need to examine

Table 1. Real wage indices, manufacturing workers

	1970	1971	1973	1975	1977	1979	1981	1983	1985
Malaysia (a)	100	100	83	96	107	118	122	147	167
Philippines (b)	100	97	85	73	–	80	89	–	–
Philippines (c)	100	–	–	–	–	89	–	88	49
Thailand (d)	100	110	92	90	103	95	99	–	–
Thailand (e)	–	–	–	–		100	100	99	101

Sources: (a) Department of Statistics, report of the Financial Survey of Limited Companies;
(b) Wage and Position Classification Office (WAPCO) estimates;
(c) Survey of Key Establishments in Manufacturing (SKEM) estimates;
(d) Sumalee, P. (1984);
(e) Legal minimum wage for Bangkok, quoted in Edgren (1989a).

more closely the impact of structural adjustment programmes on the small-scale and informal sectors, where urban employment is concentrated, especially to study the adjustment process at the enterprise level. Its implications for labour demand, skill enhancement and labour mobility at the firm-level need careful analysis. Finally, the paper strongly advocates that manpower planning in terms of providing guide-lines for investment in education and skill development can only be meaningfully undertaken by analysing existing labour market imbalances for skilled manpower and the labour processes involved in skill formation. However, existing labour market information needs to be supplemented by macro-level analysis of actual and expected structural changes, so as to anticipate demand for new skills as well as to upgrade the skill and educational capability of the labour force to face up to these changes.

Figure 1. South Asia

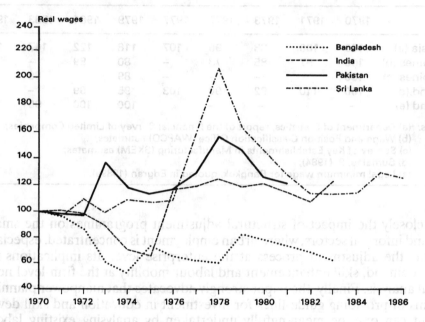

Source: Edgren (1980a).

Figure 2. East Asia

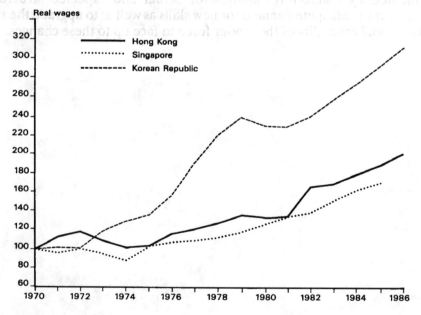

Source: Edgren (1989a).

Notes

[1] This paper relies heavily on Edgren (1989a) and the papers presented by Edgren (1989b) and Amjad (1989) at the Third Meeting of Asian Employment Planners organised by ILO-ARTEP at New Delhi, 20-22 Nov. 1989.

[2] See, for example, the World Bank (1988 and 1989) reports on employment for India and Pakistan, and A.N. Mathur: "The effects of legal and contractual regulations on employment in Indian industry", in ILO-ARTEP: *Restructuring, employment and industrial relations,* New Delhi, 1989.

[3] ILO-UNTC: *Economic and social effects of multinational enterprises in export processing zones,* Geneva, 1988.

[4] D. Mazumdar: *Labour markets in structural adjustment in Malaysia*, Washington, DC, Economic Development Institute, 1989 (mimeo.).

[5] ILO-ARTEP: *Structural adjustment: By whom, for whom,* New Delhi, 1987, pp. 49-51.

[6] I. Islam: "Industrial restructuring and industrial relations in ASEAN: A firm-level chronicle", in ILO-ARTEP: *Restructuring, employment and industrial relations,* 1989, op. cit., p. 131.

[7] ILO-ARTEP: *Survey of large-scale manufacturing sector (A study of contract labour),* Employment and Manpower Strategy Project PAK/88/007 (New Delhi, Oct. 1989).

[8] Exceptions from this rule are the Republic of Korea and Malaysia, where the large-scale manufacturing sector expanded employment very rapidly.

[9] For details, see Hallgren et al. (1989).

[10] See Amjad (1989), for estimates for Asian countries.

[11] For a recent review, see Rodgers (1989).

[12] C. Sussangkarn: *The Thai labour market: A study of seasonality and segmentation,* Bangkok, Thailand Development Research Institute (TDRI), July 1987; idem: *Labour market segmentation and the prospects for open unemployment,* Bangkok, TDRI, 1986.

[13] A.M. Nimbalkar: *Labour market monitoring and analysis for minimising mismatch of skilled manpower: Suggested system for India,* New Delhi, ILO-ARTEP, July 1989.

References

Amjad, R. (ed.). 1987. *Human resource planning: The Asian experience*, Asian Employment Programme, New Delhi, ILO-ARTEP.

— —, 1989. *Urban planning and employment generation in the Asian megalopolis,* paper presented at the Third Meeting of Asian Employment Planners, 20-22 Nov. 1989, organised by ILO-ARTEP, New Delhi.

Dougherty, C. 1990. *Education and skill development: Planning issues,* paper presented at the Asian Development Bank-World Bank Seminar on Vocational and Technical Education and Training, Manila, 22-27 Jan. 1990.

Edgren, G. 1989a. *Restructuring, employment and industrial relations: Adjustment issues in Asian countries,* New Delhi, ILO-ARTEP.

— —, 1989b. *Employment challenges in the 1990s,* paper presented at the Third Meeting of Asian Employment Planners, 20-22 Nov. 1989, organised by ILO-ARTEP, New Delhi.

Hallgren, O. et al. 1989. *Employment in urban micro-enterprises: Some perspectives,* paper presented at the Third Meeting of Asian Employment Planners, 20-22 Nov. 1989, organised by ILO-ARTEP, New Delhi.

Nimbalkar, A.M. 1989. *Labour market monitoring and analysis for minimising mismatch of skilled manpower: Suggested system for India*, HRD Working Paper, New Delhi, ILO-ARTEP, July 1989.

Rodgers, G. (ed.). 1989. *Urban poverty and the labour market: Access to jobs and incomes in Asian and Latin American cities*, World Employment Programme/International Institute for Labour Studies, Geneva, ILO.

Singh, A. 1989. *Urbanisation, poverty and employment: The large metropolis in the Third World*, Population and Labour Policies Programme, Working Paper No. 165, World Employment Programme Research Working Papers, Geneva, ILO.

Sumalee, P. 1984. *Labour market changes in Thailand*, ASEAN-Australia Working Papers No. 11, ASEAN-Australia Joint Research Project, Kuala Lumpur and Canberra.

Sussangkaran, C. 1986. *Labour market segmentation and the prospects for open* unemployment, Bangkok, TDRI.

— —, C. 1987. *The Thai labour market: A study of seasonality and segmentation*, Bangkok, TDRI.

World Bank, 1988. *Employment issues in Pakistan,* Washington, DC, World Bank Report No. 7523-PAK, Dec. 1988.

— —, 1989. *India: Poverty, employment and social services*, Washington, DC, World Bank Report No. 7617, May 1989.

Privatisation and labour market adjustment

One of the most pervasive and contentious aspects of supply-side structural adjustment programmes has been the deliberate, and often painfully extensive, cuts in public sector expenditure and employment and the "privatisation", by various means, of large sectors of the national economy. The labour market issues raised by this twin theme are very considerable indeed, and as expected led to an animated debate in the workshop. Derek Robinson's paper presents a somewhat worrying analysis of the process, drawing on his experience in working on the practical realities in Africa and in South-East Asia. He responded to our request to propose items for future work within the ILO, and his conclusions are presented at the end of his paper. In the early 1990s the terms of the debate on privatisation and the role of the public sector will surely evolve, so that stark private-versus-public positions will be replaced by attempts to combine two concerns: the social and distributional objectives that underlaid the earlier pursuit of "nationalisation", and the apparent efficiency-flexibility properties of "private enterprise". But what is beyond doubt is that in the context of structural adjustment programmes, the public sector has been under unprecedented attack. It is in that context that the labour market implications deserve to be considered to see what labour policies are required in a period of public sector retrenchment.

13

Labour market implications of public expenditure constraints and privatisation

by Derek Robinson *

Constraints on public expenditure may have direct effects on the labour market through public sector employment and pay, or indirect effects through reductions in employment resulting from lower government demand for goods or services produced by the private sector. There may also be indirect effects if taxation is reduced following a cut in government expenditure. The main concern here is with the direct effects.

Constraints on government expenditure in developing countries are increasingly imposed because of governments' difficulties in raising domestic funds to finance their expenditure, and the increasing cost and difficulties of raising external funds to meet both internal and external deficits. In most countries the absence of a well-developed domestic capital market means there is little opportunity for government to borrow internally. The downturn in economic activity further limited government's ability to raise additional funds through taxation, although in many cases improvements in tax collection could increase receipts. There has also been a marked shift in attitudes towards government expenditure and the role of government in assisting development. Rather than fulfilling the role of the main contributor to economic development, by providing necessary infrastructure and undertaking economic activity which would otherwise be left undone - because of the smallness of the private sector or its unwillingness to participate in economic activity - government economic activity is now frequently regarded as wasteful, inefficient and harmful. This conclusion is not always derived from empirical analysis.

Direct effects of government expenditure constraints

The public sector can be seen as composed of three main groups. The *civil service* comprises those employees engaged in the central administration

* Institute of Economics and Statistics, University of Oxford, Oxford.

of the State, which may in some countries include regional and local government, and often includes the uniformed sectors such as armed forces, police and fire services. In most developing countries there is a second group of employees engaged in the provision of social services such as health and education. These two groups form the *public service*. The third group are those employed in parastatal organisations or public enterprises (PEs). These are engaged in the production of goods or services for sale and may be undertakings formed under special legislative provisions such as nationalised industries, or legally exist as ordinary public companies in which the government is the sole or major shareholder. Some of these - such as electricity, water supply, telecommunications or railways - are publicly owned in many countries. Others may undertake activities which are usually performed by privately owned companies in many countries, but have been placed under public ownership in particular cases, because the private sector did not generate enough economic activity, or because the government for political reasons favoured public rather than private ownership. Constraints on government expenditure may affect the three groups differently.

Constraints may lead to reductions in government expenditure on capital items, or on labour or non-labour items of current expenditure. Often there is a tendency first to reduce investment, then non-labour items of current expenditure such as supplies, and finally labour costs or the total pay-bill, including allowances and benefits. Reductions in subsidies to PEs are here regarded as equivalent to a reduction in total labour expenditure if the effect is to contain the total pay-bill in PEs. Reductions usually take the form of reductions in real terms, as money expenditure increases less quickly than the rate of inflation.

Reductions in capital investment may affect the labour market by reducing the numbers employed in the public sector, if public investment is undertaken by public sector employees, or private sector employment if the investment is publicly funded but carried out by the private sector. Reductions in non-labour current expenditure may have relatively little impact on the labour market, but lead to a serious deterioration in the level or quality of public services (Bevan et al., 1986). This has happened, for example, in the Gambia, Ghana, Mali and the United Republic of Tanzania.

In many developing countries there was considerable expansion of employment in the public service in the 1960s and 1970s. Some growth was to be expected as countries obtained independence and sought to improve the social and economic infrastructures. Policies to generate economic expansion through government encouragement of a small, poorly developed, inadequate private sector required an expansion of civil service employment. The provision of improved - but often still inadequate - health and education services necessitated a large expansion of employment in the public services. The expansion of PEs reflected a belief that they would provide additional government revenue, accorded with the prevailing view that a strong active public sector was often a necessary condition for economic development, was necessary to make good the deficiencies of the small private sector, and perhaps met a perceived government need to have forms of patronage (van de Walle, 1989).

In many countries, public service employment also expanded as a result of deliberate government measures to provide employment opportunities for an increasing number of educated nationals who were unable to obtain employment in the private sector. This may have led to reductions in job requirements and effort inputs, as employment expanded faster than the provision of services. In some cases, the employment expansion may have been too fast for the administrative system to handle it effectively, so that underemployment and inefficient labour utilisation occurred.

This was often worsened by the deterioration in real pay of public service employees. In many countries, the expansion in numbers employed, associated with limitations on government's ability to raise sufficient public funds to maintain real pay levels, has led to drastic reductions in real pay. For example, between 1975 and 1985, the real value of public service salary scales fell by more than 50 per cent in Benin, Ethiopia (except for the lowest grades), the Gambia, Nigeria (78 per cent for the highest grade), and the Sudan. Reductions of around two-thirds occurred in the Gambia, and of more than 75 per cent in Sierra Leone and the United Republic of Tanzania. In Ghana, the real salary of a Permanent Secretary in 1985 was only one-eighth of the 1977 level. In Somalia the reductions were around 95 per cent and in Uganda about 97 per cent for the highest grade (Robinson, 1990; Klitgaard, 1989). Individual employees may have suffered somewhat lower reductions because of salary scale increments or promotion, but in many countries there were still drastic reductions in real living standards of public service employees. This undoubtedly led to demoralisation of employees and reductions in efficiency. In the extreme cases, public service employees simply cannot survive on their pay and are obliged to resort to other sources of income (Robinson, 1990).

Private sector employees may also have suffered large decreases in real wages, as in Somalia and Uganda. The experience of public service employees may therefore be regarded as similar to that of other employees, and while the large reductions in real wages may be undesirable and give rise to great hardship, internal equity considerations may suggest that no special treatment should be afforded to public service employees. However, against this, it might be argued that the provision of certain basic public services, including public administration, is so essential for the proper functioning of an economy that there might be situations when especially favourable treatment should be given to public service employees, in order to maintain morale and efficiency at levels which ensure the proper provision of their services. A competent public administration can contribute to economic development (as well as the implementation of government policies for social improvements) no less than the building of economic infrastructures.

While the public sector pay-bill (including subsidies to PEs) was expanded by increases in the numbers employed, it was contained by reductions in real pay. A significant labour market effect of constraint in government expenditure has been to reduce real public service salaries, often drastically. Salary scale revisions and increases did not match inflation. The combination of undue employment expansion in earlier periods with currently severe limitations on government resources has, therefore, in many countries, led to the emergence of a public service wage fund determined by the ability of government to obtain revenue. Further constraints on government expenditure in real terms (and even more so if they are in money terms) mean - with this budget-based public service wage fund - that reductions in staff or further reductions in real pay must occur.

Further reductions in real pay will lead to yet further reductions in efficiency and motivation. In some countries, the public service is already facing acute shortages of certain occupations, with potential recruits able to obtain jobs in the private sector, while there is an excess of applicants for other posts. In broad terms, the civil service is faced by increasing numbers of applicants for posts in general clerical or administrative positions, as the numbers receiving higher general education continue to grow, while there are shortages of those with technical and professional qualifications. Although data are fragmentary and poor, it appears that, in many countries, civil service pay for many occupations is lower than that in parastatal organisations, which in turn pay less than firms in the private sector, although the public service may have relatively higher pay for the very lowest grades (Klitgaard, 1989; Collier, 1989; Lindauer et al., 1988; Robinson, 1990). Reductions in real wages, or wage levels which are much below the levels paid in the private sector, can lead to shortages of some skills in the public service. The opportunity for public service employees, or potential recruits, to find alternative employment will influence the extent to which relatively low public sector pay leads to skill shortages.

There has been a general government concern to narrow the distribution of pay by granting proportionately larger increases to the lowest paid groups in its employ (Robinson, 1990; Klitgaard, 1989; Lindauer et al., 1988). This pursuit of a social objective may have created major difficulties in some countries, as higher graded posts in the public service now receive significantly less than higher posts in the private sector. It would be possible, in principle, to remedy the position for the highest grades, as improvements to their real pay would add relatively little to the total pay-bill. This would, however, require a reversal of the moves towards narrow wage dispersion, and would generate strong pressures for similar treatment from other groups of employees.

It is probably beyond the means of some, perhaps many governments, to remedy the decrease in real pay for all its public service employees, even if this was considered desirable. Full restoration to the real levels pertaining at some date in the past may be inappropriate, if it was thought that relative real pay levels between the public service and other sections in society were at that time unduly favourable to the public service, or if this would lead to large surpluses over real reservation wages or the real labour supply price. However, some improvement, and often a large improvement on current real pay levels, may be appropriate and a necessary condition for improvement in public service efficiency in a number of countries. This has led to proposals that there should be a trade-off between public service employment and improvements in the real pay of the remaining workforce. The wage-fund concept remains reasonably intact.

A general pattern of policy measures adopted by governments faced by budget constraints is that first there are reductions in capital expenditure, and then in current expenditure on non-labour costs so that supplies of complementary inputs are reduced. This often has seriously adverse effects on the ability to provide public services as when medical supplies are cut to health services (Bevan et al., 1986). Then a wage freeze is often imposed on the public service, and finally reductions in employment are sought by restricting or stopping recruitment, and in the last resort by retrenchment in which non-permanent employees take the first round of pressure.

The straightforward trade-off approach involves reductions in the numbers employed. Its advocates refer to the overstaffing in the public service and conclude that reductions in the numbers employed need not therefore lead to any worsening of provision of public services. In some cases, in principle, this may be correct, but there are no reliable data to indicate the "proper" numbers of public service employees necessary to provide a given level of services. Staffing levels based on work measurement techniques do not exist, and most public services in developing countries are not equipped to provide them. Nevertheless, there have been reductions in civil service employment in some countries based on somewhat arbitrary notions of overstaffing, or determined by budgetary considerations.

In some cases overstaffing or improper padding of employment may be inferred from the presence of "ghost" workers, individuals who appear on the payroll but who do not actually attend work, or, in some cases, may not actually exist (Collier, 1989). In the Central African Republic a verified payroll has been established, and this led to the removal of more than 1,000 names and a reduction of 2 per cent in the number of civil servants. In Guinea some 5,000-8,000 "ghosts" have been removed from the civil service payroll. Similar action has taken place in Togo. Other countries such as Uganda and Ghana have initiated a census of civil service employees to discover just how many employees there are, and where they are located.

In some countries the first stage of employment reductions has been a freeze on recruitment, either by abandoning the public sector employment guarantee to university (and in some countries secondary school) graduates, or by failing to recruit new employees to fill vacancies. This increases unemployment, and may have some effect on private sector wages in occupations for which those adversely affected by the ending of the employment guarantee are qualified. A universal freeze on recruitment may have similar effects in increasing the supply of labour to the private sector, but may also have undesirable effects on public service efficiency. Key posts may be left unfilled so that efficiency suffers. Attempts to allow recruitment to fill "necessary" vacancies are difficult to implement. If the freeze also applies to internal promotions, so that no empty posts can be filled, not only may there be the same undesirable effects on efficiency, but motivation and morale may also be adversely affected. The United Republic of Tanzania sought to avoid the worst effects of a recruitment freeze by allowing some recruitment for specialist technical occupations, and by allowing a specified number of promotions.

If the freeze applies only to budgeted posts, rather than those actually filled, there may be few savings. This is also true if there is a reduction in the number of budgeted posts, but this falls entirely on unfilled positions. Even if it applies to budgeted and filled posts, employment may not be reduced by the expected numbers if departments have the ability to finance temporary employment by transfer of funds. Central control of actual employment levels, and in some cases use of government funds, is weak in many developing countries. Recruitment freezes may therefore have undesirable effects on public service efficiency and be difficult to implement. Even if successfully applied, they may make relatively little impact on total government expenditure if the attrition rate of public service employees is low. Governments may therefore seek to obtain larger reductions in expenditure more quickly by reducing the numbers employed through redundancies, dismissals or voluntary retirements.

The labour market implications of civil service redundancies depend on the numbers dismissed, their occupations or skills, ages, and terms of redundancy. Frequently those first laid off are those with temporary or casual status, often in the lower grades and less skilled occupations. This may be both expected and appropriate. The notion of casual or temporary employment status is that these employees act as a buffer in the fluctuations in public service demand for labour, even though in many countries the practice has been that many casual workers remain in public service employment for long periods. It is often easier, on both political and industrial relations grounds, to dismiss a whole class or group of workers, as this avoids the difficulties of selecting individuals. Retrenchment of permanent or established civil servants may also be sought. This may be contrary to existing legislation, and is certainly often contrary to established practice and expectations.

If large numbers of civil servants are retrenched, there will be an immediate labour market effect if they seek to obtain other jobs. In some cases, as for example in Nigeria, the terms of retrenchment may include provisions designed to encourage civil servants to start up in self-employment. This has also been proposed in the Sudan. This approach requires considerable investment of time and resources to provide suitable training. There is obviously no scope for them to start up as self-employed civil servants, so that some new skills are needed or existing skills need to be converted to different use. Training in managing self-employed activities may be expensive and government may have to call on specialised agencies to provide appropriate training.

Retrenchment will presumably have the same effects in reducing employment opportunities in the public sector as a recruitment freeze, and in addition there may be former public service employees searching for private sector jobs. The type of public employment subject to retrenchment will determine the types of employees laid off. If cuts fall on the civil service, the particular skills and abilities of the individuals may be less directly related to private employers' job requirements than if retrenchments take place in parastatals. Although some technical grades in the civil service may have easily transferable skills, they are less likely to be retrenched, as these tend to be the grades where the civil service has recruitment and retention difficulties and are therefore less likely to be overstaffed. Retrenched civil servants may therefore have difficulties in finding suitable employment elsewhere. If employees in PEs are retrenched, they may have skills sought by the private sector and their employment experience may give them an advantage in job applications. Alternatively, if employers believe that public service employees have become accustomed to low levels of effort and poor industrial discipline their previous experience may be a disadvantage. The World Bank, as part of its assistance to privatisation programmes, is examining alternative employment opportunities for displaced PE employees in Togo which envisage both retraining and provision of credit to help them start small enterprises. Credit facilities are provided in Senegal, and are being considered in Ghana. In Benin retraining programmes are provided and credits are available for agricultural investments (Nellis and Kikeri, 1989). The reorganisation and privatisation of the Japanese National Railways led to a reduction in employment of 61,000, from 276,000 to 215,000. The Government set a target of 30,000 of these to be absorbed in the public sector, and the other 31,000 were assisted by retraining and other means to find jobs in the private sector or self-employment. By May 1988, only 4,000 remained to be placed and almost all of them were in depressed parts of the economy (Edgren, 1989).

If public sector retrenchments take place when the private sector is facing an economic downturn, there may be stronger competition for jobs. Private sector employers will be reducing their demand for labour, and some of them may have had even greater retrenchment than the public sector. For example, in Nigeria during the early 1980s, a federal employee in either government or parastatal employment risked a 1.69 per cent chance of retrenchment, while private sector employees as a whole risked a 9.75 per cent chance (with large variations by sector, 37.1 per cent in construction, 7.5 per cent in manufacturing and less than 2 per cent in other sectors) (Collier, 1989). However, that study also reports that there was no positive relationship (and a weak negative one) between retrenchment in a State and the subsequent unemployment rate in that State, thereby suggesting that the higher incidence of retrenchments did not, in the Nigerian case, lead to greater difficulties in finding employment in so far as unemployment rates are indicators of employment prospects.

Retrenchment differs from redeployment in that with the latter government accepts direct responsibility for relocating individuals in employment, usually in the public sector, as with half of those affected by the staffing reductions in the Japanese National Railways. With retrenchment, individuals who wish to continue in labour market activity may have the responsibility for finding their own subsequent economic activity, although government may assist by providing training courses. If those affected by retrenchment are involved in "moonlighting" or some secondary form of economic activity in addition to their public service employment, the adjustment processes and the economic consequences of retrenchment may be less serious. The procedures for determining retrenchment may influence the labour market effects. If voluntary retirement is adopted, those with better alternative employment prospects, those with ambition to start up in self-employment, or those who wish to withdraw from labour force activity, may dominate; the effects on the external labour market will differ from retrenchment on a compulsory basis of those with less marketable skills who still wish to remain in the labour force.

Because public sector employees form an identifiable group with common interests, it may be extremely difficult politically to push through compulsory retrenchments. It may also be necessary to provide attractive financial terms to those affected (Edgren, 1989). There may be differences between civil service and parastatal employees. Many civil servants have permanent or established status, often enshrined in legislative form, so that retrenchment may be expensive. Similar arrangements may also exist in PEs. For example, in Ghana the "lack of money to pay severance has brought part of the privatisation programme to a halt" (Nellis and Kikeri, 1989, p. 669). The introduction of new arrangements to encourage voluntary retrenchments may impose considerable financial burdens on government for some years ahead. Short-term savings through retrenchment may therefore be much less than first thought, and indeed there may often be significant short-run increases in government expenditure. Estimates for Nigeria showed that it cost between 2.7 and 5.6 years' pay to retrench a worker with 25 or more years' service (Kahn, 1985). In Ghana, redundancy payments to 16,000 employees of the Cocoa Marketing Board were equivalent to an average of 11 years' base salary. Interest-free payments were made over a three-year period, with the effect that inflation led to a significant reduction in the real cost to government, and in the real compensation received by employees (Collier, 1989).

If there is a reversal of the previous trade-off between employment and real pay, so that reductions in employment are obtained in order to improve the real pay of the remaining employees, instead of employment expansion leading to a worsening of real pay, and retrenchments are to be obtained on a voluntary basis, it is probably more effective, although possibly less moral, for government to seek voluntary retrenchments before it improves real pay. The improvements to real pay will make public sector employment more attractive and voluntary retrenchment less so.

Summary

The main direct effect of constraint of government expenditure has been to lead to a reduction in real pay, often a severe reduction. This has made public sector employment less attractive to new recruits, and in many countries government has had increasing difficulties in recruiting and retaining sufficient numbers in certain occupations. In many countries there has also been a slow-down in recruitment to the public sector, and in some cases there have been reductions in the numbers employed. There has been a general decline in morale and motivation, leading to a decrease in efficiency. Moonlighting and corruption may have expanded as civil servants sought to maintain even a drastically reduced standard of living (Quah, 1985). The quality of public services has declined. Because private sector employment opportunities have been adversely affected in many developing countries during recent years, there has remained a high demand for public sector jobs, even though there has been the decline in real pay. The notion of rent-earning public sector employment still remains, but appears to be expressed somewhat less extravagantly than was once the case. Constraints on government expenditure led to inadequate improvements to nominal salary scales, and this had some impact on the public sector internal labour market, as there were less opportunities for joint determination of terms and conditions.

These developments have not been confined to developing countries. Elsewhere, governments adopted policies to contain or reduce government expenditure and government involvement in economic activity. Sometimes this has been the result of ideological shifts and sometimes a reflection of currently fashionable monetarist-based economic views, which give greater importance to government borrowing as a cause of inflation. For example, in the United Kingdom both these factors have led government to reduce public service employment and to contain public sector wages. Cash limits with an overt wage fund have been imposed, with the deliberate intention of forcing a choice between employment and nominal pay rises. Even though average civil service pay has risen by more than the "pay factor" each year, there have been reductions in real pay. At least as important have been the imposed changes in the pay system, so that serious inroads have been made into the principle of national standard salary scales for different parts of the public service. There is much greater importance given to local pay differences, and performance-related additional pay increments have been superimposed on shorter normal incremental salary scales which reward seniority. While there have been employment effects, it is probable that, in the longer run, it is the changes in pay systems which will be seen as the greater impact of government financial constraint although, of course, part of the reason for imposing the constraint was to obtain the changes in the pay systems.

Privatisation

Privatisation may be regarded as a collective term embracing different forms of government action. In the most obvious sense it means the transfer to private ownership of publicly owned assets. In a broader sense, or as a variant, it also includes the provision by the private sector of services or activities currently provided by the public sector. This can be extended to future services, so that activities which are currently provided by public organisations will in future be provided by private firms. Both of these include subcontracting or contracting-out activities from the public sector. Other forms of reorganisation of public sector activities might not fall within even this broad definition of privatisation, but might still be considered relevant for present purposes. For example, proposals to transfer activities from the civil service to independent agencies which would not follow established civil service staffing, grading and pay arrangements but which would still be part of the public sector do not, strictly speaking, fall within the definition of privatisation, but in some cases may have some effects or be intended to have effects similar to those of privatisation measures.

Public enterprises account for a large proportion of economic activity in many countries. A sample of 13 African countries showed that in the early 1980s PEs accounted on average for 17 per cent of GDP. In some countries the share is much higher, ranging between 40 and 60 per cent at different times in Algeria, Egypt and Zambia. In many developing countries PEs account for more than half the value added in manufacturing, and an average of 15 per cent of non-agricultural employment. A sample of 14 LDCs showed PEs as responsible for an average of 25 per cent of total investment (Nellis and Kikeri, 1989). In Asia, where the growth of PEs was particularly rapid in the seventies and early eighties, the share of their added value in GDP did not reach sizeable proportions except in the case of oil and mineral companies. In some countries, though, PEs were responsible for a significant proportion of gross domestic capital formation. In 1984-85 in India they accounted for almost 40 per cent, about a third in Nepal, Pakistan and the Philippines, 20 per cent in Bangladesh and 15 per cent in Thailand. Although the data are less reliable, PEs may have accounted for two-thirds of gross domestic investment in Malaysia during the first half of the 1980s (sources in Edgren, 1989).

Why privatise?

It does less than full justice to proponents of privatisation to suggest that their advocacy is merely the fashionable trend in political economy. PEs collectively may run at a loss in many countries, so that government financial support is required, although within the overall performance some make profits. However they often impose budgetary burdens on government, increase budget deficits, and may lead to serious misallocation of resources (see various contributors to *World Development,* Vol. 17, No. 5, 1989). Much attention is therefore now given to the efficiency gains which may result from privatisation. The "efficiency" argument has various threads.

(a) Conventional economic theory in industrial economics is giving attention to what is termed the principal-agent argument. (A good summary is given in Vickers and Yarrow, 1988.) This starts from the position that there exists a principal and an agent who do not share the same objectives. The central issue in principal-agent theory is that of information and incentives, and the optimal incentive scheme for the principal to specify for the agent, in order to maximise the achievement of the principal's objectives. There are problems in applying this to the public sector, but an assumption that profit-maximising can be replaced by maximising of public welfare is sometimes used, and administrative action to limit subsidies or control total costs can be assumed to replace the "bankruptcy control" element. In general, the complex nature of government's objectives as principal, and in some cases the power of public sector employees as pressure groups, mean that there may be less adequate constraints on the agents in the public sector, and that this permits or generates inefficiency (Edgren, 1989). Also, efficiency in public sector organisations may be only one of a number of competing government objectives.

(b) Related to this is the argument that since, in many countries, public sector activities receive government subsidies and because they believe that they will continue to do so, they have less incentive to become efficient. In this context, "efficient" can mean different things. It can mean a reduction in the level of subsidy. It can mean improvement in productivity or reduction in costs of production, which will not necessarily reduce the government subsidy, depending on the pricing policies and objectives sought by government. The benefits of higher productivity or lower costs could be passed on to the consumers, leaving the level of subsidies unchanged. Improved efficiency can be used in an allocative sense, reflecting the view that there should be no subsidies. A rigorous application of this view might lead to a similar criticism of indirect taxation.

(c) It can be argued that PEs are influenced by civil service rules, attitudes and established behaviour patterns which are more suited to an administrative or bureaucratic organisation than to a production/commercial one. This criticism can be made stronger if there are regular transfers of staff between the civil service and parastatals, and the career development and promotion patterns are primarily influenced by civil service criteria. Management of parastatals may require different types of skills and abilities, and these may be absent or undervalued in civil service-dominated approaches. The boards of directors of PEs may be dominated by civil servants with little commercial or production experience.

(d) It might be argued that in the public sector, trade unions or even unorganised workers are able to exert excessive political pressure on governments, leading to higher wages or other improvements in the terms of employment, lower effort inputs, or overstaffing through productively unnecessary employment expansion. For political reasons, therefore, governments may be unable to prevent the creation of areas of employment insulated against the economic or market forces which, it is alleged, effectively determine terms and conditions in the private sector. This can be linked to the principal-agent argument, by concluding that management in the public sector has vested interests in colluding or forming coalitions with trade unions in their organisations, to raise wages or provide other benefits in excess of the "market" level, either to placate their workforce so that they (managers) may have a quiet life, or because their own terms and conditions are related to those of their workforce. Alternatively government could collude with PE employees in return for political support.

On either view, the public sector is seen as immune to some extent from market forces, and it is concluded that this is inefficient and undesirable. The fact that in the absence of strong state intervention to impose standard levels of pay and conditions for specified occupations, there is a considerable spread of pay among private sector firms for members of the same occupational titles, and that it is therefore extremely difficult to know what level of pay and conditions would or do emerge from the market or economic forces does not seem to provide undue concern. Similarly the observed fact that employees in multinational companies typically receive higher pay and benefits than employees of nationally owned enterprises in developing countries is often not interpreted as evidence of a similar lack of response to market forces, but justified on the grounds that those workers have higher productivity levels and therefore earn the higher wages through greater efficiency. One of the other current fashions in economics, that of rent-seeking employees in the public sector, appears partial and seldom if ever concerns itself with, for example, possible rent-seeking in multinational corporations.

In most situations, we do not actually know what the wage outcome of economic or market forces for a specific group of workers with some firm-specific skills and training ought to be. Moreover, and this point weakens the position of both the advocates of this criticism, and in turn their critics, we are very uncertain how far we should rely on comparative wage figures based on occupational titles as reliable indicators of the outcome of market or institutional forces. Only if we are prepared to accept the assumption made in theoretical analysis - that all members of a specified occupation are homogeneous - can we interpret the result of wage surveys based on occupational titles which show wide wage dispersion, as evidence of distortion of economic or market forces.

(e) Related to the previous argument, or perhaps the cause of the criticisms advanced by it, is the fact that in many countries trade unions have higher membership density in the public than in the private sector. This does not necessarily mean that public sector trade unions are stronger than unions in the private sector, where both groups of workers are organised, since the government may have imposed restrictions on collective bargaining or limited or denied the right to take industrial action to public sector employees. However, in some cases public sector trade unions may have considerable industrial or political strength or influence. They can express a collective voice which may impose constraints on government's freedom or willingness to take unpopular decisions, and it may be thought that a private sector employer would be better able to resist trade unions' pressures, or to obtain concessions on such things as work standards, staffing levels or redundancies.

(f) Conversely, in some cases, privatisation may be advocated in order to improve terms and conditions of employment of some groups of employees. If there are common gradings and salary scales operating throughout public sector employment, parastatals may have considerable difficulties in recruiting, retaining and motivating a satisfactory workforce. Privatisation may then give management sufficient freedom to improve pay or other conditions and compete effectively in the labour market (Nellis and Kikeri, 1989; Klitgaard, 1989). Different areas of public sector employment compete in different occupational labour markets, and a common grading and salary structure may not provide appropriate competitive conditions in the various different markets. While it is in principle possible for government to introduce differentiated grading and salary structures for different parts of the public sector, and many countries have always operated on this basis, it may, in practice, be very difficult for it to do so. Privatisation may then be advocated as an easier way of obtaining differentiated treatment. Once in private ownership, the organisations are outside the common grading and salary arrangements.

(g) Privatisation may be advocated on budgetary grounds. If activities are run at a loss, the transfer of them to private ownership reduces government expenditure on current account, and probably on capital account as well. Many developing countries have faced large increases in the cost of international debt servicing, and internal budgetary requirements have compelled many of them to severely contain or curtail expenditure on other items. Further, if assets are sold there will be an inflow of funds to government, thereby reducing its need to raise revenue through taxation or reducing its need to borrow either internally or externally. Control of the Public Sector Borrowing Requirement is now widely regarded as an important element in monetary policy, which in turn is regarded as a, if not the, major determinant of inflation.

(h) As well as a reduction in the financial burden of the public sector, privatisation may be advocated in order to cut down the administrative burden. Some form of government oversight of public sector activities is necessary. This creates layers of administration, which impose both financial and perhaps efficiency costs.

(i) Government may seek to expand the ownership of assets and in particular to encourage more people, either as members of the general public or as employees of particular enterprises, to own shares in private companies. This may be done to encourage participation in what is regarded as wealth-generating asset ownership, or for more political reasons related either to the type of society government wishes to create, or to a view that owners of private wealth assets are more likely to be disposed to adopt certain political values and attitudes than are those who do not have individual ownership of shares in private companies.

(j) Privatisation may be used to reduce or end the provision of certain public services. The desirability or otherwise of maintaining or reducing the supply of public goods is a value-judgement, but it is none the less relevant and important. This particular reason for privatisation may not be stated explicitly.

Overall the case for privatisation is intellectually weak. A large private company, where ownership and control are divorced, operating in a monopolistic product market, is not necessarily very different from a PE. Much depends on the system of control, directives and objectives set for the PE by government, and the regulatory framework that government may impose on private monopolies. The alleged constraints or spur to efficiency imposed by capital market control and the threat of take-over may be more impressive in theory than in practice. In many developing countries, there is either no effective stock market or it is weak, poorly developed and dominated by relatively few large participants. Even in developed economies with advanced stock markets, there is little persuasive evidence that take-overs lead to improved efficiency or ensure that potential take-over victims are spurred to greater efficiency by the fear of predators. There are also examples of extremely efficient publicly owned enterprises such as the Korean National Steel Company. The case for or against public ownership or privatisation is not one that should, or indeed can, be made on *a priori* grounds or on principle. It is an empirical issue, to be determined by examination of the evidence, assessed in relation to the objectives set for the public enterprise, and evaluated in the context of a realistic view of what was feasible in the prevailing economic conditions. Moreover, general arguments that might be of reasonably general applicability in developed countries do not necessarily hold in developing economies. Even if it is the case that public sector investment crowds out private investment in developed economies (and the point is presented here rather than endorsed), it is by no means the case that the same holds true in developing economies, where public sector investment may frequently pull in private investment.

Privatisation and the labour market

If privatisation is expected to have any effect on efficiency or productivity, it must have labour market implications, in the short or the long run, or both. If it is believed that the gains to be obtained from privatisation come essentially from an improvement in management in terms of organisational or marketing skills, it is conceivable that there are no immediate labour market effects if the current management is transferred elsewhere in public sector employment and new private sector management takes over. The rest of the existing workforce could continue on exactly the same terms and conditions of employment. Similarly, if the main effect of privatisation is to remove constraints imposed by the need to follow public sector rules and behaviour patterns and if these are regarded as restricting or preventing the enterprises from achieving high efficiency, it is again conceivable that privatisation may have no immediate direct effects on the labour market. In both cases there could be longer term effects as the numbers employed in the future would probably change, and possibly rise.

In all other situations, some changes in labour market conditions would occur unless government imposed restrictions. The expected increase in efficiency, or in the extent of economic activities undertaken by the privatised concern, will have labour market effects. The very act of privatising an undertaking may also have labour market effects. While these will vary from case to case and country to country, there are some general considerations that are likely to be common.

It is useful to differentiate between those currently employed on what can be described as "civil service terms and conditions" and those in parastatals, where different rules and criteria might be applicable. In some countries the two areas of public sector employment might have the same grading and salary systems, as in Nigeria. But there may be differences in other aspects of the employment relationship, such as permanent employment or pension provisions. The main impact of privatisation proposals is on PEs, although parts of the public service can be affected by subcontracting or contracting-out.

Implications of improved efficiency

There are three main ways in which privatisation could improve productivity:
(1)   A reduction in the number employed, to remove what is seen as overstaffing created or facilitated by public ownership.
(2)   Improvements in the productivity of the workforce through changes in job requirements, work standards or performance. This may be related to (1) if the reduced workforce is required to produce the same or a higher output, but there may be no reduction in employment if the higher output from the improved productivity of a constant workforce could be sold profitably.
(3)   Reduction in wages or other terms of employment to remove what is seen as the excessively higher than market-clearing conditions enjoyed by public sector employees.

Let us consider each of these in turn.

(1) Usually overstaffing is taken to mean that the present numbers employed are more than are needed to produce the current quantity and quality of goods and services. It is a very widely held view that there is much overstaffing in many PEs in most countries (see various articles in *World Development*, Vol. 17, No. 5, 1989, but almost any discussion of this issue presents the same conclusion). An objective assessment of the existence and extent of overstaffing requires comparison of the numbers employed against a staffing complement based on some form of work measurement. All attempts to determine the "proper" or efficient staffing levels rest on value judgements about the effort input of individual jobs. These acceptable or prevailing standards vary from

country to country, industry to industry, and through time. There is inevitably a socially determined dimension to work standards. ILO philosophy is derived from the view that the determination of work standards and other conditions of employment is best done by free collective bargaining by the social partners. If there are no adequate bargaining arrangements between developed organisations of the social partners, government may provide protective legislation to ensure that adequate protection is given to workers in situations where there are excessive imbalances of power which are likely to lead to the exploitation of labour. In the absence of collectively agreed work and effort-input requirements based on some agreed form of work measurement, staffing levels are usually determined on the basis of custom and practice.

Agreement on effort inputs and job requirements as the basis of staffing levels, or support for an assertion that there is overstaffing requires agreement on what is "a fair day's work". Comparison of numbers employed and levels or value of output at two dates does not of itself permit any legitimate conclusion about changes in effort, or the appropriateness or otherwise of the current level of employment, unless there is an explicit statement of the level of effort considered normal or proper at each date. Similarly, such simple comparisons cannot establish whether one sector is more or less efficient than the other. In particular, it is necessary to take account of existing market conditions. What may appear as inefficiency resulting from public ownership may have much more to do with a monopoly position and lack of competitive pressures. Thus, privately owned enterprises enjoying monopoly conditions may be just as inefficient and have similar staffing levels or appear to be paying unduly high "rents" to employees. The benefits of monopoly are often shared among workers, management and shareholders.

Examination of the productive processes, work organisation, capital-labour mixes, technology used, market structure and so on, may establish differences in effort inputs. It may be that PEs tend to have greater capital resources than comparable private sector firms, which could lead to the assessment that productivity is higher than that of private enterprises in the same industries. There could however still be overstaffing (Edgren, 1989). The conclusion that one firm or sector has excessive staffing can be drawn if it is accepted that the effort-input requirements in the other firm or sector is appropriate or reasonable and fair. This can be done on a priori grounds - that whatever emerges from private sector activities is market determined and efficient, and therefore by definition fair, or it can be asserted that fairness has nothing to do with positive economic analysis, and the question of fairness or reasonableness is therefore irrelevant. There is then no scope or need for government intervention to establish minimum protection or standards.

In very few, if any, cases where privatisation is advocated to improve efficiency by removing overstaffing has the necessary analysis been done. In developing countries this is not perhaps surprising. Many public sector organisations do not have the expertise or experience to carry out such comparisons between sectors, and there is seldom any clear explicit statement of what is a fair and reasonable work standard. Nevertheless, on the basis of observation and impressions, there is often broad consensus that work standards, effort and job requirements are lower or less demanding in public sector employment. The important policy question that should be decided by government, when contemplating privatisation, is whether the standards pertaining in the private sector are acceptable, and whether it wishes or is willing to see these extended to the privatised enterprises. It would also be desirable if governments were to carry out analyses of relative effort, work standards and staffing levels in *both* public and private sector enterprises. This could give some indication of the extent of improvement in efficiency or productivity that might be obtained if the standards of one were introduced in the other.

This approach is consistent with the declared policy of the World Bank. "Thus, where it can be shown or reasonably expected, on the basis of enterprise-level diagnosis, that privatisation will contribute to efficiency promotion and deficit reduction, and do more than other available actions, then the Bank has supported and will continue to support privatisation" (Nellis and Kikeri, 1989, p. 665). The key issues then become the ways in which efficiency promotion or public deficit reduction will be achieved, and an assessment of their impact on the workforce. When assessing whether these measures are desirable, it is necessary to make value judgements about the acceptability of their effects on employment, pay and effort requirements.

Actually, we know very little about relative effort-input requirements and the extent of overstaffing or understaffing. For example, we have no evidence whether the level of staffing in the ILO, the World Bank, the IMF, or any of the large private companies in IMECs or developing countries, are appropriate for the level of output of goods or services currently provided by that staff. We do not know whether administrators and economists employed by the IMF are as efficient as those employed by IBM, and we have no agreed criteria by which to judge.

If there are differences in effort standards, privatisation may lead to reductions in the numbers employed. In some cases it may lead to increased output. There may therefore be a reduction in employment, and government has to decide whether this is desirable or tolerable. The reason why government placed the enterprise under public ownership might be relevant. Apart from the natural monopoly enterprises, governments may have placed productive enterprises under public control, either for ideological or political reasons, or because of market failure to create the economic conditions sought by government. One such market failure may have been the inability of the private sector to generate sufficient employment opportunities, so that both employment and output were below achievable levels. Privatisation might then require government to accept the employment and output decisions of a market-based system. Government may be unwilling to do this.

It is possible for government to impose conditions on privatisation which limit the possibilities of reductions in employment. In Malaysia, for instance, telecommunications were to be privatised. Employees were part of the civil service with the same terms and conditions, grading and salary struc-tures as the administrative civil service, health and education sectors. Pending the sale of shares to the public, a new holding company was formed to which the assets of the telecommunication side of government activity were trans-ferred. The Guide-lines on Privatisation specified that employees affected by privatisation should enjoy terms and conditions not less favourable than those in the civil service. In addition, an assurance was given that no compulsory redundancy would be permitted for five years after transfer from the public service. Thus, if there was overstaffing, it would not be possible to reduce the numbers employed for at least five years, and it may be that, if product demand grew sufficiently, any "excess" staff could be efficiently employed.

Individuals employed in telecommunications were given the choice of three options. They could transfer to some other part of public service employ-ment; they could remain with the privatised telecommunication enterprise but continue to receive civil service terms and conditions; or they could transfer to the new private company and receive the terms and conditions to be established outside the standard civil service terms, but which were to be not less favourable than the civil service. The overwhelming majority opted for the third choice. This was not surprising, since the establishment of conditions in the new enterprise not less favourable than civil service terms was interpreted to mean more favourable so that there were gains to be received from transfer, and since the five-year employment guarantee was regarded as providing safeguards against enforced redundancies. Public service pension entitlements were also protected. Similar conditions had earlier been offered to employees at the Port Kelang Container Terminal when it had been privatised, when 99 per cent chose to join the new company.

The Malaysian Government has sought to reduce the fears and possi-bility of enforced unemployment. This will no doubt be reflected in the terms on which shares in the new enterprise will be accepted by private shareholders, but demonstrates that even if it is believed there may be excess staffing it is possible for government to balance the competing claims of different groups and seek to obtain some mixture of its different objectives.

In other cases, such as some of the privatisation measures in the United Kingdom, the Government may seek to reduce what it believes to be excess staffing before offering shares to the public. This may require government to accept responsibility for higher future pension commitments if it encourages voluntary retirements, or to meet the cost of redundancies. These costs have to be offset against the receipt from the sale of shares. This may be a common problem in many developing countries.

According to some analysts, "staff reductions may be necessary prior to sale, especially where government employment policies have led to overstaf-fing. This is an, indeed *the,* issue in many countries. Purchasers see labour shedding as an important factor in cutting costs and boosting returns, while governments are most reluctant to alienate workers and add to unemployment" (Nellis and Kikeri, 1989, p. 666, emphasis in original). It is not clear why there should be staff reductions if government policies have not led to overstaffing, unless potential private owners insist that existing employees be dismissed so that new ones can be hired on worse terms and conditions. This could be supported on the grounds that it is removing unnecessary rents given to PE employees, but it would then be interesting to see whether other private sector employers, or the potential purchasers of PEs in their capacity as current employers elsewhere, are also paying similar "rents" to their workers and whether they are seeking to remove them as well.

More important is the expectation of purchasers that there will be labour shedding to cut costs and boost returns. Governments must therefore be prepared to accept higher unemployment, provide some employment guarantees to existing employees as in Malaysia, or provide training and other employment-generating measures to absorb the displaced workforce. The choice from these options will determine who bears the costs of privatisation and this must be a political as well as an economic issue.

(2) There may be opportunities to increase productivity by changing effort inputs, altering job designs or work standards or improving labour utilisation in ways that do not lead to a reduction in employment. These changes could in principle be obtained without privatisation, but in that public ownership and management is by its nature - or as a result of political pressures, bureaucratic inertia and incompetence, or for some aspect of the principal-agent theory - less efficient as an organisational system, privatisation may be advocated. If the demand for the goods or services is sufficiently strong, the existing workforce may continue to be employed to produce a higher level of output, so that the question of redundancy or lay-off does not arise. There may be transitional problems of retraining so that the new work practices can be implemented, and some workers may need retraining in order to move to other jobs within the enterprise.

Experience in the United Kingdom suggests that, in some cases, trade unions have insisted on staffing scales and effort standards under public ownership that were less efficient than those which they themselves were willing to accept when faced with the threat of privatisation, and in some cases the staffing levels imposed after privatisation were even lower than this.

This does not, however, mean that public sector activities are necessarily inefficient or that trade unions have undue power under public management. There are many instances in the private sector where collective bargaining has led to effort levels lower than those physically or technically possible. The emergence of productivity bargaining in the 1960s in the United Kingdom, and the continuing interest of management in changing staffing levels and effort inputs, perhaps through greater flexibility in labour utilisation, indicates that both of these issues are properly the concern of collective bargaining and that trade unions are concerned to establish what they regard as reasonable effort-input or job requirements. Reasonableness is a subjective concept and there might very properly be differences in its interpretation between trade unions, workers and management. Thus, in private sector employment the threat of closure and wholesale dismissal can lead to the reluctant acceptance of changes in staffing and work practices which, while offensive to trade union standards and aspirations, and regarded as unreasonable or oppressive by the workforce, are lesser evils and more acceptable than the alternative of closure or dismissals.

Demonstrating that some groups of public sector employees have been willing to reduce staffing levels or accept increased effort-input and job requirements does not establish that public sector management is inefficient, unless there is an explicit statement that the level of effort input that *should* prevail is that obtainable by management, irrespective of social criteria.

The whole basis of the establishment of work standards by the ILO comes from the belief that there are certain minimum social standards that should be observed. The notion that the interplay of economic forces, regardless of the outcome of that interplay, should determine effort and pay, and that society should accept these outcomes, regardless of their content, is repugnant to those who believe that the establishment of minimum standards or protection is no less a part of basic human rights as the entitlement to participate in a democratic political system with the freedom to organise into trade unions.

Whether public sector job requirements and staffing levels are unduly generous to existing employees is a judgement to be made in the light of prevailing general standards, notions of equity, available resources, and the objectives of government. If it were concluded that the standards afforded to public sector employees are unduly generous it would then be a question of determining the appropriate corrective measures. Privatisation is one option, but improvements in public sector management and improvements in efficiency, while retaining public ownership and management, would be another.

(3) If privatisation is advocated as a means of reducing what are perceived as excessively high wages or other terms of employment enjoyed by public sector employees, there must be a presumption that privatisation will lead to a reduction in either current wages or the rate of increase in wages. Recall that reductions in unit labour costs without cuts in money wages are expected under (2) or (3) above.

As discussed earlier in many developing countries civil service pay is less than that in publicly owned state enterprises, for similar grades or occupational titles, and these pay levels in turn are lower than those obtained in private sector "formal" employment. Reductions in money wages of existing staff after privatisation will seldom be easy. There is strong resistance to reductions in money wages among all employees in all countries, and while this might on occasions be insufficient to prevent reductions if the perceived alternative is large scale dismissals, obtaining cuts is hard, painful and rare. This is as true of private sector employment as it is for the public sector. Experience in the United Kingdom suggests that if there are no constraints, it may be possible to obtain reductions in terms and conditions by dismissing existing employees and hiring new recruits on less favourable terms. This seems to have happened in some cases of contracting out of cleaning services in the National Health

Service, and the reductions in conditions often related to holiday pay and sick pay and reductions in the number of hours worked without a corresponding reduction in tasks to be performed.

If governments allow the new private owners complete freedom, within a general legislation regarding minimum wages or other provisions, they are effectively abandoning the protection and terms they have provided to their employees. If a worsening in terms of employment then occurs the cost of privatisation is in effect borne by the employees. If government seeks to provide some protection, as in the Malaysian provision that terms and conditions must be not less favourable than those enjoyed as public service employees, then if these impose higher costs on the new private employers there will presumably be an offsetting effect in the price the new owners are prepared to offer to take over the public sector activities. In that case, the cost of privatisation will be borne by the general public.

In some cases, there may be different treatment given to different groups of public sector employees. If activities transferred to private ownership include civil service employees they may be given more protection than if activities are state enterprises. In all countries large numbers of civil service employees are given permanent employment status. It is therefore often be-lieved that the government has a special obligation not to dismiss them or transfer them to private ownership if this would worsen their current and expected terms and conditions. No such employment status relationship may be present in state enterprise, although in a few countries no distinction may be made between the two groups. The "civil service" constraint may affect employment guarantees as well as terms and wages. For example, in Turkey some state enterprises also employ civil servants transferred or seconded to them. If these activities are privatised it is understood that the employment guarantee for permanent civil servants will be maintained but no similar guarantee or protection will be given to other state enterprise employees. In Malaysia all the employees affected by the privatisation of telecommunications were civil service employees and received the assurance of not less favourable terms, no redundancy for five years and the option to remain in the civil service and not be transferred.

Whether government should impose conditions protecting the terms and conditions of transferred employees raises the same issues as those in-volved in the determination of the appropriate or efficient staffing levels. It is a choice between the outcome of the "market forces" and the application of minimum standards.

Similar considerations arise in relation to contracting-out or subcon-tracting by government. Increasingly government is seeking to replace the public provision of services by its own organisations, or as part of its own provision of services, by private sector enterprises. These are often less well organised, have little or no trade union presence, may have restrictions on collective bargaining activity and often offer lower wages and worse terms and conditions than both the public sector and larger firms in the private sector. In developing countries, in particular, employees of subcontractors may lose important protection rights. Some protective legislation applies only to those employed in enterprises above a certain size. Subcontractors may be small-scale or may be formed into small units to avoid legislation. Thus employees may lose entitlement to sick pay, redundancy or employment protection rights.

Privatisation may lead to a worsening of terms and conditions as more casual workers are employed at lower rates of pay or without social security provisions and protection. This casualisation of the workforce with its increased insecurity as well as worse conditions can lead to a serious undermining of employment protection provisions and a deterioration in employment standards. In some cases, such as Bangladesh, this has led to increased trade union resistance to further privatisation (Edgren, 1989).

Privatisation and its terms for labour

The question of whether privatisation is necessary, or even conducive to improved efficiency is one that should be answered on the basis of detailed examination not *a priori* reasoning. There should be quantified statements of the gains expected from privatisation and this will require an explanation of where the improvements are to occur and why they cannot be obtained from continued public ownership. It may be that existing public sector management is inefficient or unsuited to productive or commercial activities, but the solution may be to replace or retrain them, and/or to institute a new set of administrative rules governing their behaviour so that they are better able to achieve clearly specified and consistent government objectives (Vernon-Wortzel and Wortzel, 1989). Present systems often impose detailed control mechanisms which absorb much time but do not provide adequate control over strategic decisions or the quality of decisions (Ramamurti, 1987). If existing grading or salary systems are considered unsuitable or incapable of providing the proper incentives it may be possible to design more appropriate systems (Klitgaard, 1989). The commercialisation proposals of Nigeria indicate one way of combining public ownership with the expected benefits of exposure to competitive economic forces. Enterprises will remain in public ownership but will be required to satisfy commercial criteria for parts of their activities. It may be that it is the exposure to competitive forces rather than the nature of ownership which exerts the greater pressure for improved efficiency (Yarrow, 1989; van de Walle, 1989). In most cases there may be relatively little improvement in allocative efficiency, but there could be some distributional gains if private firms are better able to provide affordable goods or services to poorer income groups than publicly owned organisations.

In any assessment of gains and sources of improved efficiency, it will be necessary to decide how improvements are to be obtained. This means that a view has to be taken on such issues as the future employment levels, the terms and conditions of those remaining, and the effort inputs that will be required.

If privatisation takes place it may be desirable for government to impose conditions on the new owners. The Malaysian policy of maintaining terms and conditions not less favourable than those in the civil service, and an inhibition on dismissal, except for good cause under the general employment protection legislation, provides an example of government concern to avoid a worsening of conditions for employees. These safeguards will no doubt affect the price at which assets are sold to private owners, thereby spreading the cost of employment protection. Desirable as they are, these safeguards are applicable only to public service employees transferred to private sector ownership. They do not affect employees in new projects which would previously have been in the public sector but have now been transferred to the private sector. Those employed by subcontractors will also fall outside the safeguards. It would be possible for the government to enact that all subcontractors provide terms and conditions which are "fair", either the same as in the public service or equivalent to those established by collective bargaining. The United Kingdom Fair Wages Resolution of the House of Commons of 1909 did this, but it was repealed by the present Government in 1982. Notwithstanding this precedent other governments could act to prevent exploitation by subcontractors in receipt of public funds.

A key issue is who bears the cost of privatisation. Public sector subsidies, including the writing-off of existing debt of PEs prior to their sale, to encourage privatisation, affects income distribution and income transfers no less than do subsequent changes in pay and employment security of those employed in the PEs. In some cases the employees of the enterprise will bear a large part of the costs. In others they may be protected but the taxpayer or other potential recipients of government assistance may bear the burden through opportunity costs and foregone alternative government measures. If the privatised enterprise is in a monopolistic or oligopolistic product market situation and labour is organised, monopoly rents may provide income improvements to employees with consumers bearing the costs.

Poorer members of society may end up bearing a disproportionate burden of costs if privatisation leads to a reduction in publicly provided services and reductions in the social wage or social dividend. The desirability of privatisation is then a political issue.

Role of the ILO

Although there has been relatively little privatisation actually introduced in many developing countries, despite the many declared intentions, the current fashion for privatisation can be expected to continue. The difficulties of translating these intentions into reality have often proved more serious than first anticipated. Nevertheless, measures to transfer activity from public to private sectors have been a part of most financial support and structural adjustment programmes. These will lead to pressures to reduce employment, either before or after privatisation, and increase effort inputs from employees.

In some cases they may also lead to reductions in pay of the remaining employees. While seeking a reduction in government budgetary contribution to PEs, privatisation may lead to large increases in government expenditure in the short to medium term. The more that governments reduce employment prior to privatisation, the greater the political difficulties and the greater the public cost. There is recognition that reductions in employment levels are difficult to achieve, and this seems to be so even when there has been savage reductions in real public sector pay and when public sector pay levels have fallen considerably below private sector levels.

In some cases, privatisation may not be a satisfactory solution even as posed by its advocates. Improvements in organisation and administrative mechanisms within the public sector, perhaps combined with more appropriate administrative guide-lines which give PEs greater freedom to take their own decisions regarding staffing and pay levels, with soundly based controlled incentive payment systems might be much more effective. The introduction of elements of competition might in fact be much more important than ownership. Detailed analyses of the efficiency of PEs, given government objectives, should be carried out, and there needs to be much more clarification of the levels of pay and effort inputs that exist in the private sector.

However, there will still be pressure for privatisation. Governments will be concerned to obtain a proper balance between safeguarding the interests of its present employees and the general interest reflected in government subsidies and the cost of providing adequate compensation to retrenched employees. Given the widespread expectation that privatisation will lead in many instances to a reduction in employment, which may be a prime reason for privatising PEs, governments should seek to introduce measures to prevent increases in unemployment.

There are six areas in which the ILO might offer assistance to governments contemplating privatisation:

(i)   Changes in work organisation after privatisation, and any retrenchment, will create a need for training and retraining programmes. In some cases displaced individuals may be encouraged to start small-scale enterprises or become self-employed. This too will require training programmes. Advice on screening individuals and advising on appropriate career switches will be needed. The ILO should be prepared to offer technical assistance and expert advice.

(ii) There will be need for further employment-generating programmes. Most governments will seek to minimise the unemployment effects, and international organisations will be sympathetic to requests for employment pump-priming assistance. Given its great experience in employment matters the ILO is in a position to have stock lists of such schemes. Not all of those would be appropriate to any particular country, but the collective experience should be of considerable potential assistance.

(iii) The protection of employees' rights after privatisation is a major issue. The Malaysian experience suggests that it is possible to combine privatisation with safeguards of employees' accrued interests. The ILO could prepare various types of model arrangements or options for governments. These could include variants of the Malaysian approach, and also outlines of minimum protective legislation or special provisions to ensure that transferred public sector employees received at least the same protection as is provided for private sector employees in large organised firms.

(iv) In many cases the short-term costs of voluntary retrenchment will be high. Schemes showing different methods of providing reasonable compensation could be prepared.

(v) Transfer from public to private ownership will usually mean a worsening of pension provisions. The ILO could produce guide-lines on the most appropriate methods of providing reasonable guarantees of accumulated benefits.

(vi) As part of a more general policy approach, as well as of benefit to individual countries, the ILO could assist in the analysis of the performance of PEs. In many countries there are no satisfactory data on PEs, who are often not distinguished in national statistics. Little is known about their performance and few meaningful comparisons, either of their performance through time, or of their performance related to comparable firms in the private sector, can be made. Assistance in the collection and analysis of data would be of considerable benefit. In addition the ILO should provide assistance so that countries are able to compare the performance of PEs before and after privatisation. This will have fewer immediate results but is a necessity for sound policy in the longer term.

Finally, there is need for much more research, knowledge and analysis of how labour markets actually work, particularly in developing countries. Discussion of the pros and cons of privatisation frequently falls back on *a priori* assertions or theoretical conclusions drawn from the most improbable and unrealistic assumptions about the actual economic situation that exists. There is an urgent need to know just how labour markets actually operate in the real world. While this is clearly relevant to the question of privatisation and the role and working of the public sector, it is no less important for many other issues in developing economies. At present we do not know how labour markets actually operate and until we do, it is not possible to talk of "rent" or wages in excess of market-clearing levels; we do not know what a labour market for a particular occupation with some firm-specific skills is, or what level of wages emerges from such a market in the absence of whatever is meant by "distortions". Until we do, we cannot judge whether public sector wages are too high, just right, or too low, and as the civil service is always career employment with a well-developed internal labour market which provides internal supply of labour to certain posts through promotion, it takes long periods before the effects of labour market forces on the quality of recruits really emerge, and by the time they do the civil service may have suffered a near-irreversible loss of quality which can have harmful effects on the economy at large.

References

Bevan, D.L.; Collier, P.; Gunning, J.W. 1986. *Trade shocks in controlled* economies. Washington, DC, World Bank, mimeo.

Collier, P. 1989. *Public sector retrenchment: An analytic survey.* Geneva, ILO.

Edgren, G. 1989. *Privatisation, efficiency and employment,* Paper presented at the Seminar on Privatisation, Manila, 26-27 Oct. 1989, New Delhi, ILO-ARTEP.

Kahn, A. 1985. *Wages and employment in Nigeria.* Washington, DC, World Bank, mimeo.

Klitgaard, R. 1989. "Incentive myopia", in *World Development,* Vol. 17, No. 4, pp. 447-459.

Lindauer, D.; Meesook, O.; Suebsaeng, P. 1989. "Government wage policy in Africa: Some findings and policy issues", in *The World Bank Research Observer,* Vol. 3, No. 1.

Nellis, R.; Kikeri, S. 1989. "Public enterprise reform: Privatisation and the World Bank", in *World Development,* Vol. 17, No. 5, May 1989, pp. 659-672.

Quah, J.S.T. 1985. *Towards productivity and excellence: A comparative analysis of the public personnel systems in three ASEAN countries,* Paper presented to EROPA Eleventh General Assembly and Conference on Delivery of Public Services in National Development: Problems, Solution Alternatives and Structural Adjustment, Bangkok, 8-14 Dec. 1985.

Ramamurti, R. 1987. "Controlling state-owned enterprises", in *Public Enterprise,* Vol. 7, No. 2, 1987.

Robinson, D. 1990. *Civil service pay in Africa,* Geneva, ILO.van de Walle, N. 1989. "Privatization in developing countries: A review of the issues", in *World Development,* Vol. 17, No. 5, pp. 601-615.

Vernon-Wortzel, H.; Wortzel, L.H. 1989. "Privatization: Not the only answer", in *World Development,* Vol. 17, No. 5, 1989, pp. 633-641.

Vickers, J.; Yarrow, G. 1988. *Privatization: An economic analysis,* Cambridge, Massachusetts, The MIT Press.

Yarrow, G. 1989. "Does ownership matter?", in Veljanovski, C. (ed.): *Privatisation and competition: A market prospectus.* London, Institute of Economic Affairs, Hobart Paperback 28, pp. 68-69.

Conclusion

Labour markets and structural adjustments: A global view

by Ajit Singh [*]

I am very privileged to be invited to sum up the discussion to this book and to outline research priorities for the future. As the previous chapters demonstrate, the subject of labour markets and structural adjustment is a very broad one, with significant interactions with many areas of the economy and society. But in my view the importance of the issues we have been discussing goes much beyond that. Today history is being made in Europe, and I would like to suggest to you that these labour market questions and how they are resolved are going to play a crucial role in the unfolding historical developments, not only in Europe, but also in the North as a whole and in the South.

I would like to begin by putting these matters in the framework of developments in the world economy. Between 1950 and 1973, the period which my colleagues Andrew Glynn, Alan Hughes and Alan Lipietz and I have called the Golden Age,[1] there was a historically unprecedented expansion of production and consumption (at a rate of nearly 5 per cent per annum) in advanced industrial nations. Moreover, this was a long, sustained period of more or less full employment in most of these economies. A number of countries not only enjoyed full employment, but in fact had over-full employment - nearly 10 per cent of the employed labour force in countries like France and the Federal Republic of Germany came from abroad. During this period, there was an enormous expansion of world trade, and trade in manufactures grew in volume terms at the very fast rate of nearly 10 per cent per annum. Most developing countries also participated in and benefited from this world-wide prosperity. However, since 1973, the rate of growth of GDP in the OECD countries and of the world in general has nearly halved. Significantly, the recorded rate during the last 15 years is much more in line with the long-term trend of growth of industrial countries in the hundred years before the Golden Age (Reynolds, 1983; World Bank, 1987). In the 1980s, many industrial countries, particularly in Western Europe, consequently experienced high rates of unemployment, rates which were unthinkable in the Golden Age. Similarly,

* Faculty of Economics and Politics, University of Cambridge, United Kingdom.

there has been a sharp deceleration in the expansion of world trade in manufactures. There has also been a large fall in commodity prices, with serious repercussions on Southern development during the last decade.

Now why did the Golden Age happen, why did it dissipate and, more significantly, can it be recreated? I would like to suggest to you that the labour market issues - not in the narrow neoclassical sense, but broadly conceived as has been the case in the earlier chapters - are central to answers to all these questions. I shall necessarily be extremely brief and schematic in the following account.

A careful analysis of the Golden Age economic boom suggests that its length, steadiness, speed and strength were such that they cannot be accounted for by an accidental combination of favourable economic circumstances. Rather, the extraordinary economic performance of industrial countries was brought about and sustained by a unique historical conjuncture which created a specific *economic regime*.

The most important macroeconomic characteristics of the Golden Age pattern of economic development were:

(a)   The rapid and parallel growth of productivity and capital stock per worker; and

(b)   Parallel growth of real wages and productivity.

The significance of these two relations is that they guarantee both a roughly constant profit rate and roughly equal growth of consumption and production, thus ratifying and maintaining the initial rate of accumulation. However, such a macro-economic growth path could only be perpetuated if it were compatible with the behaviour of individual economic agents - firms, workers, consumers. This compatibility in the Golden Age was ensured by a social consensus around institutional arrangements in respect of the setting of wages and prices and the distribution between wages and profits, and the state fiscal, credit and welfare policies which guaranteed minimum living standards and maintained aggregate demand. In the sphere of wage setting, for example, productivity wage bargaining, which flourished during this period, played a key role both in keeping a rough constancy of the share of wages and profits in the national product and also in helping to provide an adequate rate of growth in consumer demand. Similarly, at the international level, under the leadership of a single hegemonic power for much of this period, the United States, the global economic system functioned under stable monetary and trading arrangements.

The process of the erosion of the Golden Age began well before the oil price shock of 1973. Serious difficulties arose at the levels both of the national and the international regulatory regimes; these began to interact with each other in a cumulatively adverse way, to the detriment of the system as a whole. The Bretton Woods monetary system broke down in the late 1960s, partly as a consequence of the success of the Golden Age itself - the rise of Japan, the Federal Republic of Germany and other European countries in the international market place led to serious balance-of-payments problems for the United

States, hitherto the lynch-pin of the international system. There is also evidence of a productivity slow-down by the late 1960s in several leading industrial countries, which was not matched by a deceleration in the rate of growth of real wages, thus leading to a profit squeeze.

By the early 1970s, the Golden Age system was so fragile that it disintegrated under the impact of the two oil shocks, thus pushing the world economy into a period of prolonged slow growth, which began in 1973. The social consensus of the Golden Age, which was crucial to the functioning of the economic system as a whole, broke down. For a while, after the first oil shock, the governments of the OECD countries tried to restore the Golden Age institutional consensus, by following expansionary economic policies, but this attempt was finally abandoned in 1979 (symbolised by the "Volcker shock" and the implementation of deeply contractionary monetary policies in the United States, which were subsequently widely imitated elsewhere, particularly in the United Kingdom).

In the 1980s, the leading OECD governments attempted to create a new economic system based much more on free market principles, but this does not yet command a broad social consensus in these countries. In pursuit of this objective, there has been a widespread movement towards "privatisation", "de-regulation" and the erosion of Golden Age arrangements with respect, for example, to wage bargaining and to the provisions of the welfare state (with the professed aim of increasing labour market flexibility). Although this challenge to the existing domestic rules of co-ordination within the industrial countries has inevitably proceeded at a different pace in different countries, a number of common features can be discerned.

(a)   The Golden Age presumption that workers should bargain collectively to protect wages against inflation and to collect a share of the fruits of productivity growth was challenged. Norms of indexation were repudiated (Italy), and attempts were made to weaken trade unions by legislation (for example, in the United Kingdom - prohibition of secondary picketing, the Federal Republic of Germany - collection of social security payments from strikers).

(b)   Demands for wage flexibility have been paralleled by demands for employment flexibility - an enlargement of the right to hire and fire by means of rolling back employment protection legislation (for example, in the United Kingdom, France).

(c)   Attempts to reduce the coverage and value of welfare state benefits have been general occurrences.

(d)   There has been an explicit abandonment of full employment policies, embodied in the adoption of rules about monetary growth and public sector deficits.

(e)   There has been a general trend towards extending market pressures - privatisation of nationalised industries (for example, in the United Kingdom, France, Japan), cuts in goverment subsidies to loss making firms and industries.

Viewed from the standpoint of governing economic circles in the leading OECD countries, this emerging new pattern of development has already been "successful" in some important directions. First, there has been a major change in the balance of power, both internationally and internally. Internationally, the collapse of commodity prices, the extremely high real interest rates, and the reduction of capital flows have greatly weakened the economic and political power of developing countries. In the mid-1970s, these countries were vociferously demanding a new international economic order; today, most of them (particularly in Africa and Latin America) are severely constrained by their balance-of-payments, heavily in debt and in the position of supplicants before the IMF and the World Bank. The latter two institutions are only willing to provide the much-needed foreign exchange if these countries carry out so-called "structural reforms", which usually follow the same pattern of de-nationalisation, de-regulation, internal and external liberalisation of markets, which are the hallmark of changes in the industrialsed countries. Similarly, in the latter, the bargaining position of the trade unions, and of the working class in general, has been weakened at both the work place and macroeconomic level.

The second main success of the emerging new system has been an improvement at least in terms of inflationary performance, compared with the mid-1970s. Instead of the stagflation (low growth and high inflation) of those years, the 1980s have been characterised by low growth and low inflation. This is of course directly related to the weakened bargaining power of the unions and the fall in commodity prices that accompanied the changing internal and international balance of power, referred to above.

There are, however, important weaknesses in the 1980s record. First, although unemployment rates can be expected to come down to some degree in the mid-1990s, as the rate of growth of the labour force declines due to demographic factors, they look set to remain exceptionally high in most European countries. Only a trend increase in the rate of growth of world economic activity can offer the prospect of an improvement before then.

Second, despite five years of IMF management by means such as austerity programmes and debt rescheduling, there is still no solution in sight to the debt problem of developing countries. The debtor countries have suffered enormous economic losses during this period, without being anywhere near to recovering their creditworthiness of their pre-1980 long term growth rates. A wide range of observers believe that, for many countries, the debt problem is no longer one of "liquidity" but one of "insolvency" (see Cline (1985); Singh (1986(a)).

Third, there are extremely large payments imbalances in the international economy, which have become a source of major instability on the world's currency and stock markets.

Nevertheless, as long as high unemployment rates in the advanced countries are politically acceptable, the balance of advantage (from the standpoint of conservative governments in the leading countries) lies in continuing with the current macroeconomic pattern of low growth and low inflation. For if expansionary policies were followed and the world rate of economic growth rose on a sustained basis to anywhere near its golden age level, it would lead to a tighter labour market and therefore to an increase in the power of unions; more significantly, there would be a sharp rise in commodity prices, including oil.[2] All of these in turn will rekindle inflation. For conservative policy makers, the only perceived benefit of a trend increase in the rate of growth of the world economy would be that it would greatly help towards a solution of the debt problemof developing countries. However, they fear that this would be a the expense of rising commodity prices, inflation and adverse changes in the economic and political balance of power. Since there are a variety of other ways of solving the debt problem (write offs, interest capping etc.), it is unlikely that the leading OECD countries will seek to expand the world economy for this purpose alone.

To be sure, there is a great deal of discussion about policy co-ordination among the leading industrial countries to revive the world economy. However, it is important to note that the central objective of that policy co-ordination is *not to bring about an overall increase in the rate of growth of world demand,* but rather to redistribute the current level of demand among the leading countries in a way which will reduce their huge payments imbalances, and thus help restore stability in the currency and financial markets.

If the above considerations are combined with the expected deceleration in the rate of population growth, and the structural shifts already occurring in these economies towards low productivity growth service sectors, the prospect for the OECD countries (and hence for the world economy) must be at best one of continued slow growth. This perspective assumes that the policy co-ordination currently being by the leading OECD countries is wholly successful; if it is not, the world economy is likely to grow at a still slower rate, and then even the possibility of a serious slump in the short term cannot be ruled out.

Long ago, the Italian Marxist thinker, Gramsci, talked about the pessimism of the intellect and optimism of the spirit. The above pessimistic scenario is probably the most likely outcome for the world economy in the medium term. Yet we are living through momentous times. We are seeing history being made at a breath-taking pace, overturning many of the seemingly fixed concepts and assumptions of yesterday. Perhaps in this emerging new *political* configuration, there may be more than "spiritual" reasons for thinking, or at least hoping, that the groups of leading OECD countries may become willing to take the necessary steps for recreating the Golden Age. This would, however, require an explicit abandonment of the pattern of development of the 1980s and a commitment to a very different economic and social order. In particular, growth rates approaching the Golden Age levels would only be feasible and sustainable with low inflation on the basis of a new institutional and behaviourial framework (e.g., a more co-operative relationship between the labour force, management and government) and a rather different system of international regulation (which, for example, would involve some scheme for orderly commodity price movements, hitherto rejected by the leading OECD governments).

Before turning to research priorities, it may be useful to clarify some conceptual difficulties which arose in the earlier chapters. I wish to comment briefly on the role of the labour market with respect to (a) employment, (b) prices and (c) productivity growth.

First, in relation to employment, it has been suggested, on the basis of the actual experience of developing countries in the 1980s, that labour market conditions and wage flexibility do not matter; that a fall in real wages does not increase employment. The crude neoclassical argument that real wages and employment are inversely related has certainly been decisively rejected by the events of the last decade. Thus, in sub-Saharan Africa and Latin America there have been large reductions in real wages (up to 50 per cent or more in the 1980s in countries like Mexico or United Republic of Tanzania) but no increase and actually falls in employment. In striking contrast, in Asia (particularly in the East Asian NICs) both real wages and employment have continued to increase significantly during this decade. All of this accords with the Keynesian paradigm, in which employment is a function of aggregate demand and output, rather than of wage flexibility in the labour market.

Nevertheless, it would be wrong to conclude that the nature of the labour market has no consequences for employment. Even within the Keynesian paradigm, market rigidities have important implications for prices and therefore indirectly for employment. In our open economy, which is subject to balance-of-payments fluctuations arising from changing world market conditions (the typical situation of a developing country), the lack of wage flexibility would make it more difficult for the country to use currency depreciation as an instrument for correcting such disequilibria. To the extent that imports and exports are price elastic, an inflexible labour market may oblige a balance-of-payments constrained economy to operate with a lower level of aggregate demand and employment than would otherwise be the case.

Turning to the question of the nature of the labour market and its consequences for productivity growth, there are two important views. According to the supply-side doctrine, assiduously propagated in the 1980s to the industrialised countries by the OECD and to the developing countries by the international financial institutions, the removal of wage and other rigidities in the labour market is essential for more efficient allocation of resources, and hence for promoting growth of productivity. The late Nicholas Kaldor and other Cambridge economists have, however, a rather different approach to the issue of productivity growth. In the Kaldorian view, growth of productivity in manufacturing is basically a function of the growth of output (the so-called Verdoorn's law); the latter depends on the growth of demand and investment rather than on labour mobility and other aspects of the labour market. Thus large Japanese firms, despite life-time employment for their workers and age-related payment systems, and thus highly imperfect labour markets, in the conventional sense, have an excellent record of productivity growth because of high rates of investment and growth of output.

The research priorities for the future should be based at least in part on the challenges faced by the different parts of the world economy and policy. These challenges may be summed up as follows. First, in Eastern Europe, two historic tasks must be confronted:

(1) how to make a peaceful transition to political democracy;
(2) how to institute more efficient economic organisation without sacrificing the good points of the old order.

The latter included comprehensive social security, full employment and a large degree of equity for the population at large. It will not only be a historic missed opportunity if an "efficient" market economy is achieved at the expense of employment or workers' rights; such a solution is also unlikely to be politically sustainable in the longer term.

In the developing countries, the main challenges are the two interrelated problems of employment generation and poverty. This is especially so in Latin America and sub-Saharan Africa, the two regions most affected during the 1980s by external economic shocks, caused by the sea change in economic activity which took place in the world economy after 1979. Notwithstanding the highly impressive growth of manufactured exports to the advanced countries from heavily indebted Latin American nations, such as Mexico and Brazil, during the 1980s the overall economic and employment position in Latin America was dire. The general employment problem faced by these countries can be put in the following simple terms.

Consider for illustration the case of Mexico. Despite the Government's efforts to reduce the rate of population growth, Mexico's labour force is expanding at an annual rate of 3 to 3.5 per cent. The long-term trend rate of productivity growth in Mexico has also been of the order of 3 to 3.5 per cent per annum. This means that the economy must grow at 6 to 7 per cent per annum just to provide jobs to the new labour force entrants, let alone to reduce the huge backlog of unemployment and underemployment. During the 1960s and 1970s, Mexico did manage to achieve, more or less, the required growth rates. Thus, towards the end of the 1970s, the economy was growing at nearly 8 per cent per annum, and a million net new jobs were being created each year [Singh (1988); Brailobsky and Barker (1985)]. However, between 1982 (the beginning of the debt crisis) and 1988, the average growth rate of the Mexican economy has been close to zero. This has meant a reduction in per capita income of about 15 per cent since 1982, a large fall in employment rather than a rise, a cut in real wages in industry of the order of 50 per cent, and an increase in poverty (caused in part by reduced government expenditure on health, education and other social services, as a result of the IMF stabilisation programme which the country has been following).

Thus, unless countries like Mexico and Brazil can again achieve long-term rates of growth of 5-6 per cent per annum or more, as they did in the 1960s and 1970s, the employment situation in these countries is likely to continue to deteriorate.

Although the Asian economies achieved a much faster overall rate of economic expansion in the 1980s than countries in either Latin America or sub-Saharan Africa, the employment question, and particularly that of labour standards, remains a challenge in most of them. In a number of South and Southeast Asian countries (for example, India, Pakistan and Malaysia), the employment elasticity of output in the organised manufacturing sector and in agriculture is falling. This is so even in a country like India, with a very low level of per capita income. Most of the extra jobs therefore have to come from the urban informal sector and from rural industries and services. A very important question is whether some minimum labour standards can be introduced into the informal sector - for example, in the form of partly contributory old age and/or accident insurance.

Turning to the advanced countries, the economic problems in the United States and Western Europe are at one level somewhat different. The United States has had a relatively much better employment record during the 1980s, but real wages that have not increased since 1973 (Marshall, 1987). In Western Europe, although real wages have continued to increase at much the same rate as the growth in productivity (at an average of about 2.5 per cent per annum), unemployment rates have remained stubbornly high throughout the 1980s. It is fashionable in certain quarters (e.g. the OECD) to blame "Euros-clerosis" (i.e. institutional - mainly labour market - rigidities) for this phenomenon. This, however, seems to be a strange notion when it is clear that the rate of growth of productivity in Western Europe during the 11980s has been several times that recorded in the United States, while a country like the Federal Republic of Germany has been running a huge trade and current account surplus and the United States has had a large deficit. High European unemployment is very much due to the low rate of growth of aggregate demand, which in part is due to imbalances in trade between the Federal Republic of Germany and its EC partners. The Federal Republic of Germany, the dominant economy in Western Europe, has been following a tight fiscal and monetary policy with the result that today it has a trade surplus with every single country in the EC except Ireland (Eatwell, 1989). In the context of 1992 and the ever closer integration of the EC economies, as well as the professed desire of the European Commission to create a "social Europe", the West German economic stance and the country's trade surplus constitute a major hurdle.

The foregoing analysis indicates the following kind of research agenda on labour market questions - broadly conceived - for the ILO to consider for the 1990s. It is briefly outlined below, but not in any rigid rank order of priorities.

1. *Eastern Europe.* Here, as noted above, the main research and policy task is to ensure that the transition to a market economy and to "free" labour markets is not made at the expense of workers' employment, labour standards or living conditions. In accordance with its traditional mandate, the ILO should

be concerned to ensure that in this transitional phase, which may last some time, large numbers of workers are not condemned to joblessness or to insecure jobs without welfare and appropriate labour standards. Research should be aimed at exploring institutional mechanisms which can combine labour market flexibility with worker security.

2. *Developing countries.* Here productive employment for the rapidly growing labour force is the main issue. One major question is whether it is possible to raise the employment elasticity of the growth of output in the economy as a whole without jeopardising or reducing the prospects of long-term economic growth.

Increasingly, as a consequence of urbanisation and fast labour force growth, jobs in the developing countries will have to come from the urban informal sector. The ILO has pioneered policy initiatives and research in this area for the last two decades. But this work will have to go much further in the 1990s. So far, the informal sector research has been largely descriptive, and certainly not any the less valuable for that. Future work will need to be more analytical. For example, the following kinds of macro-economic questions concerning the informal sector need to be researched and addressed. Are price formation and employment generation in the informal *manufacturing* sector (say) similar to those in the formal sector? For example, is there cost-plus pricing, as in the formal sector, or is it based more on changes in demand? To what extent does adjustment to changes in the level of overall activity in the informal *manufacturing* sector take place through movements in wages and prices, and how far does it occur through changes in quantities (output and employment)? How do these relationships differ from those observed in the formal sector? Such research will have important policy implications.

Another important area of future ILO research on this subject concerns the question of labour standards in the informal sector. At what level of per capita income is it possible to introduce minimal social security in the form of contributory health or old age insurance schemes for workers in the informal sector? What are the appropriate labour standards in the informal sector in developing country conditions?

3. *Industrialised countries*

(a) A major challenge is the creation of "Social Europe", as envisaged by Delors, in countries with very different levels of per capita income and social conditions. Is such a vision of what might be called "civilising the role of capital" also applicable and useful for the United States?

(b) The whole issue of improving wealth and income distribution in advanced industrial countries is of great importance. There ought to be consideration of proposals like that of James Meade (1989), in his recent book, in relation to new forms of labour/capital partnerships. What role can workers' pension funds and their investments in industrial and commercial concerns play in this process?

4. *The recreation of the Golden Age.* Research is needed on the social and economic conditions necessary for a faster expansion of the world

economy. This will of course benefit both North and South. As noted earlier, it will necessarily involve exploration of both a suitable regulatory framework at the international level and appropriate corporate institutional arrangements between employers, workers and governments within the leading countries themselves. On the latter set of issues, work by Guy Standing and other scholars on Sweden and other Nordic countries is clearly important.

5. *Issues of privatisation and their impact on labour markets.* Derek Robinson's chapter in this book outlines the important research issues in this area very well, and one can only endorse his views.

6. *Segmented labour markets in developing countries.* The ILO has already done pioneering research in this area. What is needed now is research on the dynamics of these markets. Low segmentation is affected by changing economic and labour market conditions. Apart from the ILO's continuing "normal" research into labour markets in developing countries, it would be useful to assess the labour adjustments at the enterprise level in response to Structural Adjustment Programmes, as well as to long-term technological developments (e.g. modes of "flexible specialisation").

7. *Issues of training and human resource development in developing countries.* The ILO's regional teams are already engaged in work in this area, and such work will need to be greatly strengthened.

Notes

[1] Glynn, A.; Hughes, A.; Lipietz, A.; and Singh, A. 1990: "The rise and fall of the Golden Age", in Marglin, and S.A.; and Schor, J. (eds.): *The end of the Golden Age* pp. 39-125. Oxford, Clarendon Press. In this and the next two sections I have borrowed passages from the above paper and from Singh (1990), in both of which the reader will find a fuller discussion of the issues.

[2] As Beckerman and Jenkinson (1986) argued, lower commodity prices played a major role in reducing inflation in the industrialised countries in the 1980s.

References

Beckerman, W.; and Jenkinson, T. 1986 . "What stopped the inflation? Unemployment or Commodity prices?", in *Economic Journal,* Vol 96, March 1986, pp 39-54.

Singh, A. 1990. "Southern competition, labour standards and industrial development in the North and the South", in *Global rules, labour standards and development* (Washington, DC, US Department of Labor, 1990) pp. 239-264.

Meade, J. E. 1989 *Agathatopis - the economics of partnership.* Aberdeen, Aberdeen University Press.